1SP
ONE SIGNAL
PUBLISHERS
ATRIA

THE WAR BELOW

LITHIUM, COPPER, AND THE GLOBAL BATTLE TO POWER OUR LIVES

ERNEST SCHEYDER

ONE SIGNAL PUBLISHERS

ATRIA

NEW YORK LONDON TORONTO SYDNEY NEW DELHI

An Imprint of Simon & Schuster, Inc.
1230 Avenue of the Americas
New York, NY 10020

First One Signal Publishers/Atria Books hardcover edition January 2024

ONE SIGNAL PUBLISHERS / ATRIA BOOKS and colophon are trademarks of Simon & Schuster, Inc.

Simon & Schuster: Celebrating 100 Years of Publishing in 2024

For information about special discounts for bulk purchases, please contact Simon & Schuster Special Sales at 1-866-506-1949 or business@simonandschuster.com.

The Simon & Schuster Speakers Bureau can bring authors to your live event. For more information or to book an event, contact the Simon & Schuster Speakers Bureau at 1-866-248-3049 or visit our website at www.simonspeakers.com.

Interior design by Kyoko Watanabe
Map by Julie Witmer

Manufactured in the United States of America

1 3 5 7 9 10 8 6 4 2

Library of Congress Cataloging-in-Publication Data has been applied for.

ISBN 978-1-6680-1180-5
ISBN 978-1-6680-1182-9 (ebook)

This is for Sharon, Maryanne, and Thérèse.

"It takes as much energy to wish as it does to plan."

—ELEANOR ROOSEVELT

CONTENTS

CANADA
Pebble copper and gold project
U.S. Department of Energy's
Critical Materials Institute
Dow Chemical, Midland, Michigan
Twin Metals copper
and nickel project
Rock Creek copper
and silver project
Sayona lithium project
Stibnite gold and antimony project
Li-Cycle recycling facility
Thacker Pass lithium project
New York
Rhyolite Ridge lithium project
Silver Peak
lithium mine
USA
U.S. Bankruptcy Court, Delaware
Mountain Pass rare earths mine
Washington, D.C.
Salton Sea lithium projects
Austin
Piedmont Lithium project
Houston
Li-Cycle recycling facility
Albemarle's Kings Mountain
lithium processing facility
Resolution copper project
Li-Cycle recycling facility
Morenci copper mine
BRAZIL
BOLIVIA
Brumadinho tailings dam
Salar de Uyuni lithium projects
Olaroz lithium mine
Atacama lithium mines
El Teniente copper mine
CHILE
ARGENTINA

THE GLOBAL BATTLE FOR GREEN ENERGY MINERALS

PROLOGUE

A Discovery

A GLINT OF LIGHT CAUGHT JERRY TIEHM'S EYE LATE ONE AFternoon as he drove through the cragged Nevada landscape and into the encroaching dark.

The New York Botanical Garden had sent the thirty-one-year-old botanist to collect samples of Nevada flowers and other vegetation for its library of plant samples known as a herbarium, the largest of its kind in the Western Hemisphere. Tiehm's assignment was simple: Find odd, unique, colorful, and hopefully undiscovered plants. He was then to flatten them using a press he kept in the back of his truck, store them between sheets of newspaper, and send them to New York, where they would be glued to large sheets of white paper, studied, catalogued, and preserved for future generations. If any plants were found to be interesting, more scientists would be sent out for further research. Then as now, Nevada's flora has long been the least explored in the United States; more is known about plants and flowers in remote Alaska than the jagged, desert corners of the Sagebrush State.[1]

"To me, it was a dream job," recalled Tiehm, who studied botany at the University of Nevada, Reno, partly to avoid being drafted for the Vietnam War.[2] "Nevada has always been the last frontier for plant collection."

It was May 18, 1983. Ronald Reagan lived in the White House. The space shuttle *Challenger* had its maiden launch the month prior and telecom provider Ameritech was preparing to make the world's first commercial cell phone call.[3] Six years prior, a scientist at Exxon (yes, *that*

Exxon) had invented the lithium-ion battery, a feat that would eventually revolutionize the world's economy and its fight against climate change. It was also an invention that would link directly with Tiehm's Nevada work that day, work that would attract one of the world's largest automakers, stoke the ire of one of America's most preeminent conservation groups, and spread worry through the corridors of power in Washington and Wall Street.

Tiehm was very much unaware of that future as he guided his burnt-orange-colored Chevrolet Blazer down a steep embankment of gravel barely recognizable as a road. All the botanist could think about was finding a safe place to camp. Those barren hills of Nevada known as the Silver Peak Range were not forgiving for those without a plan, especially in the stygian dark. But that hint of light, flickering ahead of the dusk, beckoned Tiehm.

Amid what looked to be unusual, light patches of ground surrounded by a sea of darker rock, the botanist noticed a wildflower that hugged the earth, almost like an herb.[4] Stems of about six or so inches protruded from the soil with leaves of a bluish gray hue and flowers of pale yellow.[5] Hundreds of the plants seemed grouped together densely at the site, known as Rhyolite Ridge, but Tiehm was unsure why. He had stumbled upon the plant at the peak of its blooming season, from May to June, when the golden flowers emerge resplendent for nature and dazzle the bees, spiders, and other creatures that pollinate it in the seemingly barren desert. By July, the flowers turn red with age and begin to cast off ripened seeds, propagating their next generation. Late summer brings a hibernation that lasts through the next year.[6]

Tiehm followed procedure. He collected fifteen samples of the flowers, pressed them, labeled them, and catalogued them for New York out of the bed of his truck. He pulled out his tent and camped for the night under the wide expanse of the Milky Way.[7] Back east, months later, Tiehm was reviewing his field notes and still couldn't identify the plant. James Reveal, a University of Maryland professor, who had also studied his notes, wrote to say why: Tiehm had likely discovered a species of plant previously unknown to science. Reveal, Tiehm, and a group of other botanists visited the site the following summer and collected even more samples. In 1985, Reveal announced the findings to the world in an academic journal. And in honor of its discoverer, the plant was given the moniker *Eriogonum tiehmii*, or Tiehm's buckwheat.

A small plant, Tiehm's buckwheat looms large in the green energy transition. Beneath the roots of the plant that Tiehm first discovered that warm spring day sits a massive deposit of lithium, which is used to make lithium-ion batteries that power millions of consumer electronic devices and electric vehicles. While Tiehm would eventually have seven plants named after him, it is Tiehm's buckwheat that grows only in the lithium-rich soils of those Nevada hills and nowhere else on Earth for reasons that rank among the many mysteries of the plant kingdom.[8]

When I visited Tiehm in Reno in the summer of 2022, he wore white New Balance sneakers and was dressed in a white *Hawaii Five-O* T-shirt tucked into navy-blue shorts. A pair of reading glasses rested on top of his balding head. Fit and trim, Tiehm's youthful physique and sharp mind belied his seven decades. He had no plans to retire and cede his unofficial title of "Nevada's premier modern botanist and plant explorer."[9]

Tiehm had been teaching at the University of Nevada, Reno, since 2014 and before that worked as a bellman and limousine driver for three of Reno's casinos, mostly the Peppermill.[10] He would often take long weekends away from the slot machines and poker tables to explore the state's remote landscape. "My experience in looking at plants out at the desert for fifty years is that the plants grow where they want to grow. And nowhere else," he said.

In 2016, an Australia-based company was hunting for gold in Nevada and realized that Rhyolite Ridge contained lithium. If it could be mined, it would be wildly profitable just as global demand for the white metal was set to spike. Electric vehicles from Tesla and others were increasingly seen as key tools to fight climate change. To get at that lithium, though, would require the company to dig an open-pit mine right where Tiehm found the flowers.

Thus, the paradox: What matters more, the plant or the lithium beneath it? This is a story about that choice, and the choices facing other regions across the United States and the world replete with lithium or copper, nickel, rare earths, or cobalt—metals critical to the construction of solar panels, electric vehicles, batteries, wind turbines, and an array of other products heralded as key to electrifying the world's economy and easing carbon emissions. Tiehm would later call it "blind luck" that such a rare plant sat atop this giant reserve of a key battery metal, but if that is the case, an industry hungry for lithium would surely call it misfortune. Throughout the world, supplies of metal sit atop land considered sacred, or too special, or too ecologically sensitive to disturb. Whether these lands should be dug up in an attempt to defuse climate change is one of the defining questions of our time. For the United States, which has less than 5 percent of the world's population but consumes almost 17 percent of its energy, this new green energy economy requires a collective reflection to which many are not accustomed. Other governments, too, are grappling with this transition, including China, which has 18 percent of the world's population and consumes 25 percent of its energy.[11]

Jerry Tiehm's discovery on that quiet Nevada hill in 1983 is emblematic of the stark choices at hand and a harbinger of the fight to stem climate change. "I'm now botanically immortal," Tiehm told me. "Years after I'm dead, people will still be talking about my discovery and its implications."

Tiehm had no clue just how right he was.

INTRODUCTION

A Turning Point

On Earth Day 2016, the United Nations held a signing ceremony in New York for member states to begin ratification of the Paris Climate Accords, the culmination of years of negotiations that had begun with the Framework Convention on Climate Change in 1992. Secretary-General Ban Ki-moon, U.S. Secretary of State John Kerry, and President François Hollande of France were among the scores of dignitaries that descended on the Big Apple, a collective show of unity designed to underscore the seriousness of the topic.[1] Kerry brought his granddaughter to indicate his belief that the agreement would benefit generations to come.[2]

Nearly two hundred nations had gathered in a suburb of the French capital months earlier to hash out ways the globe could speak and act with one voice on a strategy to mitigate climate change. The resulting agreement set a long-term goal of limiting the rise in average global temperatures this century to 2 degrees Celsius (3.6 Fahrenheit) and to reach net-zero global emissions by 2050. For that goal to be reached, it would mean ending the era of fossil fuels and converting the global economy to run entirely on batteries powered by wind turbines, solar panels, and other devices that churned out renewable energy. President Barack Obama called the Paris Accords one of his proudest accomplishments. "If we follow through on the commitments this agreement embodies, history will judge it as a turning point for our planet," Obama said when the accords went into effect after fifty-five countries representing 55 percent of global emissions had signed.[3]

Beyond the goals for member governments, the Paris Accords asked consumers across the globe to consider how their daily habits contributed to climate change. And that was a very good thing for the electric vehicle industry. Transportation accounts for almost a quarter of global carbon dioxide (CO_2) emissions, according to the International Energy Agency, boosting the greenhouse gas effect and warming the Earth.[4] In 2020, greenhouse gas emissions from the transportation sector accounted for roughly 27 percent of total U.S. emissions, or 1.6 billion metric tons (tonnes) of CO_2. That makes it the largest contributor to the country's emissions. The rate of the transportation sector's emissions jumped in absolute terms more than any other sector from 1990 to 2019, largely due to an increase in travel, according to U.S. Environmental Protection Agency data.[5] And distances traveled have only grown; in the United States, the number of vehicle miles traveled jumped 108 percent from 1980 to 2010.[6] These and other human-wrought changes to the Earth's environment have likely sparked a new age in the planet's history known as the Anthropocene, the age in which humans put their collective stamp on the planet and its climate.[7]

Put simply, personal automobiles that burn gasoline or diesel fuel are making the planet warmer, a fact the nearly two hundred nations that signed the Paris Accords seemed to acknowledge publicly. Lithium demand was projected to boom, with the International Energy Agency forecasting a 40 percent jump by 2040 in global demand for the white metal used to make EV batteries if the world is going to meet the goals set by the accords.[8] Other metals would be needed in far greater quantities as well. The IEA found that between 2022 and 2030 the world needed to build fifty new lithium mines, sixty new nickel mines, and at least seventeen cobalt mines.[9] The moment was ripe for EVs and other green energy devices to go mainstream; the technology was already in place, fueling global interest in the building blocks needed to go green.

As this transition began to unfold, I was reporting for Reuters about another energy transition—the U.S. shale revolution. For more than six years I had tracked the technology, the money, and the people reviving the American oil and natural gas industry. It was an in-depth assignment that took me from the news organization's offices in New York's Times Square, to a nearly two-year stretch living in North Dakota's Bakken oilfields, and then down to Texas to cover ExxonMobil and Chevron, with several Vienna secondments in between to cover the Organization of the Petroleum Exporting Countries. (The cartel's ministers at the time were curiously afraid of America's fracking renaissance.) In mid-2018, I was ready for a change and jumped at the chance to write about the metals that were set to undergird the green energy revolution. I had already reported on one major energy transition; here was a chance to cover a second one, and one that held the potential of making more of the world not only energy independent, but healthier as well.

⚡

LITHIUM-ION BATTERIES WERE first invented in 1977 by the U.S. scientist Stanley Whittingham, who was working for the oil giant Exxon in its New Jersey laboratories.[10] While Whittingham and two peers eventually were awarded the Nobel Prize in Chemistry for the invention—the Nobel Committee in 2019 lauded it for "making possible a fossil-fuel-free society"—Exxon passed on the technology in part due to concern that early versions of the battery would spontaneously combust, a problem known as "thermal runaway," one caused by lithium's reactive properties.[11] Falling oil prices also revived gasoline's appeal after the end of the Arab Oil Embargo, lessening the crunch to find an oil replacement.[12] The addition of cobalt to the battery's composition was later found to be a way to mitigate those explosions. Japan's Sony eventually ended up with the patents and in 1990 debuted a line of handheld camcorders powered by rechargeable lithium-ion batteries. These batteries were just as powerful as traditional lead-acid batteries. Thanks to lithium's electrochemical properties, they could be engineered to be lighter and smaller.

The invention helped personal electronics go mainstream. Soon, laptops, cell phones, and a range of other consumer electronics were everywhere, powered by the rechargeable batteries built with metals that can be reused thousands of times.[13] Even still, most of the world's consumers paid little attention to how much the Periodic Table of Elements affected their daily lives and, increasingly, their futures. While the United Nations declared 2019 the International Year of the Periodic Table of Chemical Elements to honor the 150th anniversary of Dmitri Mendeleev's creation of the iconic chart, the average shopper in a department store would struggle to identify which of its constituent members go into a computer battery, or an automobile, or a solar panel. Just over a quarter of Americans told a 2019 survey they had never heard of rare earths elements, the crucial materials used to build magnets that power electric vehicles.[14]

When Martin Eberhard founded Tesla Motors in 2003, the lithium-ion battery was very much fringe in the automobile sector, treated as a kind of science experiment by Ford, Chrysler, and other auto giants. Elon Musk joined Tesla the following year and started the company on a path to launching its first vehicle—the Roadster—in 2008. It was a journey that involved battery partnerships with Germany's Daimler, Japan's Toyota, and even the U.S. government, a tortuous path chronicled in *Car Wars*, John Fialka's definitive account of the early years of the EV industry.

With electric cars making oil changes, miles per gallon estimates, radiators, and other staples of the internal combustion engine a thing of the past, consumers increasingly are being forced to master a new set of terminologies, starting with the structure of the lithium-ion battery. It has four main parts: an anode, cathode, electrolyte, and separator. An anode is typically made with graphite. A cathode is made with lithium and, depending on design, a mix of nickel, manganese, cobalt, or aluminum. Between the two is an electrolyte solution often made of lithium, with a separator composed of plastic in between. Inside an EV's motor sits more than a mile of copper wiring that is used to help turn power from the battery into motion. When the battery is powering a car or other device, lithium ions flow from the anode through the separator to the cathode. The process is reversed during charging.[15]

A lithium-ion battery's power is directly related to its metal content, but unpacking the difference between kilowatts and kilowatt hours, when many have grown accustomed to thinking of a vehicle's power in "horsepower" for the past hundred years, can seem daunting. Solar panels and wind turbines also generate electricity in kilowatt hours.

To get answers, I asked the Argonne National Laboratory chemical engineer Shabbir Ahmed to help me understand not only how much lithium, copper, cobalt, nickel, and other metals goes into the average electric car but also to better understand the language of electricity.[16] Ahmed, who studied at the Bangladesh University of Engineering and Technology before earning his Ph.D. from the University of Nebraska, runs Argonne's BatPaC tool, which helps calculate the materials needed for a battery's energy storage capacity.[17]

A kilowatt is the rate of energy flow and a kilowatt-hour is a quantity of energy.[18] (In a gasoline-powered engine, the fuel injection rate can be expressed in kilowatts, while the gasoline in the fuel tank can be expressed in kilowatt-hours.) The larger the battery, the greater its electricity storage capacity. The standard Tesla Model 3—the most popular EV in the world in 2021—has a 55.4 kWh battery, meaning it can deliver 55.4 kilowatts of power for one hour.[19] How fast that battery charges depends on the charger itself; a typical household plug charges at about 1 kW, meaning it would take about fifty-five hours to charge the Model 3 in this analogy. But most commercial or public chargers operate far faster, typically 50 kW, meaning it would take slightly more than an hour to recharge that car. Some superchargers operate at 250 kW or more.[20]

"If you have more energy to store, then you need a bigger battery. And the bigger the battery, the longer the driving range you have," Ahmed explained over Zoom, his long white hair evoking Doc Brown from the 1985 film *Back to the Future*. Not surprisingly, the bigger the battery, the more metals you need. That Model 3, Ahmed explained, uses 0.11 kilograms of lithium for every kWh. (One kilogram is about 2.2 pounds.) That means that Tesla's 55.4 kWh battery was built using roughly 6 kilograms of lithium.[21] Using Ahmed's estimates, that same battery's cells also held about 42 kilograms of nickel, nearly 8 kilograms of cobalt, 8 kilograms of aluminum, nearly 55 kilograms of graphite, and about 17 kilograms of copper, with even more aluminum and copper elsewhere in the battery.

The problem for the U.S. automakers, though, was that the United

States was producing very few of these metals just as EVs and other green energy devices began to go mainstream, a concern of industry executives that has only grown since Tesla introduced the Roadster.[22] Coronavirus put these fears into overdrive, reinforcing to consumers how much their everyday lives depended on products such as pharmaceuticals, clothing, and energy, which were linked to far-flung manufacturing plants, a point driven home in *Pandemic, Inc.: Chasing the Capitalists and Thieves Who Got Rich While We Got Sick*, J. David McSwane's deep dive into the shady financial underbelly of the governmental response to COVID-19. Russia's invasion of Ukraine further focused these fears.

Energy security *used* to be about crude oil and natural gas. Now it's also about lithium, copper, and other EV metals.

Consider the following:

- Chile and Australia by 2023 were the world's largest lithium producers but relied on China to process much of that metal into a form usable for EV batteries. Two of the world's largest lithium companies are Chinese, one of which also controls a quarter of its Chilean rival SQM, which produces much of the world's lithium in the Atacama salt flats. The United States produces only small amounts of lithium at a facility first built in the 1960s and has no large-scale facilities to process it, even though it has enough untapped supply to build millions of EVs.[23] China has some lithium reserves locked in hard-to-extract deposits.[24]

- China is the world's largest copper consumer and aggressively buys the red metal, a major conductor of electricity, from Chile, Peru, and other nations. U.S. copper production dropped nearly 5 percent from 2017 through 2021 despite the country having twice as much supply as China.[25]

- Indonesia holds the world's largest supplies of nickel and has moved to block exports of the key metal to build its own EV industry.[26] The only U.S. nickel mine will be depleted by 2025 and the United States does not have a nickel refinery. The metal is key to boosting an EV battery's energy density, and thus allowing an EV to drive farther on a single charge. An EV battery made with nickel uses 40 to 60 kilograms of the metal, whereas an internal combustion engine only uses 1 to 2 kilograms.[27]

- The Democratic Republic of the Congo holds the world's largest supplies of cobalt, which is used to prevent EV battery erosion, but child labor often is used there to extract the mineral, a source of large concern for automakers, regulators, and policymakers.[28] Elon Musk vowed in 2018 that future versions of Teslas will use no cobalt as a result, though as of this writing he had not achieved that goal.[29] The United States in 2021 imported fourteen times more cobalt than it mined.[30]

- The United States started the modern rare earths industry in the years after the Second World War, but slowly let the entire industry move to China, which now controls the mining and processing of the critical elements used to make magnets that translate power into motion.[31] Without rare earths, there would be no wind turbines, no Teslas, and no F-35 fighter jets, among myriad other high-tech devices built using specialized magnets made from rare earths. China threatened in 2019 to block its export to the United States, which has one rare earths mine but no processing facilities.[32]

- No new mines for any of these metals have opened in the United States for decades, with the exception of a small Nevada copper facility in 2019.[33] Yet multiple projects have been proposed that could produce enough copper to build more than 6 million EVs, enough lithium to build more than 2 million EVs, and enough nickel to build more than 60,000 EVs.[34]

- In 2019—the last full year not affected by the coronavirus pandemic—nearly 250,000 EVs were sold in the United States.[35]

EV sales in the country were slightly above 400,000 in 2021[36] and 807,000 in 2022. That same year, total U.S. auto sales fell by 8 percent, hinting at Americans' disillusionment with internal combustion engines.[37]

- That rising EV demand will need to be met by a fresh supply of lithium and other metals. "We want to figure out what are limiting factors for accelerating the advent of a sustainable energy future and whatever those limiting factors are, Tesla will take action on those limiting factors," Musk said in April 2022. "So right now, we think mining and refining lithium appears to be a limiting factor, and it certainly is responsible for quite a bit of cost growth in the sales. It's, I think, the single biggest cost growth item right now, percentage basis, although just for those who don't totally know this, the actual content of lithium in a lithium-ion cell is maybe around 2 or 3 percent of the [battery] cell."[38] The average U.S. price for an EV jumped to $66,000 that summer, up 30 percent from the prior year, as lithium prices spiked amid rising demand and little supply.[39] Tesla imposed one of the biggest price jumps.[40]

- Despite the role such proposed U.S. projects would play in abrogating climate change and even lessening the cost of green energy products, each one faces strong, legitimate opposition from environmentalists, neighbors, Indigenous groups, or others, underscoring the dilemma facing the country as it tries to go green.[41]

- In 2021, China had either built or was building 148 of the world's 200 lithium-ion battery gigafactories. Europe had 21. North America had 11.[42] By 2029, 101 of the additional 136 lithium-ion battery plants planned for development will be in China.[43] Despite that, auto industry executives had grown increasingly concerned that at least 90 percent of the battery supply chain—including mines—needed to meet aggressive EV transformation targets for the global transportation sector didn't exist yet.[44] By 2023, China had cemented its EV supply chain prowess and it cost about 10,000 euros less to build an EV in China than in Europe.[45]

- U.S. environmental regulators have put multiple proposed domestic mines under regulatory scrutiny, even as other parts of the government consider loans for new projects, a disconnect in strategy that frustrates miners and conservationists alike. Presidents Obama and Trump blocked mining projects for environmental or cultural reasons. (Yes, even Trump.) Biden blocked some mines, yet ordered government attorneys to defend others, often without any clear indication as to what prompted the differentiation.

- The net result has been a chilling effect on U.S. mine development, even after 2022's Inflation Reduction Act linked EV tax credits to domestic production of EV minerals. (If mines can't get built, how can consumers get the EV tax credit?[46]) Automakers protested almost as soon as the measure was passed that it could take years to find adequate metals supply in the United States.[47] Opposition to mines has long forced the country to rely on metals imports, a step that ironically has boosted global greenhouse gas emissions by increasing shipping from overseas mines to processing facilities, most of which are in Asia.

"The United States must secure reliable and sustainable supplies of critical minerals and metals to ensure resilience across U.S. manufacturing and defense needs, and do so in a manner consistent with America's labor, environmental, equity and other values," Biden's White House explained in a 2021 report on gaps in the EV supply chain.[48] To achieve the climate goals set out by the Paris Accords, global demand for lithium and graphite for EV batteries will need to increase more than 4,000 percent by 2040. President Joe Biden has promised to convert the entire U.S. government fleet—about 640,000 vehicles—to EVs.

That plan alone could require a twelvefold increase in U.S. lithium production by 2030.[49]

"You can't have green energy without mining," said Mark Senti, chief executive of the Florida-based rare earths magnet company Advanced Magnet Lab Inc. "That's just the reality."[50] The United States wants to go green, but to do that, it will need to produce more metals, especially lithium, rare earths, and copper. That means more mines. And mines are very controversial in the United States. Who wants to live next to a giant hole in the ground? Mines are dusty, increase truck traffic, and use dynamite for blasting that can rattle windows and crack foundations. Many mines throughout history have polluted waterways and produced toxic waste that scarred landscapes for generations. They also require astronomical amounts of water to operate. Stewart Udall, who ran the U.S. Interior Department under Presidents John. F. Kennedy and Lyndon B. Johnson, described mining as a "search-and-destroy mission."[51]

And yet more than 90 percent of U.S. households that own a vehicle would spend less on energy and reduce their greenhouse gas emissions if that vehicle were electric-powered, a startling finding from University of Michigan scientists that laid bare the need for more metals.[52] Wall Street expects lithium demand to surge by 2030 but is skeptical that mining companies will be able to match that demand with supply, especially for lithium.[53] And the process to produce these metals can vary widely by type and is vastly different than oil and natural gas production. Given all this history, it's perhaps understandable that U.S. government officials in Washington have not spoken with one voice on the issue. While the Pentagon grew increasingly concerned at the dawn of the twenty-first century about China's control of the industry that makes rare earths and other weapons-grade minerals, one of its divisions for years, under Democratic and Republican presidencies alike, sold domestic stockpiles of minerals considered strategic.[54] Trump used the coronavirus pandemic to fast-track development of the Thacker Pass lithium project in Nevada, even while he killed the proposed Pebble Mine in Alaska, which would have been a large source of domestic copper.[55, 56] Biden froze development of the controversial

Resolution Copper mine in Arizona, even while his administration's lawyers defended it in court.

"This country has to make a decision," Senator Joe Manchin, a West Virginia Democrat, told me. "We're so pristine in America, we think someone else will do the dirty work of mining for us. But we're just in a very, very vulnerable position."[57]

China has been scouring the world the past twenty years for cobalt, lithium, copper, and other metals. After the United States pulled out of Afghanistan in 2021, Chinese mining companies began negotiating with the Taliban to develop the Mes Aynak copper deposit, about two hours outside of Kabul.[58] China's mining companies spent billions of dollars buying cobalt mines in the Congo.[59] In Argentina, China has invested in six major lithium projects.[60] As 2023 dawned, India began scouring Argentina's reserves of copper and lithium to sate its burgeoning EV industry.[61] The European Union aims to be carbon neutral by 2050, a plan relying on increased metals supply.[62] Each of these moves reflects just the latest iteration of the global hunt for metals, a hunt that has been going on for thousands of years. Paul Julius Reuter, the man who founded the news organization for which I work, signed a contract with the Shah of Persia in 1872 that gave him complete control over the mining of iron ore, copper, and other metals across the country now known as Iran. (The contract collapsed a year later under intense local opposition to a foreigner digging up the countryside.[63])

The mines opposed by the environmental lobby in the near term are, paradoxically, necessary to battle climate change in the long term. Recycling alone cannot provide the materials needed to fuel the global green energy transition.[64] Before its very eyes, the United States is watching its petroleum dependence on the Organization of the Petroleum Exporting Countries transition into a dependence on China, Congo, and others for the building blocks of green energy devices. China has threatened to block exports to the United States of rare earths, used to make the magnets that help turn power from an EV battery into motion.

The oil and natural gas revolution that swept the global economy in the late nineteenth century and early twentieth century involved little to no collective weighing of the environmental, social, and economic costs and benefits of burning fossil fuels. Indeed, while the muckraking journalist Ida Tarbell became famous for exposing the malfeasance of John D. Rockefeller Sr.'s Standard Oil, she did so primarily to point out his greed and monopolistic business practices, not the environmental harm that can be caused by oil extraction and refining. The electrification transformation now taking place does and must involve a dialogue about what society is willing to accept and what it is expecting.

And in some sense, to rely on other nations for the building blocks of green energy is to perpetuate the very kind of economic colonialism that has pervaded Western culture for centuries. In *The Nutmeg's Curse,* a seismic tome on climate change and human exploitation, Amitav Ghosh explores how what we think of as the root causes of the climate crisis (coal, crude oil, and natural gas production) extend further back to the fifteenth century and the enslavement of Banda Island residents by Dutch invaders to produce nutmeg via forced plantation farming. By imposing such a rigorous and destructive style of cultivation that eschewed traditional farming techniques and disrespected natural processes, Ghosh argues, the seeds of the climate crisis were planted.[65] Extrapolating Ghosh's core argument for the green energy transition requires grappling with where, how, and why each nation procures its own green energy building blocks, and that there likely will not be an equitable green energy transition unless the globe reckons with how the climate crisis began.

"We throw around these words 'energy transition' and 'the future of energy' and 'climate action,' but basically what we're doing right now—this generation—is having a massive overhaul of the entire global energy system while at the same time we are electrifying everything," said Amos Hochstein, an energy advisor to Obama and Biden. "The geopolitics of energy of the 20th century that centered around producing countries of oil, gas and coal is now changing . . . to the producing countries of all the inputs for solar and electric vehicles and batteries. And that is things that we haven't talked about in the 20th century. That's the nickel and magnesium and graphite and cobalt and lithium and rare earths and other critical minerals."[66]

The United States is expected to produce just 3 percent of the world's annual lithium needs by 2030, even though it holds about 24 percent of the world's lithium reserves.[67] The country should want to produce more of these metals and support a diversified, global network for production to prevent geopolitical rivals from cornering the supply of these strategic materials as the world goes green, Hochstein added. That logic, though, has been cold comfort to the many who oppose new mines, whether for religious, cultural, or environmental reasons, and who have spent decades sounding the alarm about humanity's deleterious impact on the planet's environment.

Mining does not have the best reputation. There's no way around the fact that mines are gargantuan creations that maim the Earth's surface. They are loud and they are intrusive. Going back to the dawn of time, mines have displaced thousands—perhaps millions—of people, polluted waterways, and produced trillions of tonnes of waste, some of it radioactive. In Chile, the world's largest copper producer and second-largest lithium producer, 65 percent of the country's water is used by its mining sector alone.[68] Mining is also in a perpetual state of decline, forcing its practitioners to always be searching for the next deposit of metal to dig up, process, and sell. Mining practices have improved since the turn of the twenty-first century, with many companies envisioning a day when fully electric fleets of bulldozers and dump trucks won't spew diesel exhaust into the air.

Some miners try to use their place in the burgeoning EV industry to shield their industry from any criticism. In May 2020, the mining giant Rio Tinto blew up Aboriginal rock shelters in Western Australia that had stood for more than 46,000 years. The move was entirely legal—Rio had followed the permitting process—but drew immediate outcry because the company had destroyed a site considered sacred to the traditional owners, known as the Puutu Kunti Kurrama and Pinikura peoples (PKKP).[69]

As boneheaded and disrespectful as Rio's mistake was, it paled in comparison to what had happened in Brazil the year prior at a mining complex owned by Vale, another mining giant. In January 2019, as hundreds of employees were in a Brumadinho mess hall eating lunch, the nearby B1 tailings dam collapsed and released a torrent of toxic sludge that quickly subsumed the dining hall, its inhabitants, and much of the nearby countryside. Nearly three hundred people died.[70] (Tailings dams store the detritus of the mining process. If every hundred pounds of dirt removed from the earth contain only one pound of copper, for example, that means there's generally ninety-nine pounds of waste in liquid or solid form that must be stored in perpetuity, usually in such tailings dam facilities.)

Security camera footage shows the moment the lip of the 86-meter-tall dam collapsed, followed by the base and then the entire structure. Played out in slow motion, the collapse looks like something from a children's TV show, while angles from the footage show trucks furiously straining to escape the river of deadly mud.[71] It didn't have to happen, especially because that tailings dam had been known to have structural issues since 2003. The accident reinforced the broader public's mistrust of the mining industry, especially claims that modern mining eschews the practices of the past and "is not your father's mining," a popular talking point from industry executives.

"Automakers are realizing their future is in EVs, but that the supply chain for those EVs cannot be tainted by human rights abuses and toxic pollution," said Payal Sampat of Earthworks, an environmental advocacy organization that closely tracks the global mining industry. Another organization that monitors mining is the Church of England, which uses the clout of its pension fund, worth more than £3 billion by 2024, to sway corporations to boost safety practices. The church's pension fund found late in 2019 that more than a third of the world's tailings dams were at high risk of causing catastrophic damage to their neighboring communities if they collapsed. They also found that more tailings dams had been built in the past decade than during any previous decade. (Chinese and Indian miners did not participate in the Church's study, which prompted more questions about mining safety practices in those two countries.) The mining industry, it was clear, had work to do.[72]

In the aftermath of the disaster Brazil's government outlawed the type of tailings dam design that had collapsed, but the United States did not follow suit, fueling concern in Minnesota, Arizona, and other states that similar collapses could happen there if new mines were built. "We'll be looking up at a 500-foot dam containing 1.6 billion tonnes of toxic waste and wondering when it is going to collapse and bury the community," an Arizonan said of Rio Tinto's plans to build a large copper mine and tailings waste storage site.[73] It was a fear that had petrified residents near a diamond mine's tailings dam in Jagersfontein, South Africa, for years before it actually happened one summer day in 2022 when the dam collapsed, sending a wall of muddy sludge into a nearby residential community. Rio-Rita Breytenbach, a local resident, was swept up by the muck and dragged for six miles.[74]

Are risks—even tragedies—such as these to be tolerated on the road to a green energy future? Conversely, if the United States halts mining projects, does that hasten the onslaught of climate change while also giving China and others an economic weapon? Even Hollywood is thinking about the topic, albeit in its own zany way. The 2021 satirical film *Don't Look Up* depicts the global response to the Earth's pending destruction from an inbound comet and the decision by U.S. policymakers not to blow it up because it contains highly valuable concentrations of rare earths to aid the climate fight. When a plan to harvest those minerals fails, the planet is destroyed.

Mine supporters frequently say the United States already has some of the strictest environmental standards for mining in the world. It takes as much as a decade (or longer) to obtain a federal mining permit, but in Canada the process routinely takes only a few years.[75] Mine opponents ask about the cost. *Is this mine worth it? Does this piece of land need to be dug into? Why here? Why now?* When asked at each successive mine site, the opposition adds up, essentially blocking new projects and ultimately America's efforts to honor the spirit of the Paris Accords. Yet while it can be cumbersome to obtain a U.S. federal mining permit—and there have been legislative attempts to shorten the process[76]—the benefits can be immense: Companies do not have to pay royalties on minerals they extract from most federal lands, a quirk of the law that has governed mining in the western United States since 1872.

That is one of the reasons mining is the most lucrative part of the EV supply chain, with returns in recent years above 10 percent, according to a study by the banking giant Citi. Automakers, that same study showed, make returns of less than 2 percent when building an EV.[77]

"One of the ways we address climate change is to produce more EVs, and that needs more copper. That copper mine has to be somewhere, and some will support that mine, others will oppose it," said Scot Anderson, an attorney who helps mining companies navigate the U.S. permitting process.[78]

Relying on imports—jockeying for supply on the global market—also would delay efforts to electrify the nation's automobiles and could boost greenhouse gas emissions by increasing shipping from overseas mines to processing facilities, most of which are in Asia, partially undermining the rationale behind building more EVs. In an attempt to contend with that supply chain and spur U.S. production, the Inflation Reduction Act, approved by Congress and Biden in 2022, links the country's EV tax credit to production from either the country itself or twenty free trade partners, only one of which is on the African continent.[79]

"The (EV) supply chain has to go all the way to the mines. That's where the real cost is, and people in the U.S. don't want mining in their neighborhoods," Jim Farley, the head of Ford Motor Company, told a gathering of Detroit business leaders in 2021.[80] At the time, Farley and Ford had begun to consider where exactly they would procure lithium for their ambitious electrification goals.

They started to look at Rhyolite Ridge.

CHAPTER ONE

A Choice

"You should meet James Calaway." So advised a banking contact of mine in the fall of 2018. "He knows everything there is to know about lithium and starting a lithium company."

I was transitioning from my coverage of the U.S. oil industry's fracking revolution to coverage of the miners jockeying to supply lithium and other metals for the green energy transition. It was an opportunity I looked forward to, even if it was daunting. I had already reported on one major energy transition; here was a chance to cover a second one. Opportunities like that don't come along too often. But while the politics and production of fossil fuels are well understood and similar, making a battery would require multiple metals, some made and sourced in wildly different manners. Rather than report on just oil and natural gas, I would now find myself digging into lithium, copper, nickel, cobalt, and a strange classification of seventeen minor metals known as rare earths. (Not to mention gold and silver, which had been the mining industry's mainstays for thousands of years.)

I dove into the challenge of meeting new experts, especially those like Calaway with money on the line and skin in the game. So, on my banking contact's advice, I emailed Calaway one morning in December 2018 asking if he would be open to meet over a casual coffee. Within ninety minutes, my cell phone buzzed.

"Hello, is this Ernest? This is James Calaway. I got your email."

Now, *here* was someone eager to talk about lithium.

Not only was Calaway eager to talk, he was also based in Houston, where I had decided to remain after I switched beats. Calaway and I agreed to grab lunch later that week. The first thing I noticed about Calaway were his eyeglasses, broad, rimmed glass circles evoking the style of J. K. Rowling's Harry Potter. He dressed casually, with his shirt untucked in the style of an executive who didn't care to put his brainpower into how he looked or what he wore, but into other things. (It was not at all what I was used to; ExxonMobil, for instance, has a conservative dress code.)

Calaway had spent the bulk of his career on a string of seemingly whimsical yet extraordinarily complex ideas, each helping form what he had grown to consider his life's mission: saving the planet from the ravages of extreme temperatures and climate change. It was a mission fueled in part by his family's background. A sixth-generation Texan, Calaway grew up watching his father single-mindedly build a successful oil and natural gas company in the world's energy capital. His father even gave him the middle name Derrick to evoke the towers commonly seen atop oilfield wells.

Given that lineage, the idea that Calaway would one day run not one but two companies underpinning the renewable energy revolution was remarkable. Fossil fuels, certainly not lithium or other electric vehicle building blocks, flowed through his veins. "When people think of Texas, they think of oil," Calaway told me. "But the roots of my interest in energy were in just the opposite area."[1]

An enticing offer came to Calaway in early 2016 to help build a mine in a remote Nevada desert. While the entrepreneur relished a challenge, he wasn't sure the United States had the willingness to stomach a new mine. The country had last opened a hard-rock mine in the 1970s. (Hard-rock mines are for gold, iron ore, silver, and other metals generally considered "tough," whereas soft-rock mines tend to be for coal and other fossil fuels, as well as chalk, like the famous white cliffs in Dover, England.[2]) This was not a stereotypical mining project to produce gold or iron ore, but rather lithium, a key ingredient for lithium-ion batteries. The project's significance began to crystallize. Calaway was intrigued.

⚡

FEW WERE TALKING about climate change when Calaway came of age in the 1970s. That was because nuclear weapons were widely seen as the most likely way a mass-extinction event would take place. It would be more than thirty years before Al Gore's film *An Inconvenient Truth* made the greenhouse effect a common talking point in American households.

At the University of Texas at Austin, Calaway studied economics under Walt Rostow, who had been U.S. National Security Advisor to President Lyndon B. Johnson. Inspired in part by Rostow's anti-Communist stance, Calaway found the first way he could try to save the planet: nuclear arms control. "I perceived great risk at the time between nation-states. It was just madness that we had this globe and we run the risk of nuclear attack destroying everything," he said. Rostow pushed Calaway to pursue a graduate degree at Oxford University, and for two years on the banks of the River Cherwell, Calaway immersed himself in the politics and policy of halting nuclear arms proliferation.

Ronald Reagan's 1980 presidential election changed Calaway's plans; the new president from California signaled a willingness to boost the nation's arsenal of nuclear weapons, and he did. If the world wasn't going to stop making bombs, Calaway thought the best place for humans to go was up, as in outer space. He and some retired NASA engineers formed Space Industries Inc., a private company with the goal of commercializing space travel and space living.

While Reagan's plans killed Calaway's arms control aspirations, the president made amends in 1988 by proposing to Congress the new startup company be given a $700 million contract to build and operate a private space station where NASA could run experiments on microgravity, material science, and other areas focused on how humans could eventually live full-time outside the Earth's atmosphere. It was a bold plan, years ahead of its time, that in many ways evokes the current arrangement the space agency has with SpaceX, the rocket company controlled by billionaire Elon Musk, who also controls EV giant Tesla, which overtook Toyota to become the world's most valuable carmaker in 2020.[3]

Like most things ahead of its time, Space Industries failed. The NASA bureaucracy feared it would sap funding for its own space station plans and lobbied heavily against it behind closed doors. Congress was anxious about spending too much money on a private venture literally out of this world. The final blow came in 1989 when the National Research Council—a collection of scientists that advises the U.S. president and Congress—urged that the program be scrapped. Calaway himself is quoted in press coverage from the time urging NASA not to be shortsighted and to realize a small, private space station could be the bridge to a large, public-run station, which would take years to build. (The International Space Station would not debut for another decade.)

Beyond the failure, it was Washington's inability to create a cogent, unified plan for furthering an essential area of study—in this case, space exploration—that irked Calaway the most. How could Washington's policymakers be so shortsighted? Didn't they realize this private space station would help the United States immensely in the areas of science, exploration, and automation? Did they even care beyond the next election cycle? Were different parts of the government talking to one another? (Years later, Calaway's company would be named a finalist for U.S. Department of Energy funding, even as the U.S. Fish and Wildlife Service threatened to take an action that could effectively kill the company.) Space Industries was sold off to a company that used its technology to make research equipment. A private station was never built. "That was my first experience in business recognizing that what politicians say they want and what they actually propose as law and policy are not the same thing," Calaway told me.

Years went by and Calaway focused on a string of seemingly unrelated businesses. He built, ran, and sold a software company just as the Internet was ascendant. He opened a dessert bar. He joined the board of a Houston charter school. Still, the Texan's legacy in energy and its money kept calling. With his identical twin brother, John—they each call themselves "Brother"—he started a business focused on 3D seismic technology for the oil and gas industry, a mistake, he now admits, given what he had grown to consider his raison d'être. After a few years, he quit.

"It was not morally okay for me to continue to be devoting my life to producing oil and gas that was going to harm the planet for my children and grandchildren. I just couldn't get myself to continue to do that." The entrepreneur warned his home state to diversify its economy: "The promise for young people is not in oil." But where to go next? What to do? Calaway embarked on a metaphorical wandering in the corporate wilderness, searching for where he could put his entrepreneurial skills to work.

In 2007, Calaway did what a lot of America's corporate dreamers do when they're hungry for inspiration: He went to Aspen. The Aspen Ideas Festival, founded by the historian Walter Isaacson, was focused intently that year on the ongoing wars in Iraq and Afghanistan. The region also contains a lot of oil, which held little interest to Calaway. "All the discussions were invariably about the Middle East, the Middle East, the Middle East," he recalled. "I just couldn't take it." Tucked in a corner of the agenda, Calaway found a breakout session billed to discuss electric vehicles, a topic he knew little about. General Motors had launched the all-electric EV1 in 1996, and Toyota launched the hybrid Prius model globally the following year. Both were niche products that gained instant cult status.

GM gained notoriety by deciding after only three years that the EV1 was unprofitable to produce, in part because it couldn't find enough replacement parts to repair the vehicles when they broke down, a problem that presaged the battle to create a U.S. electric vehicle supply chain. GM had all the EV1 models destroyed, fueling conspiracy theories that it was in bed with the oil industry and providing ample fodder for the 2006 documentary *Who Killed the Electric Car?*

In the television drama *Brothers & Sisters*, Sally Field's matriarchal character Nora Walker drives a Prius and frequently waxes poetic about the dangers of climate change. Field's Walker likely had little clue the lithium used to make her Prius came from South America and was processed in China before being turned into a battery cathode in Japan, a meandering supply chain little changed in the ensuing years.[4] Few knew this, including Calaway, until he went to Aspen and got hooked on the potential of electric cars to help save the planet.

"I was reading everything I could about electric cars, but there was not that much out there to read about them. I found myself going to battery conferences, and that was one of the worst things you could ever do with your life because it's all just a bunch of chemical engineers."

I won't disagree with Calaway. My first time at a battery conference—in 2018 for Reuters—was overwhelming, dizzying, and confusing. Acronyms like NCA, LCE, NCM, and BEV were bandied about like a secret language known only to the initiated. I grew to dread going to the conference happy hours, fearing that as a journalist covering the industry, I would be expected to go toe-to-toe with Ph.D. scientists on the most esoteric of EV topics. Calaway felt the same. So he started reading academic papers. He subscribed to journals. He brushed up on his chemistry. Increasingly, he started noticing a pattern. Sprinkled throughout all the papers he was reading, like pepper in a salad, was a two-letter chemical symbol: Li.

Li stands for lithium. The lightest metal, it's found near the top of the Periodic Table of Elements and is enormously good at retaining an electric charge, making it the perfect anchor for the lithium-ion battery. Calaway realized that all the chemical equations used to build those batteries contained that symbol: Li. "And I said to myself, 'Well, heck, if there's going to be an electric vehicle revolution, we're going to need a whole lot of lithium.'" In that moment, Calaway knew he had to find lithium somewhere in the world.

⚡

LITHIUM CAN BE found in several types of rock that tend to have some connection to ancient volcanoes, hinting perhaps at the primordial origins of a metal that is now seen as key to saving our planet. The Swedish chemist Johan August Arfwedson is credited with being the first to identify lithium when, in 1817, working in the laboratory of one of the founders of modern chemistry, his fellow Swede Jöns Jacob Berzelius, he successfully separated it as a salt from the mineral petalite. (Lithium is also found in spodumene, a mineral common across Australia; lepidolite, which is found in parts of China; and deposits of salty water known as brine.) A Brazilian scientist, José Bonifácio de Andrada e Silva, had previously discovered petalite on a Swedish island but had not been able to tease out the metal inside. Production of lithium gradually was refined over the next hundred years or so, but demand was always niche. Lithium was used to make greases during the Second World War, giving tanks operated by the Allies an advantage over their Nazi rivals. After the war, lithium was used to help build hydrogen bombs, the development of which by the United States made it the largest lithium producer in the world thanks to mines that would be developed in North Carolina and a brine evaporation facility in Nevada.

Buzz Aldrin, the Apollo 11 astronaut, speaks fondly in his memoir of a lithium derivative known as lithium hydroxide, largely because it helps absorb carbon dioxide—a critical function in the recesses of space.[5] For reasons that are still unclear to modern medicine, lithium has some kind of balancing effect on nerve receptors in the human brain. That is to say, it is a mood stabilizer and is commonly prescribed for those living with depression or bipolar disorder.

As a reporter, I covered the lithium industry for years before getting to hold the element in its pure metal form in 2022 at an Albemarle Corp. laboratory in North Carolina. Lithium, as a rule, likes to bond with other elements, so several intense chemical reactions are needed to transform it into a stand-alone metal. Inside Albemarle's Kings Mountain facility, the company's scientists had extracted enough lithium to form a cylinder that looked about the size of a large can of pineapple juice commonly found in grocery stores. I expected it to be heavy; at least it *looked* heavy. But picking it up, it was no heavier than a cell phone, maybe three or four pounds at most. If seeing is believing, feeling and touching brings a heightened state of believing. I immediately understood why this, the lightest element, was crucial for use in automotive batteries.

Power is an exponential of voltage; the higher the voltage, the more power you have. Because of lithium's small size and light weight, its electrons can move inside a battery at surprisingly fast speeds. That makes it rare when compared with other metals on the Periodic Table of Elements and ideally suited for use in a battery. There aren't any immediately available substitutes that can mimic all of its properties. That is why, for Calaway and an increasing number of investors and corporate executives, finding lithium was a growing obsession.

⚡

IN EARLY 2009, Calaway sat alone on a salt flat in northern Argentina. He meditated there for an hour, in one of the driest spots on the planet. Beneath him rested an enormous lithium deposit controlled by a tiny prospective mining company named Orocobre, a portmanteau of the Spanish words for gold and copper. Months earlier, geologists hired by Calaway had stumbled onto a technical report from Orocobre. The company had hoped to strike gold in the mountains of northern Argentina but in doing so found large brine deposits. Mixed in with that brine were extremely high concentrations of lithium, just waiting to be sucked out of the Earth.

"I just sensed it. I let it all in," Calaway remembers of his meditation.

He dropped $4 million to buy as much of Orocobre's stock as he could and became the company's chairman. For the next seven years, Calaway and Orocobre built one of the world's largest lithium companies, battling the slow bureaucracy of President Cristina Fernández de Kirchner's administration in the process. By 2015, the company's stock had doubled in value due largely to a deal the company struck with Japan to supply the metal to Toyota and other Japanese automakers. Calaway was tired, ready to cash out and enjoy the fruits of his labors. So he retired.

But he couldn't stay away from lithium. He also, as an American, couldn't ignore the rising interest from Washington and Detroit for America's automakers to go electric. Tesla already had proved an EV could be mass-produced. But Tesla, like Toyota with the Prius before it, relied on far-flung sources of lithium as well as nickel, copper, and other metals.

Calaway wondered if the United States could produce its own large supply of these metals, especially lithium. He wasn't sure. His answer came in the form of a phone call from Australia, where a group of investors led by the developer Bernard Rowe were eyeing the Nevada desert. Calaway's reputation as one of the few industry executives—retired or otherwise—who knew anything at all about how to build and run a lithium mine had preceded him. Ironically, Rowe's group of investors had hoped their Nevada land—known as Rhyolite Ridge—contained gold and copper, the same mix Calaway's Argentina colleagues had sought years before. What it actually contained was a claylike mixture teeming with lithium, though how much was yet unclear.

Lithium is produced either from brine, as Orocobre had done in Argentina, or by digging out hard rock. No company had yet produced commercial quantities of lithium from clay. Calaway wasn't sure it would work or even how it could work. "I thought it was a science experiment and I wasn't interested at that point in science experiments. I told them I wasn't interested."

Rowe was disappointed but said he understood. He asked, though, if he could hire the geologist Calaway had employed in the past. Calaway, ever the businessman, obliged, asking for only one favor: If the geologist found anything interesting, Calaway would be the first call. "Part of being an entrepreneur and being successful is that you maintain an openness to being proven wrong," Calaway said.

That request proved to be fateful. A few weeks later, amid the clamor of the 2016 U.S. presidential campaign when the Democratic nominee, Hillary Clinton, called climate change "an urgent threat and a defining challenge of our time," Calaway's geologist called. Not only was Rhyolite Ridge not a science experiment, it was also sitting atop an estimated 146 million tonnes of lithium—the second-largest known deposit in the country—and boron, a chemical that can be sold to make soaps and other consumer goods.[6]

That meant Rhyolite Ridge could produce two in-demand products at once, offering two ways to make money should prices for one product ebb in the future, as often happens in commodity businesses. Importantly, the deposit did not contain as much clay as originally thought, easing production worries.

"My jaw dropped," Calaway said. Rhyolite Ridge and its lithium were inside the United States and less than 100 miles from a planned Gigafactory from Tesla, which at the time was on its way to becoming the world's most valuable automaker. In a rare situation for the world of mining, the project could make money almost as soon as it opened. "That changed the dynamics a lot." Immediately, Calaway bought

$4 million of the company and took command of its board of directors, repeating steps he had taken at Orocobre, which increasingly was proving to be a test run for this new Nevada venture. The Australians had named the company Global Geosciences, but for Calaway that wouldn't do. He came up with the name ioneer and borrowed the portmanteau style of Orocobre by smashing together the words *ions* and *pioneers*.

"We were going to help produce ions for EV batteries, and we were pioneers," he said. "So I came up with 'ioneer.'"

Why lowercase?

"I wanted something unique."

And so, ioneer was born, largely thanks to a decision Calaway made from his Houston living room with executives in Melbourne about a project in rural Nevada.

Their timing was nearly perfect. When Clinton lost the 2016 U.S. presidential election, her opponent, Donald Trump, controversially moved to take the United States out of the Paris Accords, a step that ironically had the opposite effect for much of private industry.[7] Automakers and their suppliers worked overtime to prove they cared about the environment, even if Washington seemingly did not. And electric vehicles were increasingly the way to show they cared. That meant there would be a global rush on lithium and other EV metals, so it behooved the United States to start producing them at home. Calaway saw his and ioneer's shot.

"A key component of the transition away from fossil fuels that we have to make is to get electrification transportation done. It's going to be resource-intensive, and if other nations—especially our rivals—see we have a deep vulnerability in this area, they are going to take advantage of us," Calaway said.

Over the next four years, Calaway and his team set about running geological tests, hiring engineers and architects, and shuttling between investor meetings and industry conferences. Rhyolite Ridge's economics were unassailable, Calaway thought. He made sure they were backed up by independent economists and geologists in a technical report known as a Definitive Feasibility Study. Such a step usually happens just before a company breaks ground on a mine, which ioneer was eager to do. The project, ioneer said in that report, would not build a tailings dam that could potentially collapse. Instead, the company planned to remove water from the dirt it extracted for the project and stack the tailings, a safer process known as "dry stack" tailings. Even though ioneer aimed to produce lithium for electric cars that have no emissions, the project found its detractors in the environmental community. Calaway and his Australian investors largely ignored the environmentalists, content to bury themselves in the minutiae of geological reports.

But then a strange thing happened late in the summer of 2020. Amid the arid hills of Rhyolite Ridge, 225 miles north of the slot machines of Las Vegas, thousands of the flowers found nowhere else on Earth—Jerry Tiehm's namesake—died mysteriously overnight. And the capstone of Calaway's career—his attempt to leave a cleaner Earth to his children than the one he found—seemed like it was slipping away.

CHAPTER TWO

Sacred Space

LESS THAN TEN YEARS AFTER THE U.S. CIVIL WAR ENDED, A sortie of Union soldiers ambushed Apache warriors in what is now Arizona and chased them to the top of a 4,700-foot-tall cliff. Opting for honor rather than surrender, the warriors jumped to their deaths from the cliff overlooking the small settlement of what is now Superior, roughly 60 miles east of modern-day Phoenix. Today, the cliff is known as Apache Leap.[1]

That story has been passed down orally through generations of the San Carlos Apache people. Some consider the tale apocryphal, a painful allegory, perhaps, of a people's fight against power; others hold fast to its literal interpretation, believing that indeed those warriors leapt nearly a mile to their deaths in defense of their homeland and values. What is true, regardless, is that the U.S. Army and others did very little to contain their contempt for the Indigenous peoples of the region, especially the Apache, for much of the nineteenth century.

Arizona's Apache were "the tiger of the human species," according to Major General George Crook, who led the military's fight against the tribe for fifteen years.[2] Another general ordered that all male Apache be killed on sight.[3] In 1859, the U.S. Indian Agent Diego Archuleta, whose role was to serve as a liaison between the U.S. government and tribes, wrote in a letter to *The New York Times* that the Apache had "long and pointed" fingers, "like claws," with "eyes keen and wild." The Apache, Archuleta continued, were "the greatest obstacle to the operations of the mining companies and traders" in the region. Lest anyone misconstrue his animus, Archuleta doubled down: "It is a mistake to make treaties with tribes so low on the scale of humanity as the Apache, Mojaves, Navajos, Utes, etc." Shunting the tribe onto a reservation, Archuleta added, "remote from White settlements with the penalty of death sternly enforced if they pass their limits, is the only prompt, economical, and humane process."[4] And that is exactly what the U.S. government did.

President Ulysses S. Grant approved the creation of the San Carlos Apache Reservation in 1871. While it was created with nearly 1.8 million acres, that expanse did not include what is now called Apache Leap or nearby land known as Chi'chil Biłldagoteel in the Apache language—literally "a broad flat of Emory oak trees"—a place where tribal members had for generations conducted religious ceremonies.[5] Chi'chil Biłldagoteel was more than 25 miles away from the reservation's western edge, and about 40 miles from the reservation's capital. The Apache returned there to pray, as they considered the land home to angels and religious deities, known as Ga'an. Some held (and still hold) coming-of-age ceremonies there when teenage girls who have first menstruated reenact the Apache creation myth over a four-day period of prayer, song, and drumming. Wild Emory oak trees on the grounds yield acorns used for traditional food and medicine. Some Apache ancestors are buried amid the volcanic rock. Petroglyphs at the site are considered by some observants as ancestral footprints.[6] By the mid-twentieth century, part of that area had become a federal campground known as Oak Flat.

As Archuleta had predicted, mining flourished in this corner of Arizona once its original inhabitants were pushed aside. The mineral-rich region around Superior drew in many copper miners in the years after the Apache Leap tragedy, earning it the nickname "Copper Corridor." In 1912, when Arizona became the forty-eighth state admitted to the Union, its seal was designed to show mining's importance. A human figure—presumably a man—stands off-center, holding a pickax and a shovel. The sun and its rays rise above him, shining down on mountains in the distance and farmlands. Above it all, the state's motto: *DITAT DEUS, "God enriches."*

Meanwhile, the reservation languished. The San Carlos Apache themselves consider it the world's first and oldest concentration camp.[7] By 2005, about half of all children born on the reservation tested positive for drugs or alcohol.[8] Forty-three percent of the reservation's roughly ten thousand residents are unemployed and not looking for work.[9]

Superior itself was home to the Magma Mine, which in 1937 was the world's first mine to be air-conditioned, a development that let miners dig deeper into the hot expanse of the Earth. The cooling equipment still sits on the side of a hill, a hulking box of rusting metal and tubes staring down at the town. The ebbs and flows of the copper market forced Magma to close several times over the years, decimating the town's economy each time. The median annual income in the community was roughly $22,000 in 2020 with 25 percent of the population living in poverty,[10] roughly $10,000 below and 10 percentage points above, respectively, the national average.[11]

By 1995, there was a glimmer of economic hope when more than 40 billion pounds of copper were estimated to sit near the Magma Mine and underneath Oak Flat, one of the largest untapped copper deposits in the world. The grade of the copper was 1.5 percent, more than double that of nearby Arizona copper mines. That meant that for every hundred pounds of earth extracted from the mine, 1.5 pounds would be copper. The proposed mine, which was named Resolution Copper, could be twice as profitable as nearby rivals. It was a tantalizing business prospect for BHP Group, one of the world's largest mining companies. BHP bought Magma's owner in January 1996, but Magma itself closed later that year when it was considered depleted. A slump in copper prices led BHP to close its other American copper mines by 1999. The company was hopeful about this new discovery but needed to study it further, a costly undertaking. That's when it joined forces with Rio Tinto, another global mining giant, to share the financial burden of exploring the underground deposit and convincing the government to let them access the land.

⚡

THE AMBITIOUS TARGETS set forth by the Paris Climate Accords are impossible without copper given its widespread use in nearly every single green energy transition device. Even before the discovery of electricity, the red metal was ubiquitous. For nearly five thousand years, copper was the only metal known to humanity—before even gold.[12] The Mediterranean island of Cyprus was initially famed for its copper mines; the name of the metal itself is based on the Greek name for the island: Kupros. The combination of copper with tin spawned the Bronze Age and fueled the power of many of Egypt's ancient pharaohs.

Copper, one of the best electricity-conducting metals, is easy to shape and form, is corrosion-resistant, and binds well with other metals. Only silver conducts electricity better, but silver is more expensive than copper. The average 747 jetliner from Boeing has 135 miles of copper wiring, and every American household has an average of four hundred pounds of copper wiring and piping. Freeport-McMoRan's Morenci, the largest copper mine in North America, uses Caterpillar 797 trucks to haul ore; inside each of those trucks' radiators is at least four hundred pounds of the red metal.[13]

In the United States, copper mines sprouted in the nineteenth century across Michigan, Connecticut, and modern-day Arizona. The inventor Thomas Doolittle created copper wire in 1877 for the telegraph industry, allowing wires for communication far lighter than iron-based rivals. Thomas Edison's invention of the light bulb and his power plants only further boosted demand across the globe, as did Alexander Graham Bell's telephone. The demand continued to grow in the twentieth century and into the twenty-first. About 75 percent of the copper used throughout history has been mined since the Second World War.[14] And the world's lust for copper is set to only grow. In 2022, annual copper consumption was 25 million tonnes. By 2050, it's projected to more than double to 53 million tonnes.[15]

Ominously, there is not expected to be enough copper to meet that 2050 target without more mines and more recycling. If the world wants to reach carbon neutrality by 2050, the "net zero" target that was at the heart of the Paris agreement, it needs to produce more of the red metal. "People who say that there's enough copper supply out there are not taking into account the scale of the energy transition," said Dan Yergin, the famed energy historian and Pulitzer Prize–winning author. "Without some give, you're not going to be able to achieve those climate goals."[16] Wars were fought in the twentieth century over oil. Without adequate copper supply in the twenty-first century, wars could very well be fought over copper, the consultancy S&P Global has warned.[17] The United States would have to boost its copper imports from about 44 percent of its supply in 2022 to as much as 67 percent by 2035, unless it produces more of its own.[18]

⚡

IN THE 1950S, as the story goes, First Lady Mamie Eisenhower picnicked at the Oak Flat campground and enjoyed it so much she encouraged her husband to safeguard the site. President Dwight Eisenhower issued an executive order in 1955 prohibiting mining and other development at the campground.[19] President Richard Nixon renewed the ban in 1971 but modified it slightly to allow certain development, a tweak that advantaged the mining industry.[20]

The discovery of the Resolution Copper deposit in the 1990s tested that tweak. It took more than a decade for Rio Tinto and BHP to study the deposit. They bored more than a hundred exploratory drills into the Earth, at a cost of more than $1 million each.[21] They built the deepest mine shaft in the United States, a 7,000-foot-deep structure on a small sliver of adjoining land they controlled. They discovered that if they built the mine, it would supply a quarter of the copper consumed each year in the United States, a tantalizing prospect just as the green energy revolution took shape. EVs, Rio and BHP knew, use twice as much copper as vehicles with internal combustion engines.[22] And the mining giants also knew that the upstart EV companies Nikola Corp. and Lucid Group Inc. were building manufacturing plants less than 50 miles from Superior.

Because the copper deposit is so deep, Rio and BHP also discovered it likely could not be extracted by digging from the surface but rather from below with a method known as block caving, whereby a large section of rock is undercut, creating an artificial cave that fills with its own rubble as it collapses under its own weight. That would cause a crater 2 miles wide and 1,000 feet deep, in what the mining industry terms a "glory hole." (Yes, *really*.) Thus, to harvest the copper would require the destruction of a site considered as important to the San Carlos Apache as St. Peter's Basilica is to Roman Catholics or al-Masjid al-Ḥarām is to Muslims.

"If I want to go there and be able to pray there, I should have that right. And I don't want no foreign company to come in and tell me, 'No, you can't do that,'" the San Carlos Apache elder Sandra Rambler shared with me.[23]

The mine could use as much as 590,000 acre-feet of water over the course of its life, roughly 192 billion gallons.[24] That is the equivalent of nearly 5 gallons of water for every pound of copper produced, less than other nearby mines, but an eye-popping number for a state that had been in a drought since 1994.[25] The amount of water would be enough to supply 168,000 homes for forty years.[26] The mine would also produce a pile of waste rock stored behind a tailings dam that would be 500 feet tall and cover an area of 6 square miles, nearly five times bigger than New York's Central Park. A U.S. government report on the project dryly noted "public apprehension" of that proposed tailings facility, especially in the wake of the deadly 2019 Brumadinho tailings dam collapse in Brazil.[27]

By 2013, Rio and BHP had started the U.S. federal permitting process, though as of this writing they have not obtained the permits.[28]

In December 2014, President Barack Obama signed the Carl Levin and Howard P. "Buck" McKeon National Defense Authorization Act, a Pentagon funding bill that included a clause added at the last minute to give Rio Tinto 2,422 acres containing the copper, including the campground, in exchange for 5,459 acres it owned nearby.[29] Buried on page 442 of the 698-page law was a stipulation that the land swap could not occur until an environmental report was published.[30] The Trump administration published that report five days before leaving office, sparking a legal fight among Native Americans, Washington, and Rio Tinto. Less than six weeks after taking office, the Biden administration rescinded that publication, putting the Resolution project on ice and pleasing neither supporters nor opponents of the mine.

Adding to the intrigue was that Rio Tinto had not technically decided by the time Biden froze the land swap to even build a mine—a formal step known as Final Investment Decision. "In order for us to make an investment decision, we need to know the underground geology. It's hard to do that without owning the land," Bold Baatar, head of Rio's copper division, told me. Yes, he acknowledged, the land was an area of historical significance to the San Carlos Apache. "We're absolutely not tone deaf," said Baatar, a Mongolian native who had previously worked at the banking giant J.P. Morgan.[31] "There will not be a mine until we achieve maximum effort to seek consent. We are taking this very seriously."[32]

As I learned more about the plans to develop Resolution, the tortured history of how the Apache were treated, the religious import of Chi'chil Biłldagoteel, and the essential role American copper would play in Washington's efforts to fight climate change, I saw the recipe for a perfect storm. As with the evolving tension between Calaway's Nevada lithium project and Tiehm's buckwheat, the question once again was: What matters more?

That's when I decided to visit Superior for myself.

THE HUES OF magenta, orange, and pink first caught my eye as I drove east on U.S. Route 60 into Superior after spending the previous night in Phoenix, the Arizona capital. The splashes of color were caused by rays from the rising morning sun striking the mammoth cliff that loomed over the town like a tidal wave. I turned off the state highway and onto Superior's Main Street, which seemed to dead-end right into the cliff itself. A restaurant, Miners on Main, advertised happy hour at its Tiki Deck outdoor lounge. Bruzzi Vineyard Tasting Room offered rosés to sample. A Chilean developer in 2010 had bought a dilapidated boardinghouse and transformed it into the Hotel Magma, a boutique lodge with bespoke light fixtures, flocked wallpaper, and copper ceilings.[33] But the hotel was quiet, devoid of hustle and bustle.

The town of three thousand had once been a mecca for mining, which the restaurant's name and hotel's ceilings evoked. It hoped, with the help of Rio and BHP, to recapture that former glory. Even while more than half of the buildings in Superior's downtown sat empty, several Tesla charging ports hinted at the town's aspirations to be part of the electric vehicle boom.

Rio, of course, knew this. In 2004, it had taken a 55 percent stake in the Resolution Copper project to BHP's 45 percent, giving it effective control over strategy, budget, and most important, outreach to the local communities, including Superior and the San Carlos Apache.[34] Rio and BHP by 2021 had spent more than $2 billion on the project, without producing an ounce of copper.[35] By 2022, Wall Street thought the project was nearly worthless.[36]

In its bid to win over local hearts and minds, Rio had promised to hire fourteen hundred workers—nearly half of the town's population—with an average salary of $100,000, more than quadruple the 2020 average. That number, more than any other, was forefront for Mila Besich.

First elected in 2016 as Superior's mayor, Besich was a fourth-generation Superior resident. She spoke firmly, though her soft eyes belied her singular purpose: to bring jobs home. Much of Superior, like Besich, is Democratic and Hispanic; the town and its mayor voted overwhelmingly for Joe Biden in the 2020 U.S. presidential election despite the surrounding county voting overwhelmingly for Donald Trump.

The same congressional law that approved the land swap also stipulated that the town of Superior could buy more than 600 acres from the federal government to build affordable housing and expand the local airport and industrial park, part of a long-term plan by Besich and fellow town officials to diversify Superior's economy into tourism and manufacturing. But that plan was on hold until Rio got the green light to move forward with its mine. By the time we met in person, Besich's patience was wearing thin.

We chatted in the town hall, which was housed inside a former middle school. Our chat was in what used to be the school's auditorium, with a mural on the wall depicting the shirtless torso of a miner with a drill bit in place of legs glaring down at us. The mural proclaimed, in

Spanish: *La Cultura Es El Oro Del Pueblo. Culture is the gold of the people.* In case anyone missed how important mining was to the community, the mural was there as a reinforcement.[37]

"Has Oak Flat," I asked, "in your family's history always been considered a religious site?"

"No," she replied, bluntly. "It was a place that we might have gone for a summer picnic. Long-term residents, especially my parents' age group, will tell you that they never really saw these types of traditional ceremonies going on, up until more recently, when the Resolution Copper project was proposed. It just doesn't seem genuine that all of a sudden, all these sacred ceremonies are happening when this becomes legislation. And that's been very frustrating for our community, because I think we're trying to be very respectful of the tribes. But at the same time, we're very concerned that the longer the politics weigh out on this, the longer that this goes on, it really leaves Superior in a bit of purgatory."

Besich was alleging that Oak Flat, that Chi'chil Biłldagoteel, had not been a place for religious observation going back generations—that it was *not* sacred—and that those now leaping to its defense did so only to use it as a convenient weapon in their broader fight against copper mining. "What's sacred to my community is that people have a job and have a home," she said, not mincing words.

It seemed, I said, that the Resolution saga sat on a fault line of politics, religion, and the economy. Besich didn't disagree. "We're very caught in the middle of this. And I really believe that President Biden is going to have to make some courageous decisions. If the long-term goal is to bring in more efficient vehicles . . . we're going to need American copper to do that. . . . The federal government has a responsibility to make sure that Rio Tinto does the right thing and the responsibility to make sure that we are mining America's natural resources in a safe and responsible way."

In addition to being mayor, Besich worked with a local nonprofit board that advocated for the mining industry. That didn't mean, though, that she acquiesced to Rio Tinto. Quite the opposite. Besich and town councilors pushed back when Rio at first offered Superior $350,000 a year in subsidies, far below the more than $1 million annually an economic study showed the mine would cost the town for what would be a rising need for more police, firefighters, and road maintenance. Rio agreed to boost its payments to the town, guarantee Superior's water supply, and fund the school district—which enrolled 362 students in 2023[38]—with $1.2 million annually from 2019 through 2023.[39]

Rio and Resolution Copper had also, with the town's insistence, paid $50 million to remove contaminated waste rock from the old Magma operation stored just outside a residential area, as well as an arsenic-tainted smelter that had melted copper for almost five decades before it closed in 1971.[40] The company knew the decrepit smelter—for which it was not responsible—was an eyesore and a health hazard that had to be cleaned up before it could get the community's tacit support for its mine.[41]

"Rio's had to learn over the last few years that it cannot take host communities for granted," Besich said. If the mine can be developed in a way that helps the economy and protects the environment, well, then build it. That was the crux of Besich's requests to Biden. "These jobs will help our small businesses continue to thrive as this project goes into construction and then eventually into production," Besich said.

That, of course, was easier said than done.

⚡

ONE OF THOSE small businesses that Besich hoped would be helped by the mine's opening was Superior Lumber & Hardware, which had hitched its future to Resolution. And the controversy was making Darrin Lewis anxious. A tall, gangly man with a quiet demeanor, Lewis had flipped houses for years in Arizona before moving to Superior in early 2020.[42] With the benefit of hindsight, his decision to buy the hardware store and its lumber yard in January of that year for $800,000 was ill-timed; the coronavirus pandemic quickly spread and shuttered the global economy.

Sales plummeted, which surprised Lewis as he expected the opposite with his customers locked in their homes and many eyeing renovation projects. "Well, we didn't see that," he told me inside the

5,500-square-foot store. It had low-hung ceilings and shelves filled with a hodgepodge of construction equipment. Built with cinder-block walls, the outside was painted a mixture of peach and orange, with the building's name in fading black 1930s Art Deco font. I struggled to wonder how anyone could find anything in the abyss, let alone specialized equipment to undertake a complex home renovation. The uncertainty about the town's economy, though, had kept Lewis from updating and expanding the store, he said.

That's when Rio stepped in, buying up lumber and other goods that accounted for a third of the store's sales in 2020 and 2021. "Our bread and butter are from the mine," he said. "I sank everything I have into this place. It would absolutely devastate us if this mine doesn't open."

Like most people in the town, Lewis had been closely tracking the fate of the Resolution project. He bought his store knowing full well that Obama had approved the land swap and that Trump was about to give it final approval, which he did two weeks after Lewis closed on the shop. But then Biden stepped in, much to Lewis's discontent. "It was supposed to be a foregone deal. But the next thing we know, they pull the rug out from under us. We're in this indecision mode until we find out what's going on."

I understood where Lewis was coming from, especially with $800,000 to pay back. But I asked him, as I had with Besich, what he thought of the complexities about the nation's need for copper contrasted with the San Carlos Apache's religious rites at the campground and their religious rights as Americans.

"I respect that. I respect that a lot. And to be honest, it's a thing I think about. Am I just focused on the money here? But when I look at it, at the end of the day, I look at the way copper is going, and the way copper is going to be needed in the future. And I see it as inevitable. Somebody is going to mine it eventually."

He paused, then summoned an absent party.

"If I had one thing to say to President Biden, it would be: 'Let the mine open,'" he said.

By late 2021, the project was still mired in uncertainty. Lewis put Superior Lumber up for sale, asking $450,000. It was a far cry from the

$800,000 he had paid for the business less than two years prior. The business, he said, took in between $400,000 and $700,000 in revenue each year, solid numbers but a far cry from Home Depot or other larger rivals. And it was also a sales stream largely dependent on Rio Tinto, which had no idea whether it would ever be able to build a mine. On December 17, 2021, the hardware store's Facebook page shared the Web link to the real estate listing, which boasted: "Opportunity knocks! This is an amazing property in Superior, which is beginning to boom. . . . This is your chance to be part of a growing community, rich with history and character."

Almost immediately, the sale sparked concern.

"You're selling?" Besich posted on Facebook.

"Yes, we're going to see how it goes . . . not sure what to expect . . . ," the store's account, run by Lewis and his wife, Paula, replied.

"GLWTS!" a customer posted below the thread. *Good Luck with That Shit.*[43]

No one seemed interested. Soon, Lewis cut the price to $375,000. By May 2022, he had pulled the listing. Just as the Resolution Copper project had lured him into Superior, it now seemed that its purgatory—as Besich called it—had sucked him in, too.

I asked Lewis, just before we parted ways, what he thought Americans and the rest of the world should think about the brewing tension in Superior. He paused and turned his head in thought before responding: "If you come up here to love and give, the town's going to give back to you. It you come up here to take, the town is going to take from you."

⚡

THE SHORT DRIVE from Superior's downtown to Oak Flat is jaw-dropping. U.S. Route 60 slowly climbs into the clouds, surrounded by the cragged, jutting peaks of the Superstition Mountains. Cactus and sagebrush line the roads. Apache Leap looms in the distance. Queen Creek flows through the rocky crevasses; long ago the waterway, which is dry part of the year, had carved a deep path on its journey toward Superior. An arched bridge at one point passes over a deep ravine formed by the waters. I drove up the road in the late afternoon when the sun was warm and beginning its evening retreat. The rays bounced off the narrow canyon walls that were growing taller around me, volcanic rocks pointing like fat fingers to the skies above.[44] Hikers followed a trail just off the road, one that eventually traced its way down to the river. The highway passed through all 1,217 feet of Queen Creek Tunnel, built in 1952, before emerging into an even larger canyon, the jutting mountains looming around me on both sides. About 2 miles later, I turned right onto North Magma Shaft 9 Road, headed for Oak Flat, for Chi'chil Biłldagoteel, where Dr. Wendsler Nosie and other mine opponents known as Apache Stronghold had been camped out since November 2019. It took me a few seconds to realize that this road also led to the mine shaft that Rio Tinto had dug for the Resolution project. Both sides *literally* used the same road.

I turned left onto the campground where a U.S. Forest Service sign welcomed me. Farther down, a hand-painted sign on plywood declared that Chi'chil Biłldagoteel was the physical embodiment of the Earth's spirit. A traditional teepee and two wikiups, also known as wigwams, rested nearby. I found Nosie sitting at a campfire with a handful of others on a quiet Monday. (I had been told by multiple people that the camp's numbers rose on weekends.) Nosie wore a black bandana tightly around his head, his long black hair peeking out the back and flowing onto his shoulders. We had spoken a few times earlier that year via phone and I introduced myself in person. By then, Nosie had long grown accustomed to journalists visiting, often for short stints, to talk about copper, the mine, and Chi'chil Biłldagoteel. His face told me what I already knew: that he had long grown disaffected by the news media's portrayal of his cause.[45]

We ended up talking for more than two hours, not only at the campfire but on a walk through the site. There was something special about that place; it had a unique energy, a vibe, and an ethereal presence that I had not felt before. I could understand why Nosie and the San Carlos Apache placed such a high value on the site and why Nosie decided to make it his de facto home, especially after Apache equipment at the site was vandalized in 2018.[46] As we talked, birds fluttered through trees in the soft spring air. Even though the highway was relatively close, all you could hear at the campground was the sound of silence. We left the campfire and walked atop a nearby rock formation, the expanse of an immense plain of rock and sagebrush before us.

I asked Nosie about claims from some other tribes in the area (and claims whispered by Rio Tinto officials) that Oak Flat had not been a site for religious ceremonies for generations. The former historian for the San Carlos Apache had also claimed the site held no historical import.[47] But Nosie pointed out that the U.S. government shunted at least ten different Apache tribes that had lived across what is now Texas, California, Mexico, Arizona, and New Mexico onto the reservation in the nineteenth century, and not all of them had exactly the same culture or beliefs.[48] It was akin, he continued, to asking someone from Russia about Italian culture. And, he added, many Apache ancestors were forced to assimilate and leave behind their traditional beliefs. "You're going to have those that grow up in a world of Christianity, and adapt to it," he said.

"What we're saying is, is that this is the home of the angels, the deities, they live here," he continued, waving his hands around Oak Flat, which he described as a buffer zone between the traditional Apache equivalents of heaven and Earth. "When we talk about the deities, they're no different than the deities that are part of Christianity. . . . But in the church, they bring them in as a statue, they bring them in as a picture. And they respect them. But they came from somewhere, they didn't come from the church. There was a place that they resided and lived. When America embraces their Christianity, a lot of their angels are, more or less, from the other side of the world, and yet these angels are no different than those angels. But the difference is that it's here, you know, it resides in these places."

And the ceremonies held at the site, especially those for teenage girls, connected directly with the traditional Apache sense of the divine, which Nosie described to me as intrinsically linked to the feminine. "Our ceremonies remind us that we're to take care of the female places," he said. "And that's why it's so important for us not to lose this place. This is where the Creator, which is God, put the deities here. . . .

Because if Resolution Copper gets this place, the whole thing subsides, then you just killed the angels, you just killed everything that was the beginning. Because there are those places that are unique throughout the world. And this is one of them here."

The region, I pointed out, had historically had copper mining. But Nosie challenged me to think farther back in history, to before mines opened in the area that is now Arizona. "My people go back thousands and thousands of years. We know what this place looked like.

"Now we have tributaries that are contaminated, the environments are impacted," he said. "Let's not even forget the human beings, as so many people in these mining towns have died from cancer clusters. What's sad is that there's so many people in these copper towns that cannot move. So they're the ones that are directly assaulted by what contamination comes, whether it be through air, water, or land. And those are the ones that are suffering. . . . If you take anybody that comes from the East Coast or the north where there's no mining industry, and they come through here, they're going to say there's no way that they can bring up their kids here because it's all a contaminated place."

I asked Nosie his thoughts about Besich's contention that what matters most is the economy, getting the region's residents employed and housed. "She's stuck in this capitalist world, and that's more of her religion than what is really the true religion. That's what happens when you're brought up in a capitalistic way of life. . . . If you destroy all of this, it's gone. Everything that's left is gone."

Who cares, Nosie was saying, if you have a high-paying job if the environment is destroyed? It was the starkest of black-and-white arguments, and one that partly relied on the bad actions of past mining companies. But Nosie didn't have to look too far into the past to draw from examples of major environmental harm by mining companies to bolster his cause.

The proposed mine itself was a symptom of a way of life that cared only for money, he said. "That means everything here that is left, all water, all light, the beauty of environment, what brings people back here and then the holy and sacredness of this, is totally gone."

Native Americans had long had to contend with mining companies seeking to dig rocks out of their historical lands. In the years after the Second World War uranium mining surged across the U.S. Southwest, especially on lands within and near the Navajo Nation.[49] Uranium was used for atomic bombs but also for clean, renewable power generation at nuclear plants. Yet the uranium mining literally poisoned several generations of Navajo, a tragedy chronicled with nuance and respect by Peter Eichstaedt in *If You Poison Us: Uranium and Native Americans*.[50]

Pope Francis, spiritual leader of the world's more than one billion Roman Catholics, had held a conference to discuss the mining industry at the Vatican in 2019 during which he decried in part the industry's "fallacious" business model as one that disrespected lands traditionally held by Indigenous groups. Mining companies, the pontiff said, should serve humanity—not vice versa. Indigenous groups should not be pressured "to abandon their homelands to make room for . . . mining projects which are undertaken without regard for the degradation of nature and culture."[51] Despite their obvious religious differences, it seemed Francis and Nosie may have had an area of agreement when it came to Chi'chil Biłldagoteel.

As Nosie talked, all I could think about was where we were sitting. Would it be a giant crater one day? Would the dull red copper thousands of feet beneath us be inside my cell phone in forty years? Rio had repeatedly promised Nosie and other tribal members that they would be able to access the campground for the next few decades if the land exchange went through, because not only would it take more time to get federal mining permits, but the "glory hole" crater would happen gradually, not immediately. That meant little to a community with a collective memory that lasts centuries, not one that fixates on the quarterly corporate earnings cycle. The promises from the company, for better or for worse, evoked the promises other mining companies had made and broken over the past few centuries to local communities. Mark Twain, for example, is said to once have mused, "A mine is a hole in the ground owned by a liar."[52]

Nor was Nosie swayed by the EV transition and its insatiable demand for lithium, nickel, and yes, copper. If the United States and the world needed to go green to fight climate change, I asked, shouldn't that necessitate more mining?

"That's a really scary question," he replied softly, peering over the campfire. "Because the answer to that question is that if we say that we need Resolution Copper to do this because we need all this copper . . . that means that the people of this country are greedy. It tells me that we're disobedient and we're messed up. . . . And that should be a warning to not only leaders of this country but the people of this country who are fathers, grandfathers, grandmothers, and mothers to begin to control the ugliness of being greedy. What we have is enough."

The argument, in essence, evoked Joni Mitchell:

They paved paradise
And put up a parking lot.[53]

The youngest of seven children, Nosie grew up in the late 1950s and early 1960s seeing his older siblings fall victim to U.S. government policies that forcibly relocated them to larger cities, part of a ploy to assimilate them and other Native Americans into American culture and, by extension, erase their Apache culture. While that practice largely ended in 1968 with the passage of the Indian Civil Rights Act, it stamped an indelible mark on young Wendsler, who vowed not to become what he called a prisoner of war.

Those and other strictures are likely why many in Superior and other non-Indigenous communities had never heard of sacred ceremonies at Oak Flat, he said. "One thing I was not going to give them was my religion. I was meant to be close to those religious ways. And that's right here," he said, gesturing around. "And so that's who I am. I just didn't want to leave this world as a prisoner."

(Pejoratives against the Apache hadn't subsided in the twenty-first century, it should be noted. The U.S. military's code name for Osama bin Laden during the 2011 raid that killed him was "Geronimo."[54] Also known as Goyaalé, Geronimo was a famed Apache who died in 1909 as a prisoner of war in U.S. Army custody. "I should have fought until I was the last man alive," Geronimo whispered on his deathbed.[55])

Nor was Oak Flat the first time Nosie had protested against the government. He had been put on trial in 1997 for allegedly trespassing on Arizona's Mount Graham, where a powerful telescope had been built by the University of Arizona and the Vatican. That mountain, much like Oak Flat, held spiritual significance, Nosie said. He had visited the site to pray. He was acquitted.[56]

At Oak Flat, Nosie had been camped out for nearly two years by the time we met in person; the Forest Service had largely looked the other way. (Camping at federal campgrounds typically is supposed to be limited to fourteen days.[57]) He had previously served as chairman of the San Carlos Apache, but by 2021 he had essentially eclipsed that role and now held even more power as a kind of Geronimo for his people, standing up against what he saw as a foreign invader encroaching on his traditional homeland. At one point, he alleged that Senator John McCain threatened to withhold federal funding for the San Carlos Apache if they did not support the Resolution project.[58] At other times in our chats, he said he saw himself as a preacher leading a religious movement.

In lawsuits against the mine, the lead plaintiff was not the tribe, but the activist group known as Apache Stronghold. Composed of Nosie and many other Apache camped at the site, it also included conservationists, environmentalists, and others in Arizona and around the country. He acknowledged that he had not talked to anyone from Rio, part of a long-standing assertion by Indigenous groups in the United States that the only proper form of negotiation was between tribal leadership and U.S. officials, what is known as government-to-government consultation. Nosie also said he hadn't talked to Elon Musk or any other automotive executive, but he cautioned them to do more to learn where "their copper is coming from."

"This has become a war between a religious and a corporate way of life," he said, again in his soft timbre that belied the power he held. "We're all being tested by the Creator. This country is on call."

I kept asking myself: Who was right and who was wrong here? Who should decide? The pain that Nosie and other Apache relayed to me was visceral and endemic, even. Who should get to make a decision about whether their religious site was worth destroying for a metal that could help stem climate change?

If the mine eventually was approved, Nosie vowed to do everything he could to stop it. That plan echoed other Apache who said they would barricade themselves on the land to block development, seeing the 2016 protests by opponents of the Dakota Access Pipeline in North Dakota as a model to emulate. "When you love something, you won't let it go," Nosie said. "I don't want them to take my religion away. I definitely am not going to. If anything, I'll go down in this crater when it drops."

The more I reported on the Resolution Copper saga, the more I became convinced these issues were intractable. It wasn't my job to decide which side was right or wrong—or even if one side was right or wrong. But I felt a need to ask all sides about allegations others were making.

The previous day I had made a stop at the San Carlos Apache Cultural Museum, located on the tribal reservation. Marlowe Cassadore, the center's director, had walked me through several displays stuffed with historical artifacts of the San Carlos Apache.[59] He recounted how, as a boy, he remembered his grandmother visiting Oak Flat for weeks at a time to gather Emory acorns, which are used to make traditional medicines. During the coronavirus pandemic, Apache would also gather other plants at the site for medicinal purposes, he said.

"People have been making journeys up there to get those plants," he said of Oak Flat. "And there is a sacredness to it. But Apache usually do not really talk about that."

The mine, he feared, could become the latest in a string of negatives to befall the Apache, the latest violation of the tribe's spirituality, culture, and identity. "The U.S. government and the state of Arizona had a policy to kill all Apache at one time," he said, referring to the order from the nineteenth-century U.S. Army general. "So we're not really supposed to be here. But we are."

I had that in mind as I wrapped up my conversation with Nosie atop a few boulders near the Oak Flat campground. Two of the Rio mine's headframes were a few hundred yards away in the distance. "All this is going to be destroyed," Nosie said, "if that happens."

⚡

THE HEADFRAMES WERE giant braces in the sky, artifices that represented the brawn and might of modern mining. Here, in the shadow of Nosie's protest camp, Rio Tinto had dug a 7,000-foot mineshaft, partly an exercise, executives said, to see if they could dig the deepest of its kind on the continent.

Toward the edge of the small sliver of land that Rio controlled (the company was granted the right to explore the land in the 2014 law), there was a small viewing platform that looked over Nosie's camp and, by extension, the area that would eventually be swallowed up by the mine. It looked, to the naked eye, like a garden of rocks and sagebrush as far as the eye could see, beautiful in its strangeness and stillness. The platform had first been built for the 2008 visit of Britain's Prince Andrew, Duke of York, during a trade mission to promote U.K. business interests in the state.[60]

My journey to the bottom of Rio's Number 10 mine shaft started with a long safety briefing and a change of clothes. Seven thousand feet deep, the company's officials explained, finds the Earth with an entirely unique climate where temperatures average about 180 degrees Fahrenheit. Air-conditioning runs constantly to keep the air close to 80 degrees Fahrenheit. It had cost $350 million just to dig the Number 10 shaft.

"You're gonna wanna put these on," one of the safety officials said to me, pointing to thick rain pants, boots, and a jacket. The outfit was made complete by a hard hat equipped with light, as well as a small oxygen tank. We made our way to an elevator just underneath the headframe. McCain himself had taken the same elevator down more than seven years prior. Since then, the project had been in a holding pattern, with pumps running constantly to suck out water and engineers ensuring the shaft's stability. No actual mining had taken place.

The elevator car had, I discovered, two decks. Each held four people, and our team of eight split in two. After we all loaded up, our elevator operator pulled a lever to let out five audible beeps from a bell system. "The bell system says what level we're going to. We just rang to say we're going to the very bottom," he said. For the next fifteen minutes, our elevator descended at roughly 500 feet per minute into the dark, the occasional splash of water or hot air infiltrating the tiny cart rumbling into the bowels of the planet.

We emerged at the bottom into what seemed like a rain forest, thick blankets of 100 percent humidity enveloping our group as soon as we touched bottom. Water was everywhere: on the muddy floors, dripping from the ceiling, flowing down the walls. Inadvertently, Rio had bored into an ancient lake that had been trapped underground by impermeable rock. The humidity was the result of that misstep.[61] Just outside the colossal shaft was a corridor of roughly 170 feet or so with several offshoots where Rio's staff were scurrying about, performing tasks of the day. Pumps ran constantly in the dank zone, with more than 600 gallons of water each minute (about 1 million gallons a day) pumped to treatment plants on the surface and then sold to local farmers. Rio was drawing water from the copper deposit, a necessary step before any mining could begin. While Rio didn't yet own the land containing the copper, it was drying it out to prepare it for an invasion of drilling and digging equipment. The mine also had an electrical substation at its base, Wi-Fi for workers to call the surface from their cell phones, and hardened emergency shelters with enough oxygen, food, and water for several days if the shaft collapsed. The giant hum of pumps of all types permeated the air, making it nearly impossible to talk.

It was the deepest place I had ever been in the Earth since my trip to Chile's El Teniente underground copper mine, the world's largest, a few years prior. A small room off the corridor held an excavator that sat fallow, waiting in the hopes that one day it could break through and dig into the giant copper deposit that lay just beyond. A second shaft lay at the end of the corridor, the legacy of the old Magma operation that Rio had repurposed for its Resolution project. Everywhere I looked, walls were coated in a type of concrete designed to hold back potential cave-ins. (Darrin Lewis's hardware store had sold Rio lumber for its casing.) It was a feat of engineering that showed just what was possible here in the deep, dark reaches.

Given all this engineering prowess, I wondered if a glory hole was inevitable. If Rio billed itself as a master mining company, couldn't it find a way to extract the copper without harming the Apache religious site? That seemed like a win for both sides. (Although not causing a crater probably would have meant not mining as much copper.) I put that question to Vicky Peacey, a Rio permitting manager overseeing the Resolution project. Her response was vague though not necessarily evasive, giving the company just enough wiggle room to go either way in the future: "The land exchange gives us the opportunity to collect more data, then we can refine our plans and look for ways that we can do further avoidance and minimization" of site damage.[62]

Changes in mine plans have not been uncommon in the mining industry. The Buckhorn Mine in Washington State, near the British Columbia border, was first proposed as an open-pit gold mine in the 1990s before developers changed tack amid intense pressure from conservationists and agreed to construct an underground mine.[63]

If all went as Rio hoped, it would take ten years to build the mine, once it had all the permits in hand, and then the mine itself would operate for forty to fifty years. The company would then spend five to ten years on a process known as reclamation, which is an attempt by miners to make the land look as it did before the mine existed.[64]

Resolution was just the latest U.S. expansion project for Rio Tinto. The company announced in late 2019 that it would spend $1.5 billion to extend the life of its more than hundred-year-old Kennecott mine in Utah, from 2026 to 2032. "We like copper. We like the U.S.," Jean-Sébastien Jacques, Rio Tinto's chief executive at the time, told me.[65] Chile and Peru were the world's largest copper producers as of 2021, with China coming in third and the United States a distant fourth, per the U.S. Geological Survey.

Rio's rivals were also eyeing the United States. Trump's pro-mining policies and the rising popularity of electric vehicles were drawing mining companies back to the country after years of looking internationally. It was an approach that in some ways mirrored the U.S. fracking boom, when oil and natural gas companies bored into Texas, North Dakota, and Oklahoma after decades of global pursuits. In 2019, more than $1.1 billion had been committed by companies toward U.S. copper mining projects. The Arizona-based Freeport-McMoRan Inc. owned and operated copper mines in Chile, Peru, and Indonesia, but had started to pivot home, seeing the United States as core to its future. "Fifteen years ago, U.S. mining was thought to be a dead industry, but now it's a profitable area for us," Richard Adkerson, Freeport's chief executive, told me.[66]

⚡

BIDEN'S MOVE TO step into the Resolution saga came amid a particularly testy time for Rio Tinto, which Nosie and other San Carlos Apache used powerfully for their cause.

In May 2020, the company destroyed caves used as shelters by the PKKP peoples in Western Australia's Pilbara region. It wasn't surreptitious at all; rather, it was completely legal, with Rio receiving all the necessary permits to destroy the Juukan Gorge caves to expand a mine. The caves had existed for more than 46,000 years, a standing testament to one of the world's oldest living cultures and the only place in Australia's interior to show signs of continual human habitation since the last Ice Age. A belt made from human hair was found at the site, and genes in that hair proved a strong genetic link between its source and the PKKP.[67]

The United Nations said that Rio's actions echoed the Taliban's destruction of the Bamiyan Buddha statues in 2001.[68] The PKKP bemoaned the "devastating blow," and said they had lost a connection to their ancestors and traditional lands. Rio, for its part, fell back on the fact that it had destroyed the site legally and said it was sorry only that the "recently expressed concerns of the PKKP did not arise through the engagements that have taken place over many years."[69] Retribution for Rio was swift, the public outcry harsh. Within a year, Rio had fired its chief executive and the chairman of its board of directors, showing how seriously the company's investors reacted.[70] Many including Nosie, the National Congress of the American Indians, and even a nonprofit group advocating for hiking trails took note, saying that they felt history was repeating itself, that Rio was making the same mistakes.[71]

"Like the rock shelters at Juukan Gorge, Oak Flat is a sacred and holy place that Resolution Copper greedily seeks," Terry Rambler, the San Carlos Apache chairman, wrote to Australian legislators in August 2020, demanding that they "hold Rio Tinto fully accountable for the irreparable damage that it has wrought."[72]

Jakob Stausholm, who became Rio's CEO after the Juukan Gorge fiasco, was sensitive to those charges. In September 2021, he flew to Arizona, hoping to meet Rambler, Nosie, and others opposed to Resolution. We chatted over Zoom while he was there, Stausholm dressed in running gear with sweat beading down his head; he had just returned from a run in the Phoenix heat. Rio and Stausholm had vowed to obtain what's known as Free, Prior, and Informed Consent (FPIC) from the San Carlos Apache, industry jargon that essentially means a mining company will get permission from local Indigenous peoples for a new project. Rio had failed to fully get it from PKKP, a mistake Stausholm told me would not be repeated with Resolution. "If we haven't explained ourselves well enough, then we need to explain ourselves better," he said in his Danish accent. "We're trying to find a win-win. I do think that's in everyone's interest. But I reckon that we still have work to do." I asked him if he would keep the copper inside the United States for smelting; he said yes.

Rambler refused to meet with Stausholm, saying he preferred to work with Democrats in Congress to change the 2014 legislation that approved the land swap in the first place. "If they wanted to meet, they should have met way before anything was done" in 2014, Rambler said. "My focus now is on changing that law."[73]

It was not the only problem Stausholm had, though. Deep in Serbia's Jadar Valley sat a mineral known as jadarite found nowhere else on Earth. For reasons not entirely clear to geologists, jadarite contains high levels of lithium, a tantalizing prospect for Rio, especially since Europe had few active lithium mines. The company had already spent $450 million on the project, most of that going to develop technology to extract lithium from the jadarite. But in early 2022, the Serbian government bowed to environmentalists and canceled the entire project.[74] Suddenly not one, but two of the company's more promising ventures were imperiled.[75]

The company's name itself hearkens back to environmental mistakes linked to its founding. *Rio tinto* is a Spanish term for "red river." In 1873, a group of British investors bought the rights to a mine along the Rio Tinto in Spain, where the water had flowed red for years due to acidic mine seepage into the waterway.[76] The company has grown rapidly since then, but the name endures.

By early 2022, Rio was not only fighting the San Carlos Apache, the PKKP, and the Serbian people, but also its own employees. Stausholm, in a shrewd move meant to break ties with his predecessor, had hired an external diversity firm when he became CEO to investigate Rio's culture. It was also a risky move, especially considering the potential for embarrassing dirt to be revealed. But Stausholm intended to get as much potential bad news out as fast as he could. The report, which was published on Rio's corporate website, showed that almost half of respondents to the employee survey had been bullied.[77] One employee shared a shocking story about her own harassment:

> When I first started [here], one of the men . . . asked me for a blow job. I told his direct report and leader who said "I'm sure he was just joking. We'll make sure you're not alone with him."

Stausholm, for his part, expressed surprise, but vowed change. "Now I know what I know, and I clearly have an obligation to address it." In Arizona, the report gave Resolution's opponents more ammunition.

⚡

AS THE 2020 presidential election heated up, Arizona and its eleven electoral votes became increasingly important for Joe Biden and Donald Trump. While the state had voted for a Democratic presidential candidate only once since 1952, its electorate increasingly had skewed more centrist. Even the tiniest bit of extra support from one group could make all the difference. Biden, sensing this, made a play for the votes of the Apache and other Native American tribes in the state. And he came armed with promises.[78]

On October 8, with less than a month before Election Day, Biden and his running mate, Senator Kamala Harris of California, met for thirty minutes with Arizona's tribal leaders in Phoenix's Heard Museum, which holds a vast collection of Native American art. Rambler cornered both Biden and Harris to discuss renewable energy and climate change. Resolution had not yet formally been approved, so there was nothing specific to request, but Rambler took the opportunity to get to know the politicians and to plant a seed. The next week, Biden's campaign released a list of nearly two hundred tribes that had endorsed their presidential ticket, among them the San Carlos Apache.[79]

There was aggressive politicking elsewhere, too. Unknown to Rambler or the other tribal leaders, Biden's campaign had privately been reaching out to mining companies across the country, promising them it would support boosting U.S. production of copper and other metals used to make green energy products such as solar panels and EVs in an acknowledgment that the building blocks of new technologies don't just appear out of thin air. And miners, for the most part, believed Biden's campaign, even though the candidate himself never publicly discussed mining. Glencore, which controlled Minnesota's controversial PolyMet Mining project, made the decision not to scale back in the United States even if Biden won. Employees at U.S. lithium companies, which were desperate for Washington's support, nearly doubled their donations to Democrats from 2016.[80] The National Mining Association, a trade group for U.S. miners, went so far as to co-opt Biden's campaign slogan and declare: "Building back better involves miners."[81]

The San Carlos Apache—who mine the gemstone peridot on their reservation—by that point had been fighting the Resolution project since at least 2005. The tribal council had voted unanimously in 2019 to oppose it, and tribal members since 2014 (the year Obama approved the land swap) had held an annual 45-mile march from their reservation's capital to the campground to bring attention to their cause, which was steadily growing.[82] They did not hide how much they opposed the Resolution project, and Mormons, Jews, and other faith groups agreed with them, seeing it as a matter of religious import. (Rambler told me, for example, that he was a member of the Church of Jesus Christ of Latter-day Saints and did not practice the traditional Apache religion.)

Biden promised Rambler and the other tribal leaders at the October 2020 meeting that they would have a voice in his administration. "We need you. We need you. . . . And you're going to have a seat at the table if we get elected." Harris took the promise a step further, vowing to defer to tribal leaders' experience and vision. "We are going to work together on the climate and what we know the original people always knew, which is that we have to protect this Earth, and we have to be smart about it. We will take your lead; you will always have a seat at the table." Biden and Harris narrowly won Arizona (despite the attempts of "fraudulent electors" and January 6 rioters), thanks in part to the overwhelming support of the state's Indigenous voters.[83]

On January 15, with less than five days left in office, Trump published through the U.S. Forest Service that final environmental report.[84] The agency said it had sought to balance the rising demand for copper with its commitment to respect the environment. Importantly, federal law did not allow the agency to consider whether to reject the mine or not, but rather to reject parts of the mine's operational plans that it thought could harm nature.[85] In language only a regulator could muster, the Forest Service admitted that reviewing the proposed mine was "complex." The region's Native American tribes were consulted, the agency said, "to best address the negative impacts to sacred tribal lands." The Forest Service had "sought to address these impacts in consultation" with Rio Tinto, but a press release announcing the move did not say if concrete changes were made.[86] The process to get to that publication had been long and meandering, but ultimately it was released just before Trump left the White House, a step he had taken with another proposed mine from Lithium Americas in Nevada.[87]

The process had started back in 2014, when Obama signed the Pentagon funding bill that set the whole matter in motion. Supporters had tried for years to introduce legislation that would authorize the land swap, but they had always failed. President George W. Bush's administration had supported legislation that would have allowed it, but Obama took the opposite tack in 2009. John McCain, who had just lost the presidency to Obama and was also Arizona's senior senator, was furious. Career bureaucrats had supported the project under Bush with only minor points of concern and noting that building the mine would be a boon to the region's sagging economy. "I've been around long enough to know how this works," McCain said. "They know that if they delay long enough . . . [Rio Tinto] will walk away. The people of Arizona, the country, and the world will suffer."[88]

While the Republican-led U.S. House of Representatives approved the land swap in October 2011, the legislation languished in the Senate, which was led by Democrats at the time.[89] McCain would in the ensuing years bemoan the repeated failure of the land-exchange legislation, saying it was among the "top three or four" most "frustrating issues" he had to contend with in Congress.[90]

In the fall of 2014, the senator visited the town of Superior and made a direct economic case for the mine, noting that many in the town were "struggling to find opportunities to better their lives and those of their families." Things were worse for the reservation, he noted, with more than 70 percent unemployment and many struggling with addiction. "The Resolution Copper project has the potential to utterly transform these communities," McCain pleaded after going deep into the mine shaft to visit what Rio had dug already.[91] His stand-alone bill never succeeded.[92]

But at the end of that year, McCain had a plan to win. He and his fellow Arizona senator Jeff Flake (who had previously lobbied on behalf of a Namibian mine owned in large part by Rio Tinto[93]), tucked a clause into the Pentagon funding bill near midnight as the bill was under debate that included the land-exchange provision.[94] That late in the game meant there was little anyone could do to stop it—if they even noticed. Obama, who had opposed McCain's stand-alone legislation on the land exchange, had no choice but to approve the entire Pentagon bill. Had he vetoed it over concerns about the Apache and Resolution, he would have blocked funding for the entire U.S. military.

Outrage was swift and immediate. Interior Secretary Sally Jewell said she was "profoundly disappointed." "The tribe's sacred land has now been placed in great jeopardy." Jewell said she hoped to work with

Rio Tinto "to better understand their plans for development and to see what additional measures they can take to work with the tribes, including forgoing development in these sacred areas."[95]

Lawmakers, including Senator Bernie Sanders of Vermont and Representative Raul Grijalva of Arizona, introduced legislation to prevent the land swap, but those bills gained little traction.[96] Obama's administration tried to slow down the approval process by listing the campground in 2016 on the National Register of Historic Places.[97] But the train had left the metaphorical station by that point, and Trump won the presidential election—and control over the Resolution environmental review—a few months later.

Under Trump, U.S. officials began moving the project forward, and Rio was keen to publicly say and do the right thing. In 2017, one of its executives testified to the U.S. Congress that it would smelt any copper mined from Resolution in Utah.[98] The promise was designed to address concerns that U.S. copper could be shipped to China, fears that were only fueled by Rio's largest shareholder—a Chinese government-controlled aluminum producer.[99]

Nosie and Apache Stronghold were honing their legal argument; Rambler repeatedly sent letters to the U.S. Forest Service throughout 2019 and 2020, urging more review. "Without water, without our church, I fear for the very survival and existence of Apache life, culture, and religion," Rambler wrote to government officials in December 2019.[100]

On January 12, 2021, sensing that Trump was about to publish the environmental report, Apache Stronghold sued the U.S. government in federal court, hoping to block the report and thus the land swap. Rambler also wrote a separate letter to the government, warning of "potentially disastrous environmental impacts" from the mine.[101] The group also filed a property lien, essentially claiming that the government did not own the land it was about to give away to Rio in the land swap.[102]

Trump published the report on January 15. A federal judge declined to stop him, setting in motion a sixty-day countdown to transfer the land. The judge declined to consider the broader issue of the land swap before that sixty-day window was up.[103] A few weeks later, he sided with the government, essentially saying it could give its land away to anyone it wanted.[104]

Apache Stronghold's lawyer said the group was "undaunted."[105] Indeed, Rambler knew he had a card to play. And he did. Not long after the 2021 inauguration, Rambler contacted Harris with one request: "I asked them to unpublish the FEIS," he said, referring to the Resolution Final Environmental Impact Statement. "The Trump administration had rushed this to publication," Rambler said. The newly inaugurated Biden reversed Trump, essentially unpublishing what had been published. It wasn't clear if the report even could be unpublished. Could the genie be put back in the bottle? But Biden had done it, buying time for the Apache. Biden also had put a Minnesota copper mine project from Antofagasta in his crosshairs, going back on his campaign's implicit promise to the mining industry and upholding a public promise he had made to Indigenous groups.

The court case continued, though, when Apache Stronghold appealed the federal judge's ruling to a San Francisco appeals court. Eventually, Biden would have to do something with the report, per Congress. But the appeals court, wary of the separation of powers, was loath to step in. "It'd be nice if Congress or someone would make more sense out of this," one of the appeals court judges said at an October 2021 hearing, an acknowledgment that the case was indeed complex, as the Forest Service had bluntly stated in 2021.[106]

Interestingly, Biden's government attorneys defended the government's right to give the land away. It was just the latest sign of a dualistic approach by Biden to mining for EV metals. While Biden had unpublished the environmental report and frozen the land swap, Justice Department attorneys controlled by the president were telling the appeals court that government statutes should supersede any treaty or prior agreement that Washington had with the San Carlos Apache or other Indigenous groups. It was enough to give someone whiplash, to be sure, and an inconsistency that would come to define Biden's EV minerals strategy.[107] The appeals court in June 2022 ruled for Rio and the U.S. government. Apache Stronghold had lost the battle but vowed to appeal all the way to the U.S. Supreme Court, if necessary. The saga of Chi'chil Biłldagoteel exposed complex, deep-seated issues that needed to be addressed if the world hoped to go green. And central to all those issues was one simple question: What exactly is "good" mining?

CHAPTER THREE

Radical Work

"LET ME TELL YOU SOMETHING. YOU SELL BLOOD DIAMONDS, too."[1] Leonardo DiCaprio's Danny Archer spoke those words to Jennifer Connelly's Maddy Bowen in the 2006 film *Blood Diamond*, which sparked a global conversation about how, where, and why diamonds are procured for products ranging from engagement rings to lasers. The quote was an acerbic rejoinder to Bowen's brash confidence that she bore no culpability for Africa's rough-and-tumble diamond trade. Indeed, as DiCaprio's character underscored, she did, because she and billions of others bought products every day mined out of the Earth.

Michael J. Kowalski had already begun to consider those issues about seven years before the film debuted, eventually deciding that he and the company he ran had a role to play in making sure the metals they bought were extracted and processed responsibly. Kowalski had taken the reins in 1999 of Tiffany & Co., the iconic retailer known the world over for its rings, necklaces, watches, and myriad other jewelry products made from gold, silver, platinum, and other metals wrapped in proprietary blue-hued bags and boxes. The company made most of its own jewelry, thus helping it ensure not only product quality but safe working conditions and fair labor practices for staff. What Tiffany did not control, though, was the mining of metals for its products. For Kowalski, that was a problem.

"We began to realize that the jewelry industry broadly and Tiffany specifically didn't have a strong understanding of the metals supply chain and the sourcing of the building blocks for the products we sold,"

Kowalski said.[2] It was a reputational risk to the company's bottom line. After all, buying an engagement or wedding ring is one of the most intimate purchases a person can ever make. Buying a ring made with gold that came from a mine where workers made only pennies per day or toiled in atrocious conditions was sure to zap any brand loyalty many of Tiffany's customers had. Kowalski was an economist by training, not a mining engineer.[3] He had no clue how to run a mine.

"Jewelry is an emotionally laden product, and you want to feel absolutely secure in its origin story," he said. "We understood that we could use the power of the Tiffany brand to raise awareness. When a prestigious brand like Tiffany says something, that carries weight."

Mines are giant behemoths carved into the Earth's crust that belch dust and toxins. But they also birth treasures, the building blocks for products used by Tiffany and every other manufacturer on the planet. Much of what every human touches every single day comes from the ground—typically through a mine or a farm. Kowalski realized this, as well as the inherent risk for Tiffany if it did not do more to encourage responsible mining. It was not enough for Tiffany to stop buying metals from unsavory places; Kowalski came to understand that Tiffany had to use its clout and purchasing power to force all mines to honor workers and the environment.

Kowalski started in what he considered obvious areas. In 2002, Tiffany banned the sale of jewelry made from coral, a stance that over time was embraced by more of its jewelry peers.[4] Coral is, after all, a kind of underwater forest helping to filter the world's oceans and provide shelter for a plethora of fish and other creatures. To actively encourage the mining of coral sent a signal that Tiffany did not care about the ocean and thus the world itself. For Kowalski, that wouldn't do.

In the absence of global mining standards, Tiffany signed a deal in 2002 to buy most of its silver and gold from Rio Tinto's Bingham Canyon Mine in Utah, near Salt Lake City.[5] The mine, operating since 1906, had grown to become the deepest open pit in the world, at depths of nearly 4,000 feet.[6] "It was a legacy mine, and no one was putting a big hole in the middle of the Amazon," Kowalski said. "It was responsibly managed and had a smelter on-site." Some environmental groups were irked that Tiffany did business with the mine, especially one located right outside a major U.S. metropolis. But where should the company get its metals and at what standards? Tiffany was feeling its way through the metaphorical dark. "We were willing to do the right thing, but there were not standards telling us where to get the gold," Kowalski said.

In February 2004, the environmental group Earthworks and the global relief organization Oxfam America launched an international campaign targeting the jewelry industry. Titled No Dirty Gold, the campaign planned to target Tiffany and its jeweler peers in an attempt to sway where they purchased the yellow metal. On Valentine's Day that year, the groups handed out cards to shoppers at jewelry stores across three major American cities bearing the imperative: *Don't tarnish your love with dirty gold.*[7]

Kowalski, who had already been thinking about gold sourcing, took notice. He called Steve D'Esposito, the president of Earthworks, around that time asking how he and Tiffany could help.[8] The environmentalists were shocked. Not only was one of the jewelry companies they had expected to target now asking to join forces with them, but it was also one of the world's most iconic jewelry companies. Movies had been made about the company. Its trademark blue literally was trademarked.[9]

Soon the new partners both had their first target. Late that March, Tiffany paid for a full-page ad in *The Washington Post* that was essentially a blown-up letter written from Kowalski to Dale Bosworth, the head at the time of the U.S. Forest Service. Topped by the Tiffany & Co. logo, the letter implored Bosworth not to approve the proposed Rock Creek Mine in eastern Montana, despite the immense amounts of copper and silver that it would produce. Kowalski wrote:

> This huge mine would discharge millions of gallons of wastewater per day conveying pollutants to the Clark Fork River and ultimately into Lake Pend Oreille in Idaho, a national treasure in its own right. Vast quantities of mine tailings—a polite term for toxic sludge—would be stored in a holding facility of questionable durability. Wildlife already struggling to survive would face new perils.[10]

It was a major broadside from one of the mining industry's biggest customers. Mining companies were incensed. "I was stunned that a person of Mr. Kowalski's stature and obvious business acumen would write a letter like that," said Laura Skaer, who ran the Northwest Mining Association, a trade group for mining companies in the U.S. Northwest.[11] But it worked. As of early 2024, the Rock Creek mine had yet to win regulatory approval.

In 2008, Kowalski went a step further and publicly opposed plans by a Canadian company to build the Pebble Mine in Alaska.[12] The project would unearth one of the world's largest copper and gold deposits, supplying Tiffany and other jewelers the metals they needed for decades to come. But it had been wildly controversial since the deposit was discovered in 1987, with opponents alarmed it would ravage pristine Alaskan wilderness that is home to the state's extensive salmon fishing industry. The proposed mine site also sits near an active fault line, fueling fears random earthquakes could topple tailings dams and cause cave-ins. "There are certain places where mines should just never be built, and Bristol Bay in Alaska is just one of those places," Kowalski said.[13] "The thought that one could put an enormous gold mine with a tailings dam in a geologically active zone at the headwaters of one of the world's greatest salmon fisheries was a devil's bargain."

By 2011, Tiffany had convinced fifty of its fellow jewelers to oppose the Pebble project.[14] When President Barack Obama's administration announced in 2014 that it was considering canceling the Pebble project, Tiffany took out another full-page advertisement, this time in not only *The Washington Post* but *The Seattle Times* and the *San Francisco Chronicle,* that read in part: "We know there will be other gold and copper mines to develop. But we will never find a more majestic and productive place than Bristol Bay."[15]

Coral was a relatively easy thing to ban given the importance of coral reefs to the ecological health of the world's oceans. And opposing the Rock Creek and Pebble projects made logical sense just given the risk of ecological harm. But Tiffany couldn't simply fight all gold, silver, and platinum mines. It had to find a way to buy from the best mines, and it had to insist that standards be set for responsible mining. The Bingham Canyon deal worked as a type of makeshift answer to the broader problem, but eventually Tiffany and other manufacturers would have to buy from other mines across the world and be comfortable that the product they bought was produced using standards understood and accepted widely.

Tiffany's business depended on a consistent supply of metals. They had to come from somewhere. "We wanted to do the right thing. But we were a retailer and a manufacturer, not a miner. What is a commonly accepted definition of responsible mining? There wasn't a clear answer anywhere," Kowalski said. In 2006, Earthworks and Tiffany expanded their relationship by starting a long journey into setting the best mining standards. A previous attempt to use the Responsible Jewelry Council—a trade group for jewelry companies—to set mining standards did not succeed, largely because jewelers are, after all, jewelers, not miners. Kowalski wanted a third-party organization to help set what he described to me as "an aspirational system of what a mine should look like."

"If the world was really concerned about mining, we realized we needed to go far beyond jewelry," Kowalski said. Taking inspiration from the Forest Stewardship Council, which sets standards for timber harvesting and forest management, Tiffany and Earthworks in 2006 helped to form the Initiative for Responsible Mining Assurance, commonly known as IRMA. IRMA aimed to succeed where others failed by bringing together mining companies; their customers, including jewelers, automakers, and tech firms; environmental groups and other nongovernmental organizations; local communities, including Indigenous groups; and labor unions. The intent was to set the best standards for how a mine should operate.

From the beginning, it was a motley crew. Mining companies in the same room as environmentalists? Manufacturers in the same room as labor unions? None of these groups historically had been chummy with each other. When I first heard about the scheme, I was suspicious. It sounded like something devised by 1960s hippies without any concept of how the world actually worked. Yet all of them created and agreed to adhere to ten Principles of Engagement, with the first one declaring:

We are committed to and recognize the value of a multi-sector process and solutions with the participation of all sectors.[16]

Each of the five groups, or sectors, gained two slots on IRMA's board of directors. (A sixth group—investors—was added in 2020.[17]) Each member had a vote on a standard. If a contentious issue for a mining standard up for debate had two no votes, that meant an issue was blocked and all parties had to essentially go back to the drawing board. For example, if the two nongovernmental organizations on the board disagreed with water standards proposed by the mining industry's two representatives, the issue was tabled until everyone could agree. Those operating rules were designed to spur consensus and compromise, but they also ensured IRMA got off to a slow start. For the first few years, the IRMA members wrestled with how and why they would craft the standards, as well as how many there should be. By 2011, IRMA's members had made at least one consequential decision: they would hire someone. Aimee Boulanger, a former Earthworks mining activist, joined as executive director. From the start, she was skeptical that Kowalski's vision for IRMA could succeed. "I said, 'This is probably not going to work.' The trust between mining companies and the communities who are affected . . . is too deeply broken," Boulanger said.[18] But she decided that if the United States wasn't going to update its 1872 Mining Law, there was an opportunity to use the free market to craft better industry standards. So she took the job.

IRMA's aims exceeded anything that had been attempted before. Rather than duking it out in a courtroom or the court of public opinion, all sides would have to work together to decide what the mine of the future could look like and how best it could operate. If the world needed more mines—and it did and does for the foreseeable future—then the only option was to decide how best to mine. That, at least, was the intention behind IRMA. "When you walk into a room with people who—especially in this day and age right now—see the world differently and yet who are kind to one another . . . that's radical work," Boulanger said.[19]

Slowly, the members started to work together. Consultants were hired to help the IRMA board craft standards for twenty-six areas they had agreed to codify, things such as water quality, worker health and safety, Indigenous consent, emergency preparedness, and air quality. The two biggest areas of disagreement were water quality and mine waste, specifically because they were two areas that could be quantified. Environmental and community groups wanted to set firm standards for salt disposal levels in water and where mine waste could be stored. But the mining industry pushed back, believing that one global standard for water quality wouldn't fit, and that standards should vary depending on geography. Liberia and Alaska, for instance, have vastly different topographies. "Sometimes you get salts running off mine sites and into water streams. Now, if that's going into a saltwater environment, it may not matter. If it's going into a freshwater environment, it may matter a great deal. So that's a simple example of how context actually does make quite a big difference," said Jon Samuel, an IRMA board member and an executive at Anglo American, a large miner of platinum, nickel, and iron ore.[20] "I do think there were certainly some people in the mining industry who thought this was never going to work."

"Water is always the one where everybody disagrees. It was always a chapter in IRMA that would be returned to, over and over," said Nuskamata, a member of the Nuxalk and Secwepemc Nations in British Columbia.[21]

IRMA in 2014 published a rough draft of its standards for the world to tear apart.[22] "It wasn't perfect, but it was a compromise and the first time all these groups had put standards in place," Boulanger said. The group received more than a thousand public comments about the draft standards. The Stillwater platinum mine in Montana agreed to undergo a mock audit in 2015, essentially agreeing to be IRMA's guinea pig. "The Standard is thorough and demanding," IRMA said in its report after the Stillwater mock audit, which cost $60,000. IRMA thought that the cost probably would have to rise to $100,000 for deeper on-site analysis.[23] IRMA did a second mock audit the following year at another platinum mine, this one in Zimbabwe owned by Anglo American.[24] By 2016, a second version of the draft standards was published—a decade after Kowalski had phoned Earthworks.

Disagreements over finalizing the standards, however, almost blew up IRMA in 2018. "Twelve years in, and we were at the precipice of all that effort crumbling before us," Boulanger recalled.[25] Mining companies threatened to exercise their veto, but not before IRMA organized two sets of three-day meetings—one for water and one for waste—for more debate, this time with scientists from the Mining Association of Canada, Columbia University, the World Wildlife Fund, and elsewhere. The attempt to forge compromise worked. "We didn't reach agreement that week, but that was the week when it was accepted that everybody was acting in good faith. And that allowed the specialists to actually chart out the alternative routes forward, which was what allowed us to get unstuck," Anglo American's Samuel said.[26] More public comments were solicited, and more tension erupted behind the scenes. But, once again, it didn't scuttle the process; groups that historically had been at each other's throat formalized the two-hundred-page *Standard for Responsible Mining* in June 2018. (IRMA's board of directors never reached an impasse.)

Tiffany and its jewelry peers were thrilled at the progression, having realized that their prodding in 2006 was redounding to the benefit of even more consumers. "We believe IRMA will address a current gap in the mining industry by providing an independent certification system that consumers can trust and that sets a high bar for social and environmental performance," Tiffany told its shareholders in 2016.[27] IRMA hadn't been formed to necessarily approve or disapprove mines; rather, it had been formed to bring transparency to an industry that had historically been myopic at best and duplicitous at worst. And the standards were launching just as the green energy transition was taking off.

⚡

IRMA REVIEWS ARE funded by mining companies, who hire independent, IRMA-approved consultants to visit mine sites and contrast what's happening on the ground with the IRMA standards. Results are publicly posted on IRMA's website for everyone to see, so it quickly becomes obvious if a mining company is cheating or trying to bend the rules to its favor. By early 2023, lithium mines in South America run by Albemarle, SQM, and Livent, as well as other mines for multiple metals across the globe owned by Anglo American, were under IRMA review. Only two mines had received IRMA scores.[28] (No U.S. or Canadian mine—proposed or operating—was undergoing an IRMA review.) A mine is ranked on a scale of 0 to 100 after an audit, with the latter being perfect. Regardless of a mine's ranking, a detailed IRMA audit report is released as a form of transparency and a prod for improvement. And that data has been increasingly sought after by the EV industry.

"The big car companies are now starting to want that," said Jessica Duran of Carrizal Mining, which mines zinc, copper, silver, and lead in Mexico.[29] In 2020, the company's Zimapán mine was the first ever to be reviewed under IRMA's final standards. It failed, sort of. While Zimapán hadn't scored above 50, the mine was given a label of "Achievement level: Transparency" because the entire world—including its EV customers—now knew exactly how the mine stacked up to these new standards. "I think we were very happy with the result in the end, because it taught us a lot and it also set a very clear path on what we needed to be doing," Duran said.[30] Zimapán's neighbors, for instance, didn't have a copy of the mine's emergency operation plan, so they had no clue what the mine planned to do if one of its tailings ponds suddenly collapsed. IRMA prodded them to change that and other areas.

Using funding from the tech giant Microsoft, IRMA also released a digital tool for mines to test themselves privately before they underwent IRMA certification. "Our purpose is not to fail a mine," Boulanger said. "Our goal is to create financial value and incentive for you to do better."[31]

Automakers began to realize that if they were going to build more EVs, they would need to pay particular attention to where they bought lithium, copper, and other metals to build those EVs. And having a third party independently verify whether mines adhered to commonly accepted standards for human rights and environmental protection gave the automakers themselves a bit of cover. Yet just because an automaker or manufacturer joined the group did not necessarily require that group to buy metal from an IRMA-approved mine, though that was clearly the intent when Kowalski and Earthworks envisioned it back in 2006. As of 2024, there simply weren't enough mines that had put themselves forward for IRMA certification. IRMA was designed to spread sunlight throughout the entire supply chain for EV minerals, not block a mine. In theory, if a consumer didn't want to buy a Tesla until she understood how cobalt mines in the Democratic Republic of the Congo produced the cobalt inside the Model Y, that would prod Tesla to require Glencore—from whom it buys cobalt extracted from the DRC—to undergo an IRMA audit.[32]

BMW and Ford Motor were among the first automakers to say they would abide by IRMA standards, and Microsoft did as well. General Motors, Volkswagen, and Mercedes-Benz joined later. The Ford Foundation (unaffiliated with the automaker) and the clothing giant Patagonia helped fund IRMA, as did dues from its members, capped at $15,000 annually. Ford, especially, promised to work with miners to promote what it deemed responsible mining.[33]

"Everything we make and everything that goes into our products throughout the supply chain must not only comply with local laws, but follow our commitment to sustainability and human rights protection," a Ford executive said in 2021 when the company became the first American automaker to join IRMA. Ford would work with IRMA, it said, to insist that miners meet its "consistent, clear, shared expectations for responsible practices."[34]

It became increasingly apparent that IRMA standards were a potent tool for those opposed to mines across the globe, while also giving automakers and other manufacturers a sense of relief that they were buying ethically sourced lithium, copper, and other metals for the green energy transition. IRMA was certainly a transparency tool. What it didn't do was make a decision for regulators or everyday consumers. They would have to take the reams of data that came from IRMA and make decisions for themselves.

In September of the same year that Ford joined IRMA, the automaker met with James Calaway and ioneer in the Cosmopolitan hotel on the Las Vegas Strip to discuss buying lithium from Rhyolite Ridge. Ford peppered Calaway with questions about Tiehm's buckwheat, especially how ioneer hoped to protect the rare flower while also providing lithium. No major U.S. automaker had yet signed a binding lithium supply deal, and Calaway was hungry to ink one with Ford. Yet the meeting ended with no deal.

By the following year, though, Ford pivoted back to ioneer and offered to buy its lithium, a decision seemingly at odds with the company's stance to support IRMA standards given the fight over Tiehm's buckwheat. When Ford asked ioneer to undergo an IRMA audit, ioneer said it wanted to use standards set by the Mining Association of Canada, which was controlled by mining companies. "We felt the Canadian standards were better for us," Calaway told me.[35] In the end, Ford realized it needed ioneer's lithium. The deal was set. Even if Ford wanted to buy lithium only from IRMA-audited mines, there just weren't that many and certainly not enough to fuel the entire green energy transition.

"There's not enough of that volume in IRMA-audited mines. We are getting there, but we're not there yet," Boulanger said. For IRMA, ioneer not going through an IRMA audit was an obvious loophole, but one its officials were working fast to rectify by the time Ford inked the ioneer deal. The nonprofit had been crafting standards not only for new mines, but for new smelters. For new mines especially, environmental harm and Indigenous rights would be major components of any score. Yet would ioneer actually agree to abide by these new standards, especially after the Ford deal had been signed and sealed? "Mining is really difficult, and yes, it causes harm. But we do have the technology to do things better; we just need the whole value chain to support us," Boulanger said.[36] And that meant more than just the auto industry.

CHAPTER FOUR

The Leaf Blower

"HAVE YOU HEARD ABOUT LEAF BLOWERS?!"

The unexpected question came from a former colleague as we were catching up over drinks in the summer of 2018. I had, indeed, heard about leaf blowers. I also heard them every time they were used in city parks, or a suburban backyard, or any other location teeming with copious amounts of leaves, grass clippings, or other lawn detritus. They were loud, but at least seemed to be the ideal way to clean up the aforementioned junk.

"Well," my former colleague said, "they're horrible for the environment. They're basically spewing out way more pollutants than an average car, and they're everywhere. They're just horrible. They need to be outlawed."

I had never heard of this War Against Leaf Blowers, but I soon found myself diving into research, fascinated by the arguments for and against the tiny devices that, apparently, had outsized influence over our global environment. Leaf blowers, as we know them, tend to be powered by gasoline with cheap, convenient two-stroke engines that also power small boat motors, chain saws, and lawn mowers. They're called "two stroke" because the engine finishes one cycle of internal combustion for every two movements of the motor's piston. But the engines don't have internal lubrication (like gasoline-powered automobiles), so the gasoline needs to be mixed with oil. About a third of that fuel mix isn't burned off in that two-step process, so the engine spews out a gnarly mix of air pollutants that can include carbon monoxide and chemicals that can contribute to smog and cause acid rain.[1]

Engine-powered devices can, of course, operate faster than rakes. They're great for professional landscapers who have dozens of homes and businesses to maintain. They're also great for average homeowners, many of whom probably don't have two hours every Saturday to scrape their grass or flower beds. The road to perdition apparently is cleared by leaf blowers.

Two prominent scientists described leaf blowers as an "obvious source" of emissions during a conference hosted by the U.S. Environmental Protection Agency.[2] A contributing opinion writer for *The New York Times* bemoaned that leaf blowers fill the air "with the stench of gasoline and death" and compared the devices to "mechanical locusts" that descend upon neighborhoods "the way the grasshoppers of old would arrive."[3] A report from the automotive website Edmunds found that the average, run-of-the-mill gasoline-powered leaf blower coughs out more pollutants than a Ford pickup truck. Blowing leaves around your yard for a half hour with a two-stroke leaf blower would emit roughly the same amount of hydrocarbons as driving that Ford pickup from Texas to Alaska, Edmunds found. What makes that study so fascinating (and alarming) is that it was conducted in 2011, and the Ford Motor Co. has made improvements to its environmental standards since then. But the basic design of the gasoline-powered two-stroke engine has remained largely the same. (Adding air filters would make them heavier, thus abrogating the whole appeal.[4])

Communities across the United States have considered banning them. Some, like Washington, D.C., actually did.[5] The state of California is phasing out all gasoline-powered lawn equipment by 2024.[6] Lorena Gonzalez, who as a member of the California State Assembly co-authored the 2021 bill phasing out California's gasoline-guzzling lawn devices, called them "super polluters" that are bad for the environment and contribute to the climate crisis.[7]

Even the loud *whrrrrrrrrrrr* of a gasoline-powered leaf blower—

which can be louder in some instances than an airplane taking off—can jar the psyche and contribute to several health problems, including increased stress and cardiovascular disease.[8]

As I dug further into the War Against Leaf Blowers, I came across some advice from *The Washington Post*: switching to electric, the newspaper said, would "sharply reduce" air pollution.[9] Electric leaf blowers tend to be lighter than their gasoline-powered peers, and produce less noise. Thanks also to advances in lithium-ion batteries (the same type of battery that powers electric vehicles), their average cost was coming down and battery life was increasing. By 2022, I found myself with a yard of my own to care for and figured it made sense to investigate an electric-powered Ryobi.

Ryobi makes dozens of home power tools, including drills, trimmers, rototillers, and yes, leaf blowers. In the United States, the brand is primarily sold at Home Depot, the large chain of hardware stores known for its orange motif. Ryobi developed a line of products that can use the same battery packs, which is the appeal. Want to buy a few of their power tools? You can buy the same battery for each one, swapping it in and out depending on the lawn or home project you're trying to tackle. More than 280 in all. While not unique to Ryobi, this scheme—branded as ONE+—quickly took off and became a top seller for the Atlanta-based chain.[10]

And so, in the summer of 2022, I found myself staring at a long aisle of Ryobi ONE+ products in my local Home Depot. I settled on the 18 Volt Cordless Variable-Speed Jet Fan Leaf Blower, paying $129.00 (plus tax).[11] The contraption, the Ryobi packaging declared, would whip up a wind at more than 100 miles per hour. Plenty of power for those pesky leaves. But then the real question—especially as I wrote this book—came into focus. Where was Ryobi getting the lithium, copper, and other metals to build the lithium-ion battery for this leaf blower? If they were sourced from the other side of the world, what's the leaf blower's carbon footprint, and is it more or less than if I had bought a gasoline-powered blower? And how were those metals mined and processed? Were they extracted with fair labor and using environmentally safe practices? Those questions are increasingly being asked for the manufacturing process of electric vehicles, but given the widespread implications for the green energy transition, EVs were just the tip of the iceberg. Everything, it increasingly seems, is going electric, so the sourcing of these metals matters, and some governments are starting to act. The European Union moved in late 2022 to set a tariff on imports of products from countries that don't curb greenhouse gas emissions, with China seen as a key target.[12] (Automakers, it should be noted, rarely have information on whether countries of origin have curbed greenhouse gas emissions readily available for consumers casually perusing EVs.) But standing there in the hardware store aisle, I didn't have the benefit of the European Union or any other government forcing ethical supply chains, at least not yet. I decided to dive into the provenance of this Ryobi battery myself.

Ryobi Limited is a Japanese manufacturing company that has very little to do with the leaf blower I bought. The company had long since licensed its name to a Hong Kong–based company known as Techtronic Industries Company Limited, commonly known as TTI Group. By 2022, the company was making not only Ryobi power tools, but vacuums sold under the Oreck, Hoover, and Dirt Devil brand names.

When I bought my leaf blower, Home Depot included some technical information meant, it seemed, like legalese. One of the forms was a so-called Technical Data Sheet that seemed like it might have the information I was after. It did, partly. The form promised at the top to have "Product and Company Identification." I knew already that the battery was 18 volts and that its capacity was 4 amps. I learned that its model number was "P108" and that it had been released in May 2016. While TTI's headquarters were in Hong Kong, I learned TTI had offices in Anderson, South Carolina.[13]

TTI had further outsourced the battery's manufacturing to a subsidiary of Samsung, the South Korean conglomerate. Samsung had given the battery the commercial product name of INR18650-20Q M and had built it in Negeri Sembilan, a Malaysian state near the national capital, Kuala Lumpur. The battery, according to the data sheet, contained copper and aluminum. Its anode was made with graphite. And its cathode was made with lithium, nickel, cobalt, and manganese. Those metals are commonly used in lithium-ion batteries, so their use wasn't surprising or uncommon. The battery should, the safety sheet warned, be kept out of a fire. If one of the battery cells inside the pack itself were to break open, there was a risk that hydrofluoric acid or carbon monoxide could be released. Do not, under any circumstances, swallow the liquid lithium electrolyte inside the battery.

None of this information was particularly revelatory. It was all standard product and safety information. None of it told me what part of the world had once held the minerals that were now powering the leaf blower deployed in my backyard. Had the lithium been sourced in Chile, then shipped to a battery cell manufacturer in China before being shipped to Malaysia? Was the copper from Peru, where rural farmers have bitterly complained that the mining industry's trucks kick up dust that pollutes crops?[14] Had the nickel come from Indonesia, where rain forests have been cut down to make room for new mines?[15] What about the cobalt? Did a seven-year-old extract it from a makeshift mine in the Democratic Republic of the Congo?

I called TTI at the number listed in the literature that accompanied my leaf blower, left a message, and never heard back.

While many consumers, especially in America, give little thought to how many of the products they buy are built, that was slowly beginning to change in the wake of the coronavirus pandemic. A Nike shirt may have been made in Vietnam, but where was the cotton grown, for instance? Increasingly, brands were being asked for these kinds of details. And with a wholesale shift occurring in the global economy toward electrification, new electric-focused brands were being required to do so as well. But was America ready to produce more of its own metals to build leaf blowers like mine? Were some places too special to mine?

CHAPTER FIVE

A Longing

Becky Rom was raised in a small apartment above her father's outfitter store in downtown Ely, Minnesota, about 250 miles north of Minneapolis. Born in the post–Second World War era, Rom came of age as John Kennedy was in the White House and the United States was in a period of rampant growth. The boom years of the 1950s were propelling the country's economy into an era that would bring vast technological developments fed, in part, by a burgeoning supply of metals.

Rom became an attorney and spent her career in the Minneapolis area. By the time we met in 2022, Rom was spending her golden years fighting a proposed underground copper, cobalt, and nickel mine that a Chilean company aimed to build practically in her backyard. Standing about five feet five inches tall, Rom had salt-and-pepper hair and an affinity for shades of blue. She was decked out in blue hiking pants that she unzipped later in the day at the knees, transforming them into blue shorts. She wore a blue Patagonia vest that covered a blue T-shirt with the logo of the Wilderness Society. She drove a blue gasoline-powered Audi SUV and she swapped out her glasses for blue-tinted sunglasses when not driving. She starts her days with a cup of hot green tea. A typical Saturday morning will find her at Ely's yoga studio. On weekdays she works the phones calling members of Congress, state legislators, fellow conservationists, and others, all to preach a sermon she has been reciting for more than fifty years: northern Minnesota is no place for a copper mine.

"We don't deny the reality of the green energy transition. But we would have to sacrifice everything we hold dear to have a mine here," she told me.[1] "There is only one place in America like the Boundary Waters, and it is so important because its waterways are so interconnected. It's not rational to have a mine like this in this region. You can't be the gateway to this pristine wilderness and have copper mining."[2]

The only daughter of Bill and Barb, Becky and her three brothers grew up working in the family business, Canoe Country Outfitters, which opened in 1946 and sold gear for customers to explore the million acres of northern Minnesota now known as the Boundary Waters Canoe Area Wilderness. At night, they would pack containers with night crawler worms for fishing expeditions, arrange sleeping bags and tents, and clean and polish canoes.[3]

While serving in the U.S. Navy during the war, Bill Rom had the kernel of an idea to open his outfitter shop. Inspired in part by the work of Sigurd Olson, a conservationist known for his ardent beliefs in wilderness preservation, Bill Rom thought that if Americans could experience the Boundary Waters firsthand, they would appreciate its majesty and beauty and be led to preserve it for posterity.

Minnesota's mining industry was in its prime at that time, having supplied much of the iron ore used to build tanks, ships, and other tools deployed by the Allied Forces in Europe, Asia, and Africa during the Second World War. Mining also underpinned much of the state's economy, especially in the rural north, giving that region the moniker the Iron Range.[4] Yet mining and nature exploration began to grow rapidly and in tandem during the mid-twentieth century. By the time Bill Rom sold his business in 1976, he had six thousand customers and five hundred aluminum canoes. His nickname, given by a popular pulp magazine, was the "Canoe King of Ely."[5]

In 1912, Becky's grandfather was crushed when a piece of ore calved off a ceiling unexpectedly while he was working in an underground mine. He struggled for nearly a week inside a local hospital before dying. Bill Rom was only a month old, and his father's absence left an indelible mark on him and later, by extension, on Becky Rom herself. That history also meant that the family were third-generation Minnesotans, a status that would help them fend off charges they are not invested in the state or its economy. "We're as grounded as anyone here," she told me.[6]

Even as Minnesota's mining industry flexed its muscle in the postwar years, so, too, did conservationists like Olson. In the late 1950s, the Wilderness Society and other environmental groups proposed blocking off millions of acres in the region from mining. In a way, they had history on their side.

A federal law passed in 1872 had allowed mining on wide swaths of federal land, including in Minnesota. A year later, Minnesota was removed, posing an encumbrance on the mining industry. In 1909, President Theodore Roosevelt had banned mining in the nearby Superior National Forest. Also, that same year, the United States and Canada signed the Boundary Waters Treaty, which stipulated that neither country could pollute waterways that flowed freely between the two.[7] By the late 1950s, conservationists felt the moment was right to push for a broader area of preservation with the Wilderness Act, which aimed to block new roads, as well as motorized travel—including powerboats and personal vehicles—across more than a million acres of forest and wetland.

For residents of a region so used to exploring at will, it was a deeply controversial bill. In 1962, while a seventh-grade student at Ely's Washington Junior High School, Rom was asked to defend the proposed bill in front of a school assembly. She spoke passionately for its provisions, especially what it would mean for the region's outfitter economy. Another student argued the other side. Afterward, her fellow students voted. Rom lost, 148 to 2. Her boyfriend at the time then changed his mind, leaving the vote at 148 to 1. Rather than be scarred by the experience, Rom said it emboldened her. "I learned you could still be friends with someone even if you disagreed with them," she said.[8]

At fourteen, Rom was the first girl to become an official wilderness guide in the state of Minnesota, a path encouraged by her father. She would lead customers into the woods, help them carry their canoes over portages, and cook dinner for them over their campfires.[9] "I had an extraordinary father that gave me opportunities other girls didn't have at that time," Rom said.[10]

The next summer, as Rom again served as a wilderness guide, Congress debated and ultimately passed the Wilderness Act. President Johnson signed it in September. But it was a follow-up bill in 1978 that further inflamed passions. That Carter-era piece of legislation increased restrictions on logging and motorboat access to the area. The area today is the most visited wilderness region in the United States.

It was in 1966, though, that the genesis of Rom's activism had been planted, and she didn't even realize it at the time. Quietly, the U.S. Bureau of Land Management issued two federal leases to International Nickel Co., a company that wanted to mine copper on land adjacent to the Boundary Waters for twenty-year terms. No mining was conducted, though. President Reagan's administration renewed the leases for ten years in 1989, with President Bush's administration renewing them for the same time span in 2004.[11]

The inaction and renewals were due, in part, to a slump in copper prices caused by rampant industry overgrowth in the late twentieth century. There was too much copper on the global market. But that was before the rise of China's economy and the beginnings of the green energy revolution in the early twenty-first century. Copper, soon, was very much in demand.[12] And northern Minnesota was beginning to look very appealing. The leases had traded hands a few times by November 2008, when President Obama was elected. A company known as Duluth Metals Ltd. in 2010 further studied the deposit and formed the Twin Metals Limited partnership with Antofagasta, which is controlled by Chile's richest family.[13] Antofagasta bought the entire project in 2014.[14]

For conservationists like Rom, there was that perennial concern: the Boundary Waters. For Antofagasta to access that copper and nickel, an underground mine would have to be dug at depths up to 4,500 feet. The proposed mine site also sat just underneath the watershed for Minnesota's Rainy River, which drains into the Boundary Waters and, eventually, into Canada's Hudson Bay. The physical nature of the deposit also concerned Rom and others because it contained sulfide that, when exposed to water, forms acid.

No longer was Rom's opposition based merely on a dislike of mining trucks or dynamite blasting. For her, the issue crystallized into a concern that the Twin Metals mine waste would pollute the Rainy River and flow, like the arteries of the human body, throughout the million acres of the Boundary Waters, forever spoiling the region. Nor did it matter that the United States requires all mining companies to buy financial instruments known as bonds to fund cleanup in the case of accidents or spills. "How do you bond for the Boundary Waters? It's massive," Rom bluntly told me.[15]

⚡

THE TOWN OF Ely owes its founding to a gold rush, of all things. In 1865, as the Civil War ebbed, rumors of rich veins of gold drew prospectors from across the country. While there didn't end up being much in the way of gold, there were ample supplies of iron ore, which is used to make steel. Ely's mining boom had begun.[16] Underground mines popped up in and around Ely, and throughout much of the region. The town's population surged, fueled by the high salaries that miners grew to expect for their backbreaking, dangerous work.

Ely's miners pulled about 80 million tonnes of rock out of the ground, at first using open-pit mines and then extending underground via shafts that were dug across the region. Five mines eventually dotted the edge of the town before the last one, the Pioneer Mine, closed in 1967. All five eventually filled with rainwater and formed a lake now known as Miners Lake, which is abutted by Miners Drive.[17]

It's that history that some in Ely have long hoped would come back. On the outskirts of Ely, Seraphine Rolando and Bill Erzar have been doing their best to keep that flame alive. The two retired miners run Ely's Pioneer Museum, which sits atop one of the old Pioneer Mine shafts. A few days a week, the pair regale visitors with stories of Ely's mining past, including the good, the bad, and the downright ugly. Looming over the building is an old A-frame that used to support a gondola with two levels, each carrying twenty-five men at a time down into the dark of the Earth where they would mine hematite iron ore during ten-hour shifts.

I visited on a warm spring day in June 2022 about an hour before the pair were set to close up shop. Before I had a chance to fully explain why I was in town, Erzar took me by the arm and showed me around the museum's various exhibits. There were pictures of miners in the 1890s chipping away at ore with candles on their hard hats. He showed me a yellowing map that traced the export of Minnesota's iron ore to places across the globe, destined to build ships, skyscrapers, bridges, and roads. There was a giant poster outlining a 1916 workers' strike over safety equipment. Erzar, a stocky man with a broad white mustache, showed me a Minneapolis *Star Tribune* article about the time in 1955 when his father was nearly swept away underground when mud breached a mine's walls.[18] The experience did not deter Erzar, then seven years old, from spending thirty-four years working in Minnesota's iron ore mines, albeit at a mine owned by U.S. Steel about an hour south. When Ely's last mine closed on April 1, 1967—April Fool's Day—about 450 workers were put out of work, causing the local economy to reel.[19] It came three years after President Johnson included the Boundary Waters in the new National Wilderness Preservation system, causing a bit of a one-two punch for those who saw mining as Ely's and the region's raison d'être.

"Mining built this town, whether people like it or not," he told me. "We want jobs here to bring back our young people." The town's population peaked near 6,200 in 1930 thanks to the prewar mining years. By 2022, it had dropped to near 3,200. A mural in downtown Ely depicts a miner with a red hard hat equipped with a searchlight, a visual reminder of the town's past.[20]

Erzar spoke of the Twin Metals project in almost religious tones, praying and wishing that by extracting the copper and nickel and cobalt from deep underground it would conjure an Ely that once was. In a way, Erzar's fight evokes the tension that grew amid the 2016 U.S. presidential election, with some segments of the population in regions that have grown economically stressed pining for a past that no longer exists.

"If this mine is not going to harm the environment, then let's do it," Erzar told me, his voice growing animated. "We swim in these lakes, drink the water from these lakes. We don't want pollution here, and we should not depend on Russia or China for these metals." At that last point, he pulled out his iPhone and waved it around, an implicit acknowledgment that he knew the device he held in his hand was composed of a bevy of metals, few of which are extracted from U.S. soils. Despite Erzar's and Rolando's longing, it's not clear a mine would be a boon to the area's economy. A 2020 study by a Harvard University economist found that mining would have a "negative effect on the regional economy," not only its employment but also the income of the area's residents.[21] Ominously for Twin Metals, Erzar, Rolando, and others supporting the mining, the study found that any attempt to create a regional economy based on copper mining would fall far short of an outdoors-based economy.[22] That's an argument that Rom, and many like her, had trumpeted for years, and it had been received like a Ping-Pong ball in Washington.

In 2012, with the leases to the site set to expire in two years, the owners at the time applied to the Obama administration to have them renewed for yet another ten years. Only this time, Washington took a different approach, finding that because no mining had actually taken place, the leases did not have to be renewed. And because the leases did not have to be renewed, Obama officials were free to reject the leases, which they did in December 2016, a month before Trump took office.[23] Obama officials also launched a plan to block mining in the region for twenty years, in case someone else besides Antofagasta got control of the site and its copper. "The Boundary Waters is a natural treasure, special to the 150,000 who canoe, fish, and recreate there each year, and is the economic life blood to local businesses that depend on a pristine natural resource," said Tom Vilsack, Obama's secretary of agriculture. He asked government scientists to conduct "a careful environmental analysis and engage the public on whether future mining should be authorized on any federal land next door to the Boundary Waters."[24]

That study was canceled by Trump when he took office the following year, with officials from the new administration starting work to end it only a few weeks into office.[25] Antofagasta swapped emails with senior Trump advisors. A senior member of the family that controlled Antofagasta bought a $5.5 million mansion in Washington, D.C., and rented it out to Trump's daughter Ivanka and her husband, Jared Kushner.[26] At the same time, his administration had begun reconsidering the leases.

By June 2019, Trump's administration had renewed the leases for Twin Metals, underscoring the dizzying tug-of-war that had engulfed the project.[27] Trump's Interior Department said it was rectifying "a flawed decision rushed out the door" by Obama officials.[28]

The decision only further crystallized the zeal from Rom and her fellow mine opponents against Trump, who had narrowly lost Minnesota in 2016 and wanted to win it in 2020. After Trump lost, President Biden brought a familiar face back to the debate: Tom Vilsack, who was again named the secretary of agriculture. (Here's where the bureaucracy of Washington gets even more tricky, so buckle up.) Vilsack's Department of Agriculture oversees the U.S. Forest Service, which controls the surface land at the site. But the U.S. Bureau of Land Management, which is part of the Interior Department, controls the underground copper, cobalt, and nickel deposit and must approve plans to extract minerals. The White House can ban mining in the region for twenty years, but only Congress has the power to permanently ban it, and thus the Twin Metals drama spilled over to Capitol Hill.

Deb Haaland, Biden's secretary of the interior, declined to discuss the project when asked at a 2021 congressional hearing by Representative Pete Stauber, a Minnesota Republican whose district included Ely and the Twin Metals mine site.

"Secretary Haaland . . . why does the administration no longer plan to use domestic miners to source these minerals?" Stauber asked Haaland at the congressional hearing.[29]

"Congressman, thank you so much for the question, and what I can say is that President Biden does support energy independence in our country. We agree that securing the supply of critical minerals for the future of our energy needs is very important to America's energy independence."

"Madame Secretary, would you rather source these minerals in our country? . . . Wouldn't you want to mine these minerals in the United States, rather than source them out to foreign nations?"

"I truly appreciate your question and your information, Congressman. And of course we're happy to continue to speak to you about this issue."

When he was a presidential candidate in 2020, Biden's campaign had quietly told Twin Metals and other U.S. mining projects that he would support boosting domestic production of metals used to make electric vehicles, solar panels, and other projects crucial to his climate plans. It seemed intended as a play to shore up support with labor unions in Minnesota, Arizona, and other swing states that happened to contain large reserves of copper and nickel.[30]

It was a quiet back-channel campaign that nonetheless worried conservationists, especially because the Obama administration had set rigorous environmental regulations that slowed U.S. mining sector growth during its time in office. Biden, who served as Obama's vice president and was well regarded in conservation circles, had been expected to continue in that vein.[31]

But the necessities of the green energy transition seemed to be a positive harbinger for the mining industry. Indeed, Wall Street projected that a Biden victory would spark a multiyear boon for copper, as EVs use twice as much of the red metal as internal combustion engines. (And if Trump won reelection, the industry thought the same. Either candidate was palatable.) Twin Metals had taken Biden's whisper campaign as a sure bet and publicly stated it was sure it could safely develop the mine.[32]

Biden, of course, won. He said nothing publicly after the election or inauguration about Twin Metals. But in May 2021, his administration began a whisper campaign that mirrored the whisper campaign to miners from the previous fall, only this outreach was to conservationists. The administration spread word that it aimed to rely on ally countries to supply the bulk of the metals needed to build electric vehicles and focus on processing them domestically into battery parts, part of a strategy designed to placate environmentalists.[33]

Rather than focus on permitting more U.S. mines, Biden's team grew more focused on creating jobs that process minerals. Such a plan would cut U.S. reliance on the industry leader, China, for EV materials while also enticing unions with manufacturing work. For opponents of Twin Metals, that was a big boost.[34]

"It rings hollow when I hear everyone use this as a national defense argument, that we have to build new mines to have a greener economy," said Representative Betty McCollum, a Democrat whose district was in the Minneapolis region.[35] McCollum had introduced a bill to permanently ban sulfide-ore copper mining in the basin that feeds the Boundary Waters, a bill designed to parallel an approach that the White House was seemingly pursuing.

Vilsack delayed a decision for months after Biden appointed him, saying at first that he was undecided. Biden is "trying to find the balance between preserving a pristine area, and at the same time looking for ways in which job growth, economic growth can take place in rural areas. And that's what we're going to attempt to do," he said.[36] Several months later, he added that he needed Haaland's lawyers to issue him a legal decision.[37] Haaland herself in public said little beyond what she had told Stauber in the congressional hearing that previous spring. Biden himself had yet to take a public stance on the mining of critical minerals.

But things started to move by the fall. That October, Vilsack blocked copper mining in the Boundary Waters for an initial two years, while requesting the Interior Department ban mining in the area for the next twenty years.[38] The environmental study that Trump had canceled was revived.[39] Breaking her silence on the mine the following January, Haaland canceled the Twin Metals leases for the Boundary Waters, handing a major win to Rom and other environmentalists. Saying the leases were "improperly renewed" by Trump, the secretary stressed that her department has a responsibility to "ensure that no lessee receives special treatment."[40] The decision was widely seen as evidence that Biden had grown increasingly comfortable prioritizing domestic conservation efforts even as demand for minerals used to build electric vehicles headed skyward.

McCollum, who was shepherding her bill to permanently block copper mining in the Boundary Waters through Congress, praised the ruling. But Stauber, the Minnesota Republican whose congressional district includes the mine site, blasted the decision as one he believed was based on politics, not science. "This administration has decided to leave American, blue-collar workers behind and bow to pressure from radicals who prefer to rely on foreign adversarial nations for these minerals," Stauber said.[41]

The saga presented a quandary for the United States. It had enough metals buried in its lands to build millions of its own electric vehicles. Going into 2022, the question centered around whether the country would tap these reserves.[42]

Even labor unions, a group that Biden supported strongly, tried to influence the White House. The administration's electrification goal "means good-paying union jobs for working people in responsible mining operations that will both supply battery minerals and protect the environment," said Tom Conway, head of the United Steelworkers, a union that represents some U.S. miners, including those who wanted to build the Twin Metals mine.[43]

Rom took a victory lap. "It is heartening to have an administration making decisions with integrity. Twin Metals' leases should never have been reinstated in the first place, and this announcement should stop the Twin Metals mine threat," she said.[44]

For Twin Metals and its parent, Antofagasta, the incongruity of Biden's approach to mining was too much. Two months after the project was killed, Julie Padilla, a Twin Metals executive, testified before a congressional panel that the United States was "no longer considered to have a stable regulatory climate."[45] It was a pointed statement, one clearly premeditated and carefully worded. The United States had long held itself out as a place where norms and rules and laws are followed. But Twin Metals and Antofagasta were saying that was a mirage, a farce, and a self-perception not grounded in fact. Regulatory decisions, the company was alleging, simply were made at the whim of whoever sat in the White House.

"The precedent set by these actions shows that a company can . . . spend a decade developing a project only to see it be arbitrarily canceled without any environmental review," Padilla tersely told the U.S. Senate's Committee on Energy and Natural Resources.[46] Padilla added that Twin Metals laid off a third of its workforce after losing the leases and halted "millions of dollars in local contractor work" after Biden's decision.[47] The statements echoed those of Padilla's boss, Antofagasta's chief executive,

Iván Arriagada, who earlier that week vowed to fight Biden's decision. He bluntly said he expected the mine to open by the end of the decade, even after Biden's actions and ignoring the fact that the project did not have the required permits.[48]

Ironically, Padilla gave her testimony to Congress the same day Biden invoked a Cold War–era defense law to boost U.S. mining, saying the country depended on "unreliable foreign sources" for the building blocks of green energy technologies.[49] "We need to end our long-term reliance on China and other countries for inputs that will power the future," Biden said. While funds could not be used to dig new mines, buy minerals for government stockpiles, or bypass regulatory or permitting standards, the decision would, the White House hoped, send a strong signal that Biden supported mining. Only he had just killed Twin Metals, fueling a round of head scratching throughout the mining industry.

⚡

ABOUT 250 MILES separates Minneapolis and St. Paul from Ely. Heading north on Interstate 35, from the Twin Cities to the boundary region with Canada, gives an approximate sense of the state's beauty, its history, its economy, and its future. Plastered on automobile license plates is the state's unofficial motto: "Land of 10,000 Lakes." And it's not hard to see why while driving north. The entire state is an outdoor enthusiast's dream: forests and ponds and lakes and rivers grow increasingly plentiful the farther north one drives.

The state's name itself is derived from the Dakota language, with *Mnisota* translating as "Clear Water."[50] For thousands of years before European settlers breached the area, the Indigenous inhabitants knew Mnisota to be a place where the water itself mattered and nurtured their communities.[51] In 1909, the United States and Canada, which was then a dominion of the United Kingdom, signed a treaty to oversee the flow of waters shared by the two countries. The International Boundary Water Treaty prohibited either nation from "any interference with or diversion from their natural channel of such waters."[52] Britain's King Edward VII gave his approval to the treaty the following year. While water was important to the region, so, too, were the minerals buried underneath the soil, a reality that the state began to realize as the nineteenth century gave way to the twentieth and taconite iron mines grew across Minnesota.

To get to the Iron Range, take Exit 237 off the interstate and jump onto State Route 33, heading north. Drive over the St. Louis River, the Great Lake's largest tributary, and keep heading north until you reach Eveleth, home to the U.S. Hockey Hall of Fame. Even if you don't stop to admire hockey's history, you won't miss the mines. Hulking, gargantuan open-pit taconite mines are easily visible from he highway. Dust permeates the air. I put my car's air filtration system on internal for the few minutes I was in the area.

Eveleth's economy relies on these mines, which are owned by U.S. Steel, Cliffs-Cleveland, and others. And they are extremely prone to the vagaries of the global mining market. These mines produce iron ore pellets, which are used to make steel. It's a different mining process than the one Twin Metals wants to use to extract copper, but nonetheless wildly disruptive. One does not linger in Eveleth longer than one must.

Just outside Ely sits the North American Bear Center, which holds educational seminars on the region's black bear population. Entering the town, it seems far more like a naturalist's playground than a place for miners to buy supplies after a long shift. Piragis Northwoods Company sells canoes, clothes, hats, and other sundries for exploring the woods and waters. Several other competing shops do the same. It's a town that seemingly long ago left behind its mining traditions and politely forgot that Miners Lake, the former quarry filled with rainwater, and Miners Drive sit just off its downtown.

It's on Miners Drive that Twin Metals built its two-story, LEED-certified headquarters with hues of copper adorning the outside and solar panels on the roof. The building lacks a sign indicating what it is. Visitors are asked to park their vehicles backward, in accord with mining industry safety standards. (Backing a vehicle up in an emergency is considered a safety hazard.) The air was muggy and the sky was clear when I visited the Twin Metals offices in 2022. I had spent the night prior in Ely in a lodge that caters to canoe enthusiasts and campers.

The building's lobby was festooned with posters filled with information on copper's history, going back to the ancient Egyptians. A stack of bumper stickers sat near an unstaffed receptionist's desk: "We Support Twin Metals." A mural facing the entrance was an artist's interpretation of the underground metal deposit that the company hoped to mine, with different shades of color evoking different types of rock. A blackish hue delineated a layer of impermeable rock known as gabbro, which Twin Metals hopes to drill through to get to the copper, which is its own color and sits below the black. Under the copper was a grayish layer of granite. Each stratum is clearly marked out, as if the mural were designed by Twin Metals itself to showcase how each layer is separate and distinct. The reality, though, is more complex.

Nicole Hoffman was hunched over boxes of wax-lined cardboard filled with cylindrical cores of rock in a large industrial garage toward the back of the building. She grabbed a mister and soaked one of the pieces of rock resting between us. Parts glistened in the glow of the garage's fluorescent lights.

"That's the sulfide mineral right there that contains the copper and nickel," she explained to me.[53]

"That's pretty good?" I asked.

"Oh ya!" she said cheerily. Hoffman stood about five feet eight and had dirty-blond hair tied back. A Minnesota native, she had moved to Ely in 2012 and never left. She, her two-year-old son, and her husband lived nearby, with an abandoned iron ore mine pit about 100 feet deep in their backyard. It seemed very on brand for a person who has devoted her life to geology. Hoffman took me around the Twin Metals garage and showed me rock sample after rock sample, and explained why she supported the mine, beyond her paycheck.

Eons ago, the Midcontinent Rift was formed when what is now the North American continent nearly ripped apart. Had that happened, North America would have split into two continents, similar to South

America and Africa. But instead, the continent came back together and lava from deep within the Earth's center erupted upward and mixed with other rock, leaving behind a matrix of copper, nickel, and other minerals highly prized by the auto industry in an area of modern-day northwest Minnesota known as the Duluth Complex.

The copper and nickel that Twin Metals hoped to mine is partially underneath the nearby Birch Lake. Twin Metals aimed to drill a diagonal shaft that would intersect with the copper and nickel deposit at a depth of more than 400 feet, far below the water table and any aquifers. Hoffman repeated the company line, which has been said multiple times, that the metal can be extracted safely. I asked Hoffman what she thinks about the charge from environmentalists that Twin Metals, and its Chilean owner, Antofagasta, cares little about Minnesota's land and water.

"It's not true," she rejoined. "Antofagasta depends on us to tell them what's important here and what's not."

Hoffman's colleague Kevin Boerst soon joined us. Wearing a Hawaiian shirt and a thin beard, he looked more like a character from the television show *Stranger Things* than he did a geologist working for a multibillion-dollar corporation. Yet he had been doing that for more than fifteen years, working alongside Hoffman and others to drill hole after hole into the Minnesota earth and further study the copper and nickel deposit by extracting more than 1.8 million feet of core samples that are logged and stacked for future study. When he joined, there were only 7 holes in the ground. By the time I visited in 2022, there were more than 496 holes, the result of his and Hoffman's painstaking work.

"We are studying areas of weakness that'll be good to know when we mine," Hoffman told me. I asked to see some of that digging in person, so Hoffman's boss, Dean DeBeltz, volunteered to take me later that day. DeBeltz, an Ely native, had worked in mining for most of his career. His father was a miner. His grandfather worked with the grandfather of Amy Klobuchar, Minnesota's senior U.S. senator. On weekends, he fished for walleye in the Boundary Waters. During the time we spent together in his truck, DeBeltz stressed over and over his belief that the mine can be developed safely. It was an almost palpable feeling that seemed to ooze out of him.

"If we can't prove that this mine can be developed safely, then we shouldn't build it," he told me. "Regulators should follow the science."[54] It's that last line that made me chuckle, as it clearly had been cribbed from talking points that had grown common during the coronavirus pandemic. DeBeltz wore a polo shirt with a Twin Metals logo and light khaki pants. As we left the Twin Metals offices, he and a colleague handed me a Twin Metals coffee mug that was emblazoned with a logo from when the company had celebrated its ten-year anniversary . . . in 2020. And yet no copper or nickel had been mined by 2024. And unlike other controversial U.S. mining projects, Twin Metals had yet to actually start the permitting process because it was still battling over whether it could access the land holding the metals. DeBeltz drove a Ford pickup powered by gasoline, and as we drove to see where Hoffman had set up shop that afternoon, we crossed a small bridge near Ely and turned right down a dirt road to meet Hoffman, who had erected a tent from the back of her pickup truck about 1,300 feet from the main road.

Hoffman and Boerst guided a device known as an acoustic televiewer (ATV) down a predrilled hole to scan the deposit and collect more data. It was the middle of black fly season and I kept swatting gnats from my face; I could only imagine how Hoffman—who was pregnant at the time—felt, but she didn't let on to any discomfort. Slowly, she guided the ATV down the hole at a rate of 97 feet per minute; the hole was 2,500 feet deep. After she was done, each hole would be cemented over, in accordance with state law.

I asked DeBeltz what facilities would be around us if the mine were approved. A few ventilation shafts, he told me, and a 120-acre concentrator plant to treat the copper that came out of the ground. Light pierced through the birch trees and birds chirped in the distance. "And that'd be it," he said, as if to underscore his belief that a 120-acre concentrator plant wouldn't be too much for this wooded area.

DeBeltz recommended I read Jim Bowyer's *The Irresponsible Pursuit of Paradise,* which chronicled how wealthy nations "smugly enjoy high levels of consumption with minimal exposure to the environmental impacts of that consumption" by asking poorer nations to mine copper and other minerals in their own backyards.[55] The book's thesis has practically become a rallying cry for many companies in the United States trying to open new mines. Using the playbook of the social justice movement, and drawing heavily from environmentalists' talking points, they ask a question that seems logical on the surface: Why should the United States rely on other countries to procure the building blocks of carbon-reducing technologies?

On the drive back to Ely, DeBeltz pulled into the South Kawishiwi River Campground, a federal campground along the banks of the river, which flows south into Birch Lake. He got out and looked around, admiring the views. He told me about the times he camped there as a child and how he wanted future generations to enjoy it, too. The Twin Metals mine would be right below us, which didn't seem to faze him at all. "You'll still be able to swim here, camp here, fish here, when this mine opens," DeBeltz told me as the wind tousled his hair. "Why wouldn't you want that?"[56]

Rom herself had taken me to this same spot the day before during our tour of the area. We used the campground's dock to board a pontoon boat and peruse the lake before boating to a nearby outdoors school that was helping rehabilitate veterans with post-traumatic stress disorder. The water was like glass, smooth and brilliantly reflecting the sun. "Isn't this just glorious?" Rom asked me as she basked in the summer rays. "I hope this place never changes."

⚡

AS MY TIME in Ely ended, I drove to the Stony Ridge Cafe, which sits on the edge of Shagawa Lake and serves more than fifty different types of hamburgers. (I had the Norseman burger, which features "a mango habanero glaze, triple smoked bacon, pineapple rings, and Muenster cheese.") A mother duck and her hatchlings paddled near the shore; the lake's waters were dusted with poplar tree cotton. Other birds swam through the waters around small powerboats, docked and waiting. I filmed them with my phone, intending to share them on social media later. (I forgot.) But to get a better shot as the ducks swam away, I walked out onto the dock and breathed in the lake around me.

Somewhere, deep beneath me, sat enough copper, cobalt, and nickel to build thousands of electric vehicles, lawn mowers, leaf blowers, wind turbines, solar panels, and other gadgets and gizmos of the green energy revolution that so many said were so crucial for the planet's survival. And I wondered if the metals under my feet would be or could be taken out safely so future generations of birds could take their broods across this lake. Two elderly men walked nearby with tackle boxes in hand and life jackets tied around their torsos. They jumped into a small aluminum boat with an outboard motor and, after it whirled to life, putted off into the center of the lake. Hoping, no doubt, for a good catch.

CHAPTER SIX

A Single Point of Failure

THE GLASS-AND-BRICK TEN-STORY BUILDING AT 824 NORTH Market Street in downtown Wilmington, Delaware, has, at various times, hosted a pharmacy, a sandwich shop, a bank, a cell phone company, and other retail and professional businesses.[1] The United States Bankruptcy Court, though, is the 1982-era building's largest and most well-known tenant. Strewn throughout multiple floors are courtrooms where companies come to file for Chapter 11 bankruptcy protection, usually when their debts engulf their assets to such a degree that they can no longer stay open. The point of a bankruptcy filing is to give debtors a fresh start, if possible, while at the same time making creditors whole, if possible. Assets might have to be sold to settle some of those debts, which in some industrial bankruptcies can include a liability to care for a site littered with toxins or poisons. This, of course, takes a deft approach. To be able to wade through arcane contracts, weigh competing claims, and consider complexities such as environmental remediation and local economic development requires a particular legal skill.

This court in Delaware thrives off those complexities. Its judges, clerks, attorneys' bar, and myriad other legal professionals handle many of the nation's bankruptcies because the state and its tax regime is a favored destination for incorporation, an engine that helps power the state capital's economy.[2] And 824 North Market Street's Courtroom Number 6 is where a company known as Molycorp found itself sitting before the Honorable Christopher S. Sontchi, a U.S. Bankruptcy Judge, at 2 p.m. on June 23, 2017.[3]

With roots that traced back to the years just after the First World War and a list of past owners that includes the oil giant Chevron, Molycorp had grown to be one of the world's largest miners and processors of rare earths. Broadly, rare earths are a group of seventeen metals found on the Periodic Table of Elements that are expensive, difficult, and environmentally dangerous to produce: lanthanum, cerium, praseodymium, neodymium, promethium, samarium, europium, gadolinium, terbium, dysprosium, holmium, erbium, thulium, ytterbium, lutetium, scandium, and yttrium. There are no known substitutes.

They are used in every single part of the economy and in a wide range of consumer electronics, typically in small amounts. The pepper added to the steak, if you will. They are used in televisions and other electronics, as well as ceramics, glass, the atomic energy industry, and gasoline refining. In the 1960s, U.S. military scientists invented a type of magnet made with rare earths that was far smaller and lighter than its iron-based peers, opening a new wave of possibilities for lighter, cheaper electronics.[4] Electric vehicles, computers, and computer displays, among many other tech gadgets, require rare earths magnets to function. Each wind turbine uses at least two tonnes of magnets built with rare earths.[5] The modern military uses them in laser-guided missiles, night-vision goggles, X-ray technologies, and other pieces of weaponry.[6] The Lockheed Martin–produced F-35 fighter jet, for example, contains 417 kilograms of rare earths, all of which are sourced from China.[7] Apple uses Chinese rare earths for its iPhone's haptic engine, which makes the phone vibrate. General Dynamics Corp. uses rare earths to build the Virginia-class submarine. And while their name implies they are found in very few places in the world, that is a misnomer, for the metals themselves are not particularly rare across the planet. (Cerium, for example, is as abundant as copper in the Earth's crust.[8]) What is rare is to find them in large quantities.

In the mid-twentieth century, several of these seventeen types of rare earths were found in large quantities in what has become the Mountain Pass mine, located 76 miles south of Las Vegas just over the California border. There, Molycorp built an engine of American economic might, helping to supply the U.S. military, the country's nuclear power industry, and its nascent consumer electronics manufacturers, one of which found in 1964 that europium could be used to brighten the color red in phosphor for cathode ray tubes in televisions.[9] By the 1980s, Molycorp's Mountain Pass mine supplied 70 percent of the world's rare earths.[10] Much of this research and progress was due to the collaboration between U.S. government scientists and industry, a collaboration that was allowed to wane late in the 1980s and into the 1990s. China had slowly over the second half of the twentieth century begun developing its own rare earths industry and encouraging its manufacturers (and international companies that moved there) to use Chinese-derived rare earths. For Beijing, rare earths were increasingly seen as a powerful economic weapon.

And it was the use of that economic weapon that forced Molycorp to that Delaware courtroom in the summer of 2017, where a consortium of Chinese-backed investors lay waiting.

⚡

MODERN DEMAND FOR rare earths was sparked by, of all things, lamp manufacturers.[11]

In the 1880s, the Austrian chemist Carl Auer von Welsbach discovered that by mixing thorium and certain types of rare earths, one could make filaments for gas-powered lamps. He further refined the process and created flints known as "misch metal" used in cigarette lighters.[12] The process was mimicked by an American company known as Lindsay Light, which began to source rare earths from monazite deposits in India after the First World War interrupted imports from Germany. The lamps were wildly popular in the era before light bulbs.[13] (And fluorescent light bulbs themselves are made using rare earths.)

Rare earths were first identified near Ytterby, Sweden, in 1788 when odd black rocks were extracted from a mine. They were called "rare" as they had not been previously discovered and "earths" as that was the geological term at the time for rocks that would dissolve in acid.[14] (In 2023, a Swedish mining company said it had found a rare earths reserve of roughly 1 million tonnes, a godsend for a continent that had stopped producing the metals.[15])

Rare earths then as now are most commonly derived from the minerals monazite and bastnaesite. Monazite is typically found in India, Madagascar, the U.S. Southeast, and Australia. Unfortunately, though, it's commonly also found with thorium, which is radioactive and thus harder and more expensive to process. The United States and China have the largest bastnaesite reserves. And those reserves usually have only small levels of radiation.

Especially after the rise of electricity, new uses for rare earths were popping up. They could be used in electrodes to help brighten searchlights and movie projectors, which gobbled up roughly half the global supply by 1941.[16] They could also be used in glass polishing. During the Second World War, thorium's value came to the fore during the race to build an atomic bomb. The world's new technologies and weapons were increasingly needing rare earths, something that was obvious to the United States, which was sourcing nearly all its rare earths—including the thorium used to build the first atomic bomb—from India.[17]

"In view of the difficulties in obtaining imported monazite, the consumers are making every effort to locate domestic deposits of commercial size," according to a 1946 report from the U.S. government.[18] This was also obvious to the newly formed Indian government, which by the end of the war was the dominant supplier of the strategic minerals to the United States and much of the world, originally sourcing them from black sand beach deposits on its southwest coast in what today is the state of Kerala. New Delhi aimed to take stock of its national resources by imposing a block on exports of monazite sands in 1946.[19] Much like China did during the late twentieth century, India also wanted to boost its own domestic manufacturing by keeping the minerals local and using them to make myriad products.

India also sought to build out its own rare earths processing industry and use its thorium to develop its own nuclear industry. (India would debut its first nuclear-powered reactor in 1956.[20]) Unfortunately for the new government, though, a food shortage in the years after the Second World War was facing the country's 340 million people, forcing an urgent need for wheat. President Harry Truman sensed a diplomatic opening[21] with the new country and sought to ship 1.8 million tonnes of grain to India as part of a humanitarian package. Some in Congress and American industry tried to tie the wheat to a relaxation of India's rare earths export ban. By 1951, Congress approved lending India $190 million to buy American-grown wheat.[22] India had held firm and did not link relaxing the embargo to the loan.[23]

Rather than learn from the experience and be on the lookout for future instances where another country—ally or foe—could exert economic influence over the United States, Washington seemed not to make the obvious connection that if its economy needed a strategic material, it should produce more of its own. It was a lesson it should have learned from the Indian rare earths saga and during the Arab Oil Embargo of the 1970s.

⚡

THE BOMBS THAT the United States exploded over Nagasaki and Hiroshima not only effectively put an end to the Second World War, they sparked an intense drive by prospectors across the world—and especially the United States—for uranium, the radioactive metal that is key to the fission process. The U.S. Atomic Energy Commission was desperate for uranium in order to counter a perceived nuclear threat from the Soviet Union, so the agency was offering lucrative terms—$10,000 in some cases[24]—for discovery of a fresh supply.[25] (That's $125,701 in 2023 dollars.) And that is what drew Herbert S. Woodward to a tiny schoolhouse in Goodsprings, Nevada, in late March 1949.[26] The Nevada Department of Education had paid an engineer by the name of Marty Hess to give a speech on the prevalence of uranium in the area, south of Las Vegas near the California border. Hess mentioned offhand that uranium can also be found commingled with cobalt, the bluish metal that had long been known in small deposits across the area. Woodward, an engineer by training, assumed that the arid lands around him had to contain some uranium.[27]

He had a problem. The easiest way to find uranium was with a Geiger counter, a device used to detect radiation and known for its staccato noise bursts. It was also expensive, and he and his schoolteacher wife,

Alice, could not afford one.[28] So Woodward struck up a partnership with P. A. "Pop" Simon, who owned a nearby motel and car service station. Simon would pay for the Geiger counter and Woodward would bring the engineering know-how to the venture.[29] From the outset, Woodward was eager, perhaps too eager. The group would scour the waste pits from old mines in the area trying to find radioactivity. They hadn't, and he nearly gave up after only two weeks. Woodward vented his frustrations to another prospector in the area, Fred B. Piehl.

Piehl suggested the group test rock samples from the area around Nevada's Sulphide Queen mine. Woodward's group, which then added several other prospectors, raced to the site and there the Geiger counter reacted loudly to the deposit. Piehl had already staked much of the land years before when he was searching for lead and gold, so Woodward expanded his search about a mile northwest of the Sulphide Queen deposit with the Geiger counter in tow. And then on April 2, 1949—Woodward's birthday—the group found what would later be described in the cold syntax of geology as "intense radioactivity along the outcrop of a vein."[30]

In a shallow pit located on the eastern edge of the Mojave Desert, a tan-colored mineral stuck out to Woodward and his team. But they didn't recognize it, so after they staked their claim (something they did for free, thanks to U.S. mining laws dating back to 1872), they sent samples to the nearby office of the U.S. Bureau of Mines, where a spectroscopic test—which tests for chemical composition of a substance—showed that the mineral was bastnaesite and that it held large concentrations of rare earths as well as fluorine. Woodward had not found uranium at all, but rather a tremendous deposit of a mineral for which there was not widespread use—yet. The reason that the Geiger counter had high readings was in part due to the thorium commingled with the other rare earths in the deposit.[31] A month later, the U.S. Geological Survey got wind of the discovery and asked to see the rock samples. Woodward and his team hosted the USGS later that summer, and in the fall the federal and California state scientists mapped the geology of the forty-acre area. On November 18, 1949, less than a week before the U.S. Thanksgiving holiday, the U.S. Department of the Interior announced Woodward's discovery, labeling it the Birthday Claim. It was the world's largest reserve of rare earths that had yet been found.[32]

The Birthday Claim sparked a rush of other prospectors to the area, who soon staked claims of their own. Most of the rare earths appeared to be near the surface, which meant that any mining company would not need to dig deep to extract them, thus saving money. That was very good news for the Molybdenum Corporation of America, which had been searching for fresh supplies of rare earths. The company, known as Molycorp, had started by mining molybdenum, a silvery metal used in fertilizer and in metal alloys, from Questa, New Mexico, in 1919. The discovery of what appeared to be an enormous supply of rare earths located conveniently between Las Vegas and Los Angeles was too much for the company's president, Marx Hirsch, to pass up.[33] Hirsch had hoped that a strong rare earths deposit would help his company develop newer uses for the metals, including adding small amounts of it to steel as a hardening agent.[34] A trade magazine described the region around Mountain Pass, optimistically, as one with a "pleasant climate, desert air and sunshine, just off a main highway, near a nice motel and restaurant, a mill virtually ready to go, a high-grade, unique ore deposit without overburden, and the pleasure spots of Las Vegas, Nev., just over the hill."[35] By 1951, Molycorp had bought the rights to the Birthday Claim and by 1952 had begun digging at Mountain Pass. The company estimated it had bought more than 3 billion pounds of rare earths.[36] Few expected competition. The same trade magazine that in 1952 had boasted of the "pleasant climate" near Mountain Pass only anticipated potential competition from mines in that region of the United States, not China. "Unless the thousands of prospectors and would-be prospectors who are now carrying gamma-ray detectors to all kinds of places discover enough rare earths to make the mass market severely competitive, it seems clear that Molycorp can look forward to both a profitable and interesting future."[37] And for a time, it did.

Much of Molycorp's growth was due to the company's symbiotic relationship with the Ames Laboratory, which was formed in 1947 at what is now known as Iowa State University. The lab grew out of research from scientists involved in the Second World War's Manhattan Project and it focused on ways to better separate and process rare earths from one another, sharing much of this research with private industry.[38] Unlike the process to extract gold from rock, though, rare earths are expensive and laborious to produce.

Gold production typically involves mining ore and then putting that ore on a giant pad where an acid solution is applied. The gold leaches from the ore and is collected at the bottom of the pad and, after a few other processing steps, turned into an ingot.

Rare earths require a few more steps. At Mountain Pass, after mining, bastnaesite ore is crushed down to the size of small pebbles, then further crushed into a silt-like powder. That powder is mixed with hydrochloric acid and other chemicals and then placed in a liquid solution to initiate a process known as flotation to remove other minerals that might be in the rock. (At Mountain Pass, roughly 8 to 10 percent of the rock contains rare earths.) The bastnaesite floats to the top of the tank with the liquid solution in the form of a bubbly froth, which is then scraped off the surface and then further refined.[39] Each of the seventeen rare earths has its own process, and they typically must be extracted in a precise order. Getting neodymium, for instance, requires separating out cerium first. After all this, rare earths oxides are produced in the form of a powder that needs even more processing to be turned into rare earths metals that can be used to make magnets, alloys, and other materials. In all, it takes ten days from mining to the production of rare earths, a time-consuming and costly process.[40]

Much of this process was perfected in part with the help of U.S. government scientists at the Ames lab in Iowa, which by the mid-1960s was known as the "birthplace of the modern rare earths industry,"[41] conducting research into lasers, magnets, and other emerging technologies. It was a technological prowess that Molycorp used to its advantage, fueling growth of not only its own business but also American industry. Molycorp expanded its production of rare earths in the 1960s, especially europium for the growing television market. It also bought several smaller rivals. Using new technological developments, Molycorp kept adding different rare earths to its product slate, a development that showed its increasing comfort with the complex and onerous rare earths production process.[42]

In 1960, the United States consumed 1,600 tonnes of the specialized metals, a number that had jumped to 20,900 tonnes by 1980.[43] And the research that Ames produced prodded other breakthroughs as well. Air Force scientists in 1965 invented the samarium-cobalt permanent magnet, which was able to be made stronger and smaller than iron-based magnets, key for aircraft design. Cobalt at the time was difficult to obtain due to conflict in the country then known as Zaire, fueling even more research into rare earths magnets. In 1983, General Motors and Japan's Sumitomo Special Metals each announced the invention of neodymium-iron-boron magnets, a monumental breakthrough just as the personal computing age was dawning.[44] All this growth did not go unnoticed by Wall Street or by China. In 1977, the Union Oil Company of California, known as Unocal, bought Molycorp for $240 million ($1.25 billion in 2023 dollars) and said it would operate the company as a stand-alone entity.

⚡

IN 1951, THE same year that Molycorp bought the Birthday Claim just outside Las Vegas, New York's Columbia University awarded a Ph.D. in chemistry to Xu Guangxian, which he earned after an M.S. from Washington University in St. Louis in 1949. The U.S. Congress was on the verge of passing a law that would prevent Chinese students who had studied in the United States from returning to newly Communist China,[45] so Xu and his wife, the chemist Gao Xiaoxia, left New York for Beijing, where Xu was hired at Peking University.[46] After the couple was imprisoned for six years during the Cultural Revolution, Xu was freed and sent to study rare earths, where he dove into research specifically linked to praseodymium and rubidium. Eventually, Xu's findings would help China bolster the processing and separation of its rare earths deposits, which by the mid-1970s were found to be among the world's largest.[47]

Methodically, China began to grow its rare earths industry. In 1985, the China Rare Earth Information Center was established to essentially mimic U.S. rare earths research at the Ames lab in Iowa. The country's rare earths production epicenter was in Inner Mongolia's Bayan Obo, where a large iron ore mine was discovered to also contain large bastnaesite reserves. Thus, China could produce iron ore for steel at the same time it produced rare earths, a huge cost savings that gave the country a strategic advantage. The country's rare earths production jumped 40 percent each year from 1978 to 1989.[48] U.S., Canadian, and Japanese companies also began to partner with Chinese peers, bringing their rare earths technologies to mainland China and helping to boost that country's nascent rare earths sector.[49]

Mountain Pass was still a top global rare earths producer, with minerals that were used by U.S. soldiers in the first Gulf War. But the Pentagon's growing technological prowess thanks to rare earths caught Beijing off guard, encouraging China to double down on rare earths research.[50] Chinese leader Deng Xiaoping made the prescient observation in the 1980s, "The Middle East has oil. China has rare earths,"[51] and encouraged his country to further exploit this economic advantage.[52] In 1999, his successor, Jiang Zemin, advised his country to "Improve the development and application of rare earths and change the resource advantage into economic superiority."[53]

Just as Chinese scientists boosted their rare earths research, American universities began to focus less on them, in part to study biofuels and other renewable energy technologies. The transition started slowly, with the U.S. government pulling funding in the late 1960s for a key rare earths trade publication.[54] While private industry stepped in to fund it, the publication was dead by 2002.[55] By the 1990s, Ames academics had stopped teaching a popular rare earths class to Iowa students.[56] The U.S. Bureau of Mines, which oversaw industry-related research and safety standards, closed in 1996 as part of a round of budget cuts.[57] Mark Smith, Molycorp's chief executive officer, complained to Congress in March 2010 that his company's seventeen scientists were competing with China's six thousand rare earths–focused scientists. At the time, Molycorp was not mining its Mountain Pass facility, given the weak market.[58] "I can't find any students from any university in the United States that have any rare earths experience," he told the U.S. House of Representatives' Committee on Science and Technology.[59] At that same hearing, Karl Gschneidner, an Ames professor who was widely considered one of the most preeminent U.S. rare earths scholars, warned of an "intellectual vacuum" caused by his peers retiring, dying, or simply moving on to study other areas.[60] That same year, the U.S. government's National Defense Stockpile had sold off its rare earths; the minerals themselves had never been declared as strategic for the government's purposes.[61]

China's labor, environmental, and safety standards were below those of the United States, giving the country a distinct price advantage. Near Bayan Obo, a tailings waste pond more than 5 miles wide held the gooey, dangerous detritus of the country's rare earths production.[62] A study published in 2014 found abnormally high levels of fluoride in the region around the mine, especially in dust particles.[63] A BBC reporter who visited the site in 2015 bluntly described the scene: "Hidden in an unknown corner of Inner Mongolia is a toxic, nightmarish lake created by the world's thirst for smartphones, consumer gadgets, and green tech."[64] By 2010, more than 9.1 million tonnes of mostly untreated wastewater were dumped in the region around Bayan Obo each year. Locals avoid eating fish sourced from the nearby Yellow River, one of the country's main waterways.[65]

Outside Bayan Obo, a network of illegal rare earths mines sprung up around China, often by exploiting nearby residents to work at the facilities and sell the metals on the black market.[66]

In the United States, the creation of the U.S. Environmental Protection Agency in 1970 intensified regulatory pressure on the U.S. rare earths industry. The extensive and sloppy waste ponds that China had built near Bayan Obo were certainly not allowed near Mountain Pass, and the California mine's owners found themselves running up against environmental regulations and, at least one way, consciously violating them. In 1980, Molycorp built a 14-mile pipeline from its mine site to the nearby Ivanpah Lake, a dry lake bed that straddles Interstate 15 on its way to Las Vegas. While the company's wastewater disposal permit allowed saltwater to be sent through that pipeline to Ivanpah evaporation ponds, for the next sixteen years Molycorp sent wastewater it knew was infused with radioactive particles and heavy metals from the rare earths production process onto the lake bed.[67] Between 1984 and 1993, forty spills totaling 727,000 gallons were caused by Molycorp's Mountain Pass facility.[68] California state officials fined the company $100,000 in 1994 for improper waste management.[69] Officials had thought the spillage was only saltwater, since that was all the company was allowed to dispose of and thus they asked only for sporadic tests. Efforts to clean the pipe in the summer of 1996 caused even more ruptures and officials discovered eleven more pipeline ruptures that had leaked 380,000 gallons of radioactive water into the Mojave Desert, some of it in parts of the desert that were home to rare tortoises.[70] Molycorp dragged its feet for more than a year while the radioactive wastewater lay on the Ivanpah lake bed due in part to back-and-forth squabbling with regulators. By July 1997, cleanup crews using hand tools had packed 1,840 steel drums of waste, more than half of which was radioactive, and sent it off to a landfill.[71] The mine was temporarily shut down in 1998 and Molycorp was ordered to pay a $410,000 fine.[72] Since 1984, nearly a million gallons of radioactive wastewater had leaked from the pipeline, imposing a stain on the company's efforts to anchor the U.S. rare earths industry.[73]

Back in the late 1990s, the Center for Biological Diversity—the same group that would in the twenty-first century fight ioneer's planned Nevada lithium mine—had rung the alarm about Molycorp's use of that pipeline. But after the company promised to close the line and take other steps for remediation, the environmental group was placated. Rare earths mining was dirty, but at least its products were used in green energy devices, a spokesman for the group reasoned.[74]

Amid the mounting regulatory pressure, Molycorp announced an ambitious plan in the spring of 1999 to slash the amount of water it used by 62 percent and the amount of wastewater it generated by 50 percent, part of what it saw as its thirty-year plan. The company also promised to stop transporting waste through pipelines and clean the water on-site, an ambitious target.[75] Broader market forces intervened, spurred by intense Chinese pricing pressure. The site closed in 2002, its equipment left to rust in the warm California sun.[76]

⚡

GENERAL MOTORS MADE a surprise announcement in early December 2021: It would buy rare earths magnets for its future electric vehicles from two U.S.-based manufacturing facilities.[77] It was an unexpected yet ambitious goal for the automaker, which had publicly aspired earlier that year to sell only emissions-free light-duty vehicles by 2035, in line with goals President Biden had set for the federal government's own vehicle fleet.[78]

The surprise was twofold. First, there were no U.S.-based manufacturing facilities to supply the automaker with the neodymium-iron-boron (NdFeB) magnets used to turn power from an electric vehicle's battery into motion, effectively serving as a de facto motor. And second, the reason there was no such facility in the United States was because of General Motors itself. In an ironic twist, GM once was a global leader in the rare earths magnet industry through its Magnequench division. But in 1995, GM agreed to sell the division and its patents to a consortium that included two Chinese partners, including one led by the son-in-law of the former Chinese leader Deng Xiaoping.

The Magnequench deal helped GM sell more cars in China but also gave China access to the rare earths magnet technology that had first been developed in the United States, another example of Chinese manufacturers eager to grow in a sector increasingly seen as an afterthought by American industry. The Committee on Foreign Investment in the United States, the regulatory body tasked with policing such deals, approved the buyout with the stipulation that Magnequench keep its Indiana magnet facility open for several years. When that window expired, the Indiana plant closed, and magnet production was moved to mainland China.[79]

"The United States now has no domestic supplier of rare earth metals, which are essential for precision-guided munitions. I would say that is a clear national security concern," James Inhofe, a Republican senator from Oklahoma, bemoaned in 2005.[80]

When GM sold the Magnequench division, it had little idea that its products would be so crucial to its survival less than thirty years later. Indeed, rare earths magnets primarily were used by GM at the time in the motors that move car seats up and back. While the U.S. military used rare earths magnets in multiple pieces of weaponry, including missile-tracking systems, the Pentagon said in 2008 it was "not aware of any foreign vulnerabilities within its supply chains."[81]

GM's December 2021 deal sought to undo that step by reviving a U.S. rare earths industry, even though GM no longer controlled any of the magnet patents. "The more we can recover natural resources for batteries and EVs from North America, process them here and manufacture them . . . the more value we can create," said Shilpan Amin, then GM's vice president of global purchasing and supply chain. "Our strategy is to control our own destiny."[82]

GM's plans to, as Amin called it, control its "own destiny" were certainly ironic given the company's Magnequench sale in the 1980s. The new plans linked back to California's Mountain Pass and, indirectly, China itself.

⚡

FROM 2005 TO 2009, with America's rare earths industry essentially mothballed as Mountain Pass lay dormant, China further restricted rare earths exports to encourage non-Chinese companies to buy Chinese products that contained Chinese rare earths.[83] Unocal, which owned Mountain Pass, was bought by Chevron in 2005 for $18 billion, besting an offer from Chinese state-owned oil company CNOOC.[84] Mining was not Chevron's focus, and by 2008 the oil giant agreed to sell Mountain Pass for $80 million to a consortium that included banking giant Goldman Sachs.[85] In July 2010, that consortium—which had also taken the Molycorp name—raised $394 million in a public stock offering, with executives presenting the company as the main bulwark against China's growing rare earths power.[86] The money, the new company said, would help it reopen the mine and improve its environmental safeguards.[87]

Meanwhile, Australia's Lynas had been mining rare earths from a deposit in Western Australia known as Mount Weld, and in 2010 agreed to sell much of its supply to Japan, locking out other nations.[88] Lynas aimed to do what Molycorp did as well by using China as a foil. "We are truly independent from China," said Amanda Lacaze, who helped revive the company when she became CEO in 2014. "We aim to remain a leader in the rare earths market. There will be significant growth outside China so long as customers are confident in supply."[89]

Molycorp got an unexpected boost from China in September 2010, when the country cut off Japan's access to its rare earths temporarily.[90] Global prices for rare earths spiked. The new Molycorp was ebullient; China's move had caused a global scramble for the weapons-grade minerals, and Molycorp executives intended to capitalize. Its shares more than doubled in the six months after its IPO.[91] "In my almost 25 years in this business I have never seen the number of opportunities that are available like they are today," Mark Smith, Molycorp's then chief executive, told Reuters in December 2010.[92] Rare earths prices had skyrocketed three months prior after China halted exports of the strategic minerals to Japan following a diplomatic spat, a situation that the Pentagon had long feared could be visited upon the United States. The fear was even bleeding into popular culture. The 2012 release of the video game *Call of Duty: Black Ops II* explored a scenario where China's global rare earths monopoly sparks a war on the African continent.[93]

Amid the surge in prices, Japan's Sumitomo had invested $130 million in Molycorp, and Hitachi Metals formed a joint venture with the company to ensure a steady supply of rare earths.[94] Molycorp had launched a $1.55 billion expansion project not long after going public that it labeled Project Phoenix, hoping it would be able to make rare earths safer and cheaper than the site's previous owners.[95] By 2012, the company aimed to be producing 20 percent of the world's rare earths needs.[96] The new Molycorp also paid $1.31 billion in March 2012 for a Canadian rare earths processor known as Neo Material Technologies Inc.[97] It was all part of Smith's vision for the new Molycorp to have a "mine to magnets" strategy and to regain ground ceded to China.

"Every supply and demand fundamental I look at says this is sustainable," Smith boasted.[98] Yet despite the massive spending and high hopes, the new equipment fizzled largely because Molycorp's board of directors pushed workers to move too fast without properly testing it.[99] Molycorp knew it had a great mine with Mountain Pass, but Project Phoenix never reached its production targets.[100] China boosted exports in 2012, sending global prices tanking.[101] Smith, the CEO, left the company in December 2012 after the U.S. Securities and Exchange Commission said it was investigating "the accuracy of the company's public disclosures."[102] Also in 2012, the U.S. Environmental Protection Agency made an unannounced inspection of Molycorp's Mountain Pass facility and found lead and iron had leaked into stormwater at the site. The worry had been that the water could leak out and contaminate the neighboring land. The company was fined $27,300.[103]

Molycorp lost $197.2 million in 2013. By 2014, it christened some of the new equipment and expected to be cash flow positive by the end of 2015.[104] It would never reach that target. China's reversal of its decision blocking rare earths exports flooded the global market, causing a price crash that tore into Molycorp's balance sheet. In June 2015, nearly two years to the day before it appeared in Judge Sontchi's Delaware courtroom, the company filed for Chapter 11 bankruptcy protection, saying that while its assets exceeded $2.49 billion, it owed $1.79 billion to more than a thousand creditors, including owing Wells Fargo nearly $750 million.[105] Thus started a twenty-four-month process to find out if the company—with assets all over the world, including the only American rare earths mine—would be sold off in parts.

⚡

THE FIRST SHOE to drop came in August 2016, when part of Molycorp emerged from bankruptcy protection and branded itself as Neo Performance Materials, the name of the same company that Molycorp had bought in 2012. This new Neo would also be led by the same people who had sold the old Neo to Molycorp and, for the most part, contain nearly all the assets of the old Neo, an ironic twist that further helped enrich Neo's management.[106] That deal, though, did not include the Mountain Pass mine in California, which was seemingly anathema to many creditors and potential buyers, one of which called the mine the "anchor" that had dragged the entire company into bankruptcy.[107] Molycorp wanted to sell off the mine's assets to the highest bidder to pay off its debts. Sontchi, the Delaware judge, said the fate of the Mountain Pass mining site was "fluid."[108]

JHL Capital Group, a Chicago hedge fund and one of Molycorp's bondholders, had agreed with other bondholders to pay $1 million for the mineral rights at the Mountain Pass site, though not the site itself. JHL representatives also told the court in March 2016 that they were considering making a bid for the entire complex with an unnamed foreign entity.[109] Despite the site's strategic significance, no one initially came forward in bankruptcy court to buy it, a situation that the bankruptcy trustee increasingly was anxious about.[110] After months of behind-the-scenes negotiations, the court decided in February 2017 to hold an auction for Mountain Pass.[111]

An investment firm with ties to Vladimir Iorich, a Russian-born billionaire who had become a German citizen, floated an offer of $40 million.[112] Iorich's proposed buyout immediately drew U.S. national security concerns; the Committee on Foreign Investment in the United States (CFIUS) was widely expected to scrutinize that bid or any other. Later that spring, Iorich withdrew his offer without much explanation.[113]

In stepped Tom Clarke, an entrepreneur and environmentalist who had made a fortune operating nursing homes in Virginia. He also had been buying old coal mines across the country and cleaning them up, experience he thought could help at Mountain Pass. Working with Paul Harner, the bankruptcy trustee, Clarke agreed to become what's known as a "stalking horse," whereby he'd bid first to set the floor for the auction. Clarke offered $1.2 million and said he would assume up to $100 million worth of environmental liabilities at the site, drawing from his coal experience. But then, as the proceedings wore on and Clarke seemed to be close to nabbing control of Mountain Pass, a company known as MP Mine Operations LLC stepped in to say it was also interested.

MP Mine Operations was a consortium of JHL, the Chicago hedge fund, an investment fund known as QVT Financial, and Chinese rare earths company Shenghe Resources Holding Co. Ltd.[114] MP's two American investors had no experience in mining, but Shenghe did, as it was one of the largest rare earths companies in the world. It seemed that the foreign entity that JHL had teased the previous year in court was China-based Shenghe. And it was that mining experience that was crucial for MP Mine Operations.

The bidders met at a Philadelphia law firm on June 14, 2017, for the auction. Vincent Marriott, a lawyer who was running the auction for the court, laid out the terms of how the auction would go. While Clarke's bid had set the floor initially at $1.2 million, MP Mine Operations had filed to come into the auction with a bid of $1.4 million, which served as a new floor. Bidding had to go up at increments of $50,000, and thus would start at $1.45 million.[115]

Before the verbal sparring could commence, Clarke's lawyer, Oscar Pinkas, tried to stop it.[116] The night before, Clarke and Pinkas had filed a motion with Judge Sontchi trying to disqualify MP Mine's bid, alleging, among other things, that Shenghe was being used by the Chinese government to exert control over Mountain Pass.[117] While MP Mine Operations had told the court it did not believe its relationship with Shenghe would spark a review by CFIUS, it also did not dwell on the fact that Shenghe held 9.9 percent of MP Mine Operations. (At the time, CFIUS regulations were narrowly tailored to national security, not necessarily economic security. But in 2020, Washington expanded the remit for CFIUS to include both, and specifically to target U.S. businesses that produce critical technologies.[118])

Could the auction happen before the judge ruled? Marriott thought so, stating his belief that the auction was separate from the bankruptcy proceedings. "Unless and until I get an order from the court suspending the auction, it is our intention to proceed with it, starting now," Marriott told the auction.

Again, Pinkas tried to derail the auction, asking for a break to talk with Clarke. When the court reconvened, Pinkas pointed out an unknown person in the room. "We'd like to understand their role at the auction." Thanks to the arcane rules of bankruptcy court auctions, only direct investors could be in the room.

The subject of Pinkas's inquiry was Wang Quangen, the founder of and a large shareholder in Shenghe, which itself was an investor in MP Mine Operations with the nearly 10 percent stake. Considered one of the world's top rare earths processing experts, Wang and Shenghe had rare earths investments across the globe. Pinkas seemingly intended, but not directly, to highlight Shenghe's ties to Beijing. Shenghe's largest shareholder was the Chinese Academy of Geological Sciences, which is controlled by the Chinese government.

"So Shenghe is a current investor in [MP Mine Operations] and has an ownership interest in it?" Pinkas asked.

"Yes. Shenghe is a current minority investor in MPMO. That is correct," said the attorney Matthew Clemente, using the acronym for his client.

"Was that disclosed in the bid package? I didn't see that anywhere," Pinkas replied.

"Oscar, this is wasting time," said Marriott, clearly eager to get on with the auction and net the highest price.

"Vince, it's not," Pinkas retorted, using the court-appointed auction overseer's first name. "The bid procedures specifically say the identity of each bidder at the auction will be fully disclosed to the noticed parties, of which we are one."

Not directly responding, Marriott insisted: "Oscar, are you going to bid?" He warned Clarke's attorney that unless a bid was made, the auction would end in his rivals' favor.

Partially relenting, Pinkas bid $1.45 million to start the auction, but he wanted to know what would happen if the judge ultimately ruled in his favor. Would he have to pay the auction price, or the $1.2 million initial bid? Marriott, growing exasperated, instructed Pinkas to bid without any preconditions, knowing that whatever the judge's ruling was, he and Clarke would be bound by the auction's results.

"I don't know how this auction could be subject to anything other than the court's order. So, on that basis, the bid is $1.45 million," Pinkas said.

Marriott, incredulously: "I'm not hearing what I need to hear, Oscar. I'm going to give you one more chance to say what you need to say for me to consider it a bid, and then I'm going to determine the auction is over."

Pinkas asked for a five-minute break.

"No. No more breaks. You had plenty of time. What you're really trying to do is stall to see whether Sontchi actually comes up with a decision during the period of time."

"I'm trying to strategically discuss with my client because you've made clear it doesn't matter what Sontchi decides," Pinkas retorted.

At that, the client—Clarke—stepped in and agreed that the bid would be nonnegotiable and irrevocable. Clemente, the MP lawyer, bid $1.5 million. Over the course of the next hour or so, the parties jostled back and forth. MP pushed the bid up to $1.8 million.

Clarke responded with a $5 million bid. Then MP bid $5.2 million. Clarke went to $7.5 million, followed by an incremental counter from MP. Clarke then jumped to $10 million, clearly eager to win control of Mountain Pass. His lawyer ran out of the room to call Judge Sontchi, returning a few minutes later.

"We continue to object to the entire process," Pinkas told the room.

"What does that mean?" Marriott said.

"Feels like we're bidding against a ghost," Clemente, the MP Mine Operations lawyer, said.

Pinkas: "We feel the same way."

Several hours into the hearing, both sides were drained. The bidding had climbed to $10.6 million from Clarke's side. MP responded.

"$10.8."

"$12 million."

"$12.2."

"$15 million."

"$15.2 million."

"$16 million."

"$16.2 million."

Clarke: "I'm texting my wife. I've got to get permission. Can we take a break?"

Marriott asked if the reason for the break "is because you need authority from your other investor."

"I need authority," Clarke said.

"We'll take a five-minute break," Marriott allowed.

That break, though, was blood in the water for MP's lawyers. Clarke had signaled that even he had a limit. He pushed his bid to $20 million when he returned, but MP responded with $20.5 million.

"I'm done bidding," Clarke said.

After six hours of arguments, Clarke had finally capitulated. In the back of the room sat Jim Litinsky, the man who controlled the Chicago hedge fund JHL, which itself led the MP investor consortium. He had said nothing during the hearing, letting his lawyers talk for him.

⚡

NINE DAYS LATER, attorneys for all sides appeared before Sontchi in the Delaware court. Marriott was relieved to present the auction's results to the judge after years of back-and-forth negotiations. "This, we believe, to be a highly successful conclusion," he told the court.[119]

In addition to the cash, MP had committed to shoulder the site's environmental liability. Importantly for the court, it would keep the mine alive. And it would get to do this all for the price of $20.5 million, far less than the value of the equipment then sitting fallow at the site. It was a minute sum compared to the billions of dollars that Molycorp had plowed not only into its California mine, but the complexities of starting a rare earths company.

"We are supportive of the sale," Joseph Huston, a lawyer representing California's San Bernardino County, told the court. "We think that the purchase price is, frankly, remarkable."

If the sale collapsed, San Bernardino County feared it would have to rush to a judge for permission to take over the site to prevent leaks of any chemicals stored there. But here was a company willing to shoulder all that risk, saving the court, the state, the county, and other government agencies the time, headache, and money.

Pinkas told the court via telephone that he did not object to the sale and felt that his client's repeated attempts to buy the mine and the competition that it sparked "had helped to save Mountain

Pass. . . . Your Honor, I wouldn't really call us disgruntled sitting here today."

The proceedings served as a fait accompli. MP would buy Mountain Pass and try, with China's help, to succeed where Molycorp failed. Sontchi, a law professor who was first appointed to the bankruptcy court in 2006, was pleased. "It is an excellent result that the trustee has achieved with a very difficult asset, to say the least, to sell," the judge said, before deadpanning: "I was expecting to spend all afternoon with you people."

California's Mountain Pass, a mine that held so much promise for America's role in the green energy transition, had a new owner. "We are adjourned," the judge said, less than forty minutes after the proceedings had started.

A consortium led by a Chicago hedge fund and a Chinese mining company now owned the only American source of metals used in nearly every single consumer electronic device—and, more important, in U.S. military weapons—by bidding a comparatively trifling $50,000 more than an American rival.[120]

INTERSTATE 15 MEANDERS south from Las Vegas past a series of cast-off casinos and through a taupe desert into California, where a checkpoint inspects vehicles for invasive plants that could harm the state's large agricultural industry. The highway continues past a field of solar panels in the Ivanpah lake bed before bending to the right and slowly gaining altitude to nearly 5,000 feet into the Clark Mountain Range, where signs direct you to take Exit 281 for Mountain Pass. Just as the 1950s-era trade publication had made clear, Mountain Pass is not inconveniently located. The mine's gigantic pit and pile of waste rock sit only a few hundred feet from the interstate, its hulking equipment housed in large warehouses nestled into the side of the mountains. It did not seem like a giant encumbrance to convince miners to work at the site; this was not frigid Northern Canada or the rugged Outback of Western Australia. Sin City lay conveniently nearby for entertainment, and the beaches of Los Angeles were only a few hours away in the opposite direction.

It was a sunny, windy day in January 2020 when I drove up that highway to visit Mountain Pass for the first time. Flags of the United States and MP Materials—the new name for MP Mine Operations—fluttered in the air near a security guard's station. After donning some safety equipment, I met Jim Litinsky at the site's main office building. A confident man in his early forties with jet-black hair and a wide smile, Litinsky wore jeans and an industrial dress shirt with reflective green stripes down the side, mimicking the uniform typical of many front-line miners. A Chicago native, Litinsky had earned a J.D. and an M.B.A. before founding the JHL hedge fund in 2006 that managed an investment portfolio worth more than $1.5 billion with holdings in companies such as Barrick Gold Corp. and the New York Times Co. In Mountain Pass, he said, he saw a chance to succeed where others had failed.

"At the time when we were buying it in 2017 . . . no one thought that this could be economic," Litinsky said, gesturing around the complex.[121] By 2020, the company had restarted mining at the site and begun producing a lightly refined blend of concentrated rare earths that it was selling to the Chinese company that had helped buy the facility. That was partly because the equipment that was installed at the site by Molycorp's Project Phoenix didn't work properly, Litinsky said. MP Materials' engineers, he added, were working to make it work and, thus, cut the reliance on China.

Some of the buildings sat largely empty in the shadow of nearby mountains, waiting for some kind of future use. The giant hole in the ground that is the Mountain Pass mining pit plumbed down more than 500 feet with a wide road for colossal Caterpillar trucks and dozers that snaked to the narrow bottom. Its new owners planned to go deeper and expand the pit's circumference by relocating nearby buildings. While at the bottom of the pit, wearing a hard hat and reflective vest, I felt heavily engulfed by the sheer size of the operation. I was surrounded by canyon walls on all sides, the sun partially blocked out and the wind muted by the obstruction.

MP's giant equipment took rock out of that hole in the ground, then moved it through the rare earths production process to create the rare earths oxide concentrate that was sold to China's Shenghe. Just outside the mill sat giant white sacks containing 1,500 kilograms each of that concentrate. A forklift sped around the site, putting each sack one at a time onto a flatbed truck that still bore the Molycorp name and blue and red logo.

As if in concert, or perhaps reciting a mantra, each staff member I met on-site told me of his or her pride working to revive Mountain Pass, with a goal to supply "the U.S. government, Tesla, and Toyota" with rare earths. Nearby, in a building the size of two and a half football fields, sat dozens of holding tanks that Molycorp had installed as part of Project Phoenix. A large chlor-alkali facility designed to process wastewater was in a nearby building. They were, essentially, the only equipment in North America that could make rare earths metals, but they sat unused, the victim of Molycorp's rushed implementation.

"MP Materials bought a white elephant of a processing plant. No one can get it to work the way it was designed to work," a prominent rare earths industry analyst had told me just before my visit to the site.[122]

Litinsky repeatedly made the assertion during our talk that Molycorp's failure (and, implicitly, that of Chevron, Unocal, and Molybdenum Corp.) was a failure of execution, not environmental pollution. The mine's new owners, the MP Materials that Litinsky controlled, he said, were using different chemicals, different processing techniques, and managing production schedules far differently than anyone who had owned the site before. In fact, he pushed back hard when I asked about the environmental fines and other troubles that the site's previous owners faced.

"They never got a lot of the pieces of their process going," Litinsky said of Molycorp. "There was no environmental challenge. So, I just want to be very clear. That's an unfair characterization. The predecessor [owner] did not have an environmental challenge."

It was a confusing line to draw in the sand, especially because the production of rare earths by definition yields small amounts of not only radioactive waste, but also fluoride waste, which can be toxic in large quantities. The past pipeline spills, for example, meant that the Mountain Pass site couldn't send radioactive waste to the nearby flat desert terrain known as playas; it had to be stored on-site or shipped out of state. That was a problem that Litinsky would seemingly have to contend with, but so far, it didn't seem like he had.

The company had been selling fluoride waste to Chinese buyers, the legacy of the site's past environmental missteps. It wasn't clear to me how MP Materials planned to deal with those challenges once it started making rare earths metals in California again.

Still, having any rare earths production in the country was better than none, which Litinsky and his team realized and repeated ad nauseam not only to me, but in interviews across Wall Street and with dozens of reporters. The United States was in a "green arms race for the future. And we need to lead that as a matter of national security." It was clear that Litinsky saw his role at Mountain Pass as more than that of a typical investor. Given the import of the products that his new company aimed to sell, he believed that what he had done for the site was directly underpinning the United States and its green energy goals. "We feel like we're heroes that haven't necessarily gotten a lot of support," he said. "If the U.S. is going to have a rare earths capability, it will start with us. We'll lead it."

China's global control of the rare earths industry exposed what Litinsky termed "a single point of failure" in the green energy supply chain, a vulnerability that Americans needed to come to grips with, and, in doing so, support mining and other production steps needed to turn rocks into high-tech gadgets. "The Chinese are ahead in the green arms race. They recognize that there's sort of an economic Cold War going on in the world, and they want to lead in the industries of tomorrow."

Couching the push for American support for the newly reopened mine in the threat of China as a boogeyman seemed to make sense from a national security perspective. But MP in 2017 signed a deal to sell the rare earths concentrates it produces to Shenghe, part of what's known as a "take or pay" deal. The agreement, which was renewed in 2022, linked MP's revenue and profit to China.[123] MP Materials relied on Shenghe to process all the rock it dug out of the California desert. That meant shipping roughly 40,000 tonnes of concentrated rare earths per year from California to China. As part of the deal, Shenghe would get to keep all of MP Materials' profit until it recouped its initial $50 million investment.[124]

Amid the clamor of the site's restart, MP said in July 2020 that it would go public on the New York Stock Exchange, mimicking an approach taken by previous owners of the Mountain Pass site. The IPO aimed to bring in nearly $500 million for the company itself and nearly $1 billion more for investors, including Litinsky. Backed by the venture capitalist and former Facebook executive Chamath Palihapitiya, the stock offering was an aggressive target during the coronavirus pandemic, but one that paradoxically made use of fears about supply chains for products key to Americans' everyday lives.[125] It was an immense turnaround from the $20.5 million paid for the mine in bankruptcy court. Joining Litinsky on the new public company's board of directors were Richard Myers, who served as chairman of the Joint Chiefs of Staff under President George W. Bush, and Maryanne Lavan, an executive at defense contractor Lockheed Martin, which used rare earths magnets to build fighter jets for the Pentagon.[126]

Some investors on Wall Street grew skittish in the months after the IPO. One, known as Grizzly Research, published a twenty-seven-page exposé in October 2021 claiming that MP Materials' connection to China posed national security concerns for the United States. That report dragged MP's stock down more than 13 percent.[127] "MP is a repacked [*sic*] failed business that was dumped on investors at elevated prices. The idea that MP is the only feasible competitor to Chinese producers seems like a complete charade given that its biggest client and significant shareholder is controlled by the Chinese Treasury Department," the Grizzly analysts wrote.[128]

Parts of the U.S. government also looked warily at the company. Tom Lograsso, the head of the U.S. Department of Energy's Critical Minerals Institute—the focal point of the U.S. government's rare earths research and a facility that typically works closely with private industry—expressed concerns in early 2020 about Shenghe's involvement in the project. "Clearly, the MP Materials ownership structure is an issue," Lograsso told me not long after I toured the site.[129]

Litinsky saw Shenghe's help as forged in the cold calculus of an economic investment. "Had we not had a Chinese technical partner helping us do this relaunch, there's no way this could have been done," he said when we met.[130] Shenghe was just a technical partner with no seats on the company's board of directors and no power to control where MP Materials sold its product, he said repeatedly. Of the more than two hundred employees at Mountain Pass, only a handful were non-Americans, he added. Except, Shenghe was the only company buying the one product that MP Materials sold.

Litinsky was relying on China, yes. But he was also attacking China. It was a distinction that seemed curious given everything that was going on in the world. General Motors, for instance, had signed the deal with MP Materials in 2021 for a supply of rare earths magnets, which the company had never made before.

The complex chemistry that MP Materials was hoping to revive in California was part of a simplification process designed to partly reverse Project Phoenix. At the time of our interview, Litinsky told me he hoped to fix the on-site processing equipment by the end of 2020. In 2021, the company pushed that goal to 2022. When GM signed the deal with MP Materials in late 2021, the company said on-site processing could come in the next few years. MP promised GM it would now not only process rare earths but make rare earths magnets—a process for which it had no experience and had no patents. That seemed to only heighten the urgency to help Mountain Pass succeed, even if a Chinese company was an investor.

Given the widespread use of rare earths in weaponry, the Pentagon in April 2020 said it would give MP Materials financial support for rare earths processing in California. MP said it would use the money for design work.[131] That decision was reversed a month later after the Pentagon privately told MP it needed to conduct "further research," a step widely seen as the Pentagon responding to concern from Senator Ted Cruz, a Texas Republican, and other politicians about MP's Chinese ties.[132] By July 2020, the Pentagon decided to resume funding MP, finding that financially supporting the company and its rare earths project was in the U.S. government's best interest.[133]

Other countries were not idly standing by amid the burgeoning rare earths war between the United States and China. Late in the summer of 2020, just as Biden was announcing his ambitious EV targets, the Russian government said it would invest $1.5 billion in eleven rare earths projects to wean its economy off nearly all imports of the strategic metals by 2025. Moscow bluntly declared that it aimed to be the world's second-largest rare earths producer by that year, and it would achieve that goal by exploiting its reserves of the metals, estimated at 12 million tonnes, roughly 10 percent of the global total.[134] In late 2021, Beijing toyed with the idea of blocking rare earths exports to the United States in a bid to stop Lockheed Martin and other defense contractors from making fighter jets and other tools of war for the Pentagon.[135]

Back in the United States, Senators Mark Kelly and Tom Cotton introduced a bill in early 2022 that would block defense contractors from buying Chinese rare earths, an attempt to indirectly boost the nascent U.S. rare earths sector.[136] A bill introduced the previous year in the House of Representatives would have expanded tax credits to companies that produced magnets made from rare earths in the United States. Representative Eric Swalwell, a California Democrat, introduced the bill with Representative Guy Reschenthaler, a Pennsylvania Republican.[137] Both bills showed a rare moment of bipartisanship. Neither ever passed. The legislation was the latest in a string of attempts going back to at least the 1970s by the U.S. Congress—some successful, some not—to pass legislation that would improve America's production and stockpile of critical minerals.[138]

Despite the bipartisan congressional concern, the Pentagon and White House continued to support MP Materials. Later in 2022, Litinsky found himself a guest at a virtual White House roundtable, where he would publicly meet with the president for the first time and receive not only praise but more money from the administration. The path to a green energy future, it seemed, had overlapping loyalties.

CHAPTER SEVEN

Bright Green Lies?

LESS THAN TEN DAYS AFTER TAKING OFFICE, DONALD J. TRUMP fulfilled a promise he made on the campaign trail to slash what he considered excessive government regulation of the environment, finance, and health care. For each new regulation proposed by career government staff, two existing ones would have to be cut. The White House would be the arbiter of which ones would go or stay, but career staff members were responsible for proposing them to 1600 Pennsylvania Avenue.[1]

The new president called his executive order "the largest ever cut by far in terms of regulation"[2] that the country would experience. To those who feared the fox had entered the henhouse, Trump retorted: "There will be regulation, there will be control, but it will be a normalized control where you can open your business and expand your business very easily. And that's what our country has been all about."[3]

The message was received loud and clear just a few blocks away from the White House at the Stewart Lee Udall Building, the New Deal–era Moderne-style complex that houses the U.S. Department of the Interior. Founded in 1849, the Interior Department's numerous agencies, including the Bureau of Land Management, manage much of the federal government's land, earning it the nickname "landlord of the West."[4]

In August 2017, eight months after Trump signed his executive order, Deputy Secretary of the Interior David Bernhardt signed Order No. 3355, which drew inspiration from Trump's order. Projects that required environmental oversight from the federal government, typically obtained through the National Environmental Policy Act review process, known as NEPA, had grown too long, too confusing, and too complex, the deputy secretary wrote in the four-page order.

"This order recognized that the purpose of NEPA's requirements was not the generation of paperwork, but the adoption of sound decisions based on an informed understanding of environmental consequences," Bernhardt later recalled in *You Report to Me: Accountability for the Failing Administrative State,* his memoir of the Trump administration.[5]

Bernhardt had experience with government regulations he considered burdensome and onerous. At sixteen he successfully convinced his town council to give a youth center he was forming a break on taxes for arcade games, which would be cost prohibitive to his new endeavor. He attended law school in his native Colorado and had an internship at the U.S. Supreme Court. At thirty-seven, he became the Interior Department's solicitor, essentially its top lawyer, under the George W. Bush administration, after which he spent years as an oil and gas lobbyist.

In his role as the Interior Department's deputy secretary under Trump—basically the department's chief operating officer—Bernhardt was responsible for an efficient flow of the minutiae of bureaucracy across the sprawling department and its seventy thousand employees. Order No. 3355 was designed, he told his staff, to end the "impediments to efficient development of public and private projects that can be created by needlessly complex NEPA analysis." He set length limits of 150 pages for environmental review reports. ("Complex" cases could go to 300 pages.) Agencies within the Interior Department would have one year to finish those reports from the time they announced they were working on them.[6] Bernhardt, who was promoted by Trump in 2019 to run the entire department, said the order would improve its internal management.[7]

That decision had far-ranging implications that are still not fully understood. But what is known is that the rank-and-file Interior Department employees saw Trump and Bernhardt's orders as a clarion call to move faster. And that would have tremendous implications for

North America's largest lithium deposit and one of the world's largest automakers.

⚡

IN 1975, WITH the nation reeling from Watergate and the Three Mile Island nuclear accident still four years in the future, Chevron started digging in a northern Nevada valley between the old rim of an ancient volcano now known as the Double H Mountains and the cragged tops of the Montana Mountains.[8] Chevron had hoped to find uranium mingled with the sedimentary clays that defined the geology of much of that area. It was a logical bet, for uranium in nature likes to bind with clays, especially in the western United States.[9] Chevron's potential for success, at least on paper, was high, and the company used aircraft equipped with radiation sensors to do most of its testing, thus cutting down on the need for major digging.[10]

The U.S. Geological Survey thought that because of the presence of the ancient volcano rim, the site could also have unusually high concentrations of lithium, at the time commonly used in pharmaceuticals and lubricants. So Chevron expanded its mission; from 1980 to 1987 it started to dig through the clays for lithium as well. The tests were wildly successful: The entire area had large reserves of the white metal. Standing in the way, though, was all that clay, from which lithium had never been extracted. Prices for the metal also were in the doldrums. In 1986, Chevron leased its claims and by 1991 had sold them entirely.[11]

The location of Thacker Pass—in a valley between two mountains, making it effectively a bowl—was a large part of the appeal. State Road 293 ran right through it, making transport access a breeze. There was a large power line. A rail spur was not too far away. The area had very few residents, but a well-stocked town was only a forty-minute drive away. "Logistics and infrastructure can be constraining at some project sites, but here I could see things coming together," a lithium executive would later recall of Thacker Pass. "It has all these pluses that showed its potential."[12]

The rights to the rural valley, located about 20 miles south as the crow flies of Nevada's border with Oregon and in one of the least-populated counties in the United States, were traded among a handful of smaller companies until 2007, when Western Lithium USA Corp. started drilling again to find out just precisely where in Thacker Pass was the best place to find lithium. Western Lithium drilled exploration holes to study the lithium deposit. In June 2015, the company paid $65 million for a smaller rival named Lithium Americas Corp. that was building a lithium project in Argentina; in November, Mauricio Macri would be elected president and move fast to gain the confidence of Argentina's business sector after years of uncertainty that had plagued lithium projects, including the one James Calaway built with Orocobre. Macri had abolished export taxes on commodities, including lithium, as well as made other regulatory and fiscal changes. The company said it was "impressed with the rate of positive change and commitment of strong support on all levels. These are important indications of a very strong future for the mining industry in Argentina." In early 2016, Western Lithium took the name of the company it had bought, rebranding itself as Lithium Americas and mapping out a plan to develop two lithium projects.[13]

Having the Argentina project was important because it was a traditional lithium brine deposit and thus would, presumably, be easier to build and open. While additional testing in Nevada showed that the company was sitting on more lithium than any other place in North America, it also showed it was the largest deposit of lithium bound with clay anywhere in the world, at nearly a fifty-year supply.[14] And lithium had never been coaxed out of clay before in commercial quantities. If the company was going to undertake in Nevada what was, essentially, a science experiment, it helped to have another major source of lithium to generate sales from presumably first, thus the Argentina deal. The challenge was set.

By March 2018, Lithium Americas had begun the formal application process for its U.S. permits to extract lithium from Thacker Pass, a process that required more than forty environmental studies to set baselines for water, sound, noise, and other factors that were likely to change once a mine opened.[15] (Here it should be noted that the company never intended to buy the land from or swap it with the U.S. government, the way Rio Tinto wanted to swap land in Arizona for its Resolution Copper project.) A finance group known as Orion Mine Finance did hold a royalty on the project, meaning Lithium Americas will be paying the financier in perpetuity, not U.S. taxpayers who owned the land.[16] As the permit review process got under way, Trump's Interior Department went into action.

⚡

FROM THE BEGINNING, the orders from Trump and Bernhardt were quiet whispers in the ears of staff reviewing the proposed mine. At the Bureau of Land Management's Winnemucca, Nevada, office—which was leading the review of the proposed mine—staff were keenly aware of their need to get the project reviewed quickly and within budget.

One of the main ways they cut corners, oddly, involved sage grouse, small birds that evoke chickens and are known for a flamboyant mating dance amid sagebrush. And the western United States—especially Thacker Pass—is covered in sagebrush. Male sage grouse return to the same spot year after year to their nests in the sagebrush, known as leks, to perform for hens and to mate. The sagebrush helps shelter them from predators, and the birds are known to be easily disturbed by human activity, especially artificial light.[17]

Given the overlap between the proposed mine site and the leks for sage grouse, a thorough regulatory review would be typical. But what is thorough? And how far to investigate to prove that the mine wouldn't affect the birds? (By definition, digging an open-pit mine would presumably irk the neighbors, even those with wings.) A federal rule known as the Greater Sage Grouse Amendment prescribes buffer distances for mines to keep away from leks. The BLM staff quietly ruled, though, that Lithium Americas was not subject to those buffer rules because the company had "valid rights" to the entire site, though legal justification for the decision was never given. In interagency emails, staff acknowledged to themselves that the proposed mine would not be compliant with "seasonal timing restrictions," i.e., rules that prohibit lek disturbances during certain times of year. They moved the project forward.[18]

The regulators also admitted, in internal documents, that the mine could have an enormous effect on the visual beauty of the region. That matters, from a regulatory perspective, thanks to what are known as Visual Resource Management standards. While the Bureau's staff had said they would have to change their environmental report on the proposed mine to reflect this, they didn't in the end. Making those changes "would definitely delay" publication of a draft version of their environmental report "because it seriously impacts our ability to meet the 3355 deadline" without straining staff with overtime work, Ken Loda, a BLM geologist, wrote to a colleague in May 2019, citing the Bernhardt memo.[19] "This is where the project triangle fall [*sic*] down," his colleague Robin Michel replied. "The focus is on fast, so quality and cost go out the window."[20]

By January 2020, regulators asked the public for thoughts on the project's impact on the environment, a necessary regulatory step that showed the permitting process was moving forward. The regulators did not even slow down the timeline for public comment due to the coronavirus pandemic, irking the state's two U.S. senators.[21] Loda grew frustrated by the timeline imposed on his office. "[W]e're not going to make the one-year deadline," he wrote to BLM colleagues in April 2020.[22] "I'm thoroughly frustrated trying to keep this process moving given the complexities of this proposal and the issues needing to be addressed. . . . [W]e're still struggling to adequately address a couple of the environmental issues."[23]

If all went as planned, the company would receive approval within a year, something that executives praised as a "major accomplishment milestone."[24] Just over two weeks later, with Argentina's economy in a recession and debt mounting at Lithium Americas, the company sold a controlling stake in its Argentina project to China's Ganfeng Lithium Co., a step designed to let it focus almost entirely on Nevada.[25] Lithium Americas was bullish, expecting to begin construction at Thacker Pass in 2021, close the mine forty-one years later, and then spend a few years trying to return the site to something akin to what it had looked like before digging commenced.

Later that year, during the U.S. 2020 presidential election campaign and the coronavirus pandemic, Loda decided his office did not need to make any changes to its report on how the mine could affect the region. "We have concluded that an amendment . . . is unnecessary," Loda wrote in June 2020.[26] The day prior, the Bureau of Land Management's public affairs office had told regulators to "scrub" from all their files any references to their 2019 finding that the mine could affect the region's visual beauty.[27] Whether or not this is what Trump and Bernhardt had intended, the front-line troops had interpreted it their own way and acted.

⚡

FIVE DAYS BEFORE he left office (and nine days after the events of January 6), Donald Trump approved Lithium Americas' plans to build the Thacker Pass lithium mine. The project had been hurtling through the permit review process, much to the chagrin of a group of hyperfocused environmentalists who decided that, despite the cold of the northern Nevada January, they would head to the site and camp out in protest.

The approved mine aimed to produce, once fully operational, as much as 66,000 tonnes of lithium carbonate each year.[28] That wasn't the main number that environmentalists fixated on, though. Rather, they noticed that the 5,694-acre project would require roughly 308,666 tonnes of molten sulfur to be imported to the site every year. Almost 300 million tonnes of tailings would be stored nearby in a 350-foot-tall mountain. The company would eventually need 5,200 acre-feet of water each year, though it had rights to only 15.5 acre-feet at the time.[29] The immense amount of sulfur that Lithium Americas planned to import into northern Nevada would be used to leach the metal from the sedimentary clay rock, a novel approach that had not yet worked commercially.

As you'd imagine, the timing of Trump's decision and the details of the plan sparked immediate outcry, even though Lithium Americas and its predecessors had started the permit review process years prior. In politics, as in life, optics matter. Trump, it seemed, did the company no favors by approving the mine when he did.

Edward Bartell, a rancher who raised cattle in the area, blasted the decision. His worry and that of other ranchers was primarily the water level in the region, especially since the Thacker Pass project would require more than 2,600 acre-feet of water initially before growing to consume 5,200 acre-feet.[30] That would not only severely harm ranchers' ability to water their cattle, he worried, but would also hurt native species in the area, including a threatened species of trout. The ranchers and their attorneys attacked the government regulators' review of the proposed mine in a lawsuit filed less than a month after Trump's approval as "a one-sided, deeply-flawed, and incomplete analysis and characterization of the proposed project and its likely adverse environmental impacts."[31] The part of Nevada where Lithium Americas wanted to put its mine, Bartell and his co-plaintiffs told a federal court, was "a spectacular area with a rich geological and ecological diversity, wildlife habitat, and recreation opportunities."[32] It would, they argued, turn the area into a barren desert.[33] Trump's decision should be overturned, Bartell implored.

While that court drama was unfolding, a small gathering at the mine site was under way, one that evoked North Dakota, of all places. Five years prior I had extensively covered the Dakota Access Pipeline saga for Reuters. In North Dakota, a protest against the oil pipeline had started with a handful of people around a fire and within a year had blossomed to more than five thousand camped out in the frozen north. As outcry spread about Trump's Thacker Pass decision, I wondered if the same pattern could be taking shape in northern Nevada. Still, so far there had only been a small group at Thacker Pass protesting the proposed mine. I decided to watch and wait.

But then the protestors appeared on the front page of *The New York Times,* giving their cause instant legitimacy and global recognition.[34] Max Wilbert, a Seattle native, wilderness guide, and self-described community organizer, talked about his fight against Thacker Pass in almost religious terms and labeled it the prime example of the tension facing the United States and the world amid the green energy transition. Bill McKibben, the famed environmentalist, called it a "fascinating controversy" in a piece for *The New Yorker.*[35] "Blowing up a mountain isn't green, no matter how much marketing spin people put on it," Wilbert said.[36] Wilbert wasn't the first to oppose a mine, nor would he be the last. The fight in southern Nevada between ioneer and Tiehm's buckwheat, the clash in Arizona between the San Carlos Apache and Rio Tinto, and the Minnesota skirmish over Antofagasta's plans to dig underneath a national waterway all pointed to this broader tension. But each of those causes had been simmering for years. This newfound media attention buoyed Wilbert.

In late July 2020, Chief Judge Miranda Du of the federal court in Reno, Nevada, denied part of the request from Bartell and his fellow ranchers. The judge ruled that Lithium Americas could start excavating the site while she considered the broader question of whether Trump had made a mistake in approving the mine. The ruling declared that excavation work would not affect the site too much while Du considered the broader issue.[37] A few days later, the case grew when Du ruled that Wilbert's group and Indigenous tribes in the area could join the lawsuit and add their concerns that not only would the mine harm the region's ecology, but it would also destroy a historical site where Native Americans had been massacred in the nineteenth century. Considering all of this, Du said, would take time, a bad sign for Lithium Americas.[38]

"The green transition is just all about money. There's no talks about the environment, or endangered species, or how damaging all this will be for the ecosystem," said Gary McKinney, a member of the People of Red Mountain tribe. "If a mine like that is to go in, it'll add to the whole storyline of these mines here in Nevada not caring about Indigenous people or their sacred objects."[39]

As the case wound its way through courts, so, too, did the camp's notoriety. At its peak, organizers estimated there were two hundred people, most of them arriving for weekends and leaving for the workweek. The camp was led by Wilbert and Will Falk, an attorney who had previously been a public defender in Kenosha, Wisconsin. They both had learned of the proposed mine late in the summer of 2020. Wilbert and Falk were members of an environmental group named Deep Green Resistance that, I would come to find out, made Greenpeace seem downright rigid and corporate. Indeed, Deep Green Resistance described itself publicly as "radical," a moniker from which its members did not shy.

While Greenpeace fights aggressively against fossil fuel companies with stunts that include shutting down waterways, airports, banks, and highways, it still sees itself firmly planted in the twenty-first century. Deep Green Resistance, by contrast, espouses a deeply ingrained belief that the world is at maximum peril from climate change and rather than end fossil fuel consumption, the only way to prevent the Earth from cooking itself to death is to tear down the industrial underpinnings of modern society and return to an agrarian way of life.

In practice, that means that Wilbert and Deep Green Resistance espouse a phaseout of all vehicles, technologies, and farming practices that in their view contribute to the spewing of carbon into the globe's atmosphere and thus contribute to climate change. Wilbert co-wrote a 2021 book called *Bright Green Lies* that unpacks the authors' views that the modern environmental movement's proposed solutions to climate change—including lithium-ion batteries—are "lies that allow us to maintain an unsustainable way of living while pretending that we are not killing the planet."[40] They argue that "wind and solar power will not stop the murder of the planet."[41]

Eventually, Wilbert and others opposed to the mine were forced to leave the site by federal agencies that owned it. Huge chunks of the land were cordoned off with metal fencing and signs that blared: ACCESS RESTRICTED: Active Mine Site, Thacker Pass Project. Wilbert and Falk were fined nearly $50,000 for running the camp, an amount that essentially amounted to a charge for trespassing.[42] By July 2022 the company had not undertaken any extensive site work, perhaps waiting for that broader ruling from Judge Du, which the company said it expected by the end of September 2022.[43] Cows ignored the warning signs and moved freely through fence gaps, seeking out the best patches of grass in the arid expanse.

⚡

In the summer of 2022, I headed northeast from Reno on Interstate 80 toward Nevada's border with Oregon to see Thacker Pass for myself.

While Wilbert's initial protest camp had been disbanded, he still visited for several weeks at a time and set up a few miles away from the former camp, a one-man protest in the wilderness.

By then, the Thacker Pass lithium project had started to divide other environmentalists, too. Great Basin Resource Watch, a non-profit focused on biodiversity in the U.S. West and a group that had joined with Bartell and other ranchers in the initial lawsuit, had recently parted ways with its co-founder, Glenn Miller, after he came out in support of Lithium Americas. The move got attention, especially because a prominent environmentalist was publicly backing an open-pit mine. "Everyone is deeply concerned about climate change. It's a question about values, and I go with the need for lithium," Miller, who had retired as a professor from the University of Nevada, Reno, had told me. "This is one of the least impactive mine plans I've ever seen."[44]

As I drove north, keeping Miller's comments in the back of my mind, I spotted several billboards on the side of Interstate 80: LIFE OVER LITHIUM: PROTECT THACKER PASS. PEEHEE MU'HUH, one said. They were funded, I noticed, by the People of Red Mountain, not Wilbert or Deep Green Resistance. It was a hot and hazy August day, and I had the windows open in my rental truck as I came upon what seemed to be the rim of an ancient volcano on my left.

Thacker Pass is part of the vast McDermitt volcanic formation, an extinct supervolcano with four large calderas of rhyolitic rock infused with lithium. Water would mix with the rock and leach out lithium before pooling inside the calderas' basin over hundreds of thousands of years to form a lake that also eventually filled with clays and other sedimentary rocks. Today, there's a 160-meter-thick layer of lithium-rich clay throughout much of the Thacker Pass formation.[45] All that a developer would need to do would be to remove topsoil above that layer and find an economic way to commercially produce that lithium. It was enticing for sure, especially given that it was the largest U.S. deposit of lithium, at concentrations that rivaled any other global deposit.[46]

I took a wrong turn off the state highway and found myself bouncing around a dirt road that took me through random back parts of the terrain. There were peaks and valleys all around, the descendants, it seemed, of the volcanoes from ages ago. Up and down back hills I drove. A random elkhorn darted in front of me at one point. Sagebrush was everywhere. I eventually came across a giant valley filled with farmland. A hawk was drinking from a flooded pothole in the road before flying away as I drove closer. There was beautiful farmland all around, and I could understand in part why Bartell and his fellow farmers and ranchers were some of the most ardent opponents of the plans from Lithium Americas.

One of the farms I drove past was flying a U.S. flag as well as a Trump Let's Go Brandon flag. I also passed the Humboldt Hunting Club, to which Wilbert later told me he had received an invitation for a party. The agrarian, outdoors culture was strongly evident, and I was thankful for the accidental detour on my way to Wilbert's makeshift camp, which I eventually found tucked behind a craggy hill under the harsh Nevada sun. Wilbert, who is about five feet nine, was shirtless as I drove up, wearing brown shorts, a green felt fedora with a feather in it, and hiking sandals. Camped out under the shade of a large boulder, he was crafting press releases on his computer in the quiet of the afternoon.

A hawk circled overhead as I found a spot in the shade to chat with Wilbert. We talked about the legal philosophy underpinning much of his work: that nature itself has identity and personhood. The book he co-wrote, *Bright Green Lies,* describes a conscious pronoun choice when referencing nature. Rather than using "that" to refer to a tree, for instance, the book used "who," because "we believe that how we speak of the world profoundly affects how we perceive and experience the world, which in turn profoundly affects how we act in the world."[47] (It is a stance shared by some others: New Zealand granted personhood status to the Whanganui River in 2007.[48])

Stubborn in his ways up to a polite point, Wilbert never raised his voice or grew animated when discussing the proposed mine or Lithium Americas or Donald Trump or the Bureau of Land Management. He simply described it as his mission to stop them all. He in the past had opposed a proposed oil sands project in Utah; coal exports from Washington State; and the Dakota Access Pipeline, a saga that captivated the world for more than a year and placed Indigenous rights firmly in the center of any conversation about energy.

"We need a planned contraction of the economy, planned negative economic growth," he said. The sun had shifted and started to beat down on both of us near the rocks of Thacker Pass. At the time we met, he had recently gotten engaged. During our chats, he mentioned that not having children was one way for a person to reduce his or her carbon footprint. Sensing an opening, I asked his plans. He acknowledged he did not want biological children and might adopt instead.

"We need to, basically, deliberately abandon industrialism as rapidly as we can, or else we're headed for disaster," he told me. "It's very clear that green technology is not sufficient to address the global warming issue." Here I should pause and note Wilbert's views on his own use of modern technology and conveniences. (We all are thinking it.) Yes, he drives a gasoline-powered vehicle and uses a cell phone. No, he does not see those steps as hypocritical.

"To me, personal purity is less important in the moment than effectiveness," Wilbert explained. "I think it's important that we move in the direction that we want to see." In Oregon, where he lived, he rented a small cabin near Eugene, hunted frequently, made herbal medicines, fished, and farmed to source most of his food, part of a plan to, in his words, "model a consumerist alternative."[49]

He used an older iPhone and MacBook when we met, and the juxtaposition between my 2022 Toyota Tacoma rental truck and his 1999 Toyota Tacoma with 380,000 miles was plainly evident. (On the back of his truck were two bumper stickers: NEVADA IS NOT A WASTELAND, which ostensibly referred to plans to store nuclear waste in Yucca Mountain, and WE ARE THE GRANDDAUGHTERS OF ALL THE WITCHES YOU WERE NEVER ABLE TO BURN.) He viewed automobiles as luxury goods and said the world should stop producing them.

"I don't really feel like I'm a radical," he said. "I feel like the radicals are the people who are like, 'Oh, let's just throw something else under the hood of the car and keep on driving.' That, to me, is a Band-Aid on the problem." Perhaps aware that the most common response to his viewpoints would be to question his own use of modern technologies, he referenced struggles by those in past generations, implicitly linking his cause with theirs. "A lot of abolitionists wore clothes that were made of cotton produced by slaves, because that was what was on the market, and they didn't want to be naked all the time."

"That's an interesting perspective," I replied.

"The American Indians, who were fighting colonization, used firearms that came from the Europeans because they were largely superior weapons in many cases than what was otherwise available to them."

"Right," I said.

"For me, it's a question of effectiveness in the situation. I would have chosen to walk here from Oregon, but that would have taken six months or something. And I daydream all the time of taking a baseball bat and slamming my laptop, like in *Office Space*. And if I never had to check my email again, I would be happy. But that's the world we live in."

He noted, correctly, that "the amount of energy that an individual has at their disposal today is orders of magnitude above what a couple generations ago had." It's also true that life expectancy is far higher now in every part of the world, based in part on modern medicines, transportation, and food cultivation. At one point, Wilbert mentioned a need for population control via better sex education, and pointed to Iran (of all places). In Iran during the 1980s, family planning programs had cut the country's population growth rate from about 3 percent annually to about 0.7 percent by 2010 through a social program that encouraged vasectomies, tubal ligations, birth control pills, and condoms.[50]

Even as Wilbert and Deep Green Resistance navigated their own personal use of modern technologies while they fought against the companies making those technologies, their views on gender threatened to derail the entire opposition to Thacker Pass. Wilbert and his peers have taken strong views on the transgender discourse enveloping much of American and global societies. Rather than cloak their beliefs or try to supplant them amid their fight against a lithium mine, they put them out there, front and center. "Point out that . . . men who call themselves 'transgender' are still men, and suddenly you're toxic," Wilbert and his co-authors wrote in a 2019 essay.[51]

The problem for Wilbert and his peers is that many of their allies in the fight against Thacker Pass and Lithium Americas were Indigenous communities that held strong beliefs on the existence of a third gender, known as "two spirit." The tension was exposed largely by a 2022 report from *E&E News*, the Washington-based energy and environmental trade publication, but it had reverberations far beyond the D.C. Beltway.[52] Deep Green Resistance had publicly stated on its website that it adhered to a "radical feminist" philosophy that supported biological women. That meant, in practice, that transgender women should not be allowed to use women's restrooms, per the organization's logic. Wisdom might have dictated that the group heavily cloak these beliefs before publicly linking themselves with Native American groups to fight Thacker Pass, but they did little to scrub the Internet or social media accounts. Wilbert and Falk had formed an organization called Protect Thacker Pass to work with local Indigenous groups at the camp and in lawsuits but did not mention that they were affiliated with Deep Green Resistance.

One tribe, the People of Red Mountain—the same tribe that paid for the Interstate 80 billboard—said that Wilbert and Falk should have disclosed their connection. "I felt that [Deep Green Resistance] took the wind out of our sails because it was serious between [Deep Green Resistance] and that community, and that wasn't our fight, so we were left out in the open," McKinney, the tribal spokesman said. "And it was over transphobia."[53]

But one of Deep Green Resistance's co-founders linked the issues, saying that people who "want to violate the basic boundaries of women" were akin to those who have "violated the boundaries of forests and rivers and prairies." Within a few weeks, Falk had filed a motion in U.S. federal court to withdraw as an attorney representing the People of Red Mountain. The tribe also had abandoned their protest camp. The fight against Thacker Pass, while not completely dead, had suffered a blow due to an unlikely addition to the nation's internal battle over electric vehicles, mining, and the green energy transition.[54]

⚡

AS THE SUN moved through the sky and began its downward march to the horizon, Wilbert asked if I wanted to hike around the mine site. We both packed knapsacks with water and snacks and headed off. He wore hiking sandals and I my running sneakers. We chatted about marathon training as we kicked up small clouds of dust while traipsing up hills and through clumps of sagebrush.

Wilbert's disdain for the modern environmental movement was palpable, and sometimes his analogies veered into the extreme. The modern climate movement is a "toxic mimic of environmentalism" the way sexual assault is a "toxic mimic of real, authentic sexuality and connection with another human being." He compared the Thacker Pass project to a kind of "neocolonial" mining project because a Canadian company wanted to dig in a relatively poor part of the United States. Climate change advocates are "sociopaths" who take advantage of others without sacrificing themselves. (At one point in our conversation, I asked if he had ever read Karl Marx's *Communist Manifesto*. He said he had not.)

Wilbert drew a comparison that he saw as clear-cut between average Germans during the Second World War who did not question Hitler's regime and environmentalists today who do not question how and where metals for green technologies are procured. Elon Musk, the Tesla CEO, had "some serious social problems." The Enlightenment was, ultimately, dangerous because it traded pagan traditions of land being sacred for a more "mechanistic worldview to understandings of the natural world." At one point we came across chunks of white clay poking out of the ground. I picked one up and examined the lithium inside; these rocks dotted the landscape, a visual embodiment of the site's potential.

We reached the edge of the mountains opposite the McDermitt Caldera as the hues of the setting sun splashed purple and orange around us. The wind whispered through the air. A coyote howled in the distance. Birds fluttered from nearby nests. It was idyllic in the truest sense of the word. It was hard to imagine North America's largest lithium mine one day being at that spot.

I had been waiting for the right moment to ask Wilbert about the controversy generated by his views and how they affected his partnerships with Indigenous groups. To my surprise, as we sat there overlooking the valley, he brought the topic up unprompted. He described the *E&E News* article as "pretty inaccurate and silly" while also saying "it's been so long since I read it," as if to imply he did not remember it fully. While Wilbert said he was "not a spokesperson . . . for a gender-critical perspective or a radical-feminist perspective," he had put his name on the 2019 essay. They were views that he said the various Indigenous groups were aware of, even though the article directly quoted tribal leaders who said they weren't.

"There are a lot of people in my life who are either lesbian or gay or identify as nonbinary or what have you," he said. "I really resent anyone's attempts to sort of paint me as some sort of caricature of a bigot, or violent person, or something like that. . . . It's not the issue I came here to fight. It's not the issue that I've really dedicated my life to."

Why can't, he asked, folks with different viewpoints stand against a perceived common foe? "We're gonna work with anyone who basically isn't a total asshole," he said, adding that he would even work with a white supremacist, if that white supremacist also was opposed to the lithium mine. "I would rather talk to them and be around them in the hopes of converting their views and changing their worldview," he said.

He caught himself before I had a chance to point it out: "If I were a person of color and I was in that situation, I might just not want to be around that person or be near them at all."

I asked Wilbert directly if he believed that women's spaces should be for biological women only. He nodded yes. I then asked how that viewpoint has affected his advocacy with Indigenous tribes in the area, especially considering many tribes have views on gender that do not always align with Western traditions. It was inaccurate, he said, to imply that the relationship was sundered. "Since the beginning of the campaign, going back for many years, there's been people who didn't want to work with me for all kinds of different reasons, including this gender issue. And that's fine." But it was not, he said, "a super-divisive wedge."

For all of Wilbert's stipulations, he seemed to be purposefully obscuring from himself the fact that he was missing the forest for the trees, that his views on a wildly controversial social issue were detracting from his and others' broader fight against this large mining project. He seemed to think it was something fomented by the mine's proponents to discredit him. "The [Lithium Americas] corporation and the government are very happy whenever there's conflict like this, whenever there's infighting in a social movement that is getting in their way, economically," he said.

By that point it was dusk, and the stars were beginning to peek out. We had several miles to walk back to our makeshift camp. Once back, Wilbert made a dinner of macaroni and cheese over a natural gas–powered camp stove. I had a sandwich that I had stuffed in my bag earlier that day. The sun had already set, and the Milky Way's band was carpeting the expanse above. It was the first time in as long as I could remember that I had seen a full starscape, a reality that exposed my own lack of travel outside of light-polluted places.

As we sat in the dark, Wilbert recounted to me a dream he had before he had even set foot in Thacker Pass. He had seen a grainy photo of the area, but otherwise knew little of what Thacker Pass looked like. In the dream, a powerful force overtook him and whisked him to a mountain overlooking Thacker Pass. "I sat there for sixteen million years, and just sort of had the experience of watching the coming and going of animals and then human beings." And then, he continued, the vision morphed into some kind of nightmare, with "a series of explosions, mountain slides, and other things opening the land and blasting it for open-pit mining."

I asked Wilbert, after a long silence, if he thought a mine would eventually be built at Thacker Pass. He admitted that, probably, yes, a mine of some size was likely. Perhaps his vision had been his own private harbinger, an unconscious way for him to accept his cause would fail.

That night Wilbert crawled into the bed of his twenty-three-year-old Tacoma and I crawled into the bed of my brand-new Tacoma and slept underneath the stars. I fell asleep to the howling of a coyote before the moon rose overhead like a bright flashlight and blocked out the Milky Way.

The next morning, as we prepared to part ways, Wilbert asked if I was interested in seeing the area where a massacre had taken place in the nineteenth century. The area had been named Peehee Mu'huh, or "Rotten Moon," the name that had been on the highway billboard I saw while driving to the site. Oral traditions detail how the entrails of Paiute tribal members were spread out in a crescent formation at the site after a massacre by another tribe in the nineteenth century. The horror of what happened there would be compounded, Wilbert and the Pauite said, by the construction of a lithium mine.[55]

We drove several miles away from the site where the mine was proposed, then turned left onto a pothole-filled dirt road as we climbed toward a giant rock formation that evoked a finger pointing into the sky. We were several hundred feet, at least, above the nearby plains and could see clearly the two mountains that flanked Thacker Pass miles away in the distance. When we parked, I asked Wilbert if we were at the right spot.

"Yup, this is it," he said. The area where Lithium Americas hoped to drill was barely visible in the distance. We sat in the quiet wind for a few minutes before I left, heading north.

⚡

IN AUGUST 2022, Senator Catherine Cortez Masto of Nevada was in the midst of a brutal reelection fight against Adam Laxalt, a former Republican state attorney general who, while in that office, filed a court brief opposing the state of Massachusetts's investigation seeking to link ExxonMobil with climate change.[56] The race had national implications as the U.S. Senate was split fifty-fifty, with Vice President Kamala Harris able to make a tie-breaking vote. If Cortez Masto lost, the Democrats could lose the Senate. The senator had long fought to show she was receptive to the green energy transition, going so far as to secure provisions in the bipartisan infrastructure deal passed in 2021 that helped fund U.S. production of EV batteries and bolster America's supply chains for those batteries, supply chains that include lithium.[57]

Cortez Masto had also extracted a promise from Senator Joe Manchin of West Virginia, chair of the powerful Senate Energy and Natural Resources committee, to block a proposed royalty for minerals extracted on federal land from the Build Back Better legislation, which was under hot debate at the time in Washington. (That legislation went through various deaths and rebirths before passing in 2022 as the Inflation Reduction Act.) Manchin kept his promise to Cortez Masto and the final version did not include a measure proposed in the U.S. House that would have set an 8 percent gross royalty on existing mines and 4 percent on new ones. Supporters projected that the measure, which would also set a 7-cent fee for every ton of rock moved, would raise about $2 billion over ten years. Some members of Congress had proposed the change in the hope of passing one of the most substantial changes to the law that has governed U.S. mining since 1872, which had not set royalties in order to encourage development of the western United States. But Cortez Masto helped block it.[58]

Nicknamed the Silver State, Nevada had long been one of the largest U.S. sources of that metal and gold. So, to oppose the mining of those metals would be akin to opposing gambling in the state, i.e., a *sure way* to lose an election. But lithium posed a different needle to thread for a moderate politician in a moderate state amid a heated midterm election. Thacker Pass, which is surrounded by wealthy ranchers who make large political donations and Indigenous tribes who often vote in blocs, seemed to play a large role in this fence-sitting, despite the fact that Cortez Masto has said the United States should produce more lithium.[59] The senator had visited Lithium Americas in Reno in late 2019, smiling for the camera with the company's executives after a tour of a production facility.[60]

"If we don't start embracing this new technology, we are going to be left behind," Cortez Masto said during the tour, part of a show of support for then pending federal legislation to streamline permitting for new mines. (Which, as of this writing, has not passed.)[61]

So that August, I read with interest a new poll from Suffolk University that showed Cortez Masto 7 percentage points ahead of Laxalt, a bit of good news for the incumbent Democrat. I shared that poll in a post on Twitter with a comment that noted the senator's strong support for Thacker Pass. A few minutes later, while I was walking my dog, my phone rang.

"Hi, I'm looking for Ernest Scheyder with Reuters. This is Josh Marcus-Blank with Senator Cortez Masto's campaign. Thanks for your tweet earlier today, but I'm calling to ask you to delete it." The request caught me off guard, especially considering Cortez Masto had visited with the company's executives,[62] sponsored several pieces of EV supply chain legislation, and gone to bat to defend the status quo of the 1872 Mining Law. Lithium Americas itself had touted to its shareholders in late 2021 the senator's "endorsement of our emerging industry."[63] Had I made a mistake? "Thanks for the call," I told him. "I could be wrong, but hasn't the senator voiced support for the project? If I'm wrong, I'm wrong, and I'll delete the tweet."

"Off the record, she hasn't taken a stance on the mine itself and we would appreciate it if you deleted the tweet." (Here I should pause and note that "off the record" must be agreed to by both parties; I had not agreed.)

While my dog, Theo, pulled incessantly at the leash, I told Marcus-Blank I'd get back to him once I was back at my desk. Once there, things grew more curious. Indeed, Cortez Masto had sponsored legislation, as I recalled. On the Internet, in living color, I found the photo of Cortez Masto during that September 2019 visit to the company's Reno facility. And while the senator had waxed poetic on many occasions about the need to boost U.S. minerals production for the green energy revolution, it seemed that supporting specific mines—especially *this* specific mine—was a bridge too far.

Most mining in the western United States is governed by the General Mining Law of 1872, which was written to prod development of the then underdeveloped western edge of the country. It is the guiding piece of legislation for all hard-rock mining on U.S. government land in the region, roughly 350 million acres.[64] It also stipulates that companies mining on federal land don't need to pay royalties, something that had irked huge swaths of Washington for ages.[65]

Senator Martin Heinrich of New Mexico strongly supported the creation of a royalty for minerals extracted on federal land, especially to fund the cleanup of abandoned mines. "Every day that goes by without a hard-rock royalty in place means more toxic metals in our western watersheds," said Heinrich, who was not up for reelection in 2022 and thus did not have to balance the powerful and opposing forces of the ranching, Indigenous, and climate change communities.[66]

I deleted the tweet but followed it up with another one indicating that Cortez Masto had not actually voiced support for the project even though she had said the United States had to produce more lithium. It would seem Thacker Pass had wormed its way into the fight for control of the U.S. Senate.

Cortez Masto defeated Laxalt by only 7,928 votes out of 1,020,850 cast.

⚡

JON EVANS HAS a jawline that could cut paper and, evoking his military roots, a hairstyle that is neat and trimmed closely on the sides. His grandparents emigrated from Eastern Europe to the United States and insisted that their children and grandchildren use education as a tool to better themselves and find a solid life. Evans's father got the message; he earned a Ph.D. in organic chemistry and encouraged his own children to enter the science or engineering fields.

Young Jon, though, wanted to be a stockbroker. Eventually, Dr. Evans won out after convincing his son that, with a knowledge base in a STEM field, he could go into business, research, or even—yes—Wall Street. Evans settled on mechanical engineering. He paid for his schooling with help from the U.S. military in the form of a four-year Reserve Officers' Training Corps scholarship. In exchange for the government money, Evans would serve three years in the U.S. Army, where he saw combat duty during the first Gulf War as an armored calvary officer.

"Running a tank at twenty-two years old matures you quite a bit," he recalled.[67]

After his time in the military, General Electric recruited the young veteran for its plastics business, which the conglomerate eventually sold. Evans then spent two short years in pharmaceutical sales before a recruiter reached out in 2008 with an interesting opportunity: Would Evans be interested in running the lithium business at the Philadelphia-based FMC?

Evans was intrigued, but he knew little about lithium beyond where it was on the Periodic Table of Elements. The 2008 Financial Crisis was also roiling the world, stunting the growth of the portable electronics industry, which many had assumed would begin to supplant lubricants, pharmaceuticals, and glass as some of the dominant uses for the metal. Evans took the job anyway, relocating his family and diving in headfirst to compete with Chile's SQM and Rockwood Holdings, a predecessor company to Albemarle. At the time, those three were the only lithium producers of note around the globe. His competitors and employees became his friends, including Eric Norris, who went on to run Albemarle's lithium business, and Joe Lowry, who became a highly sought-after industry consultant. Albemarle, SQM, and FMC (which spun off its lithium division as the company Livent in 2019) are still considered titans in the lithium industry.

"It truly was a bit of an oligarchy," Evans said. "It was a very small world."

After FMC's chief executive retired in 2010, Evans chafed under new management and began itching for a new opportunity. A private equity firm that controlled the do-it-yourself legal company LegalZoom and the men's clothier Hugo Boss recruited Evans in 2013 to run some portfolio companies, including a life sciences firm and an HVAC company. He sold or spun off three companies, earned enough money to pay off his house and fund his kids' college tuition. But even then, lithium was calling him back.

In 2016, Lithium Americas was trying to develop a lithium project in northern Argentina, an area that Evans knew a lot about given his time at FMC. (Interestingly, China's Ganfeng—which had been a small firm only a few years prior—was helping Lithium Americas build that Argentina project and had become the largest shareholder in the company. "They had been small, but it's amazing how things change," Evans said.)

That same year, the company was bought by Western Lithium, which was aiming to develop the Thacker Pass lithium mining project in northern Nevada. Evans joined the company in 2017 as a board member. The next year he became its president. As he grew into the role, so did his vision for what a new lithium mine could mean for the United States.

"I knew that someday, people would want to have supply chains that weren't as distributed as they had become," he said. The coronavirus pandemic turbocharged that reality. So, too, did the fight against climate change, though Evans like many other executives had not realized how quickly national and international policy would work in their favor. "Now, every time you look at EV penetration numbers, they just keep on growing. And here we have a U.S. asset that's become really important to supply those needs." Suddenly, energy security was about far more than just oil or gas. "Ten or fifteen years ago, you would never have thought that lithium would be a national security issue. Today, it is."

Cognizant of my time with Wilbert at Thacker Pass, as well as the numerous legal grenades the sides had lobbed against each other, I asked Evans what he thought. He didn't hold back.

"This project, our project at Thacker Pass, didn't become a hot potato until those two guys [Wilbert and Falk] showed up and garnered support from *The New York Times,* which wanted to use their fight as some kind of platform. And then they were throwing anything they could against the wall to make it stick, to make our project stop. All these guys are focused on is deindustrialization."

Evans noted that the Sierra Club, the Center for Biological Diversity, and other conservation groups were not opposing Thacker Pass. Evans said he believed part of Wilbert's attack was an attack on the Biden administration. He referenced recent social media attacks on U.S. rare earths projects, funded by China and other foreign governments, heavily implying without proof that perhaps Wilbert was being funded by the same people. The Chinese government, for example, had been linked to online attacks against rare earths projects in Texas and Oklahoma.[68]

"There are people who don't want the Thacker Pass project developed for political reasons. I don't think that's beyond the realm of reality," he told me. "Why would you want to allow a country to become independent in a certain area? I think that logic plays into things here, too." Evans was frustrated that at least one tribe continued to use Will Falk as its attorney, even after other tribes had cut ties.

Perhaps, he told me, some tribes wanted money. He didn't know. But he said the idea was ludicrous that some tribe—any tribe—could use the concept of Free, Prior, and Informed Consent (FPIC) to block any mine. And Evans was convinced it didn't have the support of policymakers in Washington. That, of course, was the rub for Biden's team and to a lesser extent the teams of Biden's two predecessors; at some point, some decision has to be made, or else other nations will happily sell you EV metals and use them as economic weapons.

"The issue is massive for the U.S. government, because there's a lot of lithium on Indian land," Evans said. (One Nevada tribe, it should be noted, gave its support to the Thacker Pass project after Lithium Americas promised to build it an 8,000-square-foot community center.)[69]

I asked Evans what he thought about the ability of the United States to become a lithium powerhouse. Was it possible? He thought so but then paused. "It's not like we don't know how to mine lithium here, to process it. We just choose not to do it. We need to choose to do it again. We've just put up our own barriers." Evans also—like James Calaway at ioneer—thought that lithium could be his legacy, his way of helping the planet. "As an American, there's no reason why you can't have that development here," he said.

While the courts and Max Wilbert may have stood in his way initially, Evans found a reason to celebrate at the dawn of 2023. General Motors, one of the world's largest automakers, said in January it would help Evans and Lithium Americas develop the Thacker Pass mine. GM also said it would buy $650 million worth of shares in Lithium Americas, supplanting China's Ganfeng as the company's largest shareholder and removing a glaring point of tension with Washington regulators considering whether to lend money to Lithium Americas. GM, Evans told me, was the "right and holistic partner" for his growing company and one it picked after interviewing more than fifty others for more than a year. "It was worth it to wait," he said.[70]

The GM deal was contingent on a favorable court ruling, which Judge Du issued eight days later. Mine construction could begin, Du ruled in a victory for Evans and the company, though some minor geological tests still were needed. Lithium Americas had defeated Wilbert, ranchers, conservationists, and several Indigenous tribes, but they all vowed to fight the decision. "We need to find truly just and sustainable solutions for the climate crisis, and not by digging ourselves deeper into the biodiversity crisis," said Greta Anderson, a member of the Western Watersheds Project, one of the plaintiffs whom Du ruled against.[71]

⚡

COWS WERE OUT for their morning jaunts as I drove away from Wilbert and into the Sunday-morning sun. I turned on my radio but couldn't find any stations on the FM or AM dials. I kept driving for twenty minutes or so until I came to the small town of Orovada. The town's only school teaches students in kindergarten through eighth grade and sits right on the road leading out of the proposed mine site. (Lithium Americas promised to move the school, at a cost of at least $10 million.[72])

With my gasoline tank running low and with me in desperate need of caffeine, I stopped at Orovada's Sawtooth Station, which sold Shell-branded gasoline and potent java. Toward the back of the lot on which Sawtooth sat, tucked in the rear corner and surrounded by green parking barricades, sat two EV charging stations. Here, in the middle of nowhere, next to one of North America's largest lithium supplies, the future had started to creep ever closer.

CHAPTER EIGHT

A Rebirth

ROUGHLY 130 MILES NORTH OF BOISE, UP STATE ROUTE 55 AND over a series of packed dirt roads that beat into the rugged mountains of central Idaho, sits Yellow Pine, a hamlet at an elevation of nearly a mile and with a year-round population of 32.[1] The community's post office, while open six days a week, annually handles an average of only seventy packages.[2] The Corner Restaurant—at the corner of Johnson Creek Road and Profile Street—is open only four days a week. When I visited in the summer of 2022, a flag proudly fluttered from a pole affixed to a neighboring house: TRUMP 2024: FUCK YOUR FEELINGS. The town's numbers swell each August for the annual Yellow Pine Music & Harmonica Festival, when thousands of people head to the remote Idaho countryside to play a tune or two.[3] Outside of that, Yellow Pine is quiet, a waystation for the occasional motorcyclist in summer or snowmobiler in winter.

Yellow Pine used to have a sibling community in Stibnite, about 14 miles southeast, but Stibnite effectively does not exist anymore, leaving Yellow Pine the lone voice crying in this very remote wilderness. All of Stibnite's wood-framed homes were carted off decades ago on the backs of trucks. Stibnite's church, gym, community center, canteen, and small store have vanished. But during the Second World War,[4] both Stibnite and Yellow Pine thrived due in no small part to the insatiable demand from the Allied Powers for antimony, a metal used in hardening bullets, tanks, ball bearings, and other armaments, as well as in flame retardants. It was a growth sparked, indirectly, by China.

Since the early twentieth century, China has been the world's largest antimony producer thanks to mining in the Xikuangshan district in the country's Hunan Province, which has reserves of 2 million tonnes.[5] The First World War increased global appetite for antimony and led the United States to rely more on its own mines, especially small facilities in Nevada, as well as producers in China and Bolivia. But the rise in popularity of the internal combustion engine, and with it, the lead-acid battery made with antimony, saw a spike in demand for the metal during the 1930s. That pushed the rising global appetite for antimony into an acute hunger when Japan invaded China during the Second World War, stoking a perfect storm of supply-and-demand imbalance. Japan blocked exports of the strategic metal, sparking a hunt for alternate reserves. In 1939, Congress and President Franklin Roosevelt passed the Strategic and Critical Materials Stock Piling Act, which directed the U.S. military and Department of the Interior to craft a list of minerals and materials crucial for the national defense. Antimony was placed on the list, and the U.S. Bureau of Mines started scouring the country for supply.[6]

The mountains near Yellow Pine and Stibnite had been known to have a large concentration of gold and antimony ever since the Thunder Mountain gold rush of 1900. That gold rush failed largely due to the complex geology and the sheer remoteness of northern Idaho; just transporting digging equipment to the site proved an insurmountable cost.[7] Several companies staked claims over the next thirty years before a San Francisco–based firm, Bradley Mining Co., optioned for the rights to mine in the area in the 1930s. Like those who had gone before, Bradley found it challenging to profitably separate gold from antimony. The bill that Roosevelt had signed in 1939 proved fortuitous. Government geologists digging nearby found fresh deposits of not only antimony, but also tungsten, another in-demand wartime mineral. Using the powers allocated by Roosevelt's bill, the U.S. government subsidized Bradley's production, which went into overdrive. By April 1941—before the United States was even at war—Bradley had drilled its first underground mining shaft, with production beginning by August. By 1942, with underground mining running at full tilt, the company and government were preparing to expand the operation with a giant open-pit mine, a step that required a river to be diverted. By 1943, with the path of a major river relocated, the open pit had been dug and was producing antimony and tungsten. Rock was excavated from the pit and hauled 2 miles south to a processing plant where it was crushed, ground, and then treated with chemicals to produce a thick concentrate of each metal that was sent to a rail station 80 miles away. So it went for the entire war, twenty-four hours a day.[8] While antimony helped make bullets, most importantly, it also was applied in liquid form to the wooden decks of aircraft carriers.[9] (The Grenfell Tower fire in London in 2017 reinforced how important antimony could be as a fire retardant; parts of the building were not treated with the metal and seventy-two people died when a small fire spread to the building's insulation and engulfed the entire structure.[10])

As the mine grew alongside the East Fork of the South Fork of the Salmon River, so did the community. By the end of 1943, 1,500 people lived in Stibnite in communal bunkhouses, as well as more than a hundred single-family wood-frame houses that included free utilities. A school and post office opened, as did other community staples. The village hospital got the state's first X-ray machine. Stibnite elected a five-person Village Board. Men who were drafted could perform their military service by working at the mine, an appeal for those with families. Despite the cold winters, a warm, thriving community emerged in Stibnite and, to a lesser extent, nearby Yellow Pine, all to support the war effort. By the end of the fighting in 1945, Bradley and U.S. officials had mined all of the tungsten in the area. They had also mined nearly 10,000 tonnes of antimony, accounting for roughly 90 percent of U.S. wartime demand.[11]

That growth came in the years before U.S. environmental laws had been cemented. It also came amid the fever of war, the desire to win at any cost. A hundred-mile power line, for instance, was built quickly in 1943 to connect the mine to a steady, cheap supply of hydroelectric power, with little to no public comment or review of how the line could affect the rural state's ecology. Such a rushed job is unimaginable in the twenty-first-century U.S. bureaucratic structure.[12]

Stibnite stayed open after the Second World War and helped fuel the Allies during the Korean conflict as well. The open-pit mine closed in 1952, and while the processing equipment kept going for a few years, cycling through stockpiled rock, it, too, was shut down and dismantled. Stibnite was abandoned by 1958.[13] The site sat fallow until the 1970s, after which some parts were mined by a handful of smaller companies, including one that eventually was bought (and later sold) by Mobil Oil Corp.[14] Much of the site had suffered environmental harm during the wartime efforts. More than 10 million tonnes of tailings had not been stored properly and had been leaching chemicals into waterways. Some of the waste rock actually *was* in streams, dumped there in the decades before the U.S. Environmental Protection Agency was created, and slowly discharging arsenic and other poisons into the Idaho wilderness. Old mining equipment, including a smelter, was buried underground.[15] Numerous wildfires had caused massive erosion that had pulled sediment down from higher elevations, blocking waterways that long had been used by salmon to spawn. Stibnite was designated a Superfund site, partly explaining why it was bounced between successive owners over the years even though large gold and antimony reserves remained. If the site could be cleaned up and the antimony and gold mined together, it could become very profitable. Especially with the rising price of gold and the rising demand from the burgeoning electronics sector for antimony, which at the turn of the twenty-first century was increasingly being seen as a vital, if niche, mineral for technologies of the future.

Antimony can be harmful to human health, thus requiring special handling when mining and processing. World Health Organization guidelines, for example, consider concentrations of antimony over 20 parts per billion to be unhealthy. Chinese mining safety standards do not always overlap with what those in some Western societies might consider best practices, and a 2011 study of the Xikuangshan antimony mines found concentrations of antimony in drinking water samples collected in a 300-square-kilometer radius ranging from 8.1 to 152 parts per billion, with most nearby residents absorbing the metal when they ate rice or vegetables, or drank water.[16] The challenge for the Stibnite project was whether the antimony that was present there could be produced safely. Slowly, over the course of about twenty years, a small company known as Midas Gold began to buy up competing claims in the Stibnite region. And by 2016, that had caught the eye of John Paulson.

⚡

AFTER LEAVING NEVADA, I continued my drive north into Oregon and then to Idaho, which in 1890 had adopted the state motto *Esto Perpetua, "Let it be perpetual."*[17] For years, the state tried to balance with mixed success the preservation and production of its natural resources, whether that was the extraction of minerals, such as gold and antimony, timber from logging, or even potatoes, which Idaho produces more of than any other state.

After spending the night in Cascade, I struck out the next morning for Yellow Pine to see the old Stibnite mine site. It was a beautiful drive, with the sun shining through young pine trees swaying in the crisp August mountain air. I headed north on Warm Lake Road, rarely encountering another vehicle, my cell phone reception coming in and out. The road climbed a mountain that had clearly been the victim of wildfire in the recent past; the acrid smell of smoke still hung in the air and dead tree trunks stuck out of the earth like desiccated matchsticks. I turned left when I reached the unpaved Johnson Creek Road, passing a U.S. Forest Service ranger station and a sign indicating I had 25 miles to go until I reached Yellow Pine. I put my rental truck in four-wheel drive; I had been warned that good tires were advised. The road at times took a sharp downward turn with grades of 10 percent or more. Narrow creeks appeared right on the edge of the road, seemingly tempting my truck to dive in. I had a hard time believing a mine could have existed in this remote backcountry. How were supplies delivered? How was ore trucked out? I was used to rural America, having been raised in Maine, but this was an entirely different kind of rural, one that embraced its middle-of-nowhere isolation while hungering for large industry. A small indication of that came every few miles on Johnson Creek Road, where a series of small boxes had been placed, each labeled Emergency Response Kit. I would later learn that they were filled with equipment to clean up oil spills should an industrial truck have an accident. Eventually the road grew to parallel Johnson Creek, and I passed the occasional salmon trap and dam along the way. If there was any confusion about the reason I was headed north, the name of a tributary said it loud and clear: Antimony Creek.

Yellow Pine itself emerged out of a row of pine trees, an open expanse of buildings, some of which seemed abandoned. The restaurant was open and two staff members were outside. I parked my truck and noticed an SUV across the street. That's when Mckinsey Lyon got out and headed my way.[18]

"You made it!" Lyon said, a broad smile across her face. Lyon, who worked for a mining company known as Perpetua Resources Corp., wore hiking gear. A native Idahoan, Lyon explained over lunch how the road that I'd just traveled on wasn't destined to be used once again by mining trucks, as it was in the Second World War. "You're not going to use that road for supplies once this mine opens," she said. The company hoped to build a new road to an old mine site, Lyon explained, just the first phase of its extensive plans for northern Idaho.

Up until 2021, Perpetua had been based in Canada and known as Midas Gold. King Midas, as the legend goes, ruled an area in what is modern-day Turkey and was given the power to turn anything he touched into gold.[19] It's essentially a parable about greed. The company grew to realize that connection might not ingratiate itself with the local community and regulators. Importantly, the name also fixated on a metal—gold—that was not essential for the green energy transition. Evoking Idaho's state motto, Midas became Perpetua Resources in February of that year, moved its headquarters to Boise, and listed its stock on the Nasdaq exchange in New York. The new company pledged to focus itself on developing "the critical resources our country needs for a more secure and sustainable future."[20] It was a shrewd strategy; the company was effectively cloaking its gold plans behind the green energy veneer of antimony, a tactical response to the Biden administration's focus on the green energy transition.

"We have been planning on antimony being a part of this project forever. It just happens to be that we, all of a sudden, got an administration who wanted to talk critical minerals, and we saw it as a viable path," Lyon told me.[21] "So, are we putting that message now a little bit more forward? Yeah, absolutely we are, because that makes this project more urgent." Perpetua's plans for Stibnite offered an interesting detour on America's path toward critical materials production. Here was a company willing to assume the cost and risk of cleaning up a site that the U.S. government itself had polluted and then allowed others to pollute. The company likely would never receive permission to mine just gold in that quiet corner of Idaho; it was the antimony that made all the difference.

Cleanup alone could cost $100 million, a cost that U.S. taxpayers likely weren't going to be asked to pay, given other pressing needs. The entire project was expected as of this writing to cost about $1.3 billion. But the site had at least 6 million ounces of gold, worth more than $11.4 billion based on prices at the end of 2023, and 189 million pounds of antimony, worth about $990 million on the same timeframe.[22] Perpetua's sales pitch was this: Let us fix what happened to this site, and, in return, we want to mine those metals.

We left the restaurant and piled into Lyon's SUV for the 14 mile, hour-long drive to the Stibnite mine site, where Perpetua had been working slowly on cleaning up some acreage. The road was a single lane, and at every mile marker Lyon had to radio to a control tower our location to avoid us encountering someone driving in the other direction, and partly as a proof of life, with some parts of the road on embankments that went down hundreds of feet. The views at times were incredible, with the Idaho expanse splayed out before us, a carpet of green.

Lyon, a mother of three in her early forties, spoke with obvious pride for her state and its economy. Before working for Perpetua, she worked as a state lobbyist and with the state's former Democratic governor. She had, she admitted, been coy to tell friends that she'd taken a job at a mining company when she joined Perpetua, fearful of any blowback. But that changed when she pivoted the company's message to one focused on helping to clean up this old site and produce metals for the green energy transition. In addition to its use in weapons, antimony was being used to make the glass used in solar panels and cell phones; to coat copper wiring in electric vehicles; and in semiconductors. About a year before we met, Perpetua had doubled down on this approach by agreeing to supply antimony to a Bill Gates–backed startup firm known as Ambri that had developed a liquid metal battery technology that required only antimony and salt.[23] The appeal of Ambri's technology is that it could store power from a solar panel or wind turbine far longer than lithium-ion batteries, further democratizing power generation.

"So many of us in the industry now grew up watching *Captain Planet*," Lyon said, referencing the children's TV show from the 1990s that promoted conservation. "We grew up in an age of assumed environmental responsibility. And you also have a company comprised almost entirely of Idahoans. This is our backyard."

It also is the backyard of Indigenous groups that have lived in what is now Idaho for centuries, and many tribes were increasingly opposed to Perpetua's plans. The Nez Perce tribe used to roam across thousands of acres in this part of the North American continent until the pioneers on the Oregon Trail started to come through in the nineteenth century, disturbing their ancestral homelands. Miners soon followed, bringing with them fresh concerns for the Nez Perce and other tribes, who saw their lands shrink during successive treaties with Washington in 1855 and 1863.[24] The Nez Perce, who refer to themselves as the Nimiipuu, place great value on salmon and have invested heavily since the Second World War on efforts to restore fish stocks in the area, as well as in hatcheries and trucks and other equipment to carry salmon over the region's dams to help on the final leg of their 900-mile journey from the Pacific Ocean to the mountains of Idaho. The tribe speaks of the salmon in religious terms in oral histories passed down from generation to generation. "Salmon saved us. When he saved us, he also said that he would give himself to us, and when he gave himself to us, he would lose his voice. And so then we would have to be his voice," said a Nez Perce tribal leader.[25]

Even with Perpetua's offer to clean up the legacy pollution, the Nez

Perce are not convinced. Rather, they worry that the mine will cause even more damage over the next twenty years, an opinion buttressed in part by a U.S. Environmental Protection Agency finding that the mine itself would pollute streams and groundwater with mercury and other heavy metals.[26] Perpetua disputed the charges but changed its mine proposal to include more protective covers for waste rock to limit water contamination. It also shrank the proposed size of the mine by 13 percent and the amount of rock it would hope to mine by 10 percent.[27] Perpetua hoped, it said, that antimony and gold would start flowing once again from the site by 2027.

Despite the Nez Perce's opposition to Perpetua and even the San Carlos Apache's opposition to Resolution, many Indigenous leaders across North America and, indeed, the world have slowly warmed to their communities' role in the green energy transition. It's a strategy that implicitly is centered on the power that comes from being at the table, from knowing that traditional tribal lands often contain reserves of copper, lithium, antimony, and other EV metals—and that by controlling how they are produced tribes can reap not only the financial rewards but safeguard their production.

"Many Indigenous folks are already pressed to the edge, their traditional food sources are at risk, the Industrial Revolution did not serve them well, and now you're asking them to participate in a positive way in the green energy transition by mining their land. You'll of course have a conflict there unless you come up with an equitable solution that works for everyone," Aimee Boulanger, the head of the Initiative for Responsible Mining Assurance, told me.[28]

While we drove around Stibnite, I asked Lyon what she thought about the Nez Perce's claims, especially their concerns that Perpetua could actually make things worse. She was driven, she said, by what she saw as both sides' goal to improve water quality in the area, which could only redound to the salmon's benefit. "There's too much common ground for wanting to see fish passages restored, for wanting to see water quality improved, and for finding opportunities to try to repair the relationship between tribes and industry," she said.

But that was cold comfort for the Nez Perce, as it also had been for the San Carlos Apache in Arizona, the People of Red Mountain in Nevada, and other Indigenous groups.

Lyon and I spent the next several hours driving throughout the Stibnite project. While much of it technically sits on private land, a key portion is controlled by the U.S. government and a public road goes right through it. I could have driven through it myself, but Lyon's explanations helped me better understand what Perpetua aimed to do. Ambitiously, the company planned to redivert the river that had been moved during the Second World War, allowing salmon to spawn once again by swimming through the existing open-pit mine that had been abandoned after the war. It also planned to put a new liner on old waste rock piles, move other waste rock piles, restore hills that had eroded, and clean up other parts of the site poisoned by the leaching of heavy metals. Critics pointed out that Perpetua also planned to dig new open-air mining pits and expand the entire footprint of the existing site, disturbing what is now virgin land. To do all this cleanup, Perpetua had been asking for the federal government to guarantee it couldn't be sued down the road for the past environmental harm for which it was not responsible, a step linked to what's known as Good Samaritan legislation.[29] "We don't want to inherit the legal liability for people that came generations ago," Lyon said. The company also ran the risk of cleaning up the site and then not getting the necessary mining permits.

"There's lost trust between the public and industry. There was also this really important component of wanting to show how serious we are. And we're willing to invest in it as a signal that this is what is the vision that is driving the company," she said.

I shared with Lyon my leaf blower story, about trying to find out just where the metals came from to build the contraption that I had been using to blow leaves off my back patio. "There's just no transparency at all in these supply chains," she said, decrying what she labeled as the "neocolonial economics" of relying on other nations, a term similar to the one that supporters of the Twin Metals project in Minnesota had cited to me. "We really should be thinking longer and harder about where do our things come from. And do I want it enough to accept its production in the United States. Or do I need it enough? Maybe that's the better way to think of it. If we need it, don't we have an obligation to produce it here? And I think the answer is yes."

For Lyon and Perpetua, it was a matter of what she called social justice to mine more domestically, especially to produce minerals under the environmental standards that were now common across the country. I asked Lyon about the tension spreading across the United States, about where and how the country hoped to procure strategic minerals for the green energy transition. She acknowledged that, yes, some places in the country probably were too special to mine. Why dig up a religious site? Or a major recreational zone? But, she kept stressing, why not mine an area that has been mined before such as Stibnite? That might, she hoped, fuel some kind of détente between the mining industry and conservation groups, two groups that for decades had grown accustomed to fighting with each other.

"That can be uncomfortable, because for the mining industry, that means we're going to have to partner with some environmentalists and think about how we do our projects differently. And for the environmental side, it means they're going to have to pick a different enemy. If you want to change the climate, industry has to be part of the solution."

⚡

AS MUCH AS talk about the green energy revolution in 2021 helped Perpetua, its tack truly started to change in 2016 when the financier John Paulson lent the company about $40 million.[30] Based on the terms of the agreement, Paulson would be able to convert the value of the loan into shares in the company at $0.26 per share if he wished to do so anytime during the next seven years. It was an enormously lucrative deal for Paulson, as the company's shares were then trading around $2.40. The deal, which also gave Paulson control of two seats on the company's board of directors, meant that Paulson was effectively getting stock at a steep discount. The reason the company agreed to this could be gleaned from its balance sheet. Perpetua (then known as Midas) at the time had only $4.5 million in the bank; Paulson's loan gave the company a financial lifeline.[31] The financier also began to shape the company's management. Later that year, Laurel Sayer was appointed president, becoming one of the few women to lead a major American mining project.[32] (By 2022, two thirds of the company's six-person executive team comprised women, virtually unheard of in the global mining industry.[33])

Paulson lent even more money in March 2020, bringing the total that he had lent to the company to about $60 million. Shares were trading around $3.63. In August of that year, the company released what is known as a Draft Environmental Impact Statement on its Idaho mining project. The required report was a detailed analysis of how the company thought its mine could affect the region's ecology, including its rivers, mountains, and streams. It was also a big step forward in the project and showed Wall Street that the company was making progress—not just making talk. Paulson pounced, converting his entire loan into stock and instantly becoming the company's largest shareholder, able to chart the company's direction in whichever way he felt best. He also vowed not to sell the stock, no matter how high (or, implicitly, low) it went.[34]

Interestingly, the announcement of the stock conversion did not mention the green energy transition, even though by 2020 it was well under way. Antimony was listed as a mineral "essential to the economic and national security of the U.S.," but not as something key for solar panels, wind turbines, and EV batteries. For Paulson, it was all about gold.[35]

Paulson, a native of Queens, New York, built his hedge fund in the late 1990s and early 2000s after working at Bear Stearns. Around 2006, he noticed some troubling macroeconomic data around U.S. housing prices and subprime mortgages. His next step, in which he took a complex bet against an index that tracked the strength (or weakness) of the subprime-mortgage market, was expertly chronicled by Gregory Zuckerman in *The Greatest Trade Ever*. By 2007, Paulson's funds had turned that bet into $15 billion, with at least $3 billion of that estimated to be his personal cut.[36] It was widely considered the most lucrative bet in the history in investing.[37] Paulson then turned to gold by following the housing bet with a bet that gold prices would jump. They did, and in 2010 Paulson was estimated to have pulled in $5 billion, making his firm one of the largest hedge funds on Wall Street.[38]

Some of Paulson's future bets on gold stumbled, and he has had ill-timed investments in other sectors, notably pharmaceuticals, but his earlier wins in gold had made him something of a bull about the metal. The gold sector at that time was filled with overpaid executives who had little sense for strategy. Many paid themselves handsomely and spent corporate funds with abandon, a strategy that Paulson himself began to publicly call out.

In 2017, less than a year after he had taken the stake in Perpetua, Paulson initiated what has since become known as a "war" on poor gold mining returns. Investors, according to this plan of attack, should get more directly involved in the strategy of gold mining companies they invest in; they should speak out against mergers that could waste money; and they should forcefully oppose high executive compensation.[39] Pointedly, Paulson held up his recent investments in Perpetua as examples the rest of the mining industry should emulate.[40]

Given this stance, I was curious what Paulson thought of the broader tension over critical minerals projects creeping across the United States. Perpetua had consciously chosen to brand its Idaho mine as key to the country's green future—a strategy that seemingly had Paulson's blessing. To find out, I visited the investor's Manhattan offices. Located on Sixth Avenue, a few blocks from Times Square, Paulson's offices are adorned with watercolor paintings from the twentieth-century American artist Alexander Calder, a whimsical assortment of reds and blues and yellows strewn into various shapes. Marcelo Kim had been working among the art and with Paulson since 2009; in 2016, after Paulson extended Perpetua the loan, it was Kim who became its chairman. By that point, the proposed Stibnite mine had been trying for six years to win regulatory approval, but it had come nowhere close to succeeding, a timeline that clearly irked Kim: "The challenge with the U.S. is permitting. It's an antiquated process with no timeline to it."[41]

Kim, who wore a crisp white shirt with striped dress pants, stressed many of what he considered the project's positives: It was a site that had already seen mining, known in the industry as a brownfield project; it had a large gold deposit, a plus for Paulson; it would be powered by hydropower-generated electricity, reducing carbon emissions; and it would produce antimony for America's green energy revolution even if China flooded the market, with the concurrent gold production ensuring that antimony could be mined profitably. And the site would get cleaned up. "We're offering to be part of the solution. Government isn't," he said. "No one yet has cleaned up this site. There's a lot of talk, but no action."

It was a frustrating roadblock for Kim, Paulson, and their team, the inability to even feel their way through the dark of the U.S. permitting process. Despite the money already invested, Perpetua had no clue when it would receive approval (or rejection) for its mining permit application. Trump's Bureau of Land Management had promised an answer within two years of application. Yet Biden took a more open-ended approach once he took office. "Why are there so many departments? It's just so complicated," Kim said.

Without my prompting, Kim brought up actions the Biden administration had taken against proposed U.S. mines from other international mining companies, including Antofagasta's Twin Metals project and Glencore's PolyMet project, both in Minnesota. "Why is the U.S. saying no to all of the world's major mining companies? The political class is not looking at the details of all these important projects."

For all of Kim's points about permitting, he was right about one thing: Perpetua and Paulson had a leg up specifically because the Stibnite area had been mined before. And parts of the federal government seemed to acknowledge that advantage. Late in 2022 the Pentagon pivoted back to Idaho and gave Perpetua nearly $25 million to help the company complete its permitting process. The funds, which were drawn from a bill passed by Congress to help Ukraine repel Russia's ongoing invasion, were part of the Pentagon's mission, officials said, "to restore domestic industrial capabilities essential to the national defense by enabling the warfighter." Perpetua, the Pentagon added, would help "increase the resilience of our critical mineral supply chains while deterring adversarial aggression."[42] The company just needed other parts of the government—the parts that issued permits—to agree with the Pentagon.

⚡

AS WE DROVE around the middle of nowhere, Idaho, my mind couldn't help but draw parallels to Alaska, the largest state and one that holds buried beneath its soil huge reserves of oil, natural gas, copper, gold, and other minerals. It also is replete with wildlife that supports a diverse economy of subsistence fishers, many of whom belong to the region's Inuit. Each year, more than 30 million adult sockeye salmon spawn in a region about 250 miles southwest of Anchorage, the state's largest city. That region also contains one of the largest deposits of copper and gold in the world—the Pebble mining project—with more than 80 billion pounds of copper, 107 million ounces of gold, and other metals, including 5.6 billion pounds of molybdenum buried under wetlands and marshlands.[43] While gold would have largely ornamental value, the copper and to a lesser extent the molybdenum would increasingly be needed as the world went green.

Unlike Perpetua's project, though, Pebble is in a wilderness that has never been touched before. And plans to mine it have long drawn outcry from many throughout the state and region concerned that any chemical spills or leaks from the mine would destroy not only the state's land, but the waters of Bristol Bay, a key area for fishers.

The deposit was first discovered in 1987, and by 2001 a Canada-based company known as Northern Dynasty Minerals Ltd. had bought the rights to develop it. Over the next several years, Northern Dynasty conducted more geological tests and by 2007 it had drawn major investments from Rio Tinto and Anglo American, two of the world's largest mining companies.[44] That timing seemed fortuitous for Rio and Anglo, especially as copper demand was seen as on the rise. Yet from the beginning the project faced strong opposition from Alaska's powerful fishing industry, which undergirds much of the state's GDP. Salmon fishing in 2019 contributed nearly $310 million to the state's economy.[45] "If there's damage to the watershed and the fisheries, then it would be devastating to our identity as indigenous people," said an official with United Tribes of Bristol Bay, a group representing fifteen of the area's federally recognized Indigenous communities.[46]

The project divided the state in uneven ways. Republicans were not uniformly for the mine. Indeed, Senator Ted Stevens, once a powerful senior Republican in the U.S. Senate, opposed the project, which aimed to dig an open pit that would be 2 miles wide and 1,700 feet deep. A natural gas pipeline and power plant would need to be built to operate the mine site.[47] (Sarah Palin, the state's governor at the time, quietly supported it behind the scenes.[48]) It was unusual for a Republican to oppose an extractive project, but Pebble proved to be the exception, no matter how much the world needed copper. Still, the developers sought to curry favor with the locals. Anglo American launched a PR campaign with large billboards near Anchorage that declared: COEXISTENCE. MINING AND FISH CAN LIVE TOGETHER.[49]

And yet the U.S. Environmental Protection Agency found in 2012 that the Pebble project likely would destroy at least 55 miles of streams and 2,500 acres of wetlands in the region. Additionally, the agency worried about the project's planned use of tailings dams in a state that often had earthquakes.[50] What if one of the earthquakes damaged the tailings facility and caused some toxic metals to leach into Bristol Bay? That was the worry from many in the state's Indigenous and fishing communities. Most public comments sent to the EPA about the project opposed it.[51]

Given the widespread opposition to the project and the equally widespread need for copper, *National Geographic* declared the Pebble Mine "the Gettysburg of natural resource conflicts in Alaska."[52] Anglo American walked away from the project in 2013 despite having spent $541 million. The company said it would devote its time and money to "projects with the highest value and lowest risk," a stinging rebuke.[53]

President Obama's administration halted the entire project in 2014 when it stopped the Army Corps of Engineers from issuing wetlands permits, citing concerns for the state's fishing industry and ecology. Two months later, Rio Tinto also walked away from the project and donated its 19 percent stake to two Alaskan charities. That is to say, Rio thought it was better to give away its investment and did not think it could find a buyer, a startling admission about the project's viability.

In a move that mirrored what happened in Minnesota's Twin Metals, Trump officials took steps to reverse Obama in 2017. They settled several lawsuits that the EPA had filed against the mine and promised that the project would receive a fair hearing.[54] In 2019, Trump officials said they would restart the regulatory review process for the project.[55] By July 2020, as the coronavirus pandemic raged and the U.S. presidential election season was in full swing, Trump officials said they were on the verge of approving the project, calling it vital for the nation's production of copper. The mine would certainly harm part of the state's ecology, officials noted, but the company had tried to find the least damaging option.[56] Trump also began looking for more minerals the United States could get its hands on, at one point proposing to buy the island of Greenland from Denmark.[57]

Then things went sideways.

On August 4, 2020, Nick Ayers tweeted that he hoped President Trump would order the EPA to block the Pebble project. Ayers, who had served as Vice President Mike Pence's chief of staff before resigning in 2018, worried that "a Canadian company will unnecessarily mine the USA's greatest fishery at a severe cost." A few hours later, Donald Trump Jr.—the president's son—retweeted Ayers, saying that "the headwaters of Bristol Bay and the surrounding fishery are too unique and fragile to take any chances with."[58]

A few days later, at a fundraiser in New York's tony Bridgehampton enclave, Trump Jr. approached his father to make a direct plea to kill Pebble. Joined by Andrew Sabin, who had grown enormously wealthy in the metals refining business, the pair made the case that the mine project should be stopped dead in its tracks and that Alaska was not the place to dig up billions of tonnes of dirt. The president nodded but made no promises. "This mine makes no sense," Sabin told Trump. "With the Pebble mine, there's no way you could clean up the damage. The fish would be gone forever."[59]

Sabin and Trump Jr. reminded the president that he had just signed the Great American Outdoors Act, which funded conservation efforts on public lands. "At some point, they'll have to start thinking about the Republican Party and all of the incredible things we've done on conservation and many other fronts," Trump said when signing the bill.[60] If Trump really believed in the letter and spirit of the legislation he'd just signed, his son and Sabin stressed, he would stop Pebble.

Perhaps the greatest weapon the anti-Pebble forces used to convince the president, though, came from one of Trump's favorite TV channels: Fox News. On August 14, Tucker Carlson aired a five-minute segment that warned the Pebble project would cause significant damage to Alaska's fishing industry. "Suddenly you are seeing a number of Republicans, including some prominent Republicans, including some very conservative ones, saying, 'Hold on a moment, maybe Pebble Mine is not a good idea, maybe you should do whatever you can not to despoil nature, and maybe not all environmentalism is about climate,'" Carlson told his millions of viewers, including the forty-fifth president.[61] It wasn't altruistic, though: Carlson and for that matter Trump Jr. enjoyed fishing and hunting in Alaska's Bristol Bay region.[62]

Trump got Fox's message, despite Northern Dynasty and Pebble launching an advertising campaign targeted at the president in the middle of the Republican National Convention. On August 24—ten days after Carlson's broadcast—the Army Corps of Engineers said it was impossible to permit the mine under the Clean Water Act because it would "likely result in significant degradation of the environment and would likely result in significant adverse effects on the aquatic system or human environment."[63] The state's two powerful Republican senators, Lisa Murkowski and Dan Sullivan, abandoned their support for the project.[64] Shares in Northern Dynasty fell by more than 40 percent. One prominent Wall Street analyst said he no longer was confident in how much Northern Dynasty was worth as a company. (Morgan Stanley had sold its shares in Northern Dynasty a few months prior.)[65]

The company was shocked, not least because it had already spent $600 million on the project and thought it had made adequate concessions to protect Alaska's ecology, including promising not to use cyanide in the watershed.[66] "We're sitting there going, like, WTF," Ron Thiessen, Northern Dynasty's chief executive, told me.[67] "There was close to half a billion dollars lost" of the company's market value the day the Army Corps made its announcement.

Not only was Trump no longer supporting the Pebble project, but his rival in the 2020 presidential election had never supported it. Late in 2022, the EPA was advised to permanently block the project.[68] Conservationists also began buying up land around the project site in a bid to stop the company from building a needed access road.[69] The people of Alaska had spoken. A major deposit of copper, a metal that will define the green energy transition, would not be developed.

⚡

DRIVING ON THE dirt back roads of northern Idaho, the sheer remoteness of this once abandoned mine struck home to me as the right rear tire of my rental truck started to deflate. A warning alarm on the dashboard indicated the PSI was slowly decreasing in the tire. From 30 (like the other four tires) to 25, then 20, then 15, then 10, then 5.

At 5 PSI, I pulled over and accepted the reality that I would have to change this tire by myself. Thankfully, Mckinsey Lyon had stayed back when we left each other. She pulled up a few minutes later. There, on that dusty, dirt-crusted road, we changed the tire and joked about the frustration of us doing this alone away from what we all consider to be the modern conveniences of our everyday life. There was no calling AAA or other roadside assistance. I couldn't help wondering if the blown tire was a metaphor for the struggle to resuscitate a mine in this rural area.

The dangers of operating in such a remote place were even more pointedly brought home by an incident earlier that day. Twin brothers Mark and Daniel Harro had taken off in a small airplane from the Johnson Creek Airport after camping in Idaho's backcountry, the same area holding Perpetua's proposed mine. In broad daylight, with minimal winds and warm temperatures, the two-seater plane had crashed in a nearby stream. The brothers were killed, though their dog survived.[70] They took off from the same airport Perpetua hopes to use if its mine opens.

CHAPTER NINE

Lonely Are the Brave

By the time Patrick Donnelly arrived at Rhyolite Ridge late on the afternoon of September 12, 2020, it was too late. Thousands of Tiehm's buckwheat, a species found nowhere else on the planet, had fallen victim to an unknown assailant. Stems and pistils yanked from their roots lay fallow and lifeless amid the lithium-rich volcanic soil. "I was absolutely devastated when I discovered this annihilation of these beautiful little wildflowers," said Donnelly, who worked with the Center for Biological Diversity, a staunch environmental group that advocates for rare slivers of the plant and animal kingdoms. The extirpation appeared, Donnelly said, to be a "premeditated, somewhat organized, large-scale operation aimed at wiping out one of the rarest plants on Earth."[1] He spent that Saturday surveying the damage to one small cluster of the flowers, and then returned the next day to inspect the rest of Rhyolite Ridge, chronicling the massacre of hundreds more dead buckwheat.[2]

Donnelly mourned the loss as one would mourn a fellow human, a sign, perhaps, of how much he had anthropomorphized the plant. The bond started to form in June 2018, when an employee at the U.S. Department of the Interior's Bureau of Land Management—the federal agency tasked with overseeing most of the nation's federally owned lands—contacted the Center for Biological Diversity.[3] It was an unusual outreach for many reasons, not the least of which is that the Bureau of Land Management and the Center for Biological Diversity are often at odds in legal cases. Frequently, the CBD goes to bat for a fish or frog or other creature that could be harmed by something the government did or wants to do with its land.

Daniel Patterson, who joined BLM as an environmental protection specialist in 2015,[4] suggested that Donnelly file a Freedom of Information Act request for information about a rare flower known as Tiehm's buckwheat. The flower had been considered a "sensitive species" by BLM for years, reflecting the government's concern that it needed extra attention and protection. Tiehm's buckwheat also was known as a prolific seed producer and thus a great source of food for small mammals and pollinating insects and birds.[5] The FOIA request should seek, Patterson suggested, information about how that flower could be affected by the plans of a small Australia-based mining company to extract lithium and boron from Rhyolite Ridge, the remote hill in the Silver Peak Range near Nevada's border with California.

Donnelly had driven to Rhyolite Ridge not long after Patterson's 2018 tip and fell in love with Tiehm's buckwheat. "The flowers were blooming, and I got hooked," Donnelly recalled. "It's a very charismatic plant when it's flowering."[6]

Patterson also suggested that Donnelly inquire how Doug Furtado, who ran BLM's Battle Mountain District office and was responsible for permit reviews in the area, hoped to care for Tiehm's buckwheat. It was a provocative line of inquiry because very few outside of that local BLM office, Jerry Tiehm and his botany colleagues at the University of Nevada, Reno, and ioneer even knew Tiehm's buckwheat existed, let alone was at risk. Patterson was essentially contending that BLM, which at that time was overseen by President Donald Trump, was too chummy with the very industries it was meant to police, and that public lands suffered consequently.

Red flags went off at the Bureau of Land Management when Donnelly filed his FOIA request. Furtado, logically, assumed that Patterson had prodded Donnelly to dig into the potential fate of Tiehm's buckwheat. Who else could have tipped off the environmental group? Patterson was put on a five-day paid administrative leave. Ostensibly, the reason for the suspension was that Patterson had argued with a coworker, though Patterson claimed it was because he had tipped

Donnelly off. Patterson further alleged he was subjected to "harsh retaliation" that went beyond the suspensions.[7]

In October 2019, Patterson filed a whistleblower's lawsuit against BLM. "As an Environmental Protection Specialist, Mr. Patterson's professional responsibilities are in conflict with the objectives of District Manager Furtado," he alleged in a thirteen-page court filing.[8] Patterson further claimed there was a "pervasive pattern of lawlessness" at BLM and that, among other things, the agency routinely fast-tracked proposed mining projects without giving adequate or serious consideration to how they could affect the environment. Left unsaid in the filing until much later was that Patterson himself had previously worked for the CBD, a fact that seemed to implicitly set up an antagonistic relationship with his superiors at BLM.[9] (Patterson's colorful career also included time working for an Arizona labor union, the U.S. Postal Service, the fire department in Las Vegas, and a stint in Arizona's House of Representatives.) "I believe my job is to provide public information to the public," Patterson told a Nevada news website. "We have public ownership of natural resources and public land. I work for the public."[10]

By April 2020, Patterson had reached a settlement with BLM and left the agency.[11] He worked for a fire department for a few months during the coronavirus pandemic and in 2022 was an independent, write-in candidate for a seat in Nevada's state senate. (He did not win.) While Furtado remained at his BLM post and continued to oversee ioneer's project, even after Joe Biden moved into the White House, the metaphorical cat was out of the bag. CBD, and Donnelly especially, intended to learn as much as they could about Tiehm's buckwheat and, if possible, save it.

Donnelly's FOIA request had been, surprisingly, honored promptly. In November 2018, five months after Patterson's tip, he and the Center for Biological Diversity received 1,291 pages from the Bureau of Land Management related to Tiehm's buckwheat. The material was somewhat helpful, Donnelly recalled, but the real juice came from visiting government offices in person to see records that had not been digitized, especially filings related to ioneer's approval to explore for lithium on Rhyolite Ridge in five-acre increments. A lot of damage could be done to buckwheat, Donnelly thought, in five-acre increments.[12]

Three days after Patterson filed his whistleblower lawsuit in 2019, Donnelly and the CBD filed an emergency petition asking the U.S. Fish and Wildlife Service to list Tiehm's buckwheat as an endangered species.[13] "There's a lot of plants that are endangered. There are very few facing existential extinction factors that could wipe them off the face of the Earth," Donnelly recalled.[14] The company's exploration activity, which included drilling holes to test rock samples, posed an "immediate threat" to the flower's survival, Donnelly and the Center for Biological Diversity argued.[15] Only about 22,500 of the plants existed, strewn across six sites in and around Rhyolite Ridge because—ironically—they seemed to thrive in the area's lithium-rich soil.[16] Tiehm's buckwheat, it seemed, loved lithium just as much as ioneer did. And because of that, Donnelly said, it needed to be declared endangered and given all the protections that label would afford it under U.S. law. "We urge the [government] to propose Tiehm's buckwheat for listing as endangered and to designate critical habitat to ensure that it survives for future generations," Donnelly wrote.[17]

Just weeks later, in a second offensive against the company, the Center for Biological Diversity went to court and argued that the Trump administration was ignoring laws designed to protect rare plants. By giving ioneer permission to explore more than five acres of Rhyolite Ridge without giving the public a chance to comment, especially while the endangered species request was under review, Trump was breaking the law, the suit claimed. "It's wrong for the BLM to allow mining companies to destroy its habitat while other agencies are deciding whether to list the flower as endangered. We won't let it be erased from the planet for a quick buck."[18] Even if, it seemed, that "quick buck" would help produce a metal key to helping stop climate change.

Nor was ioneer the first to undertake exploratory drilling in the area. Two mine shafts at Rhyolite Ridge date back to the 1890s, though the land sat largely undisturbed until a chemical company started drilling in 1962, followed by a borax company in 1987, and then a gold miner around 2010. By 2019, ioneer had dug nearly 50,000 feet of core samples out of Rhyolite Ridge, largely to map the underground lithium deposit and groundwater.[19]

For its part, ioneer moved forward. It was not technically part of the lawsuit. Later in 2019, the company issued more stock[20] with the help of the banking giant Goldman Sachs in order to fund what's known as a Definitive Feasibility Study, a report for investors on the economics of their entire project.[21] It also agreed to sell half of the boron it produced from Rhyolite Ridge to a Chinese company once the mine was up and running. Boron, which can be used to make detergents and other household goods, was found in large concentrations at Rhyolite Ridge alongside lithium, giving the project's economics a natural hedge should prices for either commodity ebb or flow in the future.[22]

By January 2020, it became clear that the situation could devolve quickly for ioneer, which intervened in the suit and promised to take extra precautions to avoid Tiehm's buckwheat at the site. One of those precautions involved a promise to use handheld equipment, rather than industrial machinery, to repair any damage from exploration that occurred within 30 feet of any groups of the plants.[23] But, ultimately, could the lithium be extracted while at the same time the flowers were preserved? The company said yes. Donnelly said he wasn't so sure, vowing to stop the full mine from opening were even one flower harmed.[24]

In April 2020, ioneer released its Definitive Feasibility Study and projected that its Rhyolite Ridge project would not only make money, but that it would be wildly profitable. The company expected its cost to produce lithium to be about $2,510 per tonne, far below the industry average at that time of $7,000 per tonne. (By the end of 2022, lithium prices had jumped to $62,500 per tonne.[25]) Construction would begin in 2021 and the mine would be running by 2023, the company said. Tesla's massive Gigafactory was only a short drive away from Rhyolite Ridge, the company eagerly noted (though it did not have any supply agreements with the automaker). The study showed, ioneer's Calaway summarized, that "our Nevada project is poised to be one of the biggest, low-cost players in the lithium industry."[26] There was enough lithium at Rhyolite Ridge, the company said, to make nearly 400,000 electric vehicles each year for at least thirty years.[27]

It was an upbeat outlook despite the early onslaught of the coronavirus pandemic, which was trapping many of the company's investors and executives at their home base in Australia. Calaway, who was chairman of the company's board, not an employee, soon found himself the most senior ioneer-linked person physically in the United States. By July 2020, Calaway was essentially running ioneer's Rhyolite Ridge development project.[28]

Things were moving in ioneer's favor by the next month. The Bureau of Land Management had accepted the company's plan of operations, a technical, bureaucratic step that advanced the permitting process. Two years of studies had gone into that approval, and all the necessary permits were expected within a year.[29]

And then it happened.

During what he described as a routine visit to Rhyolite Ridge in September 2020, Donnelly discovered the mass extirpation of thousands of Tiehm's buckwheat. He and a colleague estimated that 18,646 had been destroyed. The flowers appeared to have been dug up by small shovels; in some cases, all that was left was a hole in the ground. Elsewhere part of the plant or its roots remained. A large number of footprints hinted that a sizable group of people had been at the site. "The lack of a large amount of uprooted biomass makes very clear that the perpetrators took the majority of the uprooted plants offsite," he later told regulators, referring to it as a "poaching incident."[30]

Donnelly neither at that time nor since has directly accused Calaway or anyone else at ioneer of killing the plants, but he has heavily implied a link.

"Some monster," Donnelly said, "destroyed thousands of these irreplaceable flowering plants."[31] To a reporter, Donnelly alleged that the perpetrators used GPS and maps to find the flowers, that the flowers' destruction was the result of a sophisticated "multi-stage, multi-person effort."[32]

The U.S. federal government, Donnelly pleaded, should immediately declare Tiehm's buckwheat an endangered species and pause ioneer's lithium permitting review until it was clear whether the remaining flowers would survive. "We await your prompt action," he wrote to government officials.[33]

For his part, Calaway was incensed, not least because of the implication that he or someone at ioneer had gone out to Rhyolite Ridge in the middle of the night to kill a bunch of plants.

"It's one hundred percent clear that this wasn't done by anybody running out there with shovels because, first of all, why would anybody do that?" Calaway said.[34] The company showed evidence that University of Nevada, Reno, researchers had visited the site earlier that month and knew that some flowers had died. Rodents, the university staff surmised, had likely gnawed away at the flowers' roots to find moisture amid the state's drought. State officials agreed, saying they found no evidence that humans were involved.[35] The university staff's theory was substantiated two months later by the U.S. Fish and Wildlife Service, which used DNA analysis to study the damaged Tiehm's buckwheat roots and, based on that study as well as animal droppings nearby, agreed that ground squirrels were the most likely culprits. There already was a well-known scurry in the area of white-tailed antelope ground squirrels that liked to burrow into the ground and gnaw on roots.[36] Rodents, not ioneer, murdered the Tiehm's buckwheat, the government officially ruled.[37]

"Regardless of the cause of the recent loss of *E. tiehmii* plants, we are very concerned about this event and how it will affect the viability of the species," the Fish and Wildlife Service wrote to the Center for Biological Diversity a month after the flowers were destroyed.[38]

Amid the initial furor over the plant's destruction, Joe Biden was elected. The new president-elect's campaign had quietly promised miners that he would support domestic mining.[39] (Calaway, a staunch Democrat, had donated money to Biden's campaign.) Publicly, Biden also had vowed stricter environmental regulations. (Donnelly, also a Democrat, did not donate to Biden, but had donated to several left-leaning advocacy groups during the 2020 campaign.[40]) The case of Tiehm's buckwheat posed a quandary. What mattered more to the incoming administration: conservation or green energy? The flower, Donnelly declared, "is a symbol of our times."[41]

More lithium would be needed to achieve Biden's ambitious green energy goals, that much was clear. The new president vowed to convert the entire U.S. government fleet of about 640,000 vehicles to run on electricity, a plan that one think tank estimated would require a twelvefold jump in U.S. lithium output by 2030.[42] Reuters reported that Biden was considering approval of mines that produce EV metals under existing environmental laws, rather than pushing for them to be tightened, as he wanted for the coal sector.

The day Biden was elected, the U.S. Fish and Wildlife Service told ioneer it wanted to work with the company to determine "how best to protect and conserve Tiehm's buckwheat throughout the life of the mining operation."[43] But once in office, the Biden administration's approach to ioneer's project proved confusing at best. In July 2021, the new administration said it was considering whether to declare that Tiehm's buckwheat was an endangered species. (The decision, which ioneer said was based on "shallow, conclusory, and incomplete" data,[44] went out for public comment and was finalized at the end of 2022.[45]) The Fish and Wildlife Service found that the mine and the damage caused by the rodents would destroy at least 70 percent of the flowers. Transplanting the flowers was also likely to fail, ironically because of the flowers' love for the lithium-rich soil.[46] It was a blow to the company, which had expected to begin construction on its mine by that year. Instead, it was now trying to stave off the extinction of a rare plant while at the same time salvage its permitting process, which was put on hold by the Bureau of Land Management while the Fish and Wildlife Service considered the endangered species listing.[47] Exasperated, Calaway and ioneer pointed out that the flower likely *would* die if climate change continued unabated. They had begun investing millions of dollars to hire full-time botanists, rent greenhouse space, and study soil composition, none of which was a traditional investment for mining companies. "We are prepared to do whatever is necessary to make this mine coexist with Tiehm's buckwheat," Calaway said.[48]

While one Biden-controlled agency was debating whether to declare Tiehm's buckwheat endangered, another was considering whether to lend hundreds of millions of dollars to the company. In December 2021, ioneer said its application for a loan from a U.S. Department of Energy program that Tesla had famously used a decade prior was moving to the third of four review stages.[49] It was a remarkable development given that another U.S. government agency was also considering a step that could kill the entire mine. Washington's left hand, it seemed, did not know what its right hand was doing, much as in the case of Lithium Americas' Thacker Pass mine in Nevada and the Resolution copper project in Arizona.

Adding to the melee of excitement and tension stemming from the federal government's mixed reaction was a deal that ioneer struck with the South Africa–based mining company Sibanye-Stillwater in September. Sibanye-Stillwater would pay ioneer $490 million for a 50 percent stake in the Rhyolite Ridge project, but only if the company got its permits. Which meant only if Tiehm's buckwheat didn't go extinct.[50]

That same month, Calaway met at the Cosmopolitan hotel in Las Vegas with representatives of Ford Motor Co., hoping to convince the automaker to buy ioneer's lithium. Earlier that year Calaway had sold a small portion of ioneer's planned lithium production to a South Korean company[51] and was hoping that Ford, which aimed to be selling 2 million EVs each year by 2026, would bite.[52] Bill Ford, the company's chairman, had said as far back as 2019 that the automaker was hunting for lithium deals.[53] The automaker's staff peppered Calaway with questions about Tiehm's buckwheat. Ford had previously committed itself to follow IRMA standards, which could prevent any agreement with ioneer. Calaway left the meeting without a deal.

As 2021 bled into 2022, Biden's administration seemed to be warming toward approving more mines, giving ioneer and its peers hope. Jennifer Granholm, the U.S. energy secretary, told a conference of energy executives and investors: "It takes forever to get a new permit. How crazy is that?" The crowd burst into ecstatic applause.[54] The secretary herself was an EV enthusiast and drove a Chevrolet Bolt that she leased. "It's the best car I've ever had," she said.[55]

Biden made his first public comments as president about the mining sector at the beginning of that year, saying more U.S. lithium production was needed to wean the country off foreign supplies. "We can't build a future that's made in America if we ourselves are dependent on China for the materials that power the products of today and tomorrow," he said. Biden also gave a grant to an experimental lithium company in

Southern California controlled by Warren Buffett, a step that would come back to haunt the president.[56]

Not long after, though, Ford reached out to Calaway. The auto giant was interested in buying lithium. Was Calaway still interested in selling?

"Yes!" he replied, but only if Ford signed what's known as a binding offtake, a contractual obligation that differed from the nonbinding offtake that too often was de rigueur in the mining industry. The deal, announced in July 2022, promised Ford enough lithium to build 175,000 electric vehicles annually once Calaway started shipping the metal in 2025. At even conservative estimates for lithium prices, the five-year deal alone was worth $800 million to ioneer.[57] (Ford had also signed a supply deal with a direct lithium-extraction project in Argentina using technology from a Bill Gates–backed startup.[58])

In the end, Ford had not been concerned enough about Tiehm's buckwheat to walk away. Helping to boost lithium production inside the United States was a key attraction, Ford said.[59] I asked Calaway how he sold the project's lithium to one of the world's largest companies despite the regulatory uncertainty. "We're not going to touch the buckwheat," Calaway replied.[60]

Donnelly, though, thought Ford was being too cavalier. He issued a statement that went right for ioneer's jugular: "Ford just bought extinction along with ioneer's lithium and needs to rethink this poor decision. There are many other lithium sources that won't end up killing off a species. Electric vehicles don't need to come at the cost of extinction."[61]

It was a shot across the bow that clearly hearkened back to Donnelly's strong implication after the extirpation in 2020 that Calaway may have had something to do with the demise of thousands of plants. It irked Calaway and ioneer's senior leadership. Why would they destroy a group of flowers when that could scuttle their chance to sell to Ford or other automakers? Even though Calaway and Donnelly had never met, or perhaps because they hadn't, the animus festered. Calaway couldn't understand why anyone would question his motives. He was trying to produce lithium to save the planet, he told himself. Publicly, he was promising the mine could safely operate and the flower could be saved. Donnelly firmly believed that the choice for our planet isn't so black-and-white, that the loss of any one species is too much. Neither side could see the veracity of the other's argument. And it was getting personal.

"That Patrick Donnelly is a son of a bitch," Calaway said. "And you can quote me."

⚡

I HAD INTERVIEWED Patrick Donnelly for years via telephone but never had met him in person until one dusty, warm afternoon in August 2022. My day started in Reno, Nevada, with a four-hour drive south through the state's mining past—through Mineral County, past abandoned gold and gravel mines, at elevations that ranged from 4,000 to 6,130 feet, through sagebrush fields and barren desert plains that evoked the sheer, lonely wonder of the U.S. West—to Silver Peak, home to what was the only existing lithium mine in the United States. Owned by Albemarle, it had been passed between successor companies since first opening in the 1960s.

Silver Peak is in the middle of nowhere, an outpost akin to something from the Mad Max films. Abandoned trucks and sedans were strewn on the sides of roads in fields leading to the town's core, which had an abandoned post office and playground, as well as a green-colored Albemarle office and industrial plant atop a small hill. The town had no gasoline station (or EV chargers), though it had a small store that doubled as the local saloon, and an RV park. Dozens of buildings, including the former Shifting Sands cantina, were boarded up and left to wither in the desert sun. Weeds crept through the community basketball and tennis courts. The children's playground was caked in dirt. A stranded car on the roadside held aloft a sign ordering: 25 MPH. SLOW THE FUCK DOWN! About two hundred called the town home. Plywood signs, spray-painted in orange and black, pointed the way to Las Vegas.

Despite being the only U.S. source of a metal that was fast rising in demand, Silver Peak had clearly not seen any benefit. Out past the center of town sat hundreds of acres of flat desert expanse, which Albemarle has been using as evaporation ponds to filter lithium from brine it pumped out from reservoirs under the Nevada landscape.

I waited for Donnelly at what could be described as a kind of five-way dirt intersection near the Albemarle offices. He arrived after a few minutes in a white SUV, got out, and shook my hand, which was coated in sunscreen from having lathered too much on my pale skin.

"We should get going," he said, nodding to the Albemarle offices nearby. "I'm not very popular in this town."

Due to the pandemic and concerns about coronavirus—Donnelly had COVID at least twice—we drove separately away from Silver Peak and into the mountains for the 20 miles to Rhyolite Ridge. The road seemed to continue to climb, making me thankful I had arranged to rent a pickup truck for the adventure; a sedan wouldn't have cut it. As we rose to an elevation of 7,100 feet, we grew closer to Piper Peak, which had purple and red hues baked into its summit in the distance.

We kept driving through a slot canyon, with cragged rocks bursting forth from the earth like broken fingers, past three random cows and what looked to be their makeshift corral. Then, I saw it. As we came down a hill and into a small valley, I noticed a mound in the distance with a covering of what appeared to be a white ash-colored substance. I could immediately understand why it had caught Jerry Tiehm's attention so many years prior. We pulled off the road and parked near that white hill, which was surrounded by fencing installed by the Bureau of Land Management. We got out of our vehicles and Donnelly started to show me around the site, past the gates and up a small hill. I had never seen Tiehm's buckwheat in person and was eager.

"Be careful where you walk," he instructed, explaining that the flower goes dormant in periods of high heat, which the area was then experiencing. We came across a small, wilted thing that looked barely indistinguishable from a dead houseplant. Tiehm's buckwheat was very much alive, though, waiting for moisture that would come in the cooler, rainy season, and soaking up the lithium and boron mixture in the interim. Donnelly's obsession with this plant at the expense of all else had reminded me of another ardent conservationist, albeit one from years earlier.

⚡

EDWARD ABBEY WAS, to put it mildly, rough around the edges. He reportedly spent two years as a soldier in the aftermath of the Second World War and received several promotions, but then was demoted twice for refusing to salute.[62] He abjured conventional niceties and routinely reached for the metaphorical jugular to prove his point, which often involved some defense of the U.S. West and its natural terrain. He was known to toss beer cans from his car onto a landscape because, in his estimation, the landscape had already been ruined by the road he was driving on. If Americans didn't respect nature and approved of roads, could they seriously mind a little trash?[63]

He once famously quipped: "If wilderness is outlawed, only outlaws can save wilderness." Importantly for posterity, he was a prolific writer whose fiction and nonfiction inspired many. He was fascinated by the idea of a singular person battling forces beyond his grasp or conception. His novel *The Brave Cowboy* was turned into the 1962 film *Lonely Are the Brave*, starring Kirk Douglas as a ranch worker who eschewed the rapid technological changes sweeping the country and endangering his way of life. It was classic Abbey, and a way for him to underscore his concern for what he thought the postwar American way of life was doing not only to the country but to the environment itself.

In 1982, he told a local Arizona TV station:

> So I hope we can save what's left of . . . the United States by legal, political means and I still think we can. I still vote in elections . . . even though there doesn't seem to be much to vote for or against, when there's not much choice. I think if enough people get sufficiently concerned, why, we can still make changes . . . needed changes in this country by political methods . . . God, I hope so.[64]

Years later, Patrick Donnelly would stumble upon Abbey's books when he was backpacking through the U.S. West, finding inspiration in the words that called for any and all means to preserve and protect the unadulterated land from the encroaching American experiment. Abbey's words had a profound effect on the young Donnelly, who as a child moved frequently with his parents as they served in ministry at Episcopal churches across the U.S. East Coast.

At twenty, Donnelly moved west and never looked back. "When I came to the West, I realized it was my place, and more particularly, the desert," he said. He took odd jobs leading trail crews and backpacking expeditions, with open skies and scenic vistas as his office. He took a job at the U.S. Bureau of Land Management as a ranger in California, and after that worked as a field instructor in Wyoming for an outdoor leadership school. A rare wet spell in the Southern California desert in 2004 brought a six-month bloom while Donnelly worked for BLM. "I just sat there and saw all these flowers constantly growing around me. It had such a tremendous effect," he recalled.

For eight years he was part of a nonprofit organization that helped repair and restore damaged outdoor areas while working toward his baccalaureate degree at the University of California, Berkeley, from which he graduated in 2014 at the age of thirty-one.

"I was interested in advocacy on the side and would go to public meetings and make a ruckus about whatever environmental issue they were debating," he said. "It was a hobby, something to do outside my primary work helping to restore nature."

Often, someone opposed to mining would show up to those public meetings in Nevada, which has long had a history as a mining-friendly state. Donnelly would chuckle at the seeming inanity of fighting mining in a state known by the nickname the Silver State, a nod to its mining past and future. "I thought he was a chump, but now I'm the chump. It's what I care about, so I'm going to fight the fight."

Berkeley had taught him to write. It also showed him how to research and petition his government. Those were the tools he deployed to become his own version of Abbey and to help save as much wilderness as he could. His thesis at Berkeley had focused on the interplay between solar power and local animals and plants. Could they live in harmony? What if they didn't? "Someone's role in life is to swing tools all day, but it's not mine," he said. "I found I was really passionate about policy."

Donnelly in 2017 took a job at the Center for Biological Diversity, which had become widely known for its entrenched advocacy for rare parts of nature. Like a dog with a bone, the CBD had a reputation for finding niche causes and never giving up. It was the perfect place for Donnelly, for it was an organization that would let him channel his inner rebel. (On his Twitter profile, he labeled himself as someone "Not going gentle into that good night.")

Donnelly is something of an introvert, so any comments related to the buckwheat were the closest things to emotion that I could tease out of him during our several chats. After his first visit to the site, when he got the first glimpses of the flower that had captivated Jerry Tiehm so many years earlier, Donnelly decided then and there, he told me, to try to fight for this rare, odd flower, no matter the odds. I asked him, as he was relaying this story to me, if his zeal for this flower and this cause had anything to do with his parents and their Episcopal ministries. He paused, as if considering what his own belief system might be. "What is religion, but finding meaning and purpose in the void of life? I find the mystery of life is unlocking biodiversity, and that's how I connect with nature," he said.

For Donnelly, connecting with nature often involved some unusual tactics. On a clear, warm April day in 2021, with the sun nearly at noon overhead, Donnelly and two companions came across a camera that had been affixed to a pole planted firmly in the ground at Rhyolite Ridge. Ostensibly, the camera and several others like it across the area were installed to monitor the remaining flowers—the ones that hadn't died during the September 2020 massacre. Donnelly approached the camera from behind and shoved his hand in front of it, his middle finger standing alone in clear view of the lens. He then walked in front of the camera's lens, his navy-blue shirt and brown Carhartt jacket clearly visible. He walked back slowly, before mischievously shouting to his colleagues: "Oh, I should moon the camera! There's no law against it."

"No! Don't do that, Patrick! Don't do—!" a female colleague implored him, a tone of exasperation in her voice.

Ignoring her, Donnelly dropped his pants and shared his backside with the camera, twisting right and left like a Care Bears character. It was an act of defiance that showed ioneer what he thought of the company. It was not what one would characterize as normal office behavior.[65]

"Ugh!" His female colleague groaned.

Despite his disdain for ioneer—and the colorful ways he showed it—Donnelly admitted to me on multiple occasions that he believed a lithium mine at Rhyolite Ridge was a foregone conclusion. He knew the lithium was important, but he believed the Tiehm's buckwheat flower was just as important. If they could coexist, all the better. In his thinking, one should not supplant the other.

For Donnelly, and the Center for Biological Diversity, saving the planet from climate change would be meaningless if the planet lost even a small fraction of the biological diversity that they saw as making the Earth unique and livable. Increasingly, the scientific community saw biodiversity as a planetary challenge on the scale of climate change, a fact underscored in late 2022 at a United Nations nature conference in Montreal where member nations agreed on a global pact to safeguard ecosystems by limiting the use of pesticides, among other steps. The conference agreement was widely seen as doing for biodiversity what the Paris Accords had done for climate.[66] "Climate change presents a near-term threat to the future of human civilization. The biodiversity crisis presents a longer-term threat to the viability of the human species," said the climate scientist Katharine Hayhoe, who chronicled the global tension over emissions in *Saving Us: A Climate Scientist's Case for Hope and Healing in a Divided World*.[67]

A rare snail, an endangered owl, a small flower: all added something to the planet that made it, well, our planet. Are we really going to choose electric cars over nature itself? For several years, investors and industry executives would whisper a quiet yes to me when I would ask some form of that question during interviews, each time prefacing the answer with a request to go on background or off the record. Even ioneer itself was cautious, cognizant that any hint that it supported the lithium more than the buckwheat would be a public relations nightmare. (But of course, the company was created to mine lithium, not to garden.) Slowly, that reticence began to melt. A prominent mining industry investor, whose fund was backed in part by the U.S. government, in late summer 2022 started to say the quiet part out loud: Maybe the flower wasn't worth saving after all.

Brian Menell, head of the mining investment firm Techmet, bluntly stated:

> We need government to say, "Sure, we love wildflowers, and we're going to respect environmental and social governance standards, because that's part of our culture." But, at some point, we've got to say, "Mister wildflower group, you had your say, and now go and shut up. We are going to develop this mine, even if we destroy the habitat of a wildflower, which everybody would regret. It's better than destroying the world with climate change."[68]

I asked Donnelly about the quote, and he chuckled a bit, saying he thought the investor was being crass. But Donnelly again noted his belief that a mine was likely to be dug at Rhyolite Ridge, which I thought perhaps was a sign of acceptance or at least of a change in strategy with the hope of influencing the mine's final design.

Calaway and ioneer, Donnelly suggested, should move their mine site a mile away from Rhyolite Ridge. When I pointed out that the lithium deposit was at Rhyolite Ridge, not a mile away, Donnelly seemed flummoxed, as if to indicate the proposal was a serious one on his part and showed he was offering what he considered a solution, in good faith. He honestly thought that by changing the mine plans, everyone would be happy. He'd go away, knowing the flower was safe.

"My goal has never been to stop a lithium mine. My goal has been to save Tiehm's buckwheat," he said. "We know we need lithium, and we know we need to fight climate change. But Tiehm's buckwheat has catalyzed a discussion about the impacts of lithium mining on biodiversity." If ioneer wanted to mine, say, gold instead, "Then we would fight them all the way and say, 'Screw those guys. You don't need gold.'"

Donnelly stands about five feet ten with dark hair and a quiet demeanor. He often wears hiking boots and hiking pants, the preferred uniform for someone who spends so much time in the middle of nowhere with rare plants and animals. When we met, he was wearing a

T-shirt emblazoned with the phrase I'M ON TEAM BUCKWHEAT TO SAVE TIEHM'S BUCKWHEAT. He was quiet in person but bombastic on Twitter. "I say and do controversial things," he told me. "I haven't made a lot of friends doing this advocacy work."

Donnelly played lead guitar for a cover band on the weekends. Sometimes they sang bluegrass. Or classic rock. Or whatever requests they got. I asked him what his favorite song was to play. Without skipping a beat, he blurted out that it was Gloria Gaynor's "I Will Survive."

Whether the flower itself survives is a question that had haunted Donnelly for years, and likely would haunt him until either he died or the plant itself went extinct. He wanted his fight to force Americans and consumers everywhere to think through the trade-offs of the clean energy revolution. "If we're going to let Tiehm's buckwheat go extinct, then the next fifty years of the energy transition look extremely dark. If it does, then it's going to leave me thinking a lot. It would force me to ask, What does this say about the rest of our fights to prevent other species from going extinct?"

A stillness fell over our conversation, and I could tell Donnelly was growing introspective, perhaps even more than he typically was. He mentioned the fights to block the Twin Metals copper mine in Minnesota, the Thacker Pass lithium mine just north of us on the Nevada-Oregon border, the Resolution copper project in Arizona.

"What does Tiehm's buckwheat say about those fights and other fights to come?" He mentioned he had been tracking ninety-eight proposed lithium mines across the U.S. West, including the Thacker Pass project. Only four had officially applied for permits as we talked. "I bet half of those ninety-eight companies are looking to see what happens to Tiehm's buckwheat. It'll be open season if we lose."

⚡

OVER THE COURSE of the next two hours, Donnelly and I walked among the hills resting just below Rhyolite Ridge, which loomed over us in the afternoon sky. The entire project, ioneer told government regulators, would encapsulate 7,166 acres, with 2,426 acres physically changed for the mine project, either for the 960-foot-deep open-pit mine itself or chemical processing equipment to produce lithium, as well as boron. Trucks would transport the lithium and boron away from the site and bring supplies to it, more than a hundred tractor-trailers each day, every single day of the year, up and down Cave Springs Road, which bisects the entire area of the mine.[69]

Donnelly and I started off on the north side of the road, where large white rocks sat atop a small hill, likely the very same outcropping of the color white that partially caught Jerry Tiehm's eye decades prior. I was disappointed not to see the flowers in full bloom given their dormancy. According to ioneer's mine Plan of Operations, a storage facility for pellets of ammonia nitrate prill that would be used to crack open the earth with explosions and expose the lithium would be built near one of the patches of flowers.[70]

The planned chemical plant on-site would use nearly 1,200 tonnes of sulfur each day, shipped from Canada's oil sands facilities to produce sulfuric acid to strip lithium and boron from the rock dug out of Rhyolite Ridge. Making sulfuric acid produces enormous amounts of steam, and ioneer plans to use that steam to make 35 megawatts of power each day. The facility would not be on Nevada's electrical grid.[71]

More than twenty haulage trucks, each capable of carrying 136 tonnes of dirt from the mining pit, would work the site, as would drill rigs, a wheel dozer, a skid steer loader, two backhoe excavators, and three water trucks to keep dust to a minimum. All that equipment would guzzle 4.7 million gallons of diesel fuel each year. Twenty light towers would keep the site illuminated for nighttime operation. Five cell phone towers would be built. When the mine closed, sometime mid-century, a quarry of about 203 acres would slowly flood with rainwater.[72]

The mine would be crisscrossed by autonomous Caterpillar trucks, making it the first new mine in North America to use unstaffed machinery. It was part of a $100 million deal between ioneer and the manufacturer known for its iconic yellow paint scheme.[73]

Not all the rock that ioneer planned to take out of Rhyolite Ridge would contain lithium or boron. The rock that is left over after processing would be stored near the mine site, eventually growing to 250 feet tall and containing about 54 million tonnes of waste rock, from which water would be removed in order to prevent a mining disaster like the one that had occurred in Brazil in 2019. The road that Donnelly and I drove on to reach the site—Cave Springs Road—would need to be moved slightly north to make way for it.[74]

With each update to the plan, ioneer took more and more steps to protect Tiehm's buckwheat. The changes were prodded in part by Donnelly and the Center for Biological Diversity, who in turn had pressured the U.S. Fish and Wildlife Service, who in turn had kept twisting the vise around ioneer, directly linking the company's ability to extract lithium with the fate of the flower. At first, ioneer had planned to move the plant, but of course there was the problem that Tiehm's buckwheat liked the lithium-rich soil of Rhyolite Ridge. In 2022, the company proposed creating what it termed "Buckwheat Exclusion Areas" to create fenced gardens for the flowers, blocking them off from the noise and dust of a mining operation. Two of these proposed fenced gardens are north of the road, though three are south of it and edge right up against the 960-foot-deep quarry that ioneer hopes to dig and would be surrounded on three sides by mine operations, an isthmus protruding into an extraction zone. The fences' distance from the flowers, ioneer proposed, would range from 13 feet to 127 feet. The company had counted 24,174 Tiehm's buckwheat plants, a number it hoped would only grow.[75]

As I walked with Donnelly just south of Cave Springs Road, I was imagining a hole in the ground one day, right where I stood. We climbed a small hill and saw a field of dormant Tiehm's buckwheat before us but did not enter for fear of disturbing it. If ioneer's plan went through, just beyond that grouping of flowers would be a gigantic quarry in the shape of a kidney bean, one that would produce a metal vital in the climate change fight.

Donnelly, not surprisingly, was not supportive of the proposal. "I'm calling it 'Vacation on Buckwheat Island.' It's just a little polygon surrounding the populations of buckwheat. There's no fucking way that's going to pass muster." He brought up again his proposal to move the mine a mile down the road, incredulous that ioneer would even think of digging closer to the plant. "We have all this data showing that the dust depositions from mines, within one mile, are disastrous for rare plants," he said. "We can't have little islands of biodiversity surrounded by an open-pit mine." (The proposal would create more of an isthmus than an island, but "Vacation on Buckwheat Isthmus" doesn't have quite the same ring.)

It was clear that Donnelly had invested so much of his life into this plant, into learning what it was, what it liked and didn't like, and how it best grew. Our visit to Rhyolite Ridge was Donnelly's forty-sixth. And that advocacy had made it, he thought, "the most famous little wildflower in the world." News outlets across the globe had chronicled the fight, underscoring the stark choice facing the United States and the globe amid the clean energy transition. "It's really highlighted and put me in the center of this debate around how to make clean energy truly clean. And so now I'm in the center of the lithium debate, and I'm not even an energy guy. I'm a biologist who looks at rare species."

Donnelly drove a fairly new SUV. He used a smartphone and other modern electronics. He did not consider himself opposed to lithium mining per se or the modern economy, so in that sense he found very little commonality with Max Wilbert's fight at Thacker Pass. "It's not a realistic argument to get rid of electricity," Donnelly said of Wilbert's cause. "They latched on to Thacker Pass because it gave them an opportunity to perpetuate their anticivilization agenda."

Donnelly was at pains to distance himself from Wilbert's strategy—"We don't communicate"—and repeatedly stressed he would walk away from Rhyolite Ridge if he knew the flower and the mine could live in harmony. But it was also clear that the flower had become his raison d'être, much like the lithium had become Calaway's. "No rare plant," Donnelly boasted, "has ever got this much attention."

CHAPTER TEN

The Neighbors

NORTH CAROLINA'S GASTON COUNTY IS A PLACE ENTIRELY divorced from the hustle of nearby Charlotte, one of America's twenty largest cities. On a map, the county's borders evoke an anvil hugged up against Charlotte's western borders. Founded in 1846, the county was named for William Gaston, a former member of the U.S. Congress and jurist who had died two years prior. Gaston for a time owned slaves in a state that would become one of the most active in the Confederacy. Yet he paradoxically was an ardent abolitionist. As a member of the state's supreme court, he ruled that a slave could defend himself against an unjust attack from the person who claimed to own him. Supreme Court Justice Benjamin Curtis cited one of Gaston's rulings that Black North Carolinians were citizens of the state when he dissented in the infamous Dred Scott case.[1]

In an 1832 address to University of North Carolina graduates, Gaston beseeched his audience to decry slavery, saying it "more than any other cause, keeps us back in the career of improvement" and "is fatal to economy and providence—it discourages skill—impairs our strength as a community and poisons morals at the fountain head."[2] Elsewhere in the speech, Gaston implored graduates to balance development with other areas, advice that would prove sage as the green energy revolution began:

> As your country grows in years, you must also cause it to grow in science, literature, arts, and refinement. It will be for you to

> develop and multiply its resources, to check the faults of manners as they rise, and to advance the cause of industry, temperance, moderation, justice, morals, and religion.[3]

Over the next two centuries, cotton mills spurred some mild industrialization, but farming remained core to the county's economy. The pastoral hills were dotted with old brick homesteads and the farms brimmed with produce and livestock. In 1916, while Europe was in the throes of the First World War, Paul Edward Hastings was born in the county on a wet July day.[4] As he grew into adulthood, Hastings developed an affinity for farming and started buying land. At first, he bought one parcel off Aderholdt Road, and then another. Eventually, he bought just over 200 acres of undulating hills, pine trees, moss-strewn cemeteries filled with veterans of the U.S. Revolutionary and Civil Wars, and small streams. Aderholdt Road divided his property in two. Beaverdam Creek ran just to the north.[5]

Lacking advanced technologies to find the best spot for a well and the funds to pay for costly drilling, Hastings turned to an ancient device to place his home by finding a well to feed it: the dowsing rod. He and his brother carried the forked stick throughout the acreage, hoping to get the sensation, the vibration, indicating a water supply. When the ancient device settled on a small patch of dirt to the west of Aderholdt Road, Hastings and his brother started digging with buckets into the soft earth. When the hole became too deep to easily enter and exit, they erected a tripod atop it, lowering and raising each other in and out. After digging for more than 30 feet, the pair hit water. Paul Hastings knew where to build his house.

Just off the main road, using timber from his land, Hastings built a modest three-bedroom cottage with a small bathroom and narrow second floor. Stones taken from his soil served as footings for the homestead. Wood shingles were nailed to the roof to keep out the rain. Hastings planted corn, okra, tomatoes, and other crops. He also started raising dairy cows.

Together, Paul Hastings and his wife, Clara, had two daughters: Sylvia and Paula. Starting at 5 a.m., before the sun rose, the family would tend to the dairy cows, milking their udders, throwing fresh hay in their stalls, mucking out manure. The ritual would be repeated later that day, a rhythm to which the Hastings family had grown accustomed. When Paula, the youngest daughter, went off to college, Paul sold the dairy cows and started raising Black Angus cattle, whose prized beef was sought after by the region's restaurants.

Paula married and had a daughter, Sonya, and together they would often spend Sunday afternoons visiting Paul and Clara on their homestead. Different seasons could find them shucking corn or picking okra. In autumn, the Hastingses and their brood would review the pumpkin patch, playfully arguing over which of the plants would make the best pie. Sonya spent summers helping her grandfather raise chickens and pigs, collecting the birds' eggs and cleaning the pigs' stalls. "There's a beauty to the land, a peace," Sonya recalled, her voice trailing back toward the memory of her long-dead grandfather.

Paul Hastings, it should be noted, was not entirely opposed to mining. Since at least 1900, it had long been known that a thin sliver of rock known as the Tin-Spodumene Belt sliced through the state and into South Carolina. While most of the belt's thick rock was closer to the South Carolina border, Hastings knew that some still rested underneath the acreage he had amassed. He went so far as to allow minor excavation, and by 1982, an underground mine 39 feet deep was probing a deposit of feldspar, cassiterite, and quartz beneath his land. Primarily, the mine's purpose was to extract tin. Lithium was present, but at the time it was a largely niche metal with little practical application. (The lithium-ion battery had been invented only a few years prior.) The mine produced little and today is sealed.[6]

"My grandfather's concept of mining was nothing like what Piedmont is proposing," Sonya said, her tone a mix of memory and anger directed at her new neighbor. Sonya herself went off to college, her visits to the family homestead growing less frequent but just as fervent. At the University of North Carolina at Chapel Hill, Sonya met Warren Snowdon, a tall, strapping student brimming with confidence. He also, not incidentally, was strong. And on a visit back to the farm, Sonya brought Warren and his muscles to help bale hay.

"This is what I married into: How much hay can you lift?!" Warren joked. But rather than scare him away, hay shucking endeared Gaston County to Warren. Even after he married Sonya and they had three children of their own, the family would drive the thirty minutes or so from Charlotte to Aderholdt Road to visit Paul and Clara, and the land.

When Paul died in 2004, at the age of eighty-eight, it wasn't clear what would happen to the acreage or whom it would pass down to. Some of Paul's descendants had bills to pay; others wanted to come back as often as they could. For the next sixteen years, the acreage remained in limbo. Warren and Sonya built a successful property management company in Charlotte. But then in March 2020, just as the coronavirus pandemic began sweeping across the United States, rumors that had lingered in the county grew more intense: An Australia-based company wanted to extract lithium somewhere nearby.

Albemarle and Livent, two companies that had operated lithium mines in a bordering county in the mid-twentieth century, thought that much of the area's lithium was uneconomical to extract. Warren and Sonya took a gamble and moved to save their family farm. They bought the acreage and the home that Paul had built all those years prior for $849,000.[7] "Others in the family didn't have the passion for the land like we do," Sonya told me. "And when you have companies like Albemarle and Livent saying the area's lithium reserves are in terrible shape, buying the land feels like a calculated risk worth taking."

⚡

IN THE SUMMER of 2020, Tesla was celebrating a breakneck period of growth and preparing for a major battery technology presentation to its shareholders. By the end of the year, despite the pandemic temporarily bringing production to a halt, the company's sales climbed by 36 percent to nearly 500,000 vehicles.[8]

More of the American public agreed with the automaker's core mission that something needed to be done about climate change. Elon Musk, Tesla's chief executive, noted that wind and solar comprised 75 percent of new electricity capacity in the United States in 2020, and that the country's reliance on coal-fired power plants was dwindling. More work needed to be done, Musk said.[9] "The past five years were the hottest on record. It's really important that we take action," he explained at the company's Battery Day, held in late September 2020. "The U.S. is moving toward sustainable energy. Over time, you will even mine with sustainable energy, and eventually it will get to an effective emission of zero."[10]

The United States had never made its own electric vehicle lithium-ion batteries from scratch. China controlled roughly 80 percent of the globe's EV battery market despite having only 23 percent of the lithium, nickel, and other metals used to make such batteries. Tesla itself had long been reliant on Panasonic for cathode battery parts using Panasonic's Asian factories. To help shorten those supply chains—which exacerbated climate change by boosting emissions from shipping—Tesla planned to build a new factory, known as a Gigafactory, in Austin, Texas, to complement its other U.S. operations. The company also planned to build a chemical plant in Texas to transform lithium mined from hard rock, known as spodumene, into a derivative of lithium known as hydroxide, which boosts a battery's range regardless of weather conditions. It would be Tesla's first foray into chemical production, a plan it hoped would cut its lithium costs by a third. The company also planned to use a new chemical process that didn't require the use of sulfuric acid, making the extraction of lithium for EV batteries far safer than the traditional method.[11]

"What we need to see is vertical integration that shortens the process path from mine to cathode," Turner Caldwell, a Tesla engineer, told the Battery Day audience. "This growth is real. We are going to make all of these batteries, and everyone needs to grow with us. The entire supply chain needs to grow with us."[12] The only problem for Tesla and Musk was that North America had no hard-rock lithium mines. It could buy lithium from some planned U.S. projects that weren't hard rock, but that would boost its costs and emissions. The company risked being accused of greenwashing if it came out that the well-heralded plans to reduce supply chains were smoke and mirrors. A U.S. supply of lithium from a hard-rock mine was crucial for Musk. And that's when Tesla called Piedmont Lithium.

Founded by a group of investment bankers and Australian stock promoters, Piedmont hoped to build one of the largest lithium mines in the United States—including an open-air pit more than 500 feet deep—in the pastoral farming community of Gaston County. There, much of the land had been transferred from generation to generation, including the Hastings family homestead. Many of the region's farmers knew that under their feet where rows of corn and other crops grew sat one of the largest lithium deposits on the continent, but for decades there was never a large need for the ultralight metal. Importantly for Tesla, Texas was far closer to North Carolina than China. Piedmont for years had been plodding along on its project development, just like the other smaller lithium projects across the United States. But Piedmont's project comprised U.S.-based spodumene, piquing Tesla's interest.

Elon Musk himself pushed for a lithium supply deal with Piedmont and instructed his staff to negotiate directly with the company. It was a godsend for a junior mining company; typically, these entrepreneurs are often begging automakers to sign supply deals.[13]

Less than a week after Tesla's Battery Day, Piedmont announced it had signed a five-year deal to supply Tesla with lithium spodumene concentrate for its new Texas chemical plant starting sometime between July 2022 and July 2023. The volume was less than half of the output Piedmont had planned, but the vote of confidence from the electric car giant turbocharged Piedmont's stock, sending it up tenfold to more than $70 per share the following year. That was a rarity for a junior mining company that had yet to produce anything. Most companies in similar positions trade for less than a dollar per share, including ioneer at the time. The Tesla connection helped Piedmont's stock shine. Wall Street fell in love. The only problem for Piedmont—and by extension, Tesla—was that it had overlooked one crucial constituency: its North Carolina neighbors, including Sonya and Warren.

Fueled by the constant need for investors to fund mining projects, Piedmont's executives spent more time wooing Wall Street than they did North Carolinians. For more than four years, the company methodically hired investment banks to find investors for its $840 million project, which would include facilities to produce battery chemicals.

At least one media outlet ran a glowing profile about Piedmont, describing it as a company at the "leading edge" of U.S. efforts to fight climate change and catch up to China's green energy prowess.[14] The White House touted Piedmont's deal with Tesla as a sign its efforts to grow America's use of electric vehicles were going mainstream.[15] But Piedmont signed the Tesla agreement before it applied for a state mining permit or a zoning variance with county officials. The company moved its headquarters to the local county that contained the lithium before it presented its plans to the county's board of commissioners.

In that void, mistrust and misinformation grew. And that's when Sonya and Warren, along with hundreds of their neighbors, started pushing back, saying they were determined not to let their bucolic paradise fall victim to the green energy transition.

⚡

I FIRST MET Sonya and Warren on a muggy July day in 2021. My cell phone had no signal, and Warren had warned me to print out directions before I got on the highway headed west from Charlotte. On a bend in Aderholdt Road, past rows of ripe corn, the home that Sonya's grandfather had built from North Carolinian stones and timber came into view. It was faded and weathered, eclipsed by poplar and pine. A small sign the size of a political ad was staked on the roadside, the words GASTON COUNTY PIT MINE encircled and crossed out.

Warren, an imposing six feet four, wore hiking boots and hiking pants with a blue-striped polo that complemented his salt-and-pepper hair. Sonya, also in hiking boots, wore camouflage pants and a white T-shirt, her dirty-blond hair resting on her shoulders. The couple, aged fifty and forty-eight, respectively, had twin teenage girls and a tween boy. The house that Sonya's grandfather had built sat nearby, looking loved and well-worn. "We want to repair it and have big plans for upgrades, but until we figure out what's going on with Piedmont, we're in limbo," Warren told me.

Twice, they said, Piedmont had offered to buy all their land. And twice the couple had refused. Their land shared a border of more than

8,000 feet with Piedmont's acreage, and only a small buffer would be needed to separate their land from the proposed mine, according to the state's mining laws. Clearly, that concerned Warren and Sonya, who worried about the effect mine blasting would have on the homestead and the corn, soybeans, and barley that grew on their land. The wind in this part of North Carolina generally blows west to east, and with Piedmont's proposed mine site just to the west, Sonya and Warren worried they would bear the brunt of airborne particles from the mine.

Over the next two hours the pair took me on a tour of their acreage, down through the creeping woods and through cornfields. We visited a small creek that separated their land from Piedmont's acreage. I could see in the distance where the company had placed markers indicating the land boundary. We walked for an hour or so, sweat beading down my back in the humid July air. At one point we came across a cemetery that had held the dead from two major American wars. Could these dead bodies be moved for a lithium mine? Would the past make way for the future?

"We don't need to destroy the United States to address climate change," Warren told me. "This mine would create an environmental issue in an attempt to address an environmental issue."

The couple were at pains to share their green credentials. Through the Natural Capital Exchange, for instance, the Snowdons sold carbon credits to Microsoft; the family would plant trees to soak up carbon and the software giant would buy the carbon credits. They were planning to install solar panels and wind turbines on their acreage. They owned a hybrid.

"We're so much greener than most other people," Warren told me, almost as if to strain a point. "And we're not opposed to lithium, we just want it someplace else."

As we talked, a hawk flew overhead, and bees swarmed through the thick summer air. Turkeys, deer, and even bald eagles—the national American bird—make their home on the Snowdon acreage. "If you destroy this land, it's going to be destroyed not only for the people, but for the animals as well."

The couple had been vaguely aware for more than four years that the company was buying up nearby acreage, but without a firm sense of what the plans were or how big the mine could get. Nevertheless, they were opposed to any mine. By the time they bought the family homestead in 2020, they had decided to oppose Piedmont, no matter the cost. And they posed a formidable challenge to Piedmont. Sonya, of course, had three generations of history baked into the land. And her husband, Warren, was a commercial real estate developer by profession, meaning he knew how the game of cutthroat land acquisitions was played.

Piecing together what Piedmont told investors, the Snowdons and others began to realize just how big a mine Piedmont wanted to build. It would be gigantic, at more than 3,600 acres. (Three times larger than Charlotte's downtown area of 1,200 acres.) The Snowdons' property would butt up against an immense open hole in the ground, with only a 15-foot barrier in between. The water table was expected to drop as the mine gobbled up billions of gallons of water. Blasting could occur at random hours, scaring away wildlife. The idyllic way of life, the reason the couple bought the land, could disappear.

So together with some neighbors, they formed Stop Piedmont Lithium, a grassroots organization with the sole purpose of living up to its name. In June 2021, just before I visited the state, the group started circulating appeals to neighbors on a one-page yellow flyer to join their cause. Not only could Piedmont's mine "permanently scar the landscape and cause serious pollution," it could "discourage other forms of economic development" because "many industries prefer to avoid areas near significant open-pit mines." Open-pit mining of lithium "is the way of the past and should have no place in our future," the flyer read. Interestingly, it also touted plans for direct lithium extraction (DLE), saying "new technology has been developed that allows for the rapid extraction of lithium from brine without using much water or land."[16]

While that last part was in debate, as EnergyX, Lilac Solutions, Standard Lithium, and other DLE developers were learning elsewhere, the Snowdons and their fellow Piedmont opponents had perhaps inadvertently deployed the core of many NIMBY arguments: *There's a better place to do this.* The flyer encouraged anyone and everyone who opposed Piedmont's mine to show up at the Gaston County Courthouse on July 20, 2021, wearing red shirts to tell the regular meeting of the county board of commissioners what they thought of Piedmont's mine. It was the first time that the company would officially unveil its plans, and tensions were running high. Sonya and Warren planned to channel that anger, and they said so in their flyer:

> Piedmont Lithium is far from having their way. They have yet to request rezoning and still require many important permits. Much of the information on their website is incomplete as well. They may seem like a powerful company, but they are a paper tiger.

⚡

ABOUT 200 FEET north of Sonya and Warren sits a ranch-style house where Hugh and Libby Carpenter first moved during the early 1970s, raised their children on its five acres, and had planned to spend their golden years. Then the phone calls started. At random hours, representatives of Piedmont would phone to ask if they'd want to sell their land.

"No," Hugh would say. "*We don't.*"[17]

I had connected with the Carpenters through their grandson Will Baldwin, who had joined with Sonya and Warren in the bid to stop Piedmont. The young Baldwin had just graduated college and clearly had a soft spot for his grandparents, neither of whom was very tech savvy and thus lacked some of the more modern ways of organizing. He stepped in for them. The day after I met with the Snowdons, I met Will and Hugh in the home's quiet living room to talk about the mine. (Libby was out on a few errands, but we'd hear from her soon enough.)

Right off the bat, Hugh—a kind man who had aged gracefully and dressed like Mister Rogers—told me what he thought of Piedmont's proposed mine. "I don't want it in my front yard," he said bluntly. While it wouldn't literally be in his front yard, it would be practically right across the street. What about the well in his backyard, would that run dry? Would the birds that he had spent years attracting with pollinator gardens and feeders fly away? And what about mine waste and pollution—where would that be stored?

At eighty-two, Hugh had no plans to leave, even if the mine was approved. So his best option was to fight it. And Hugh had the fire of a pissed-off neighbor who did not intend to lose. Piedmont, he said, was putting the cart before the horse. "Are they really a mining company or are they just prospecting to sell to the highest bidder? They haven't even applied for permits yet! They're just talking a big talk to make investors feel better."

What about the Tesla deal? I asked him. "Piedmont is not going to be able to meet that deadline. Elon Musk can't depend on this company," Hugh said. And he and his grandson had armed themselves with facts and figures about the lithium industry. If the company planned to produce 30,000 tonnes of the white metal each year, that would be only about 1 percent of the 3 million tonnes that the country would need to go fully electric. Was it worth it to dig here, now? Hugh thought not. "We don't have to have this mine here to get more lithium as a country," he said.

He and his grandson were agitating for a fight, and they intended to bring it to Piedmont the following week at the county commissioners meeting. As I said my goodbyes, they suggested I talk with someone who perhaps more than they, more than the Snowdons, had given up so much to Piedmont. Her name was Emilie Nelson.

⚡

THE FIRST THING I noticed about Nelson's home was its sheer beauty. Built in an A-frame, log cabin style, it was nestled between an open field and a densely packed forest. Nelson and her curly blond hair greeted me outside just as I pulled up. She was immediately bubbly and effervescent, the kind of person you feel like you've known forever.[18]

She asked me where I was staying and said if my hotel wasn't up to snuff, I would be welcome to stay with her and her husband. I declined the polite but kind offer and asked her to tell me about her journey with

Piedmont. She had first moved to Gaston County in 2016 when she and her husband built their home, where they intended to live forever, she told me. A large pool came the next year. Nelson had always had a love for animals, which was part of the reason she moved to the county. She had formed NC Wildlife Rehab in 2016 to care for injured or orphaned wildlife. The move to Gaston County was aimed at turbocharging her ability to care for baby flying squirrels, opossums, pigs, chickens, and other animals.[19]

A heart attack in her early thirties that led to a weeklong coma motivated Nelson to open the shelter, she told me. It was a pure labor of love, with no government aid to care for the animals. When Hurricane Florence hit the state in 2018, folks would drive for hours to bring her injured animals. In her basement and in outside cages, Nelson cared for hundreds of animals each year, often using what spare cash she had to feed them. She and her husband didn't go on vacation, instead funneling that cash into the operation. When animals recovered, some were let loose into the nearby woods that sat atop the giant lithium reserve.

When Piedmont started buying up land near her in 2017, she got anxious. Soon, Piedmont officials started to visit with offers to buy her land, stopping by at least five times. "He told us if we refused to sell, they would mine around us," Nelson told me as we chatted in her kitchen.[20] She started to mist up and turned toward the ceiling, hiding the tears.

Nelson had never encountered a landman before or knew much about the cutthroat tactics of the mining industry (which evoked many of the tactics deployed by the oil and natural gas industries during the fracking boom of 2008–2015). Nelson wasn't even convinced more lithium would be a good thing for the planet's health. "There's so many other ways to save the environment without EVs," she said.

As the uncertainty of the mine and its fate weighed on Nelson, she closed her animal shelter in January 2020. By the time we met, she was spending most of her time scouring the Internet looking for information on Piedmont's plans and coordinating against the mine with her neighbors. At one point, the couple bought a recreational vehicle to live in, worried that Piedmont might seek eminent domain to take their property by force.

I pressed Nelson a few times, asking if she wanted to sell, but she gave uncertain answers. Her dream of helping had morphed into a nightmare, and her husband's job was fully remote, so they weren't tied to the land. She lived in the uncertain middle, unclear if Piedmont's mine ever would be built. Some neighbors had vowed to her they would never sell; by the time we met, more than seventy neighbors had broken those promises, lured by Piedmont's financial offer and the fear of being the last one standing should the music stop. She'd be open to selling if Piedmont got its permits, but when we met, the company hadn't even filed an application for them.

"I was trying to help the environment and look what happened to me," she said as we toured empty animal cages and pens in her backyard, the remnants of a dream dashed.

BY EARLY 2016, an Australian company named WCP Resource Limited had been trying for years to strike gold in Yemen. The Yemen Civil War had disrupted most of WCP's plans when it erupted in 2014, pitting Iran-backed Houthi rebels against the Saudi-backed central government in Sanaa for control of the country, located on the southwestern corner of the Arabian Peninsula. The war quickly became a nightmare for Yemen's people. It also halted much of the country's industry, including its mining sector. WCP's gold project was put on ice. In early 2016, the WCP executive that had led the Yemeni project left.[21]

Even as the situation in Yemen grew worse, WCP had been looking elsewhere for fresh business prospects. The company's board of directors noted, rightly, that while gold has lasting intrinsic value, it held little direct purpose for the coming green energy transition. Governments across the globe were inching their nations away from fossil fuels and into renewable energy projects that would need more practical metals, including lithium.

And so it was in September 2016 that WCP announced it would invest in not only a continent but a country in which it had never operated: the United States. The company paid $165,000 for the option to buy or lease a total of 415 acres in a farming community just west of Charlotte.[22] It wasn't much money in the scheme of things, but WCP was hoping to piggyback onto the nostalgia for the area. Starting just after the Second World War, North Carolina grew to become the largest lithium-producing region in the world. Predecessor companies to Albemarle and Livent ran giant open-pit lithium mines and sent their rocks to be morphed into versions of the metal that could be used all over the world. Sony's camcorders used lithium produced from the region.

Lithium prices had crashed in 2010—the market was so small at that point that EVs hardly mattered to its producers. That had, in turn, scared away other small junior miners who were looking into the area to operate. WCP hoped it could succeed where others failed. In 2017, the company hired a new chief executive to help guide its new American plans. Keith Phillips had spent more than thirty years rotating through the top echelon of investment banks, including J.P. Morgan Chase, Merrill Lynch, and Bear Stearns, the last two of which were bought by Bank of America and J.P. Morgan, respectively, in the wake of the 2008 financial crisis. As an i-banker, Phillips served as a middleman, helping companies sell themselves to buyers and helping buyers find companies to sell. His specialty was companies in the so-called extractive industries, corporate jargon meaning companies that take oil, natural gas, gold, and other minerals out of the ground.

It is a highly speculative space for many reasons, not the least of which is that it's quite hard to find a deposit of any mineral large enough to extract using existing technologies that won't bankrupt developers. Many so-called junior miners thrive on this kind of exploratory work and then typically hand off their discoveries to i-bankers such as Phillips, who then work to sell the newfound discovery—or the entire company behind it—to the highest bidder, or at least to investors to help develop it. In the nearly three decades of his career, Phillips had helped sell or lend more than $100 billion—a sizable sum, and one that showed the new executive's skill set. He had also worked with Barrick and Newmont, two of the world's largest gold companies, an indication that his Rolodex was brimming with top industry connections.

Two days after the July Fourth holiday, WCP officially hired Phillips as its CEO with the express purpose of "value creation" for the company's shareholders, a Wall Street term with a very clear meaning: sell the company or get the stock price soaring. The company also said it would change its name to something that more evoked the North Carolina land it hoped to exploit: Piedmont Lithium.[23]

KEITH PHILLIPS AND I first chatted in February 2019 via telephone. I had been reaching out to various executives in the U.S. lithium industry, which was quite small back then and filled with CEOs and others trying to get favorable media attention for their projects. Phillips, who was warm and gregarious, explained that he made the jump from banking to running an actual company because he saw the broader economy starting the transition away from fossil fuels and toward renewable energy. He didn't want to miss the boat.

"Electrification is happening," he said. "Everyone producing cars in the United States would prefer to procure materials, including lithium, from domestic sources."[24]

And Phillips firmly believed that Piedmont could be a key source of the white metal. The company had geology going for it because its underground deposit was primarily filled with spodumene, which is mined and processed in a way not dissimilar to gold or silver. Giant excavators pull rocks out of the ground, then those rocks are crushed into smaller and smaller pieces, and a chemical process is then used to separate the lithium from other components in the rock. It is also, not coincidentally, an easier way to make the specialized lithium hydroxide that Tesla, BMW, and other automakers prefer. Piedmont thus found itself as the only viable U.S. source of a type of lithium that major automakers coveted.

The company had quietly bought or had the right to buy about 1,800 acres of land from about thirty-five landowners in the area, Phillips told me during our chat. They needed at least 3,000 acres, and it all had to be contiguous. Piedmont had to contend with hundreds of local landowners for its project to succeed, something that virtually none of its rivals in the junior mining space had to deal with because nearly all of them were located in the western United States, where the U.S. government was often the only landowner. "The idea of putting together a land package isn't in the DNA of bigger companies like Albemarle," he said. "These are private land deals, and it requires talking to landowners, letting them know the opportunity for them to explore and discover lithium on their property. It's a long process, with conversations that sometimes take years."[25]

Even after it changed its name and hired Phillips, Piedmont Lithium's roots were still Australian. Multiple news reports would refer to it as an "Australian mining company" and a not insignificant number of its shareholders were based Down Under, largely because the company's stock traded on the Australian Stock Exchange, in Sydney. (Levi Mochkin, who was for a time the chairman of Piedmont's board of directors, had been banned in 2001 from working in Australia's financial services industry after allegations he had rigged the prices of shares in some mining companies.[26]) As 2020 drew to a close, Piedmont decided to list its stock in the United States on the Nasdaq Stock Exchange and move its headquarters. Rather than put its new American offices in New York or Washington, though, Piedmont decided to go all in on North Carolina and set up shop near its proposed North Carolina mine, in a picturesque town called Belmont.

I asked Phillips why he had spent more time focused on investors rather than neighbors and local elected officials. The company by that point had spent $58 million on its project, not a small sum nor one that typically reflected a company unsure of its strategy. The Tesla deal, especially, had irked residents and officials.

"Why in the world would they make this deal with Tesla before they even have approval for the mine?" Tom Keigher, then chairman of the Gaston County Board of Commissioners, asked me. The company, he added, "has sort of put the proverbial cart before the horse."[27] Neither Phillips nor any other Piedmont official had made any presentation of the company's plans to the county board, fueling an information vacuum that frustrated many. Just because Piedmont planned to produce lithium, and lithium was key to America's green energy plans, didn't guarantee success in this or any other county. In 2018 and again in 2019, the company had told Wall Street it would soon apply for permits and that it was not aware of any potential roadblocks from local regulators or officials even though it had not talked to local regulators or officials. Optimistically, Piedmont predicted it would have local approval for the mine by June 2021.[28] The company also hired a voice-over actor known to sound very similar to the Academy Award–winning actor Morgan Freeman and had him narrate a promotional video for its project.[29]

"Maybe it would have been better had [commissioners] been in the loop constantly. We didn't really have the time or resources to do it and we didn't even know what to tell them, until now," Phillips told me in mid-2021.[30] Keigher and other county officials wanted to reserve judgment until Piedmont made a formal presentation, but their patience was growing thin. In July 2021, Phillips finally met with the board, and hundreds of mine opponents joined for the presentation at the Gaston County Courthouse.

The mood was tense from the beginning of the meeting, and several county commissioners tore into Piedmont for waiting so long to share its plans, a delay that seemed to imply the company believed the green energy transition would give the company carte blanche to do whatever it wanted. Phillips apologized and promised to be more communicative, but the well had already been poisoned. After his presentation, eighteen county residents spoke against the proposed mine. Only one spoke for it. More than 1,500 had already signed a petition asking the board to block it. Libby Carpenter, who lived with her husband, Hugh, near the proposed mine site, told commissioners they shouldn't let "strangers intrude into our community knowing they're going to bring destruction."[31]

The meeting was informational, and no formal vote was taken. But it did little to quell the opposition. A few weeks after the tense county meeting, Piedmont's contract with Tesla was indefinitely delayed. No specific reason was given.[32] Four days later, the Gaston County commissioners temporarily banned mining in their jurisdiction, a step designed to let them craft the county's first mining laws. Piedmont, commissioners said, could not "be trusted without adequate local controls to protect the health, safety, and welfare" of the community.[33] (By 2022, Elon Musk was openly musing that Tesla might need to "get into the mining & refining" of lithium for itself.[34])

Piedmont formally applied for a state mining permit later that month. The county's new mining laws, announced a couple of weeks later, included new stipulations for fencing, lighting, and noise mitigation, as well as rock blasting. The county thought it was a good first step, but its board vowed not to vote on a necessary zoning variance until the state approved Piedmont's permit, a process that dragged on and as of late 2023 had not been resolved.[35]

Phillips made the head-scratching claim to a North Carolina television station in 2022 that the proposed mine would pose no harm to the area. "Even if you wanted to, you couldn't build a mine that is environmentally unfriendly or unsafe. I don't think people have anything to worry about."[36] Yet the Snowdons and others felt they did have something to worry about, a fact that Piedmont increasingly began to realize. The company invested in lithium mining projects in Quebec and Ghana, and by the summer of 2022 was telling investors it expected its mines there to open before North Carolina. The company also decided to build a processing plant in Tennessee that would convert lithium from Ghana and Quebec into a form usable for automakers, a project that received $142 million from the White House.[37] Amid these announcements, Piedmont admitted it did not know when it would obtain a North Carolina mining permit.[38]

Even as Piedmont faced so much opposition in Gaston County, its rival Albemarle was moving forward on plans to reopen a mothballed lithium mine in neighboring Cleveland County, a step that mimicked the one Perpetua Resources planned for Idaho. Importantly, Albemarle had the support of the White House and local officials. It was already the world's largest lithium company and it intended to ensure it conquered the nascent American lithium industry. The company in mid-2022 said it would build a facility to process 100,000 tonnes of lithium each year. That was more of the metal than the entire company had produced at that time across the globe at facilities in China, Chile, and Australia. It would be the first large-scale U.S. lithium processing plant ever built. "We want to be, in five to ten years, the biggest producer in the U.S.," Eric Norris, who ran Albemarle's lithium businesses, told me. "Our aspirations don't end there."[39]

It was also a plan that would set Albemarle up in competition with Tesla, one of its biggest customers. Elon Musk had announced plans in 2020 for Tesla to build a lithium processing plant in Nevada that would produce the metal from 10,000 acres of clay deposits it had secured in the state. Producing lithium from clay had never been done before at a commercial scale; Lithium Americas was trying to crack the code for its Thacker Pass project. Musk gave a rudimentary explanation of the process, saying the company would mix the clay with "table salt" and water, causing a reaction from which the lithium would leach out. The company also filed a nineteen-page patent application with U.S. officials.[40] "It's a very sustainable way of obtaining lithium," Musk said.[41] Yet over the next three years, Tesla did nothing with those plans and seemed to shelve them completely when it announced in September 2022 that it wanted to build a lithium refinery in Texas, although it did not say where it would procure the lithium.[42]

"Have you heard Elon talk much about table salt lately?" Norris asked me two weeks after Tesla's Texas announcement as we were discussing Albemarle's expansion plans, which the company was extolling to Wall Street, regulators, and North Carolinians—a strategic step by Albemarle to avoid the pitfalls that had befallen Piedmont. Albemarle was at pains to show it would not make the mistakes its smaller peer had, that it knew how to build and open a lithium mine and still help the environment. Norris stressed, "This is an existing mine in a town that is very mining-oriented," a reality that clearly worked in Albemarle's favor. Tesla did not control a lithium deposit and Piedmont had never processed any lithium before, but Albemarle did both, and the company telegraphed strongly that it would use these advantages to dominate the American lithium industry that Biden and others so desperately wanted. I called local elected officials and business organizations and asked them the same questions I had put to elected leaders in Gaston

County. I tried in vain to find business owners, residents, or elected officials in Cleveland County who opposed Albemarle's plans.

The company set wildly ambitious targets for itself. In 2030, Albemarle expects to produce 600,000 tonnes of the 3.7 million tonnes of lithium it believes the world will produce.[43] That share of global production—16 percent—would give Albemarle mighty sway over the global lithium market. (ExxonMobil, by contrast, produced only 2.4 percent of the world's oil in 2022.[44])

President Biden gave Albemarle nearly $150 million tied to the bipartisan infrastructure law that Congress had approved in late 2021 to help build lithium processing equipment.[45] Biden, at a White House virtual event announcing the grant in October 2022, described Albemarle's plans as a "game changer for the battery supply chain in the United States." Pointedly, given the Piedmont morass, Biden asked Albemarle's CEO, Kent Masters, how the local community was responding to its own plans.[46]

"We'll talk to the community. We tell them what's happening. We get their input. We adjust to that, and we bring them along in the process," Masters told the president.

"Well, the reason I asked the question—I knew that, and I wanted to make sure people knew that you were reaching out, that it matters—inform the community of what you're doing and what's there and why it's going to be safe and so on. So, thank you for doing that," Biden told Masters. The president, it was clear, wanted the folks (as he would say) living near a mine to actually want the mine.

Another company received money from Biden that day: Piedmont, which by that time had bought 2,100 acres in Gaston County and spent more than $100 million on the proposed mine.[47] Yet the $142 million that Piedmont received had nothing to do with the North Carolina project, but with new plans to build its own processing plant in rural Tennessee using lithium extracted by its business partners in Quebec and Ghana, not the United States. Plans to dig a lithium mine in the hills of Gaston County had seemingly faded as a priority for the company, which now saw a future elsewhere.

CHAPTER ELEVEN

"Electricity Means Copper"

On the northern side of New York City's Bryant Park, under a canopy of London plane trees[1] and a stone's throw from the Avenue of the Americas, stands the dignified bronze sculpture of William Earl Dodge. The nearly 8-foot-tall statue depicts Dodge leaning on two books resting atop a pillar, his left hand grasping his right while his eyes gaze firmly forward. Unveiled in 1885 in the city's Herald Square, the sculpture was moved to its current location in 1941, where it rests on a granite base. It commemorates a man who was a founding member of the Young Men's Christian Association in the United States and who was well known for his views on temperance. (The sculpture's original base in Herald Square held a water fountain as a nod to Dodge's teetotalling ways.)[2]

Dodge founded a trading firm in 1834 with his father-in-law, Anson Phelps, growing an empire that led to Dodge being described as a merchant prince because of his holdings of extensive interests in multiple industries: timber, real estate, railroads, banking, cotton, and other commodities, to name a few. He even, for a brief time, represented New York's 8th Congressional District in the U.S. Congress. His legislative tenure from 1866 to 1867 was marked in part by a spirited campaign to convince a reported fifty senators and congressmen to take pledges to abstain from alcohol.[3] It would be the early twentieth century before the firm morphed into what became one of the world's largest copper mining companies: Phelps Dodge.[4]

The transformation to copper mining happened slowly. The U.S.

copper industry had pre–Revolutionary War roots in what is now Connecticut and later in Michigan. In a sign of the aggression that would be meted out repeatedly to the Indigenous communities across the American West, the U.S. government in 1842 confiscated a copper mining region in Michigan's Keweenaw Peninsula from the Ojibwe people.[5]

As the United States grew through the second half of the nineteenth century, prospectors looked west and began digging into the Arizona hills around modern-day Clifton and Morenci. They hoped to find gold, but instead found outcroppings of copper oxides that drew in even more prospectors hoping to find their fortune. It's no small surprise that the prospectors who came west for Morenci's copper inflicted much of the pain and suffering that the San Carlos Apache and other Indigenous people would later draw from to channel their opposition to the Resolution Copper project.

In 1881, two years before Dodge's death, William Church traveled from the Territory of Arizona to the Phelps, Dodge & Co. offices in New York and asked for a $50,000 loan to build a copper smelter. (That's $1.5 million in 2023 dollars.) The request from the owner of the Detroit Copper Mining Company was unusual for many reasons, not the least of which is that Dodge and his partners had up until that time not been involved in the mining business. Intrigued, they hired a geologist to explore the region around Church's mining claim, which he had named Morenci. After a glowing recommendation from the geologist, Phelps, Dodge & Co. decided to buy half of Church's company, which began to develop the Morenci mine.[6] By 1921, Phelps Dodge (the name had been simplified) bought full control of the mine, which closed temporarily during the Great Depression but came roaring back to life due to the Second World War.[7]

Morenci's rise as a major source of American copper coincided with hundreds of inventions in the late nineteenth and early twentieth centuries by Thomas Edison that utilized the red metal, including telephones, motors, and electromagnets.[8] They were creations for which the mining industry was increasingly thankful, and in 1911, the American Institute of Mining Engineers honored Edison for his life's work, including and especially the invention of the first practical incandescent light bulb in 1879. Rather than accept a typical plaque or figurine, Edison asked the mining engineers for a solid cubic foot of copper—which was crafted by Tiffany & Co. and weighed nearly five hundred pounds[9]—that the inventor installed on a pedestal in his laboratory's library.[10]

Morenci's importance to North America's copper industry became almost legend, especially after it was bought in 2007 by Freeport-McMoRan. It surprised me, then, to learn that the largest copper mine in North America—one controlled by the world's largest publicly traded copper mining company—draws water from its neighbor: the San Carlos Apache tribe.

⚡

ABOUT 200 MILES east of Phoenix sits the town of Morenci and its roughly 1,500 residents. Nearly everyone who lives in the town works for Freeport-McMoRan, or at least is connected to someone who works for the mining giant. The dusty hills surrounding the town are dotted with juniper trees and sagebrush that are baptized each year by less than 15 inches of rainfall. Rocky Mountain bighorn sheep roam the region's undulating hills, standing guard. Small roads twist and turn up and down the bumpy terrain, and I found it hard to fathom how miners in the nineteenth century—before the automobile was invented—transported hulking pieces of mining equipment around the region as they lusted for copper. It's not the natural environs that set Morenci apart, but its sprawling copper mine, which has grown steadily since the 1880s and now covers nearly 100 square miles—and counting. The size alone makes it the largest mine for any metal on the North American continent, a constant hive of activity that churned out 900 million pounds of copper in 2022.[11]

Morenci is one of five mines that the company operates in Arizona. In early July 2022, I decided to see the operation for myself to get a better sense of how a copper mine operates inside the United States, especially one with an open pit exposed to the air. I had visited an underground copper mine in Chile in 2019, but the enclosed space gave little sense of the project's scale and scope. Morenci's enormous size and its role in supplying much of the copper America consumed—and hoped to consume in the future—piqued my interest.

Morenci grew quickly in the late nineteenth century as an underground mine, winnowing its way through the Arizona copper deposits on the state's border with what is now New Mexico. In 1939, the mine went aboveground via a series of open pits that carved into the copper-bearing earth.[12] Phelps Dodge, the mine's owner for much of the twentieth century, built houses for workers and their families, as well as schools, hospitals, gymnasiums, and other accoutrements of a solid middle-class Americana. Morenci High School built its football field in 1909 on a pile of waste rock from the mine, and its athletes often used the copper operations to intimidate rivals. Morenci's copper smelter, for example, used to belch a sulfur smoke that would waft over the gridiron and cause players who did not take precautions to cough and choke for air.[13] The smelter was torn down in 1984.[14]

The mine itself today appears from high above as if it is arrayed in a long, narrow pattern that evokes a map of the mythical land of Westeros from *Game of Thrones*, with leach pads, tailings ponds, and other repositories at the mine's southern end, and its vast open pits dotting the north, each one dipping deeper into the earth in gradual slopes marked by small terraces of land known as benches that narrow every 20 feet or so until reaching the bottom of the pit. Each day, the mine's fleet of 154 mining trucks moves 815,000 tonnes (that's nearly 1.8 billion pounds) of rock, with each truck bed capable of carrying 236 tonnes (520,290 pounds) per load. (As recently as the 1970s, the company had used trains, rather than trucks, inside mine pits.) Those trucks and shovels, drills, and other equipment help Morenci and its 3,600 workers dig into three types of mineralization at the copper deposit—basically a geological way of saying how the copper appears in the rock. Much of the copper at the Morenci deposit is considered low-grade, ranging somewhere between 0.23 and 0.5 percent. That means for every hundred pounds of rock those trucks move, about a quarter to half a pound is copper. A lot of rock needs to get moved, and a lot of waste rock needs to be stored somewhere. The town of Morenci itself has had to morph around the whims of the mine; in the

1980s the entire community was relocated to make way for the mine's expansion.[15] U.S. Route 191 was moved—at the company's expense—in 2015 to make way for Morenci.[16]

The mine manager Robert "Bobby" Pollock has worked at Freeport for his entire career and is a third-generation miner. We met as I visited the mine's Command Center, where dozens of TV monitors spewed out data on how much rock the mine was moving, the production rates at processing mills, the stability of tailings piles, and a plethora of other items. A sign in the corner of the room displayed the target the twelve-hour shift workers were in the middle of achieving: moving 360,000 tonnes of rock. Just outside the Command Center sat a digital display board with Freeport's stock price constantly updated as well as a picture of Kathleen Quirk, Freeport's president, and Gabriel Boric, the president of Chile, where Freeport also has several large operations. Doors were opened with copper-coated handles, a nod to copper's antimicrobial properties.[17] The company had begun to brand itself as "Foremost in Copper," and its colossal spending on efforts to extract the red metal was evident everywhere. Morenci was and remains one of Freeport's crown jewels: At the end of 2021, the mine—despite being open for more than a century—had more than 15 billion pounds of copper left in the ground.[18] The mine also paid no royalties to the state or federal governments—just like every other Freeport-owned mine in the United States.

Morenci and Freeport's entire portfolio of mines was viewed by the company's managers as driving what they saw as a second era for copper this century, after China's rapid economic rise in the early twenty-first century powered its first era of demand. "The world is becoming much more electric," Freeport-McMoRan's chief executive, Richard Adkerson, told me. "Electricity means copper. There are still huge populations of people around the world, people living in undeveloped, underdeveloped situations, and they have aspirations of having a better life. More power, better cars, more appliances."[19] And copper from Morenci and the rest of Freeport's mines, Adkerson was saying, was key to fueling that future. He also was tying copper's future to efforts to fight climate change: "I don't think there's any question that the way societies have developed over the world is creating carbon emissions. And we're the one piece that can do something about it."[20]

After drilling and blasting Morenci's pits, Freeport then loaded rock onto trucks and hauled it to one of two basic types of processing. One method is to crush the rock in giant tumblers that turn 24/7, mill it into a fine powder, and then lightly process it into what's known as copper concentrate, before sending it to a nearby smelter, where the concentrate is melted and then put into molds for various products, including pipes. Another method is to pile the rock onto leach pads, where an acid concoction is applied via drip irrigation to tease out the copper, after which the acid solution—known as a Pregnant Leach Solution, containing 2 grams of copper for every liter—is collected at the bottom of the pad and processed into flat sheets of the red metal known as copper cathode by using electrical currents. A quarter of the nearly 100 square miles that compose the Morenci mine site holds tailings ponds that store the muddy detritus of the mining process. To prevent dust, Freeport applies magnesium chloride to the top of the gargantuan ponds, which look from the air like gigantic pyramids, wide and flat at the top with sides that angle and slope down gradually to the edge of a community of hundreds of homes. The facility is considered "zero-discharge," meaning that Freeport aims to prevent water—whether from rainfall or another source—from leaving the site. (In 2012, the company paid $6.8 million to settle charges that sulfuric acid from its tailings facility leaked and harmed birds and other wildlife.)[21]

Much of the copper that Morenci produces finds its way to the Freeport-owned El Paso Rod Mill in El Paso, Texas, where it is turned into copper wiring used in millions of products, including electric vehicles, solar panels, and wind turbines.

Morenci, I quickly learned, was a true company town. Nearly everything within its borders was paid for and operated by Freeport. If the industry's relatively high salaries were an attempt to keep its workers happy—Freeport's median pay in 2021 was 9 percent higher than the U.S. national median[22]—its community offerings aimed to keep their spouses and children content. As mine manager, Pollock also serves as the de facto town mayor because the company owns all the homes and retail stores, as well as the library, hospital, and hardware store. While Pollock gives regular updates to the town about how the company maintains certain facilities, including horse corrals, residents cannot vote for mayor or any other town official because Freeport literally is the town.[23] Freeport also owns and runs the town's recreational building, which included exercise equipment, an outdoor lap pool, climbing wall, basketball court, and indoor water park. (The monthly fee for a family: $30.) A large, decorative A-frame adorns the outside of Morenci's Community Center, a visual nod to the mine. "This is all about earning our social license to operate," Pollock told me on our visit, which coincided with hot summer weather that drove Morenci's residents to the indoor water park.

While the perks are plenty, the mine's needs are paramount. No clearer was that to me than after I visited Morenci's main office, a brown single-story structure just off U.S. Route 191. A large valley sat on the opposite side of the road and a mountain loomed to the left, slightly north. In time, Pollock told me, the mountain will edge south as the valley is filled by waste rock from Morenci's operations. As those mountains are leached of copper during the next twenty or thirty years, the mountain will grow to loom over the mine's main office and cast a shadow, part of the unending pursuit of the metal.

⚡

IN 1992, THE U.S. Congress passed, and President George H. W. Bush signed, the Reclamation Projects Authorization and Adjustment Act, a mammoth bill that included a clause reallocating certain water rights to the San Carlos Apache tribe, a huge win for the tribe in the perpetually arid state.[24] The law formalized agreements and practices that had never been codified during the previous century and gave the San Carlos Apache control over more of the water that flowed on and through their 1.8-million-acre reservation. The law created a $41 million trust fund for the tribe and also granted them the right to sell their water.[25] The San Carlos Apache now had the right to the groundwater on their reservation, as well as the surface water that flowed through their land to four rivers and tributaries.[26]

The law therefore gave the tribe greater sway over those using some of its water already, including Phelps Dodge, which had helped build a dam near the reservation earlier in the twentieth century to store water and prevent flash flooding. With its newfound control over its own water, the tribe negotiated a fifty-year supply deal with the copper mining giant starting in 1999.[27] The U.S. Department of the Interior—which controls the Bureau of Indian Affairs—called the deal a "landmark settlement" after hundreds of hours of negotiations.[28] Phelps Dodge planned to use the water for the Morenci Mine. The agreement implicitly showed that the tribe was not opposed to all copper mining per se, and that perhaps there was more nuance to the tribe's position.

Indeed, there was. I put the question to Terry Rambler, chairman of the San Carlos Apache, during one of our chats. "How," I asked, "should we ask folks to square the tribe's opposition to the Resolution Copper project while at the same time the tribe is selling water to a massive copper mine?" The answer drew on the issue of tribal sovereignty. Rambler rightly noted that tribes could do whatever they wanted with their land and their water, as a matter of choosing their own fate, and if they wanted to support one copper project and not another, that was their prerogative. (The tribe also had sold water rights to nearby housing developments.[29]) "We had a say in those things, and it's very important that people remember that we did," Rambler said.[30]

Still, how did Phelps Dodge (and its future owner, Freeport) succeed whereas Resolution Copper's owner, Rio Tinto, clearly failed again and again? While supplying water is vastly different from building a mine that would destroy a religious and cultural site, the sales agreement showed the San Carlos Apache tribe was not opposed to copper or the green energy transition as a matter of policy. And building a new mine is, as we've seen, increasingly anathema to many.

After talking to Rambler, I put the question to Adkerson, who was, perhaps understandably, reticent to talk about one of his peers and rivals, especially coming off a two-year stint as chairman of the International Council on Mining and Metals, a trade group for Rio

Tinto, Freeport, and other mining companies. "We are very close to the San Carlos Apache," Adkerson told me, underscoring the pride he said he felt in his company's relationship with Arizona's Indigenous communities. The friendship with the San Carlos Apache came despite Adkerson's personal connection to the late Senator John McCain, whom the San Carlos Apache blame for adding a clause to a Pentagon funding bill at the last minute in 2014 giving Rio Tinto access to the Oak Flat campground. (Adkerson was an honorary pallbearer at McCain's Arizona memorial service.[31])

"Resolution's at a site that the Native American groups consider to be sacred." Adkerson noted Rio's destruction of the Juukan Gorge caves in Australia. He also noted the geological complexity facing Rio should it ever win approval for the mine. "That's the difference between trying to do something new versus when you've got existing operations," Adkerson said.[32]

⚡

IN 2007, NEW Orleans–based Freeport-McMoRan bought Phoenix-based Phelps Dodge in what was a rare instance of a smaller company buying a larger rival. At the time, Phelps Dodge controlled mines across the United States, Africa, and South America. Freeport controlled only one mine: Indonesia's Grasberg, which grew by 2023 to become the world's second-largest copper mine and its largest gold mine by production. (The two metals are intermingled in the geological deposit in the western part of the province of Papua.)

Freeport feared it had been missing out on the merger mania sweeping the world's mining companies at the time. "We had been watching the industry consolidation, fewer companies, larger companies, but we had not been playing a role in it," said Adkerson, an accountant by training who became Freeport's chief executive officer in 2003.[33] Adkerson had tried to sell Freeport to Phelps Dodge, but in the process ended up doing just the opposite and acquiring the company that traced its roots all the way back to the man commemorated in that New York City statue.

"It was a minnow swallowing a whale. We had been strategically trying to decide what to do with Freeport. We didn't think it was sustainable as a one-asset company," Adkerson told me.[34] "We kept trying to get someone to buy us, but that didn't work out. And then the financial markets opened up for us to acquire Phelps Dodge. We thought it was a great match." Freeport's Grasberg mine had unusually high grades of copper and gold. That meant that when prices for either metal fell, the mine could still be profitable. The multiple mines owned by Phelps Dodge had typically lower grades, but they were more geographically diverse and thus could be wildly profitable when metals prices rose. The two portfolios could balance each other. The deal was struck. For a purchase price of $29.6 billion in a combination of stock and cash, Freeport bought Phelps Dodge in 2007.

From the beginning it was a challenge to combine the two cultures, something not uncommon in large corporate mergers. Phelps Dodge lost its name. Freeport shed its New Orleans headquarters and moved to Phoenix, near Morenci and other Arizona mines. Freeport also had to contend with the poor reputation that Phelps Dodge had engendered since its founding. While Dodge himself eschewed alcohol and was known for his benevolence, the company that bore his name had grown since his death into a nameless, faceless corporate giant known primarily for its adherence to the bottom line—and not much else. In what is considered the largest forced deportation in American history by a private company, Phelps Dodge transported 1,200 striking union members in 1917 from its Bisbee, Arizona, copper mine at gunpoint, shoving them into cattle cars and leaving them stranded 173 miles away in the New Mexico desert. In 1983, amid low copper prices that were crimping corporate profits, workers at Morenci and three other mines owned by Phelps Dodge walked out during contract negotiations. Rather than negotiate with the union workers, the company brought in temporary staff and locked out the union, fueling a nearly three-year strike that ultimately led to the company decertifying the union. Both strikes were chronicled in depth by Kim Kelly in *Fight Like Hell: The Untold History of American Labor*, the definitive account of American labor's interaction with industries such as mining.[35]

At Freeport, the company's strained legacy in Grasberg was more environmental. At an elevation of more than 16,000 feet, the mine site is in one of the most remote parts of Indonesia, and also one prone to earthquakes. Building a traditional tailings dam was too risky, so Freeport started dumping the tailings in rivers and lowlands closer to the coastline. "With its physical location, you couldn't dispose of tailings in a traditional way. And we had to come up with an approach using an existing waterway," Adkerson said. "We transported tailings to lowlands and built these levees to contain it."[36] The practice, not surprisingly, had an impact on the ecology and environment of the island that, as of this writing, is still occurring.

Slowly, the two corporate cultures commingled, but not before another large buyout. In 2012, Freeport decided it couldn't let the oil and gas boom pass it by. Just before Christmas that year, the company announced it would spend about $20 billion to buy two smaller oil companies. Prices for American crude oil at the time were near $100 a barrel, a tantalizing prospect. The deals were championed loudly by James Moffett, the company's chairman at the time and thus Adkerson's boss. Moffett bragged to Wall Street that the deal would let Freeport become a "much larger, well-capitalized platform." (Moffett owned part of one of the two companies that Freeport bought.) Wall Street grew irked for many reasons, not the least of which was that the two deals did not require shareholder approval because Freeport was issuing only 8 percent of its shares to close the transaction, below the requirement to seek shareholder approval.[37]

Moffett, a famed oil and gas wildcatter, told investors that some years gold might be sexy. Some years it might be oil or natural gas. Other years it might be copper. Essentially his argument was: Wouldn't putting all of these projects under one roof make sense?

Stock analysts, whose job it was to grade corporate strategy, did not think it made sense, especially because Moffett held shares in the oil companies that were being acquired. Financial commentators concurred, with one op-ed observing: "[T]here are no obvious synergies between excavating Indonesian gold and American oil and gas."[38]

Market volatility ended up battering the company. Freeport's stock had been trading north of $60 per share in December 2010, a few years after the Phelps Dodge deal. Oil prices started to fall to about $26 per barrel in early 2016, taking Freeport's stock with it. In January 2016, Freeport's shares were hovering below $4, and at least one analyst suspected that the company might go bankrupt. It was worth $4.8 billion but owed more than $20 billion.[39] (Moffett resigned as chairman in late 2015.[40] Adkerson himself admits in hindsight that investors "hated the deal. Their view was, 'If we wanted to invest in oil and gas we can do that.'") It was a hugely stressful situation for Adkerson and his lieutenants, who controlled some of the world's most valuable sources of oil, gold, natural gas, copper, and other raw materials. Grasberg alone could be worth $16.2 billion if sold, Freeport estimated.[41]

One other mine that Freeport controlled was also highly sought after, especially by rivals in China. "We were really in dire straits," Adkerson recalled. "It was a very scary time."[42] Freeport was, in the words of a business columnist, a desperate seller.[43]

⚡

UNDER PRESSURE FROM the corporate raider Carl Icahn, Freeport sold parts of its oil business in September 2016 for $2 billion.[44] Not long after, it sold more oil assets—this time in California—for $742 million.[45] The company had already that year sold a 13 percent stake in the Morenci mine to Japan's Sumitomo Metal Mining Co. for $1 billion in cash, a deal that boosted the Japanese company's stake in the largest North American mine to 28 percent based on its previous holdings.[46] But those sales were sideshows to the main event.

In May 2016, Adkerson and Freeport were forced by their company's tremendous debt load to sell their controlling stake in the Tenke copper and cobalt mine in the Democratic Republic of the Congo to a Chinese company known as China Molybdenum for $2.65 billion. Freeport had for years invested heavily in the Tenke operations, ruffling some feathers initially by relocating more than 1,500 residents.[47] But over time the company grew to gain the respect of local communities through its various social and community health projects, and it became widely known for its stringent worker safety program.[48] "We had made the largest investment in the Democratic Republic of the Congo. It was great to go in there and give employment, improve health, improve water for villages, build educational facilities. That's just a great feeling to have, in addition to being successful for your workforce and your stakeholders and everybody else," Adkerson told me.[49]

Freeport had already cut its budget for the Tenke project by 50 percent in 2016 due to its debt crisis as well as low copper prices.[50] It also had curtailed expansion plans at the mine, which had dug into Congo's southern copper and cobalt belt since 2009. It was a fire sale, pure and simple, and Freeport's pain fueled China Molybdenum's—and China's—gain. "We really liked having this as part of our portfolio. So, when circumstances required to sell it, everybody was disappointed," Adkerson said.[51] In 2016, Freeport was one of the largest cobalt producers in the Congo. Soon, it wasn't even in the country.

Melissa Sanderson, a former U.S. diplomat who helped run Freeport's Congo operations for four years, was among the thousands of Freeport employees shocked by the sale. "It was a disaster for the United States of America on a strategic level, and particularly to have sold to the Chinese. It was a disaster for the company. That was just a lose-lose scenario. And I will say on a personal level, I was glad I was not sitting in Richard Adkerson's chair, having to figure that out and make those kinds of choices," she said.[52] Freeport's exit from the Congo was caused in part by its rushed oil investments a few years prior, but it also came just as China was on the rise across the African continent in a mad dash for strategic metals. As important as copper was to China Molybdenum—and it was tremendously important—it was Tenke's cobalt that held immense appeal for China's Belt & Road Initiative, launched by President Xi Jinping in 2013 with the goal of using his country's infrastructure prowess to "build a broad community of shared interests" across Africa, Asia, and Latin America.[53] By 2020, fifteen of the Congo's nineteen cobalt mines were financed or owned by Chinese companies.[54]

"China, Inc., has realized how important cobalt is," said Ivan Glasenberg, who ran the rival global mining giant Glencore at the time.[55] Cobalt is a metal with a blue to green tint that for thousands of years has been used in pottery, glass, and other arts. As with rare earths, some of the first mines were located in modern-day Scandinavia. Central Africa was found to have vast amounts of not only cobalt but also copper in the nineteenth century, sparking prodigious interest from Europeans, including Leopold II, king of the Belgians, who personally ruled what came to be known as the Congo Free State with brutal efficiency, a tortured history chronicled in grim detail by Adam Hochschild in *King Leopold's Ghost*. After the Second World War, cobalt mining picked up in the United States, especially Idaho, but as of 2023 the country produced only small amounts of the metal.

That became a problem for the United States, especially amid the rise of the green energy transition, for cobalt is used prominently in EV batteries to ensure they do not overheat and catch fire.[56] The metal also helps extend the life of an EV battery.[57] But since Freeport had sold its Congo mines, it no longer controlled the world's largest source of the metal and its largest active producer. China Molybdenum did, and its track record of safety and community relations started to pale in comparison to that of its predecessor. But it was the cobalt that China did not mine that perhaps mattered most. Nearly a third of Congo's cobalt production comes from so-called artisanal miners, who are essentially everyday Congolese citizens—sometimes young children—who take pickax and shovel and dig, sometimes under their homes, sometimes in the woods, and sometimes after breaking into mine sites.[58]

"We go to the concession at night," one Congolese man recalled. "We pay the guards, and they let us dig in the pits. It is more certain to find cobalt there. If we cannot pay the money, we sneak inside the concession and dig. Sometimes we are chased by dogs, but mostly, we are not disturbed."[59]

These miners do not use sophisticated equipment and sometimes die when the tunnels they dig to reach the cobalt deposits collapse. Companies such as China Molybdenum implicitly encourage the trade by buying the metal from these amateur miners, with some of that cobalt filtering down through global supply chains and ending up in millions of consumer goods. Cobalt can irritate skin and repeated exposure to cobalt dust can cause lung scarring. Both pose challenges for any amateur miner, especially a child. Amnesty International warned in a 2016 report that:

"The children told us that they endured long hours—up to 12 hours a day—working at the mines hauling back-breaking loads of between 20 and 40 kilograms for US$1–2 per day." It continued: "Many had nothing to eat all day. Fourteen-year-old Paul, who began mining aged 12 and worked underground, told us he would often 'spend 24 hours down in the tunnels. I arrived in the morning and would leave the following morning.'"[60]

It's a problem that had grown to worry Apple, Microsoft, and other major tech companies. "Electric vehicle manufacturers and electronics companies are operating with one eye open and one eye closed. In practice it is virtually impossible for them to completely exclude artisanal cobalt, especially when it is sent to smelters and refiners in DRC and China," a human rights group warned in 2023.[61] A long-range Tesla, for example, is made using 10 pounds of cobalt, about 400 times more of the metal than is found in a cell phone.[62] Elon Musk and Tesla have been trying for years to wean their operations off cobalt, but the sheer rise in the number of EVs that will be built in coming years means more cobalt will flood the global market—much of it from Congo.[63]

That had not gone unnoticed in Washington. In late 2022, U.S. Secretary of State Anthony Blinken signed a memorandum of understanding with the DRC and Zambia to help both countries further develop their cobalt and copper mines for the electric vehicle industry. The deal seemed designed to blunt, in part, China's growing prowess in the region, something that Blinken implicitly acknowledged: "This is the future, and it is happening in the DRC and in Zambia. . . . The plan to develop an electric battery supply chain opens the door for U.S. and like-minded investment to keep more value-added in Africa. Electric vehicles help reduce carbon emissions; they support the global response to the climate crisis."[64]

The optics of Washington supporting mines in a region where China had already heavily invested, where an American company had to sell its prized assets, and where some children were active parts of the mining chain, grew to be too much for prominent U.S. politicians, especially those who wanted more mining in the United States. "America needs to develop our vast mineral wealth, right here at home, with high-wage, union-protected jobs instead of continuing to send American taxpayer dollars to countries like the Congo that use child slave labor. The only winner here is China," said Representative Pete Stauber. His district in northern Minnesota contains some of the largest deposits of copper, cobalt, and nickel found in the country, specifically the Boundary Waters area near where Twin Metals wants to mine.[65] Stauber's furor was shared by none other than Pope Francis, spiritual head of the world's 1 billion Roman Catholics. "Hands off the Democratic Republic of the Congo. Hands off Africa. Stop choking Africa: it is not a mine to be stripped or a terrain to be plundered," the pontiff said.[66]

⚡

AT FREEPORT, ADKERSON and other executives did not dwell on the past and turned their attention to Morenci and other U.S. mines in their portfolio, which they predicted held roughly half of their 235 billion pounds of copper reserves. In 2020, Freeport opened an $850 million expansion of one of its Arizona copper mines, doing what Rio Tinto and BHP had so far been unable to do at Resolution. But those projects were for copper, not cobalt. Freeport's days of producing a second valuable EV metal were seemingly over.

Not long after that expansion opened, however, Freeport faced a new problem: Who would run those mines? A wave of retirements faced the company and many of its Western peers. More than half of Western miners in 2021 were over the age of forty-five. A fifth were over sixty and nearing retirement. The U.S. government went so far as to form a committee aimed at addressing that aging workforce, as well as "public perceptions about the nature of mining." In China in 2020, just one mining school enrolled more mining students than were enrolled in all of the United States. Adkerson and other Freeport executives visited universities, trying to convince students to change their majors to mining engineering.[67]

Despite copper's role in the green energy transition, it seemed few young people in the West wanted to help procure it. "I would like to see more people want to come work for our industry," Kathleen Quirk, Freeport's president and effectively the company's co-leader alongside Adkerson, told me. "There's something for everyone in this business. It's viewed as dirty, but it's modernized a lot."[68]

The efforts failed, or at least had not succeeded, by 2023, when Freeport's copper production in the United States fell not because of weak commodity prices or weather or economic tensions, but because the company did not have enough workers. And Quirk and Adkerson warned the problem would only get worse. "Our work is hard work," Adkerson said. "It's harder to drive a big-haul truck than it is to drive an Amazon or UPS or FedEx truck."[69]

CHAPTER TWELVE

The Entrepreneur

THE SKY OVER HOUSTON WAS CLEAR AND FILLED WITH A light breeze in the early evening of April 23, 2017, as Tashi Garcia unloaded his pickup truck in Northside Village, a neighborhood just north of the city's bustling downtown.[1] As Garcia walked onto his back porch that Sunday, the shock wave from a sudden explosion pierced the air and slammed his body into the doorframe of his home. Garcia experienced ringing in his ears and thankfully wasn't seriously injured, but the unexpected shove shook him. Several windows in his house shattered; several walls cracked.[2]

"I had no idea what was happening. It was the loudest thing I've ever heard," he said.[3] Garcia lived about 350 feet away from a major rail line that bisects Houston, the largest city in Texas and a waypoint for trains traveling between the east and west coasts of the United States. A few minutes earlier, an operations manager for Union Pacific—one of the largest U.S. railroad companies—noticed that railcar UMXU 27757 was smoking while it rolled through the city. The operations manager alerted the train's conductor, who hadn't realized that part of the train convoy he was leading had caught on fire. The conductor stopped the entire train and alerted the Houston Fire Department. Then, at 6:01 p.m., the railcar exploded. First responders had the fire under control within two hours, after which the train moved to a nearby railyard where the railcar that caught fire was removed.[4] The rest of the train continued on its way. No one was killed, though a foul odor wafted across downtown Houston.[5] The incident cost Union Pacific

$25,000—$5,000 for damage to its railcar, $5,000 to clean up the area near the explosion, and $15,000 for Houston officials.[6]

Garcia hadn't known that the explosion was fueled by the lithium-ion batteries that Union Pacific was transporting from Atlanta, through Houston, and then to a recycling facility in Los Angeles. The railcar that exploded was filled with 55-gallon drums of used lithium-ion batteries, sourced from cell phones and other consumer electronics. The drums were uncovered, exposed to the elements. Federal officials had begun to realize about that time that such batteries could spontaneously combust, what is known in industry parlance as "thermal runaway" and can be caused when a lithium-ion battery is overcharged, short circuits, or is exposed to high temperatures.[7] The explosion, though relatively minor, caught the attention of *Automotive Logistics*, a trade publication based in the United Kingdom that tracks the automobile supply chain. In reporting on the Houston explosion, the publication noted presciently and ominously: "The news will concern those in the growing electric vehicle market and any supply chain operations that support it, as such vehicles are largely powered by lithium-ion batteries."[8]

While the incident sparked concerns about the potential for lithium-ion batteries to explode at random, it also underscored the danger in transporting those batteries over large distances to be recycled. When these batteries were relatively niche and not commonly used, there was little cause for alarm. A 2016 study found a failure rate of about one in a million.[9] But the number of lithium-ion cells for batteries manufactured each year had jumped from about 3 billion in 2007 to about 7 billion by 2017.[10] And as these types of batteries grew in popularity, so, too, did related explosions. Only two U.S. facilities reported lithium-ion battery–related fires in 2013. By 2020, that had jumped to sixty-five.[11] The batteries were and are, by and large, safe, especially when contrasted with vehicles powered by internal combustion engines in which passengers literally sit atop a tank of explosive liquid fuel. But as lithium-ion battery usage grew, so did the rate of explosions.

The Houston incident sparked questions of not only logistics but also infrastructure. Why, exactly, was a large railcar filled with dozens of batteries headed from one U.S. coast to the other? Were there not enough adequate facilities nearby to break down those batteries into the metals that helped build them? The answer, simply, was no.

In the years after the Houston incident, alarm grew about the potential damage that lithium-ion batteries could inflict. The electrolyte solution that sits between a battery's anode and cathode is extremely flammable, made all the more so by the high energy density inherent to a battery's core purpose. If a lithium-ion battery is damaged or overheats, the solution can ignite and fuel a fire that can be very difficult to extinguish. A cargo ship carrying more than four thousand luxury vehicles caught fire off the coast of Portugal in early 2022 and sank, with authorities suspecting thermal runaway caused by some EVs the ship was carrying.[12]

Germany's Lufthansa became one of the first airlines to ban lithium-ion batteries from cargo shipments in 2015.[13] The U.S. government banned the batteries from the cargo holds of passenger airplanes in 2019.[14] That ban came several years after batteries in a Boeing 787 Dreamliner plane had caught fire, raising concerns about the plane's safety.[15] The New York City Council considered a ban on reusing the batteries out of concern they could be more dangerous if used in a device they were not originally built for.[16] Beyond bans, the widening use of lithium-ion batteries amid the EV revolution prompted the need to consider what to do with all these batteries and how to transport them to recycling centers.

"Nobody wants to transport lithium," said Michelle Michot Foss, a fellow in energy, minerals, and materials at Rice University's Baker Institute for Public Policy. "But no one is going to invest in battery recycling everywhere, so lithium-ion batteries will end up needing to be shipped."[17]

Unlike gasoline or diesel, which are burned off when used to power internal combustion engines, the lithium, copper, and other metals in lithium-ion batteries can be reused if they can be removed from a battery and recycled. Lithium doesn't lose its ability to hold a charge just because it's been sitting in a battery for twenty years. What many countries were missing, though, was the infrastructure to accomplish that goal. If more recycling facilities to handle electronic waste were built, fewer railcars would explode, and more metals would end up back in new batteries rather than sitting in junkyards or random drawers and storage closets in the average home. In 2017, the year of the Houston railcar incident, fewer than 200,000 EVs were sold in the United States,[18] though that paled next to the hundreds of millions of cell phones and other consumer devices built with lithium-ion batteries. The United Nations estimated that of the 53.6 million tonnes of electronic waste generated globally in 2019, only 17.4 percent was collected for recycling. That left copper and other metals worth more than $57 billion by the wayside, unused and essentially wasted.[19] (A survey of six European countries found nearly half of those polled said they were hoarding household electronics that could be recycled because they expected to use them again in the future, a position ignorant of the fact that they *would* use them again in the future if they were recycled.[20]) Breaking apart a battery purposefully inflicts damage on battery cells, thus causing the very conditions that could lead to explosions. Facilities that purported to recycle such batteries would need to be prepared for this potentiality. The risk of explosion in a battery-recycling facility is far greater than just bringing an iPhone on an airplane. Even still, the green energy transition is fueled by a growing realization that more metals are needed to combat climate change, a reality that even mining companies seem to agree with. In the early 2020s, EV battery manufacturing scrap was the primary feedstock for the recycling industry. By the mid-2030s, discarded EV batteries are expected to be the primary feedstock.[21]

For the most part, mining companies agree that recycling may pose a challenge to their business model, just not anytime soon. "There's a limited period of time, in geological terms, of thirty to fifty years to develop these mineral resources. You're not going to develop them fifty years from now. There will be other ways, though lithium will continue to be required. A large part of it will come from recycling," Martín Pérez de Solay, head of Allkem, a lithium company with locations on four continents, told an industry conference in early 2022.[22]

The recycling industry, though, was not growing as fast as the green energy revolution, a fact underscored not only by the rising popularity of EVs, but also the dearth of recycling centers across the United States and the world. And that was a problem that two engineers had already started to tackle by the time that railcar blew up in Houston.

⚡

THOSE RAILCARS THAT rumble through Houston and other major global cities are the harbinger of a development that, all in all, is a positive one. Too often, old electronics are just thrown away. Without more electronics recycling, the world's landfills would mushroom to completely unmanageable size while at the same time global reserves of cobalt, nickel, and other metals would be depleted. Each year, about 50 million tonnes of electronic waste is generated, an amount roughly equivalent to every single commercial airplane ever built. Yet only about a fifth of that amount is actually recycled. Without some intervention, by 2050 the number will jump to 120 million tonnes each year.[23] In 2019, all the EVs put on the road generated about 500,000 tonnes of battery waste, a figure that could hit 8 million tonnes by 2040.[24]

Manufacturers, especially EV manufacturers, by 2020 had only begun to think about how to design products that could easily be recycled. For EVs especially this was challenging because of differences in battery chemistry designs. Some automakers may prefer nickel-rich EV batteries to boost range; other automakers may opt to design an EV with an iron-heavy battery known as an LFP, which tends to be cheaper. And for parts of electronics that are not in batteries, recycling isn't always clear-cut and easy, but it's economically essential. Recycling rare earths, for example, uses as much as 88 percent less energy compared to mining and producing the metals.[25]

Business models for lithium-ion battery recycling had yet to be set up in the early days of the green energy transition, although there were certainly plenty of successful examples to use as North Stars. Coors, the iconic beer company, launched the first aluminum beverage can in 1959 with a twist: Customers would get a penny back for each can returned. Coors knew it'd be vastly cheaper to recycle cans than make new ones.[26] Lead-acid batteries had largely become illegal to dump in many landfills by the end of the twentieth century. They're also typically made the same way, regardless of the manufacturer. Nearly all lead-acid batteries are now consequently recycled; as long ago as the 1930s, lead was presented as a loan by the industry to consumers, rather than a sale.[27] Yet as EVs and other green energy devices go mainstream, there is no widespread financial incentive to recycle their batteries or broad prohibition against dumping them in landfills.

Just as it controls the global market for green energy minerals, China holds much sway over the market for recycling lithium-ion batteries, with more than three times as much current and planned recycling capacity as the United States.[28] China has led the world on battery recycling research as well, far eclipsing Japan, South Korea, and the United States, the three closest countries by research.[29] Battery chemistries change over time, but many of the old lithium-ion batteries that will come due for recycling by 2030 have high volumes of cobalt, the metal most commonly extracted from the Democratic Republic of the Congo and under safety and labor standards opposed by many manufacturers. Thus, to recycle more batteries with cobalt is to rely less on Congo mines for new sources of the bluish metal.[30] And while the greenhouse gas emissions to produce an EV are higher than those to produce an internal combustion engine, an EV's battery can be recycled over and over—a plus for the environment.

"There is an opportunity to rethink mining to consider sources of these materials that are already out of the ground," said Lisa Jackson, who ran the U.S. Environmental Protection Agency under President Obama.[31] A chemical engineer by training, Jackson joined Apple after leaving government to oversee its efforts to reduce the tech giant's impact on the environment. In 2017, Apple had set a goal for itself to "one day end our reliance on mining altogether."[32] When we spoke in 2019, Jackson and Apple had just won a Global Climate Action Award from the United Nations, with the UN praising Apple's efforts to "make its products without taking from the Earth."[33] At the end of that year Apple signed a deal to buy aluminum from Alcoa and Rio Tinto for its Watch and iPhone products that was made without carbon, eliminating greenhouse gas emissions from a normally carbon-intensive process.[34]

Buying raw materials on the front end was one thing, but recycling old Apple products was another. Part of the problem for manufacturers is that devices containing lithium-ion batteries come in all shapes and sizes. This was a problem even for Apple, despite its reputation for being fastidious in design.

Enter Daisy, a robot designed and engineered to quickly break apart an iPhone to its glass, aluminum shell, battery, and other component parts. "The mining industry needs to know that if we're concerned about climate, water, and responsible sourcing, that we need to look for innovation," Jackson said. Daisy was part of Apple's plan to become a so-called closed-loop manufacturer, one that adhered to the principles of a "circular economy." In theory, this means that old electronics get broken down to build new ones, over and over, thus limiting the need for new mines. More an aspiration for now, perhaps, than a realistic target given the world's rising hunger for electronic devices, aiming for a circular economy nevertheless would help reduce a constant cycle of consumption and disposal, easing the burden on the planet's strained resources.

"We've trained people how to recycle certain metals, like steel and aluminum, and we make them feel guilty if they don't. But we're still mining bauxite and iron ore," said Jon Kellar, a professor at the South Dakota School of Mines and Technology.[35]

Not long after Jackson and I talked, I decided to see Daisy for myself. Inside a nondescript office park in Austin, Texas, that had no signs on the outside, Apple had set the robot up to go to work. I had arranged to meet Apple staff members outside the entrance and, after a safety briefing, we were given a tour with the understanding that we were not to take photos of Daisy in action.[36]

Daisy looked like a long robotic arm often seen in science fiction movies. It was self-contained in a glass box, was less than 20 yards in length, and used a four-step process to break apart an iPhone. Blasts of air at roughly –80 degrees Celsius (–112 Fahrenheit) were used to pop off the phone's glass screen, as well as its battery pack and haptic engine, the device made with rare earths magnets that makes a phone vibrate. Conveyer belts leading from Daisy rumbled toward large sacks where tiny battery parts and other components of an iPhone were collected, waiting to be sent to recycling facilities so the gold and other metals could be extracted. Apple said that Daisy could tear apart 1.2 million phones per year.[37] Just because Apple aimed to go closed loop didn't necessarily mean it would happen, although the company was making progress: By 2021, almost 20 percent of Apple's computers and other products were made with recycled material, the highest level ever.[38] "The demand in the future for metals is only going to increase," said Corby Anderson, a recycling expert at the Colorado School of Mines Kroll Institute for Extractive Metallurgy. "One way to meet that demand certainly is recycling, but recycling is not going to meet all that demand."[39]

Even after visiting with Apple's Daisy, I had a nagging need to know what came next. Apple wasn't breaking apart batteries at its Austin site, so what happened after? A startup company from Toronto held some answers.

⚡

AJAY KOCHHAR AND Tim Johnston had a ritual.

Several times a week, the engineers would meet up for coffee at a small shop in the basement of the Ontario offices of Hatch, the engineering and consulting firm where they both worked. It was a regular opportunity for them to brainstorm, even though the two men could not be any more opposite. The son of Indian immigrants, Kochhar has a warm, infectious smile that immediately puts one at ease. Johnston, a tall Australian, is affable but introverted, always thinking of the next big idea. These coffees were a way to unpack off-the-wall ideas that might be seen as too "zany" to bring to regular office meetings. In mid-September 2016, Johnston made an unusual request for their regular catch-ups: Would Kochhar meet off campus?

"And immediately, I thought to myself, 'Oh, Tim must be leaving,'" Kochhar said.

The son of entrepreneurs, Kochhar grew up wanting to be a medical doctor before deciding to study chemical engineering instead when he enrolled at the University of Toronto. Traditionally, such a major would have led to a career in the oil or natural gas industry, but when Kochhar enrolled in 2009 the seeds of the green energy transition had been planted. He got an offer from Hatch when he graduated in 2013 to join the "non-ferrous off-gas handling" division, which, despite the clunky name, essentially studied emerging clean technologies. He helped clients engineer processes to reduce their emissions, a key concern for nickel refineries in Ontario. "The experience forced me out of the theoretical space and to actually build things," he said.[40]

In 2013, Kochhar transferred internally at Hatch to a group that was helping mining companies and other clients build new projects. And the first project he was assigned to involved Rio Tinto's plan to build a new lithium mine in Serbia, the same project that would hobble the company during its fight in Arizona with the San Carlos Apache. Kochhar was assigned to help develop a study that would unpack just how Rio could build the facility, and as part of that experience he began to work with Johnston, who lived in Brisbane at the time. Importantly, it introduced Kochhar to the technical side of lithium production.

Within a few years, Johnston had moved to the United States and advised Kochhar to devote more of his professional focus to lithium. Demand for the metal was beginning to surge across the globe thanks to expansions by Tesla and others. A steady stream of clients came to Hatch asking for them to evaluate various lithium projects across the world, fueling Kochhar's desire to jump into the emerging space. By the time Johnston asked him for the off-site coffee in 2016, Kochhar was itching for a change.

Johnston indeed was leaving Hatch, armed with several business ideas that had been brewing in his head for some time. One of those ideas involved recycling lithium-ion batteries to separate out their component metals, especially lithium. Kochhar wasn't convinced there was a business model for recycling that could succeed, so after Johnston left, he dove into various academic papers and industry reports. He found that there wasn't yet an entrenched industry for lithium-ion battery recycling, but there likely would be one in a few years if a business model could be set up to sell recycled lithium and other metals. And Kochhar wanted to help set up that market.

Two months after Johnston left Hatch, Kochhar followed. A week later, they formed Li-Cycle, with the goal of creating a business that would focus solely on pulling metals out of old batteries. For the first year, the pair didn't take a paycheck, which proved a source of personal tension for Kochhar, who had met the woman who would become his wife just before that fateful coffee with Johnston. Potential investors balked, worried that the company would need too much up-front funding or was something too far-fetched.

"For the longest time, folks thought this was a science project," Kochhar recalled. "I could probably create a list of a thousand people we pitched unsuccessfully." They also started trying a bunch of random experiments, including shredding a battery in a kitchen blender.

The coronavirus pandemic turned out to be a godsend for Li-Cycle, Kochhar, and Johnston. By forcing the world to contend with long supply chains for everyday goods, the green energy transition was pushed into overdrive. The same forces that encouraged the United States and other Western nations to consider more mining also encouraged growth in recycling. As EVs grew increasingly more popular, so, too, did discussions about what to do with their batteries when they reached the end of their lives. Also, the manufacturing process for lithium-ion batteries produced leftover scrap waste that needed to be recycled.[41]

The year after Kochhar and Johnston founded Li-Cycle, JB Straubel, whose work in Tesla's early days was so important Elon Musk deemed him a co-founder of the company, started Redwood Materials with the similar goal of recycling old batteries. Straubel, a cerebral, behind-the-scenes type of manager, grew obsessed with finding new ways to reengineer and reuse existing batteries.[42] "An important part of our mission is to get these materials back as quickly and efficiently as possible into the battery supply chain—that's easier said than done," said Straubel,[43] who had designed Tesla's first battery and famously convinced Elon Musk at a 2003 lunch at a Los Angeles seafood restaurant to invest in the automaker.[44]

Despite their similar goals, Redwood's and Li-Cycle's strategies diverged almost from the beginning. Straubel and Redwood aimed to make cathodes for EV batteries. There was no cathode production in North America when Straubel founded Redwood or even by late 2023.[45] Straubel and Redwood hoped to use as much recycled material as possible through processes they ran in-house, but if not, they realized they would need to buy lithium and other metals from mining companies. "We're going to push the recycled percent as high as possible, but that is really going to be dependent on the availability of recycled materials," the Redwood chief executive said. "If we end up consuming 50 percent or more of virgin raw materials, that's fine."[46] Redwood saw itself, ultimately, as more of a cathode producer than a recycler; recycling became a kind of means to an end.

Li-Cycle, by contrast, stayed focused on tearing apart batteries and selling their components back to the market. "We have chosen to stick to our DNA," Kochhar told me. "We're not biting off more than we can chew."[47] Both companies received large loans from the U.S. Department of Energy, which was eager to do whatever it could to boost America's production of EV metals. "One of the benefits of recycling is it can bring metals to market more confidently than some of the mining companies that take a bit longer to go from the identification of the resource to full production," an Energy Department official said.[48]

Redwood and Li-Cycle differed in how they thought about recycling. Both start with batteries that have been crushed down to what's known as black mass—essentially shredded battery cells containing nickel, lithium, and cobalt. Yet Redwood and several other large recyclers in China use a process known as pyrometallurgical recycling, which requires large amounts of energy in order to heat and leach materials from the black mass at 1,482 degrees Celsius (2,700 Fahrenheit). That heating leaves a metal powder that is treated further with chemicals to get forms of cobalt and other metals.[49]

Conversely, the hydrometallurgical recycling techniques favored by Li-Cycle use far less energy but rely on large volumes of acids and other chemicals.[50] Li-Cycle also makes its black mass differently, using a liquid solution to break down the batteries to avoid the kind of fire that shook Garcia's home in Houston back in 2017. The acids and other chemicals, via a series of complex steps, were then used to leach out nickel sulfate, cobalt sulfate, and lithium carbonate.[51] Li-Cycle recovered as much as 95 percent of the nickel, cobalt, and lithium inside old batteries.[52]

Redwood chose to stay a private company controlled largely by Straubel. But in 2021, Li-Cycle started trading on the New York Stock Exchange after a deal that saw the company valued at $1.67 billion.[53] That helped Li-Cycle attract new investors and customers, including Glencore—one of the world's largest mining companies—as well as the battery parts makers LG Chem and the conglomerate Koch Industries.[54] Glencore also agreed to supply a steady stream of sulfuric acid to process more batteries.

And whereas Redwood chose to build a recycling and processing facility in Nevada to which old batteries were shipped, Li-Cycle opted for a so-called hub-and-spoke model, whereby they would build small facilities across the United States and Canada to collect old batteries and crush them down to black mass, which would then be sent to a centralized facility in Rochester, New York, for the black mass to be separated into metals.

Depending on the recycling process and other factors, the cost of transporting lithium-ion batteries for recycling can be as much as 70 percent of the entire recycling process, an eye-popping number that shows why Li-Cycle favored its hub-and-spoke model.[55] And just as the United States and other nations are having to grapple with the need to mine more of their own metals for the green energy transition, so, too, are they having to contend with the need to recycle more of their own batteries. That reality had been underscored by late 2020 when China—which had long accepted the world's junk—tightened its standards to stop taking recyclable materials, including e-waste, from the European Union and United States.[56]

By 2023, Li-Cycle had built spoke facilities in New York, Alabama, Ontario, and Arizona, most of which were near its customers' EV facilities. The Alabama facility, for instance, was built to handle scrap from Mercedes and other automakers rapidly building plants across the U.S. Southeast.[57] A facility near Phoenix[58] aimed to do the same for the EV market growing in the Southwest, which included a plant by the EV maker Lucid.

I met Kochhar at that 68,000-square-foot facility just outside Phoenix on a warm June day in 2022. The company had moved in a month prior. Signs with the company's name had yet to be installed outside the building. Inside, a gargantuan warehouse was filled with 3,500 pallets of battery waste stored in black drums and other containers. Some were filled with old iPhone batteries. Others held large EV batteries from Hyundai and other automakers. Massive fire sprinklers were affixed to the ceiling as a defense in case one of the batteries spontaneously combusted. What struck me immediately was that here was a giant warehouse filled with battery parts needing to be recycled—clearly, the demand was there, and recycling was not necessarily a problem for 2030 or 2040.

"It's 2022, and this warehouse is full. The limiting step for us right now is how fast we can process battery material. It's not the amount of material we have to process," Kochhar said. Several miles down the road, Li-Cycle had recently opened another location where those batteries would be turned into black mass. (U.S. safety regulations require battery collection and battery processing facilities to be separate.) That second facility was even bigger, at 140,000 square feet. Inside, a relatively narrow contraption stood in a gargantuan warehouse. Two stories in height and several hundred feet long, the device tore old batteries apart in three stages. The first stage carried batteries up a 6-foot-wide conveyer belt to a vat filled with a proprietary liquid where the battery was shredded and plastic casings were removed. Copper is removed in a second stage, with a third stage coughing out black mass. Bags of all three wait at the end. It was the first time I had ever seen black mass in person. It looked like a finely powdered charcoal. The day I visited, that crushing machine was processing about 1,100 kilograms of old batteries each hour. That black mass would eventually be sent on to the hub in Rochester, where it would be broken down further into metals.

By 2024, with its Rochester facility fully operational, Li-Cycle aimed to be producing about 8,500 tonnes each year of lithium carbonate, Kochhar casually mentioned on our tour. The number surprised me—at the time, the United States only produced about 5,000 tonnes a year at a small facility in Nevada. That's because Lithium Americas, ioneer, Piedmont, and others had not been able to get their permits, much less open new lithium mines.

"That would make you the biggest lithium producer on the continent," I said to Kochhar.

He nodded yes, smiling. *The largest source of lithium on the North American continent would not be a mine, but old batteries.* It was a shocking thing to process. "I don't think many people have clued into that," he said. And those Arizona facilities and the other spoke sites aimed to grow bigger still, with Li-Cycle eyeing expansions in Europe and Asia.

Lithium-ion battery recycling may not yet have been able to fuel Apple's dreams of a completely circular economy, but neither was it a science experiment any longer. The lithium-ion battery market was valued at $1.33 billion in 2020, a number expected to spike to $38.21 billion by 2030.[59] Traditional sources of lithium and other metals were put on notice. Yes, new mines would be needed to supply the green energy transition's initial phases. But recycling will eventually supply a larger percentage of the metals needed to build more batteries.

"All of those materials we put into a battery and into an EV don't go anywhere. They're all still there. They don't get degraded, they don't get compromised. Ninety-nine percent of those metals, or perhaps more, can be reused again and again and again. Literally hundreds, perhaps thousands of times," said Redwood's Straubel.[60]

While Kochhar, Johnston, and Li-Cycle, Straubel and Redwood, and their other recycling peers were aiming to supply even more metals to the United States and the world, other technologists were trying to produce their own lithium in new, fantastical ways that had never been done before on commercial scales. They were facing a host of problems.

CHAPTER THIRTEEN

Green Technology

"GAVIN! HOW ARE YA, MAN? GOOD TO SEE YA!"

Wearing a crisp white shirt, striped tie, and navy-blue suit, President Joe Biden sat at a small table with a large digital display before him showing Governor Gavin Newsom of California and a smattering of industry executives. Jennifer Granholm, the energy secretary, sat to Biden's right. Gina McCarthy, then the president's national climate advisor, and Kathleen Hicks, the deputy secretary of defense, sat opposite.[1]

While Biden had repeatedly detailed his plans during the 2020 presidential campaign for America's economy to transition away from fossil fuels toward green energy, he had not spoken publicly about where or how he expected the country to procure the minerals needed to achieve those goals. And trust me—I tried to figure it out. During the 2020 campaign, I embedded myself with Biden's campaign for a week in late October, tracking the then-former vice president with a small pool of about twelve other journalists across Florida, Pennsylvania, and Georgia for Reuters. At each stop, through Tampa rainstorms, windy Philadelphia afternoons, and at the Warm Springs resort where FDR went to recuperate (and eventually died), I had one question for Biden: "Does your clean energy plan require more mining?" But Biden didn't bite, the product perhaps of his unwillingness to engage on the topic or his fixation on more-pressing campaign issues at the time. (COVID-19, Russia, his son Hunter.)

Biden, of course, bested Donald Trump in the election and was inaugurated on January 20, 2021. He spent the next year saying nothing publicly about minerals or mining, even while he and Granholm talked repeatedly about the need for the United States to build and use more electric cars, solar panels, and wind turbines. I kept asking myself and my Reuters colleagues, "Just where does Biden expect the country to get these EVs?" After all, Teslas don't grow on trees.

Biden signed an executive order in August 2021 that set a goal for half of all new passenger cars and light trucks sold in 2030 to be electric, a goal that had the backing of Ford, General Motors, and Stellantis, the biggest Detroit-based automakers.[2] But very few of those automakers, or their new rivals, including Rivian and Lordstown Motors, had said where they wanted to procure minerals to build those electric cars by the time Biden signed his order. It was a glaring public oversight and one not in keeping with the auto industry's history. Henry Ford, after all, built an entire town in Brazil's Amazon to source rubber for his growing car empire.[3]

A hint came the prior month when a small startup company in southern California signed a deal to supply General Motors with lithium from deep beneath a man-made lake using experimental technology. The Salton Sea sits about 160 miles (258 km) southeast of Los Angeles. In the early twentieth century, waters from the Colorado River breached an irrigation canal to form the lake, and it's been there ever since, collecting rainwater, pesticides, and runoff from farms.[4] Superhot brines teeming with lithium, calcium, and other metals swirl a mile beneath the Salton Sea at temperatures around 371 degrees Celsius (700 Fahrenheit)—more than three times the boiling point of water. Berkshire Hathaway for years had been flashing steam off those brines to power turbines that produced electricity for much of Southern California. And those brines (essentially salty water) contained more than enough lithium to build all the EVs that Biden wanted to build and use in the country, for decades.[5]

In theory it wouldn't require large open-pit mines (which no one wants in their communities) or large evaporation ponds (which waste millions of gallons of water and take months to produce lithium). While open-pit mines are anathema to many—as seen most pointedly in Piedmont's North Carolina experience—and other lithium projects can harm watersheds and other ecosystems, so-called direct lithium extraction (DLE) technologies offered the promise of filtering out lithium from salty brine reservoirs efficiently and with minimal impact on landscapes. "While all [lithium] extraction methods have the potential for some environmental impact, DLE has the potential to have a smaller environmental impact than either surface mining or evaporative extraction," the Nature Conservancy said in a 2022 report on lithium production methods. There, on the cover of the seventy-four-page report, was a picture of Tiehm's buckwheat.[6]

So the tantalizing question was this: Did one or more types of DLE technology exist that could filter out that lithium from Southern California's hot brines, or even cooler brines in places such as Utah's Great Salt Lake and old oilfields in Arkansas? Laboratory tests for years showed that metals could be filtered from some brines, but those DLE processes had never worked where it matters most—out in the real world.[7]

"I had an over/under on whether you were going to do this today. I'm impressed," Gavin Newsom said through the video screen to Biden. "Thank you for not canceling on us." (Russia was about to invade Ukraine.)

"Are you kidding me?!" Biden said in a tone that underscored how much importance he gave to what he was about to say. Jim Litinsky, the CEO of the rare earths miner MP Materials, JB Straubel of Redwood Materials, and Alicia Knapp, who ran Berkshire's BHE Renewables business, joined the president virtually.

Newsom joined to tout his belief that lithium extraction in the United States—specifically his state—could be done in a "clean and sustainable way," a belief that he shared with the president.[8]

"We can avoid the historical injustices that too many mining operations left behind in American towns," the president said.

New sources of minerals for the EV economy, Biden was essentially saying, could not repeat the past sins of the mining industry by damaging the environment and leaving behind a wasteland for local communities to contend with. If America was going to go green, and if that greening required metals, the production of those metals must not leave destruction in its wake. It was an ambitious goal, and Biden told Knapp that Berkshire's plans for California's Salton Sea were a "big part" of his plan.

DLE technologies are comparable to common household water softeners, which remove metals from drinking water. One industry analyst told me he thinks DLE processes could supply a quarter of global lithium supply by 2030. The process can take as little as a few hours to filter the metal inside an average-sized warehouse. By contrast, traditional evaporation ponds can be hundreds of acres in size, permanently drain nearby aquifers, and take several years to produce lithium. However, most DLE technologies are more expensive to operate than evaporation ponds, which use sunlight.

Knapp told the president that Berkshire was "working to secure the most abundant source of lithium in the United States using the world's most environmentally friendly technology. . . . If this seems ambitious, it is. And there's no one better suited to take on an ambitious test like this than Berkshire Hathaway Energy."

Mere hours before Biden was inaugurated on January 20, 2021, the U.S. Department of Energy had chosen Berkshire to receive government funding for its plans to produce lithium in the Salton Sea region for the auto industry. It seemed like a parting shot from the outgoing Trump administration, and a decision that would come to haunt Biden's White House.

The grant was to fund studies into whether lithium from Salton Sea brines could be turned into lithium hydroxide. Berkshire was to fund the other half of the $30 million project. The federal grant was designed to complement one from the year prior, when Berkshire had received $6 million from the California Energy Commission, a state agency, to study whether lithium could even be removed from the Salton Sea brines at such high temperatures. Cooling the brine down would be expensive, since it would require more energy that would boost the project's cost. The science wasn't quite there, but Berkshire was hopeful.

The implications were clear: If the Salton Sea could produce lithium simply by filtering water and brine, that meant the United States didn't need to dig up places like Thacker Pass or Rhyolite Ridge, or have to decide whether sage grouse leks, Indigenous ceremonial grounds, or

Tiehm's buckwheat should be sacrificed. The country could leave behind the dirty, nasty mining practices of the past. It could truly usher in a green economy.

What Knapp didn't say, though, spoke volumes for not only Biden's plans but also the future of lithium production in the Salton Sea. For the previous thirteen months, behind closed doors, Berkshire had been tussling with the Energy Department over terms of the grant, including control of patents and whether it could one day sell its lithium business, even if the government helped to fund its creation.[9] Berkshire had not even technically accepted the grant yet, making Knapp's participation in Biden's event seem like a glaring oversight.

Energy Department staff said in emails they planned to be "substantially involved in the direction and redirection of the technical aspects of the project." Berkshire said, though, that it "would expect to manage [the project] with its existing development plans."[10]

The Energy Department warned Berkshire on December 14, 2021—two months before Biden's minerals roundtable—that talks had reached an "impasse" and that the company needed to accept the grant or risk losing it. That warning was never relayed to the White House. A senior Energy Department official asked Berkshire to meet with her in January 2022, calling the company's Salton Sea plans an important part of the government's plans to boost U.S. minerals production.

Even while bragging to Biden about Berkshire's technical prowess, Knapp failed to tell the president that the company was facing tremendous technical challenges in the Salton Sea as the region's superhot brines corroded equipment and clogged pipes. One metallurgy professor described the region's brines as a "nasty, hot soup that's sometimes acidic," pointing to the potent challenge facing Berkshire.[11]

Behind the scenes, unbeknownst to Biden, a company that was publicly hailed as key to Washington's green energy goals seemed to be opposing the Biden administration at every turn and lacking the technological know-how it purported to have. It was not only a bad omen for Biden's climate goals, but also for the economy of the Salton Sea region, which had become one of the poorest parts of California.

The same day that Biden held his minerals roundtable, the Berkshire lobbyist Jonathan Weisgall emailed a senior advisor to Energy Secretary Jennifer Granholm.

"As you know," Weisgall wrote, the "president and CEO of BHE Renewables told President Biden at the White House critical minerals roundtable just now that we have started working on two R&D demonstration grants—one from the state of California and one from the U.S Department of Energy—to show . . . that we can also recover lithium from that brine."

Despite that brag, Berkshire reached out to the Energy Department the next day and asked to change its plans in order to produce a type of lithium that was less technically challenging to make, implying it did not have the technological prowess it told Biden publicly that it had. That request—in the wake of the behind-the-scenes back-and-forth—led to Berkshire losing the grant several weeks later.

Biden's public promises that Berkshire's technology could help the Salton Sea's economy as well as his own green energy ambitions had come back to haunt him. The promise of a cutting-edge technology to produce lithium without the mess of open-pit mines or water-wasting evaporation ponds had not yet been met.

PART OF BERKSHIRE'S hope was due to other mineralogical successes in the Salton Sea region. Starting in 1932, the Cardex Western Company had extracted carbon dioxide from sand deposits about 100 meters deep, using the gas to make dry ice to cool railcars. The effort stopped in 1954 after the advent of the refrigerated railcar.

The Morton Salt Co. extracted calcium chloride (a type of salt) from the area in the 1970s.[12] And Berkshire itself produced zinc in the early 2000s from Salton Sea geothermal brines at a small test facility, with contracts to supply a Canadian zinc company. But Berkshire's project was plagued from the beginning and ultimately closed when zinc prices crashed in 2004.[13]

Given that mixed track record, lithium production was far from a surefire situation for the Salton Sea. But it was not for lack of trying. Going back to the late 1970s, scientists had tried to develop technologies that could commercially filter lithium from brine formations across the United States and the world. In the late 2000s, California and the U.S. Department of Energy had given nearly identical grants to Simbol Inc., a startup firm with an uncanny ability to attract some of the most brilliant minds in chemical processing and engineering. The company and its scientists filed more than nineteen patents related to the filtration of lithium from geothermal brines in the Salton Sea. They used the government funding to test their hunches. But ultimately, thanks in part to a skirmish with Elon Musk, they failed.

The Salton Sea's lithium kept luring scientists. A month before Biden set his 2030 goal, the auto giant General Motors signed a deal to help a small startup company from Australia known as Controlled Thermal Resources to produce lithium from the Salton Sea. GM gave few details about how much money it was spending (publicly saying only that it was making a "multimillion-dollar investment") or how much lithium it hoped to produce (saying only the Salton Sea "will supply a sizeable amount of our lithium needs.")[14]

Controlled Thermal was over the moon, bragging that its Salton Sea project (which it nicknamed, perhaps without a sense of irony, "Hell's Kitchen") could, with GM's help, be producing enough lithium by 2024 to make 60,000 tonnes of lithium each year, enough of the metal to make millions of EV batteries. That was roughly twice as much as Lithium Americas hoped to make from Thacker Pass. Controlled Thermal added that it thought that by filtering out lithium from the Salton Sea brines, it would emit fifteen times less carbon dioxide than lithium mines in Australia, at the time the world's largest producer of lithium.[15]

To start, though, Controlled Thermal needed to build a power plant, something it had never done before. To make its efforts profitable, it would need to first produce electricity. Then it could filter lithium. There was one company, however, that already had more than ten power plants in the area and was itching to produce lithium: Berkshire Hathaway, controlled by Warren Buffett, at the time one of the world's richest men. Yet Berkshire's lithium technology had its own limitations.

California had a lot riding on the efforts of Berkshire, Controlled Thermal, and a third company known as EnergySource Minerals. All wanted to produce lithium from the area, but it was Berkshire that had received the federal grant, and it was Berkshire that was chosen to join Biden and Newsom that day in February 2022.

⚡

HERBERT HENRY DOW had long been fascinated with brine, though it was bromine—used in synthetic dyes, among other products—rather than lithium that caught his attention. A prolific inventor and the son of an inventor, Dow received his first patent at the age of twenty-three. In 1897, he founded the Dow Chemical Co., which today is one of the largest chemical companies in the world. At the time, Dow used his technological prowess, his patents, and Michigan's large brine formations to produce bromine far cheaper than German rivals.[16]

In 1917, as the First World War was in its penultimate year, Dow's daughter Ruth married Leland Doan, a native of Ann Arbor and an engineer by training. Doan that same year joined his father-in-law's company, slowly rising through the ranks in various sales positions.[17] By 1930, the senior Dow was dead, succumbing to cirrhosis brought on by years of steady drinking.

After helping to guide the company through the Great Depression and the Second World War, Doan was named Dow's president in 1949. Nepotism or not, Doan, who favored small rimmed glasses atop his rotund face, proved he could run the company, helping it nearly quintuple its annual sales to about $900 million during his thirteen years at the helm.[18]

A hallmark of his leadership was regular retreats to a cabin in northern Michigan where the company's brightest minds would debate future technologies and how Dow Chemical could or should pivot to help produce them. It was an innovative approach, to be sure, especially coming so soon after a war that had taught generations of Americans to accept what they were told by authority figures. Here was a corporate leader encouraging dissent, asking for free thought, and demanding frank dialogue.

With some trepidation, an employee who had served in the war raised his hand at a retreat in the early 1950s and offered his prognostication for the future: "In fifty years, everyone is going to be walking around with a telephone in their pocket."[19]

The room erupted in laughter, cackles really. *What was this idiot thinking?*

Doan, though, wasn't laughing. He quieted the room.

"Why do you think that's going to happen?" he asked his junior staffer, the veteran.

"Well, nobody wants to be tied to a wall with a wire."

"So what's the biggest restriction to that?" *Why couldn't a mass form of communication go mobile?*

"Well, they're too heavy."

The veteran explained that he had hated traipsing around Europe during the war for thirty months carting a 40-pound battery on his back for his commander's walkie-talkie. That experience convinced him that better technologies were necessary. The problem was essentially the heavy lead-acid batteries.

That prodded Doan to turn to his head of research, Bill Bauman, with a request: "Find out what the most efficient battery material would be."

The morning after Doan's brainstorm, Bauman came back with a report. Not only was lithium extremely good at holding an electric charge, but it was also the lightest metal on the Periodic Table of Elements, making it an exceptionally good candidate for future batteries.

And Dow was already producing bromine from brines across the United States, brines that Doan, Bauman, and the company surmised would also be good sources of lithium. And so Doan put Bauman in charge of a program to study how the fast-growing chemical company could produce lithium should a mass-market need arrive in the future. While elsewhere in the world some were producing lithium using large evaporation ponds, Dow eschewed that approach for fear it would produce too many other salts (calcium and magnesium, especially) for which it had no market use.

If Dow could produce bromine from brine, then it stood to reason the company could also produce lithium from brine. Its scientists went to work for over a decade. And largely, those years were not successful. Lithium, Dow Chemical discovered, was a social creature among its friends on the Periodic Table of Elements, one that did not want to be alone. After spending gobs of money and more than a decade, Dow shelved the lithium research in the late 1960s.

But Bauman kept an interest in the white metal, and after leaving his position as Dow's chief technology officer, he set himself up as a kind of in-house scientist, a position known as a Dow Fellow. From his lab at Dow's campus in Texas, which he called the Advanced Separations Lab, Bauman began to futz around on various issues that had gnawed at him over the years, including lithium.

"We're going to figure out how to get lithium," he told his team. And they went to work. By the late 1970s, Bauman and another Dow scientist named John Lee had combined a metal salt containing aluminum with an ion exchange resin, a kind of filter for removing certain metals. After many tests, they found the right ratio of the two that could extract lithium from brine, but they did not know how it worked. However, Bauman and Lee found that they could wash off the lithium from the resin, and, voila—a supply of the metal.[20]

There still were a host of problems in the process, which were not entirely understood by the Dow team. If they didn't know what was actually happening at the molecular level, that meant it would be nearly impossible to get the process to work at a commercial scale. In 1979, a young scientist named John Burba who had just earned a Ph.D. in physical chemistry joined the team.

"My first assignment was to figure out what this crap was and figure out the structure of it and why it did what it did," Burba recalled. Working with Bauman, Lee, and the others in Dow's lab, Burba filed numerous patents that helped refine the process.[21] By 1979, the first Direct Lithium Extraction process had taken place at Dow, and the company set up a small facility in Freeport, Texas, to run tests on the new processes. Dow, at the time, also owned a facility in Arkansas to produce bromine. That bromine, it turned out, also teemed with lithium-rich brine, so Dow put a test facility there, too. It ran about nine months, and it worked, but it was expensive and had kinks to work out. And lithium prices were very low in the years before portable electronics became fashionable, never mind electric vehicles.

Dow decided to sell its brine chemical business—including all the lithium research into which Bauman, Burba, Lee, and others had poured their blood, sweat, and tears—in 1987 to a company that would eventually be known as Albemarle Corporation.[22]

Bauman retired and moved away. Burba went on to other projects at Dow. Both let lithium slip from the forefront of their minds.

In early 1992, Burba found himself hammering at the eaves of his roof. He had just left Dow Chemical and taken a job at Great Lakes Chemical Corporation. He set aside a few weeks of personal time before moving his family to Arkansas so that he could make some home repairs before selling his Texas house. Perched on a ladder, Burba heard his wife yell up that he had a phone call, so he climbed down. It was Bauman.

"John, how are you doing?"

Fine, Burba replied, asking the same question in reverse.

"I'm bored as hell. We need to come up with a better way to produce lithium."

"Sure, OK, that sounds good to me," Burba said, masking an excitement only a chemist could hold.

"All right, well, I'll jump on a plane tomorrow."

After debating the best ways to improve upon the resin that Bauman and Lee had developed, Bauman and Burba developed two new methods for lithium extraction after multiple experiments that featured kitchen utensils borrowed from Bauman's wife. But there wasn't a large market for lithium, which was primarily at that time used in glass, lubricants, and pharmaceuticals. The invention made using kitchen utensils was awarded several patents, but it sat largely unused for a few more years.

⚡

BURBA LEFT ARKANSAS in 1994 for Princeton, New Jersey, where he was hired to conduct research for FMC Corporation, which had bought Lithium Corporation of America the previous decade, at the time the world's largest producer of the metal. When he joined, he was asked to list the patents he held, at least one of which FMC had already licensed and was testing in its labs.[23]

Eager to ensure its role as a major producer of a then-niche product, FMC had struck a deal with the Argentine government to produce lithium high in the Andes Mountains in the Salar del Hombre Muerto, a giant salt pan filled with lithium-rich brine at an elevation of nearly 14,000 feet. Internal company estimates showed that a mine in North Carolina that supplied all of FMC's lithium would be depleted in perhaps five years. The pressure was on.

FMC had little experience producing lithium from brine, so it planned to mimic what a competitor had been doing at a similar facility in Nevada. Foote Mineral, which would one day be owned by Albemarle, had installed a series of evaporation ponds, each hundreds of acres in size and each evaporating out a different chemical, leaving lithium in the end.

In theory, it made sense to use the same process in Argentina. But FMC found itself in trouble almost right away. The brine in Argentina had much higher concentrations of magnesium, as well as sulfur and boron, than Foote's Nevada operations. That meant, due to a chemical process known as the Common Ion Effect, using a series of evaporation ponds wouldn't work. The magnesium, for starters, wouldn't separate out—it would stick with the lithium. Ideas being bandied about to solve the problem by injecting lime into the ponds would only produce a gelatinous substance akin to Jell-o. Burba knew this and informed his new employers, only to be rebuffed and told he didn't know what he was talking about.

Burba went back to Princeton.

Reports from the Argentina site to FMC's leadership stopped. That's when Bob Burt got on a plane. A hard-charging chief executive, Burt had taken the reins at FMC two years prior after climbing the ranks for eighteen years running the company's pesticide division and a separate division that made Bradley tanks, which were widely used during the First Gulf War.

If lithium was core to FMC's future, and if FMC needed a new source of lithium, Burt wanted to know what was going on in Argentina. But once at the site, he found a chilly reception. Workers offered to show Burt everything but the pond that he wanted to see. Eventually,

Burt grew so annoyed that he threatened to simply walk around the entire complex until he found it himself.

Begrudgingly, they took him to the test pond. And there, out in front of FMC's leader, were acres of gelatinous magnesium hydroxide. Burt, who at one point also served on the board of directors of Phelps Dodge, the copper company that would one day be bought by Freeport-McMoRan, was enraged: "You guys have successfully made twenty acres of fucking Jell-O!" he thundered while stomping on the pond, sending undulating waves to its far corner.

Back at the company's headquarters, after firing some of the scientists behind the Argentina debacle, Burt and other FMC executives realized they needed to talk to Burba. He was summoned from his lab and asked, in detail, how much lithium he and Bauman had made with their patented technology.

"We made about 2.5 grams," Burba told them, eliciting gasps. Burba's technology was effectively a science experiment. Could it work in Argentina? That's what they were really wondering.

"Can you turn it into a working process?" Burt asked Burba.

"Yes."

"You sound very certain."

"Well, I'm certain we can."

"So, what do you need to do what you need to do?"

Burba explained the staffing, the crew, and the labs he would need, before giving them the information they really wanted: "Two to three years and probably eight to ten million dollars."

Feeling the market pressure, Burt said he had six months and $4 million. "If we wait three years, this business is dead."

Within six months, Burba had proven his technology could work in the Argentine mountains and produce lithium. FMC pushed forward, approving a plan to meld Burba's DLE technology with evaporation ponds at the site, which opened in June 1998 after four years of construction. The mine, at the time, produced about a third of the world's lithium—and just as demand began to surge from the battery industry.[24]

Sony's Walkman was already selling more than 150 million devices a year by that point. Apple's iPod—with its revolutionary rechargeable lithium polymer battery and ten hours of music play time—debuted in 2001.[25]

"Argentina opened at just the right time," Burba recalled. Others across the world had noticed what he and FMC had done and wondered what it meant for them, too. Including Bolivia.

⚡

BY EARLY 2013, Burba had retired. But then the startup company Simbol came calling, searching for a leader. Founded in 2006 by the engineers Luka Erceg and John Conley—who both met while pursuing graduate work at Houston's Rice University—the company aimed to extract lithium from the Salton Sea by adding their technology to geothermal power plants. They had recruited scientists from the Lawrence Livermore National Laboratory as well.[26] It was a plan that would eventually be mimicked years later in the same region.

A company named EnergySource had, in 2012, opened a $400 million geothermal power plant in the Salton Sea, the first such plant to be built in the area in twenty years. The facility, not far from the famed Coachella Valley, was named for John Featherstone, a scientist who had pushed for years for greater development of geothermal power plants as a way to make electricity with very little by-products or waste. Geothermal power plants take superhot liquids from deep beneath the Earth's crust and flash steam off them, using the steam to spin turbines that generate electricity. The water is then reinjected underground. The facility generated nearly 50 megawatts of power, enough to supply fifty-thousand homes across the region.[27] (By 2016, there were nineteen such geothermal power plants in the Salton Sea region.[28])

Simbol's plan was basically to bolt its technology onto the Featherstone plant and extract lithium from the water that EnergySource was pulling from deep underground, at depths of more than 10,000 feet. It was a plan that made sense, on paper. In 2008, Simbol had estimated that the global lithium market would be worth $1.5 billion by 2015.[29] And the Salton Sea's brines were chock full of lithium, a tantalizing prospect for any company that could figure out how to separate the white metal from those superhot liquids.

Burba joined Simbol in part because he saw the potential for the company to make lithium that would be, in his words, "absolutely green" with "essentially no pollution."[30] It would be the continuation (or the culmination, he hoped) of work he had pioneered at Dow Chemical and FMC, a way to cement the legacy of his more than forty-year career.

By 2013, Simbol had built a small facility in the Salton Sea to test its technology. The facility ran for more than a year. One of the main problems Simbol faced was silica, a naturally occurring chemical that is one of the main components of sand. The brine needed to be cooled to extract the lithium, but when that step was taken, the silica would form glass that would clog pipes and other equipment, a major impediment.

Working with Burba and other scientists, Simbol was able to devise technology to deal with the silica. It was a big breakthrough for Simbol, and its venture capital backers at Menlo Park, California–based Mohr Davidow Ventures (MDV), were thrilled. Test projects also proved the technology was immensely successful.[31]

Given that development, and the subsequent performance of the company's test facility, it was time to start hunting for an investor that could help fund the construction of a commercial facility or, perhaps, buy the entire company. Burba thought that Elon Musk, might be interested.

Tesla at the time was buying lithium-ion battery cells from Panasonic. The automaker was also scouring the United States for a place to build its so-called Gigafactory to assemble its vehicles. Rumors swirled that, perhaps, Southern California could be the ideal spot for Elon Musk and the EV giant. Wouldn't Tesla like to have lithium sourced close by as well?

But Burba didn't know how to even reach Musk. He drafted a three-page presentation and started racking his brain for how he could get it to the elusive CEO. He soon realized that one of his connections knew a Wall Street analyst who might know a way to reach Musk. In early 2014, Burba sent the presentation through the loose network, hoping it would make its way to its intended destination.

It did.

A few months later, Deepak Ahuja, Tesla's chief financial officer, and JB Straubel, Tesla's co-founder, reached out to Burba, wanting to know more about Simbol, its technology, and the Salton Sea. By June, Tesla had made Simbol a $325 million offer, a sign that Tesla was hungry for a deal and wanted to move fast.[32] The proposal stipulated that Simbol would receive shares in Tesla worth $325 million, a common tactic that let the acquiring company keep its cash while also incentivizing the seller. If the technology that was bought as part of the deal didn't work and the acquiring company suffered as a result, so in theory would the seller.

Ahuja emailed the formal offer, telling Burba that Tesla would benefit greatly from Simbol's "people, innovative technology, and the potential to increase the supply of Li [lithium] in an environmentally friendly manner." Tucked inside the offer was a formal letter from Musk himself to Burba and Simbol's board of directors:

> I am very excited about the prospect of Tesla and Simbol coming together, and I hope that you share our view that this is a compelling opportunity to combine two innovative companies on a mission to advance clean and sustainable energy technologies worldwide. We're very impressed with what you and your management team have created at Simbol, and we look forward to discussing how you and the Simbol management team would continue to make a real difference in the world.[33]

Musk, importantly, told Burba not to talk to the media or otherwise share news of the offer.

Then things started to get interesting.

MDV, the investment firm that was a major Simbol investor, had taken stakes in several large tech companies in the 1980s and 1990s. It was used to large returns, and $325 million just wasn't going to work if this technology, indeed, could help shift the globe's economy away from fossil fuels. (Never mind that a commercial Simbol plant would alone likely cost $600 million or more and take at least three years to build.[34])

So Burba approached Musk, who openly mused how to move the deal forward without a formal counteroffer.

"How will we do this?" Musk asked Burba.[35]

"Well, we could ask Jefferies to value the project," Burba replied, referencing the New York–based investment bank. Burba's hope was that by hiring an independent party to value Simbol, Tesla would have to stick to whatever number they came back with.

"If Jefferies will value it, and we can still use stock, then we have a deal," Musk told Burba.[36]

In a twenty-page report marked "Highly Confidential," Jefferies compared and contrasted Simbol with FMC—Burba's former company and a leading lithium producer by that time in its own right—as well as Chile's SQM and Rockwood Holdings Inc.[37] Technology from those companies and others "cannot meet large EV manufacture demand for quality LiOH [lithium hydroxide], the report noted, adding that Simbol's technology was "superior" to others on the market. The report additionally forecast that the lithium hydroxide that Simbol aimed to produce would sell for an average of $13,464 per tonne by 2020, nearly double the rate in 2014, due to "persistent scarcity." Importantly, Jefferies found Simbol's plan to be far better for the environment than other lithium projects. Simbol's plan, the bank noted, did not require a mine, or mine processing plant, or large tailings ponds, or remediation costs to close.

Taking all of that into account, Jefferies said that Simbol was likely worth about $2.5 billion, a large sum that nevertheless was justified by the expected surge in global lithium demand.

Burba, who was in China at the time on business, sent the report to Musk, who reviewed it. During the working hours in China—the middle of the night in the United States—Musk called Burba to discuss the bank's report.

"I just don't want to look like an idiot to my board," Musk said.

"OK, I understand," Burba replied, noting that Jefferies had done a thorough, impartial study. "Think about it, and then let's talk."

The next week, the pair were in person again. Musk, though, was agitated. He tossed a printed version of the Jefferies report on the table in front of them.

"Someone," Musk said to the room, "told me that John Burba is a liar."

Burba was stunned.

"Someone," Musk went on, "told me that I can buy lithium for a decade at six hundred dollars a tonne."

"That's not true," Burba interjected, pointing out the bank's lithium hydroxide price estimates. Six hundred dollars per tonne, he told Musk, wouldn't even cover the cost to make the metal, let alone turn any profit. "You can't do that. It can't be done."

But Musk's mind was made up, influenced by this unknown person that Burba was already cursing in his head. Tesla would now cut its offer to $125 million, Musk said.

"I can't do that," Burba returned. "But would you at least invest in Simbol?"

"No," Musk retorted.

Burba got up and walked out. He never talked to Musk again, and he never learned who had poisoned the deal. Tesla would go on to ink deals with most of Simbol's entrenched rivals. Simbol's technology and its patents—including the important technology to remove silica from superhot brines—were eventually bought by a startup company led by the country music singer Clay Walker. As of this writing, that company and its partner Occidental Petroleum have done little to use them to produce lithium.

For Burba, the entire Simbol experience was frustrating but also instructive. He realized that while Tesla and Musk certainly wanted its technology on the cheap in the end, the timeline to build the commercial plant—at least three years, or perhaps longer—was likely a turnoff. And Tesla needed every penny it could get to build its own plants; it probably didn't have or didn't want to spend $600 million on a commercial lithium facility. (Tesla had $746 million in cash at the time Musk and Burba met.)

The solution, Burba thought, might be a portable lithium facility that could be moved around on trucks while also filtering lithium with DLE technology. He knew from his time at Dow Chemical, at FMC, and then at Simbol that lithium demand was only going to rise, and that while there were very few lithium brine deposits across the world as big as those of the Salton Sea, there were many lithium brine deposits far smaller but nevertheless rich in the battery metal.

Could a portable lithium plant be the future? Burba thought so. And so rather than take umbrage at Musk's irascible negotiating tactics—tactics that had doomed Simbol—Burba decided to start a new company, one that would succeed where so many others had failed. All he had to do was file more patents again, something he knew a lot about. It was a strategy a rival thought it also could deploy in the country estimated to hold more lithium than any other place on Earth—Bolivia.

CHAPTER FOURTEEN

An Elusive Prize

THE ROAD BETWEEN POTOSÍ AND UYUNI IN BOLIVIA IS 126 miles of strange and twisting history and struggle and hope. Scores of hairpin turns forced me to heave my body to avoid clumping up against my two seatmates in the back of a Toyota 4Runner outfitted with a snorkel and other off-road gear. The road at times was buttressed by hulking rocks that evoked pictures of the Martian landscape beamed back to Earth from *Perseverance*. Other times it was embanked by cliffs so steep I wondered if anything could survive a fall.

Faded campaign advertisements painted onto highway drainage ditches implored VOTE SI EVO 2020-2025![1] as a sign of what could have been and a reminder of how lithium fueled the undoing of a sitting president here in the Plurinational State of Bolivia, which holds more of the white metal used to make electric vehicle batteries than any other place on Earth. Road signs warned of llama and ostrich crossings. They did not promise sightings. Eventually, the curves lessened and the altitude dropped, and both helped quiet the throbbing in my head, which was unacclimated to being nearly 12,000 feet above sea level. As the landscape morphed, it at times evoked a John Wayne film, with erratic buttes giving way to large grassy plains and other geological wonders.

An advertisement for Potosína beer declared: LA CERVEZA MÁS ALTA DEL MUNDO. THE BEER AT THE TOP OF THE WORLD. And I believed it. Because here in Bolivia, anything seems possible and nothing seems possible, both polarities existing in an unclear harmony. At roughly 424,000 square miles, Bolivia is nearly the same size as Colombia.[2] But the amount of roadway in the country is roughly 56,500 miles, which lags by comparison to much smaller Ghana and Ireland.[3] As a result, getting around Bolivia—which is bisected by the Andes Mountains and nicknamed the "Tibet of the Americas"—is often a time-consuming task that stunts the nation's economic potential. One woman I met in Potosí described her more than twelve-hour ordeal to reach the regional capital despite the distance being 297 miles, roughly what separates Boston and Philadelphia.

Potosí is not only a major city, but the namesake of the regional department, the equivalent in Bolivia of a state or province. One of the main demands from locals in the Department of Potosí is more paved roads; the road I found myself on was itself a rarity.[4] As it grew straighter, a valley of muck and grass and vicuna and lamb presented itself. The hills surrounding the valley were coated white in salt, not snow, because the ground underneath is bursting with reserves of sodium chloride. When game eat the grass from this valley, the locals say, the salinity permeates their muscles and leaves an indelible taste for the dinner table. Some of the hills surrounding the valley undulated like sheets fluttering in the wind. Others looked like warts, cragged and pockmarked. This place had its own beauty, I thought, especially at dusk as the sun began to set over the hills and the moon slowly emerged in the sky and light from both converged to smother the land with an amber hue.

Potosí, in the rearview, once supplied most of the silver that kept the engine of the Spanish Empire humming. From its founding in 1545 after the discovery of a literal mountain of silver, Potosí kept a steady stream of the metal flowing to Spain, China,[5] and other eager customers across the globe. In the early seventeenth century, a new way to extract the metal was invented that involved crushing silver-bearing ore, mixing it with mercury, and then letting it bake in the sun. That new technology, and a horrific system of forced labor, helped Potosí's economy boom.[6] It was known as "the first city of capitalism." It made Spain enormously wealthy.[7]

At one point in the early seventeenth century, the city's population eclipsed that of London.[8] Today, it has about 176,000 residents, a bit smaller than Little Rock, Arkansas. While the Spanish never found

El Dorado, Potosí proved an enviable consolation prize. The empire built its first Western Hemisphere mint in the city in the late sixteenth century, pumping out legions of Spanish dollars, colloquially known as pieces of eight, and becoming the envy of buccaneers across the globe. It built exquisite architecture throughout the city that, while now time-worn, has nevertheless been preserved and honored as a UNESCO heritage site.

But slowly the city took stock of the high costs to its people of the extraction of silver. The author Eduardo Galeano tells of the 8 million who died extracting Potosí's silver in his wildly popular *Las venas abiertas de América Latina*, or *Open Veins of Latin America*, a copy of which Hugo Chávez gifted to Barack Obama in 2009. Apocryphal or not, the number is seared into the minds of Bolivians as evidence of the high cost of natural-resource extraction.

By the eighteenth century, much of the silver reserves had been depleted and the Spanish moved on to better mines in Mexico and elsewhere.[9] Sales of tin eventually overtook those of silver, but they could not match the wealth that silver had generated. It was an inevitability that Adam Smith had warned about in his capitalistic guidepost *The Wealth of Nations*, declaring: "If new mines were discovered as much superior to those of Potosí as they were superior to those of Europe, the value of silver might be so much degraded as to render even the mines of Potosí not worth the working."[10] The grass, truly, is always greener.

The silver did not produce generational wealth for Bolivians; much of that went to Spain's empire, and the country has come to suffer what's commonly known as the natural resource curse, with mineral-rich colonies often failing to provide basic education or infrastructure for their people. The Bolivia of the twenty-first century is one of the poorest countries in the Western Hemisphere. Cerro Rico, the mountain with the silver deposits, is slowly collapsing. Artisanal miners scour the more than four thousand dilapidated mine shafts within the mountain looking for scraps of silver to sell to put food on their tables.[11] They often chew coca leaves to help boost their energy levels as they toil underground.[12]

While Potosí traces its roots to the reign of Philip II, Uyuni was a relatively late bloomer. From its founding in 1890 by Syrian and Slav colonists, the small outpost served as a key railroad stop on the line to the city of Antofagasta, once Bolivia's jewel on the Pacific Ocean but now part of modern-day Chile.[13] A town of roughly 10,000, Uyuni is dotted with half-finished buildings, salt-encrusted streets, queñua trees, and quinoa, a hearty plant now known throughout the world as a superfood but one that is particularly adept at thriving in the salty cold of high Bolivian altitudes.[14] Importantly for Uyuni, it is near the Salar de Uyuni, the world's largest salt flat at more than 3,860 square miles, nearly the same size as Hawaii's Big Island.[15] Nestled between two offshoots of the Andes Mountains, the salar is a wonder to behold. The road from Potosí winds its way to Uyuni and then along the salar, an expanse that evokes a flat white carpet. It's said that the astronaut Neil Armstrong saw the salar from the moon in 1969 and thought it was a large glacier.[16] A quiet wind blows through the air providing the only auditory sensations. The stillness and wideness and *blanco* landscape force you to ask yourself if you are lucid or dreaming.

In 2017, the director Rian Johnson used the salar as the setting of the mythical planet Crait for *Star Wars: The Last Jedi*, insisting to his location scout team that the shoot utilize an area replete with salt, not snow.[17] In promoting the film, Johnson described Crait as "way out there," "very remote," and "uncharted," adding that it was a "mineral planet and so there are mines on it."[18] Bolivia, it would seem, held echoes of a mythical Star Wars planet. Except it's not in a galaxy far, far away.

Legend has it that once, long ago, the volcanic mountains surrounding the salt flat were actually giant people caught in a love triangle. Yana Pollera, so the legend passed down from generation to generation by the Indigenous Quechua people goes, had an affair with two men: Thunupa and Q'osqo. When Yana became pregnant, Thunupa and Q'osqo fought a fierce battle over paternity, frightening Yana so much that she sent her baby away. But Yana grew worried her baby might be hungry, so she flooded the salt flat with milk to feed it. The milk eventually turned to salt, leaving behind the Salar de Uyuni.[19]

Geologists tell a different story. Two branches of the Andes Mountains diverge in southern Bolivia, pinning the salar (the Spanish term for "salt flat") in the middle. Thousands of years ago, the salar was a lake now known as Lake Minchin. Water flowed in but had nowhere else to go, an environment known to geographers as an endorheic basin. Over time, the water in the lake slowly evaporated, leaving behind the salt formation.

That phenomenon is repeated every rainy season as rainwaters that wash down from nearby mountains have nowhere to go. Those waters carry with them loads of minerals from the snow-crested peaks and saturate the salar with several inches of water, forming one of the world's largest mirrors. As one of the flattest places on Earth—the salar's height deviates by only one meter across the entire expanse—satellites often use it to calibrate their sensors. Flamingoes flock to the salar from November to March to soak in the water and breed before migrating onward. As the year marches on and the dry season approaches, the water evaporates, leaving behind hexagonal salt patterns that coat the entire surface of the salar and evoke ornate household tiles.

Fortunately for Bolivia, that evaporative process has led to enormous mineral wealth. Resting underneath the hard salt floor of the salar is brine containing magnesium, the fertilizer potash, and a large share of the world's lithium. There is enough lithium in Bolivia to power billions of electronic devices. While neighboring Chile and Argentina also have lithium reserves and together the three countries are known as the "Lithium Triangle," Bolivia has the lion's share, with an estimated 19 million tonnes of lithium resources waiting to be tapped, according to the U.S. Geological Survey. But because little production had been undertaken, Bolivia's lithium is considered a resource, a technical definition that essentially means the specific amount that can be extracted has yet to be determined. It differs from a reserve, which is based on geological analysis, required by mining financiers, of the amount of a metal that can be technically recovered. Even still, having the world's largest lithium resource gives Bolivia enormous power in the green energy transition. By 2018, that lithium had entranced an American startup firm, which boasted it had the best technology to help Bolivia mass-produce the metal for the first time. However, China and Russia disagreed.

⚡

SPAIN'S COLONIES ACROSS Latin America began to break free from their colonial overlords as Madrid's empire slowly started to wither in the nineteenth century. Led in part by the Venezuelan Simón Bolívar, people across the continent formed new countries with their own laws, customs, and economies. The region of Charcas renamed itself Bolivia in honor of its liberator. The country fell into a vicious cycle of wars and alliances with its neighbors, especially Chile to its west. Most of these wars hurt Bolivia. From 1879 to 1938, Bolivia lost more than half its lands to Chile, Argentina, Paraguay, Brazil, and Peru.[20]

A war with Chile in the late nineteenth century forced Bolivia to cede its access to the Pacific Ocean, effectively making it a landlocked nation.[21] (The country maintains a navy on Lake Titicaca, the highest navigable lake in the world, which is also on the border with Peru.) As the nineteenth century ended, Bolivia waged a war with Brazil to the north. Bolivia lost, and one of the consequences was the loss of the rubber-rich Acre region. In the 1930s, as the Great Depression raged across the world, Bolivia fought Paraguay and eventually lost control of the Chaco region. Seventy-nine years later, Paraguay announced an oil discovery in Chaco.[22] That history has incited a deep mistrust of outsiders who want Bolivia's riches. In the 1990s, a Chilean company was given a license to produce borax in Bolivia's Rio Grande region. The backlash was fast and furious, with Bolivians incensed that a foreign company could get access to the mineral, also known as sodium borate and used extensively in soaps.[23]

Bolivia's sales of natural gas to its neighbors, primarily Argentina and Brazil, bolstered the national budget for a time. In the 1990s, though, a dense politician, thinking little of the past, proposed exporting natural gas to the United States via a pipeline through Chilean territory that used to belong to Bolivia. The plan failed precisely because it so alarmed Bolivians that Chileans could financially benefit from the sale of their gas on land they took from Bolivia in that nineteenth-century war. In 2018, after five years of proceedings, the United Nations International Court of Justice ruled against La Paz's attempt to compel Chile to give back its access to the sea.[24]

It is worth noting here that Bolivia's lithium reserves lie in the country's southwest corner, near the border with Chile. The specter of land loss looms large in Bolivia's collective consciousness, especially given the past wars and the fact that the border region contains a metal so prized by electric vehicle manufacturers. These ups and downs have fueled a deep resentment across Bolivia and mistrust of outsiders who are perceived—rightly or wrongly—as seeking only to exploit the country and its riches before moving on. It did not help Bolivia's relationship with Washington that the Central Intelligence Agency propped up Bolivia's military dictatorship in the 1960s.

Bolivia began to realize its lithium potential in the late 1970s and early 1980s when its own geological bureau, the U.S. Geological Survey, and other geological organizations published in-depth studies on the Salar de Uyuni and other nearby salt flats. What they found was staggering. The brines that flow roughly 32 feet beneath the salar are teeming with more lithium than any other place on Earth. They also contain large concentrations of magnesium, potash, and other minerals that can be sold for a profit.[25]

Bolivia had found itself hundreds of years earlier sitting on a literal silver mine. Now, it found itself sitting atop an ocean of lithium just as the world's economy started to question fossil fuels and flirt with renewable energy. Predictably given the country's history, a foreign-owned firm swooped in fast. Lithium Corp. of America, later bought by FMC and now known as Livent, proposed a deal in 1990 to extract all that lithium using a series of evaporation ponds. In return, the company promised 8 percent of the profits to La Paz. It was a measly offer and immediately sparked protests in the nearby town of Uyuni, which demanded more of a financial stake if the world sought the riches under its feet.

The deal collapsed and the company went next door to Argentina, where it struck a deal to produce lithium from the Salar del Hombre Muerto using a mixture of evaporation ponds and the DLE technology that John Burba helped develop.[26]

Eric Norris, an executive at the time at Lithium Corp., noted that his company left for Argentina in part because Bolivia's "political environment was not favorable," the country lacked certain infrastructure, and it was technologically challenging to extract lithium from the Salar de Uyuni. The first reason cited is ironic partly because while Argentina in 1990 was starting to experiment with market reforms, its economy would roller-coaster over the next twenty years and cause perpetual headaches for the global banking system. Bolivia, meanwhile, by 2015 had built a $15 billion reserve, earning kudos from the International Monetary Fund.[27] The second reason was head-scratching, because Lithium Corp. had known about the state of Bolivia's roads and general lack of infrastructure before it made its offer. But the third reason showed the complexity facing the country on its long road to lithium production. Its lithium has high concentrations of magnesium and other minerals, unlike the brines found in neighboring Chile, boosting the cost of extracting lithium and the use of water, a problem in the arid country.

Evo Morales was hoping to move his country forward when he was elected as Bolivia's first Indigenous president in 2005. An avowed socialist, Evo—as he was known colloquially—helped rewrite the country's constitution to give more control to Native and other groups in the country's rural east and south. In 2010, he told *The New Yorker* that the history of Potosí, once the jewel in the Spanish Empire's silver crown, was a "symbol of plunder, of exploitation, of humiliation."[28]

Evo advocated for nationalization of important industries and did just that by taking control of telecommunications and energy companies.[29] As lithium's potential crystallized, Evo grew visibly keen not to be seen as repeating the mistakes of his predecessors. "The state will never lose sovereignty when it comes to lithium," he said.[30] Morales saw the fight for Bolivia's self-determination as almost akin to the central plot of the Star Wars franchise, an ironic view given that one of the Star Wars films would eventually be filmed in Bolivia atop the lithium that could make the country a global economic powerhouse.[31]

As Evo was nearing the end of his first term in 2009, the government in La Paz announced it would spend as much as $400 million to build a state-run and state-controlled plant near the salt flat that would produce lithium. The goal was to be producing by 2014, and indeed the plant opened in 2013. The government made a point of going it alone. A senior official in Evo's Mining Ministry told Reuters that the government was not seeking partners because it sought "total control over the resource."[32]

But producing lithium is far more complicated than farming coca. That $400 million largely proved a fruitless endeavor: The site on which the pilot plant was built now holds an empty shell of a building. The lack of lithium know-how, the remote location, and the high magnesium content of the brine all complicated Evo's vision.

When the go-it-alone plan fizzled, Evo and his government in La Paz were begrudgingly forced to acknowledge outside help was needed. They launched a search in 2017 for a business partner to help Yacimientos de Litio Bolivianos, the state-run lithium firm known as YLB, exploit the Salar de Uyuni's vast treasures. In the last days of 2018, they picked Germany's ACI Systems, a family-run company that had never produced lithium before but had the backing of the German government and, implicitly, Germany's powerful auto industry. ACI also, importantly for Evo, promised to build a factory for electric vehicle batteries in Bolivia, further expanding the country's economy.[33] It was at best, though, a pipe dream. Neighboring Chile was by that time a gigantic lithium exporter but had never produced EV batteries or EV parts. Even the United States, with its iconic auto sector centered in Detroit, didn't make EV batteries.

ACI, sensing perhaps in part Evo's desperation, promised to build the battery plant, which helped it beat a Chinese company also vying for the award.[34] But there was more than enough lithium in Bolivia to go around, and more than enough hunger from the country's politicians. Less than two months later, Bolivia signed a $2.3 billion deal with a Chinese consortium to extract lithium from smaller salars that neighbor the Salar de Uyuni. That deal, pointedly, did not require any battery plants to be built.[35]

What happened next surprised even Evo.

Whether he had played his hand too hard by seeking bigger lithium deals or by pursuing an unprecedented fourth term as president, the end of 2019 brought huge protests against his rule throughout the mountainous south. Indigenous leaders in Potosí and Uyuni grew irked, feeling that all the talk of foreign lithium development had left them out. Many demanded higher lithium royalties and a greater local share of lithium sales, just as they had in 1990.[36]

Quietly, the ACI contract was canceled. The government didn't even call its now-former German contractor: ACI found out through press reports. "Until a few days ago, the project was running as planned," ACI's managing director, Wolfgang Schmutz, said when told of the news.[37] Evo resigned and fled the country amid controversies over the country's presidential election. Two months later, Bolivian officials said the Chinese deal was being reassessed as well.

The next year, Bolivia had a new president but was singing an old tune. No longer would the country seek to partner with international miners, the new head of YLB said. Instead, it wanted to hire contractors and others that could bolster its own know-how.[38] That made DLE suddenly very attractive. Rather than farm out lithium production to outsiders, Bolivia could pick a DLE technology it thought would work best and then YLB would license it for use at the Salar de Uyuni. The government could have its cake and eat it, too. At least, that was the plan.

DLE technologies had advanced since Bauman, Lee, and Burba's initial experiments, with several different types aiming to extract lithium from brine using filters, membranes, ceramic beads, or other equipment that could be housed in small warehouses. But none at that point had worked independently at commercial scale. Bolivia would be making a consequential bet that DLE could work, although it wouldn't be alone: Global automakers, mining companies, and investors such as Bill Gates and Jeff Bezos were pouring millions of dollars into DLE companies, betting they could supply the bulk of the lithium needed to power the electric vehicle revolution.[39]

In late 2021, eager to get its lithium plans finally in motion, Bolivia invited eight companies to conduct pilot tests on brine from the Salar de Uyuni. It was a bake-off in the truest sense of the word: If these companies thought their DLE technology could jump-start global lithium production, then there would be no better place to start than the country with the world's largest lithium resource.

The list included China's giant battery maker CATL, which had never produced any lithium before; Argentina's Tecpetrol; Russia's Uranium One, a subsidiary of Russia's state-owned nuclear power company; and three other Chinese companies, including Fusion Enertech, TBEA Co. Ltd., and CITIC Guoan Group Co. Two U.S. startups also made the cut: Lilac Solutions—backed by the German carmaker BMW—and a small firm based in Puerto Rico with a growing laboratory in Austin, Texas: Energy Exploration Technologies, known as EnergyX.[40]

Each of their technologies had advantages and drawbacks. With Bolivia eager for lithium riches, the question facing officials in La Paz was not merely who should help produce it, but whether the ecological costs of sucking lithium-rich brine from underneath the Salar de Uyuni—a major tourist draw—were worth it.[41]

⚡

TEAGUE EGAN IS tall and jaunty, with dirty-blond hair that could reach to his ears if styled straight but is matted over his head with gel or mousse or some other hairstyling product. The ends sometimes point nearly straight back just past his whorl, as if his head were perpetually caught in a wind tunnel and the last bits of hair froze slightly out of the flow, in defiance of intention. He talks with a slow, purposeful drawl that evokes his native south Florida and adopted Southern California—some have called it "Valley Girl" speak—but this belies the furious thought taking place underneath the hairdo. Born in 1988, Egan is a true millennial: sure of his potential, passionate about effecting change, and confident enough to believe he can achieve success.

And he is flamboyant in the truest sense of the word. In January 2021, flaunting a fur coat and walking on a Colorado tarmac near a Bombardier Challenger, he asked his nearly sixty thousand Instagram followers: "How's your aspen?" A year later, he was ringing in the new year in the hipster enclave of Tulum, Mexico, sharing videos of his shirtless beachside workouts and firework-studded celebrations with friends. His father, Michael, started working at Alamo Rent-A-Car during the tail end of the Nixon era, bought it in 1986, then sold it for $625 million in 1996. Michael had the ingenious idea to offer Alamo's customers unlimited mileage on their rental cars, upending the common practice of nickel-and-diming customers, freeing them to explore further on their vacations.[42] In doing so, Michael revolutionized what had been a staid, boring industry. Teague, who was eight years old at the time of the sale, took note.

In high school, Teague Egan played golf and ran track.[43] As a sophomore at the University of Southern California, he started a party-promoting business. Egan then expanded that business into music, signing the rapper Sammy Adams as a client. Egan named his business venture 1st Round Entertainment and intended to make it his marque brand, the way Richard Branson had used the Virgin brand for a range of businesses.[44]

"Hard to not be the man, catch me in the limelight," Adams sang on his 2010 album, *Boston Boy,* which went to number 1 on iTunes."[45]

Perhaps, though, Egan's greatest accomplishment as a twenty-two-year-old college student was convincing the National Football League Players Association to let him become an agent. On October 1, 2010, he became the youngest person to ever represent prospective talent for the American football league.[46] It was an odd arrangement. For starters, the NFLPA requires its agents to have a baccalaureate, which Egan had yet to obtain. But Egan argued persuasively that he should be granted a waiver based on his experience as a negotiator. The Sammy Adams saga worked in his favor.[47]

Egan had pledged to the Phi Psi fraternity with four football players, including Everson Griffen, who eventually would spend more than a decade playing for the Minnesota Vikings.[48] He saw in Griffen and his other pledge mates an opportunity to boost his own profile while getting them into the big leagues. It was his goal to get at least four of his friends from the powerhouse USC Trojans signed at the NFL draft that year. Never mind that he wasn't allowed to socialize with them anymore, due to NCAA rules on gift-giving. He flouted those rules and was seen often in public with members of the team.[49]

Known for darting around the USC campus with a golf cart, Egan gave his classmate and USC football player Dillon Baxter a ride one day. And given the strict rules of the NCAA, that ride constituted a gift. And gifts weren't allowed. Baxter was suspended and forbidden from playing in the Trojans' upcoming game against the Oregon Ducks (which Oregon won by 21 points).[50] Baxter, who later said he was unaware Egan was an agent, eventually left USC and cycled through several colleges.[51] He never played in an NFL game and eventually washed out of the far less prestigious Indoor Football League.

The experiment in peers representing peers as NFL agents ended not long thereafter. The NFLPA revoked the wunderkind's ability to represent talent.[52] Egan was defiant. "My aspirations and goals are bigger than anybody you have ever met in life," Egan told the *Los Angeles Times*. In 2017, Egan gave a TedTalk in Bergamo, Italy, on his newest venture, Kindness Is Cool, which partners with companies to give discounts to everyday people who help strangers. "If we get thousands or millions of people to do this, we're going to see a huge spike in the random acts of kindness," he told the audience through an Italian translator.[53]

Egan invested in Tesla when the automaker traded around $9 per share. By the time we met in Bolivia in 2022, the world's largest automaker by market value traded near $750 per share. He was living between Puerto Rico and Austin.

Michael Egan had previously advised his son to make two lists of five things each: his biggest passions and his forecast for industries he thought would see breakneck growth in the coming years. Climate change and renewable energy were on both lists.[54] By chance, he then came across several academic papers on membrane technology to filter lithium from brines. He struck up a relationship with the paper's author, who then connected him to a Bolivian professor. Egan then licensed the technology and formed EnergyX. The membrane technology was a subset of the broader classification of DLE technologies increasingly being sought after by General Motors, Ford, and other automakers to produce lithium faster and with less of an environmental footprint.

In January 2018, Egan found himself in Bolivia for the first time.

Traveling the continent with a friend, Egan came across the Salar de Uyuni and grew entranced with the natural wonder. "I was like, 'This is what I'm going to fucking conquer,'" Egan told me as he ate a plate of dehydrated, shredded llama meat at Uyuni's Lithium Club restaurant, a place that felt very on-brand given our conversation. (And a restaurant seemingly marketed to out-of-towners; the word for "lithium" in Spanish is *litio*.)

"Why Bolivia?" I asked him, pointing out that lithium deposits are common all over the world. The United States and Germany, especially, hold vast, lithium-rich brine reserves waiting to be tapped.

"It's the biggest lithium resource in the world, you know?" For Egan, tapping this gargantuan lithium deposit had become his white whale. Obstacles were not impediments but opportunities to improvise and overcome. I asked Egan if Bolivia's past troubles with lithium development, including its still-unexplained cancellation of the German company's contract, worried him. He looked at me directly and gave a pointed "No."

Bolivia, he explained, knew how important its lithium was for the world. And the world was beginning to understand how important lithium was. "People don't realize where their shit comes from! The stuff that makes their lives possible." His voice and cadence began to rise. "The only reason I know lithium is in lithium-ion batteries is because it's in the name. You need lithium!"

To impress upon his team the role he saw for his company in this energy transition, Egan had given each employee a copy of Edmund Morris's biography of Thomas Edison and, as part of a monthly book club, quizzed them on the finer points of Edison's life.[55] The attempt at drawing parallels between the inventor and the executive was plainly obvious.

There was one entrepreneur, though, to which he resisted comparison. Elizabeth Holmes, the disgraced founder of blood-testing startup Theranos, is only a few years older than Egan and, like him, was filled with self-confidence as she started a business with an unproven technology. I visited Egan in early 2022 in Austin, and while we drove to an EnergyX facility I brought up Holmes, who by that time had been arrested for fraud. "The difference with Elizabeth Holmes is that she's a psychopathic liar," Egan said.[56] "As long as your morals and ethics are high, I think, when you're trying to build a company all you can do is try your best and keep trying and trying."

He seemed to be focused on EnergyX and not the world around him, a potentially dangerous misstep for an entrepreneur looking to grow in a part of the world with rapidly shifting geopolitical fault lines. On that same trip I asked Egan what he thought of Gabriel Boric, who had recently been elected president of Chile, a country where Egan was hoping to expand EnergyX one day. He didn't know who Boric was, and when I explained that he was a thirty-five-year-old socialist who had repeatedly criticized private lithium companies during his campaign,[57] all he seemed to focus on was Boric's age. "You mean he's thirty-five?! Maybe I'll ask him to play beer pong."

⚡

EGAN IS NOT the kind of person prone to anything but confidence. Yet in early May 2022, he found himself waiting in the private dining room of Jhonny Mamani, the regional governor of Potosí, his nerves amassing deep beneath his blue pin-striped suit and starched white shirt. A plate of fricasé—a traditional Bolivian soup of pork, white corn, and freeze-dried potato known as chuño—sat barely touched before him. His eyes darted across the screen of his MacBook, the back of which was emblazoned with his company's logo. He checked his watch again.

"Are we going soon? I have to leave at three," he asked government aides. It was barely 11 a.m.

"You have to understand the concept of the *Bolivian hour*," said his Spanish translator, Valeria Arias Jaldin. "Things are always running late." Egan was told that Mamani was hosting an unrelated event just below them. He would be late. There was no apology or request for understanding; it was merely a statement of fact. *Things are always running late.* For an American on a mission, the delay was highly inconvenient. A cabinet of delicate China sat in one corner of the room. A gas fireplace blazed away in the diagonal corner, a hint perhaps of Bolivia's prowess as a natural gas producer.

To help him run EnergyX, Egan had recruited a motley crew of like-minded scientists, engineers, and a marketing specialist named Kellee Khalil. A self-driven entrepreneur like Egan, Khalil founded a company in 2012 geared to become a "trusted digital destination for modern couples planning their wedding."[58] She designed a brash, bold logo for EnergyX that is anchored by a green "X" that pivots downward. Egan liked it so much, he convinced Khalil to join full-time as EnergyX's chief marketing officer.

As Egan's nerves mounted, I sat in the corner making small talk with Khalil and swapped home renovation stories and in-progress photos. I asked her, when that part of the conversation waned, what got her interested in EnergyX.

"Bees," she replied.

In her free time, which she seemed to have very little of, Khalil explained that her apiary in upstate New York has thousands of the insects in a bid to help fight biodiversity extinction, a cause she sees as directly related to her work at EnergyX. "We have to do something to save the planet," she told me. "You know?"

Khalil was fiercely loyal to Egan and fiercely loyal to EnergyX. She mentioned casually at one point that she planned to move, at least part-time, to be closer to EnergyX's laboratory in Austin. In Potosí, waiting with Khalil ahead of a meeting with government officials, I shared a few anecdotes about my time with then candidate Joe Biden on the 2020 campaign trail for Reuters, peppering him with questions about whether his environmental goals would require more mineral extraction. Khalil smiled then leaned over and whispered in my ear, "The U.S. government isn't looked upon too favorably here in Bolivia."

I knew, of course, that La Paz and Washington weren't exactly best buds. Both capitals had long been at odds over drug policy, among other matters. (President George W. Bush had put Bolivia on a blacklist in 2008 because, he said, La Paz was not doing enough to fight drug trafficking.[59]) Lithium was only the latest tension point between the two.

Three weeks earlier, Egan and Khalil had crafted an idea to bolster their cause in the fight for Bolivian government approval: They would donate $100,000 for health and education programs in the communities around the Uyuni salt flat. Rumors had fluttered for years that Evo's 2019 ouster was linked to the U.S. government's hunger for Bolivia's lithium. Never mind that the United States already has the world's fifth-largest lithium reserves, according to the U.S. Geological Survey,[60] the street chatter had been that Washington wanted Evo out. Given those whispers, it behooved EnergyX, itself a U.S.–based company, to make as many friends as possible in the country, especially in the region closest to the lithium.

"I decided we needed to do the donation, got the governor and mayor on the phone, and did an audit of their needs," Khalil told me. EnergyX seemed determined to show that it cared about Bolivians, their economy, and their well-being. "This lithium is Bolivia's, so it should help Bolivia," Egan told me.

The Hall of Mirrors inside the Gobierno Autónomo Departamental building in downtown Potosí was adorned with gold-painted ornate wood columns and ceiling trim. A bust of Simón Bolívar, the revolutionary icon for much of South America and for whom the country is named, stared back at an assembled audience of Indigenous communities, miners, and children.

Egan entered with Khalil and other EnergyX staffers, looking for guidance from their Spanish-speaking hosts. Small children dressed like miners with hard hats and lanterns shuffled by. Several TV crews set up in the back of the room, which was stuffed with scores of Bolivians. Egan was asked to sit at a table onstage with five seats, his translator, Arias Jaldin, to his left. Khalil and I took seats together at the front of the room, facing Egan and the dais. "The U.S. government isn't doing anything to help us, you know," she whispered in my ear, as if to solidify a point. It was well known that Chinese and Russian diplomats were lobbying La Paz for the lithium contract. Vladimir Putin had twice called President Luis Arce about Bolivia's reserves of the battery metal.[61]

"Maybe Washington has other things to worry about?" I replied, an implicit reference to Russia's ongoing invasion of Ukraine, the coronavirus pandemic, and the tottering economy.

Khalil smiled and then turned to Egan sitting on the dais before us. "This is crazy!" she mouthed to him.

"I know!" he mouthed back, a smile creeping across his face, darkened by his five o'clock shadow.

Here was a young entrepreneur who only a few years earlier took the germ of an idea and formed a startup company that helped open doors to a government controlling the world's largest resource of a metal that would define the twenty-first century the way oil had defined the previous one. No longer was Egan jostling with the NCAA over golf carts. He was in the big leagues here in this moment, following the well-trodden path of mining executives before him, hoping to gain access to a natural resource and using money as the ultimate social lubricant.

"Bolivia has the necessary energy to transform this country and the entire world," Egan told the audience. "I'm confident our technology is key to unlocking the vast lithium reserves of Bolivia."

The response was bold, ecstatic applause from the audience. Egan went on to say his company would donate $50,000 to Uyuni's schools and another $50,000 to Uyuni's health care system. "Having a company like EnergyX willing to listen to our problems and work with us to find the right solutions ensures that our heritage is safe," said Eusebio López, Uyuni's mayor.[62] The funds would be earmarked to support six schools in Uyuni to teach students about lithium's chemistry. They would also help fund free eye exams. The money wouldn't be distributed until receipts were submitted proving milestones were met, Egan told me a few days later.[63]

As a gift of appreciation, the governor and mayor gave Egan a sombrero and a poncho—traditional garb worn for centuries by the region's Indigenous peoples. Sheepishly, Egan put on the clothing and accepted the gift. It was hard not to think of the ongoing tension in the United States about white men, cultural appropriation, and respect for traditional cultures. But this was a gift and one that Egan wore the rest of the day.

A young boy wearing an Indigenous headdress and hat walked toward the front of the room. He proceeded over the course of a few minutes to re-create the Tinku dance, a ritualized representation of a violent fight in some traditional Bolivian communities. It called to mind a real-life version of David Fincher's 1999 film, *Fight Club*.[64]

That dance was followed a few minutes later by a carefully choreographed dance by a dozen or so young boys, some dressed as miners, other as the Devil. It's the Devil, a government official explained to me, who is the embodiment of gold, silver, lithium, and other metals that come out of the ground in Bolivia. He is known as *tío*, or "uncle," by miners—many of whom keep red-colored dolls in their homes.[65] The Devil, it would seem, truly is in the details.

After nearly an hour, Egan and the governor signed the agreement. Egan took photos with officials and then headed for a nearby restaurant. En route, he was stopped by people asking him for a picture. At lunch, he ordered *cerveza* and *agua*. He toasted with twenty or so Indigenous community leaders and the Uyuni mayor. I sat next to Arias Jaldin and had a lively discussion about Bolivia's mistrust of neighbors, its long, fractured history of wars, and its sclerotic attempt to produce more of its own mineral wealth. The country, she bemoaned, has had a rough go of it throughout its history of mineral production, be it silver, rubber, or even its natural gas.

"What's different this time, with lithium?" I asked.

She paused then pursed her lips. Her answer startled me. "To be honest, I don't know. Hope, maybe? Hope that we will industrialize Bolivia." Her reply hung in the air as Khalil swooped by, seeking translation help with a group of Indigenous Quechua women.

"Tell them that I'm a woman in business and know what it's like to be a woman in business. We're here to help," she asked Arias Jaldin to translate. Later on, Khalil whispered to me that she planned for EnergyX to make $250,000 more in donations, a plan that would evoke the well-worn path of mining companies donating to host communities while they sought social license to operate. She also shared that she wanted EnergyX's investors to be forced to sign a pledge to abide by certain environmental, social, and governance standards, known by the acronym ESG. While I wasn't sure of the legality of such a plan, I nodded my head and smiled.

My chest was throbbing from the altitude, and I drank as much water and *cerveza* as I could get my hands on. The pencil I was using to write kept dulling; my Uniball pen kept leaking and staining my hands, given the elevation was 13,100 feet.

I glanced over at Egan, who was still wearing his poncho. The sombrero was on the table beside him. He was scrolling through his iPhone, his guests chattering away at the end of the table in a language he did not understand.

⚡

THE SALAR DE Uyuni can be an unforgiving place. In 2008, two buses happened to collide in the middle of the salt flat in broad daylight. Thirteen tourists—five Israelis, five Japanese, and three Bolivians—burned to death in a fire caused by the crash, which was linked to driver fatigue.[66]

Several miles beyond the Palacio de Sal, somewhere inside the Salar de Uyuni, sits the *Escalera al Cielo,* a large set of stairs installed by the Bolivian artist Gastón Ugalde. Designed to look ancient, the stairs go nowhere in the literal sense, but in the artistic sense were designed by Ugalde to say that Bolivia can go anywhere.[67] I joined Egan and his EnergyX crew for a drive across the salar; those stairs were our first stop. I stepped out of the SUV and onto the hard salt floor, the Andes Mountains looming in the distance. The salar went on and on, seemingly infinite.

The ground was firm and cool to the touch. The layers of salt crystals rustled and crinkled underfoot. It reminded me of the salt we used to sprinkle on my childhood home's driveway in Maine after particularly gnarly blizzards. The sun beat down relentlessly on this bleached sea, hammering my exposed skin and making it all but impossible to see without sunglasses. The nearby Palacio de Sal, a hotel of twenty-one rooms built with salt bricks, boasted as its slogan *Experiencia de Otro Mundo. Experience another world.* In the distance, I saw a tractor-trailer barrel across the flatness, belching diesel exhaust. The terrain, which is unpaved but has tracks, often serves as a highway for Bolivians traversing this corner of the mountainous country.

Egan had arranged for a film crew to track him around Bolivia and craft a thirty-second commercial to air on local television. It was all part of his campaign to convince the government in La Paz to choose the EnergyX technology to extract lithium from the salar.

We spent about an hour at the giant stairs, the crew filming Egan and other EnergyX employees with a drone and other cameras, methodically walking up and down, grabbing salt, looking to the horizon. Flat white as far as the eye could see, except for that flight of stairs. Egan fluttered in the background, directing the film crew to take different shots, different angles. Whatever could help augment the commercial that would, Egan hoped, engender goodwill among the local population.

And then Egan directed us all atop the stairs. He wanted to use a drone to film us dancing atop the stairs. Not a fan of heights—the stairs are nearly 12 feet tall—I demurred.

Egan insisted. I relented.

Slowly, we climbed to the top and then Egan yelled at some tourists in the distance to join us. The tourists, a family of five with young kids, started walking over. When they reached the top of the stairs, I asked where they were from.

"Brazil!" replied a woman herding her small children up the steps. The mother from Brazil asked Egan in English what the filming was for.

"It's an ad for Bolivia," he deadpanned.

WE PILED BACK into the 4Runners and started a drive west. For forty minutes our driver, Robbie, commanded the SUV at 60 mph across the vast white expanse. We drove past a hotel—now closed—sitting in the middle of the Salar de Uyuni. And yet even as we kept driving, the flatness of the salar remained, as if we were running just to stand still.

The salt was crystal white, and I wondered how it had no stains from standing water or the cars that drive on it constantly. The crust of the salar was only 4 to 8 inches deep in some areas. Beneath that sat the brine of potash, lithium, and other minerals. Amit Patwardhan, a former engineer with Rio Tinto who had joined EnergyX as its chief technology officer, explained that it held hundreds of years' worth of lithium.

Soon, signs in the salt warned, Area Restricto. The edge of the salar holds the pilot facility for YLB. It also is a military base, guarding one of Bolivia's most valuable natural resources.

As we drove closer to the base, the floor of the salar changed from a flat white to the consistency of cottage cheese. Amit suddenly shouted: "There's water right there!" We had stumbled upon a thinner part of the salar in an SUV that weighed more than 2.3 tonnes (2,300 kilograms). That centered the mind.

The cottage cheese, Amit explained, was formed because this part of the salar has yet to fully evaporate from the summer rains; the curdling was an early stage of crystallization. But the water levels didn't subside as we approached the military base. Rather, they seemed to increase, leaving our 4Runner no choice but to drive through. Khalil started reciting the rosary.

We drove slowly and dodged pools of deep water. Egan, who was in the 4Runner behind us, pulled alongside and asked, "Are we going?!" The boyish excitement was painted on his face. Amit flipped back, deploying his Ph.D.: "The ground seems pretty competent. Just keep a safe distance in case you need to pull us out!" Days later, one of the occupants of Egan's SUV sent me a video of our 4Runner driving through the deep part of the salar. "This is crazy!" he said, watching us in real time drive through the submerged salar to the military base. But we made it. We pulled onto a small salt-encrusted road near the base and greeted the guards. Our driver got out and offered them a bagged lunch from our trunk. We had an appointment to see the site; food helps grease the wheels.

After we passed the checkpoint, we drove by two buildings. One, with a green roof, processes potash from the Salar de Uyuni. The government-run company already used evaporation ponds to extract the fertilizer from the salar's brines. But the brine had a high concentration of magnesium, which is very difficult to separate from lithium with evaporation ponds. YLB had already spent nearly $1 billion failing to produce lithium and that was why the government launched the DLE tender contract.

The salar's waters in this area were the color of the Caribbean Sea.

Deep hues of cyan and aquamarine fluttered across the vast expanse. We drove between two lagoons for several more miles until we came upon another military post where guards' fatigues were labeled with YLB patches, a sign of the closeness of the state-run lithium company and the military.

A small rock cliff loomed; tucked underneath it was a gasoline station. And nearby sat a three-story office building with missing windows and sheets flapping in the wind. It was the same building that Evo had christened back in 2013 during his failed first attempt at Bolivian lithium production. There, in its shadow, sat a shipping container plastered with the EnergyX logo. Among the eight companies vying for the Bolivian DLE contract, only EnergyX sent a pilot laboratory to the country itself. The rest had brine shipped from the salar to their labs in China, Russia, or the United States. In early 2022, the shipping container was assembled in Austin, driven to Houston, put on a barge to Cartagena, Colombia, sent through the Panama Canal to Arica, Chile's largest port, shipped to La Paz, and then taken via truck to the salar.

It was a gargantuan journey intended by Egan to show the government he cared enough about its lithium plans that he would drag a shipping container across the equator and into the mountains. Inside the container was a makeshift chemical laboratory equipped with face shields, gas masks, an eye station, and other safety equipment. Egan made a point of noting the chlorine gas monitor. "That's really important," he quipped as he showed me LiTAS.

LiTAS was, effectively, EnergyX. It is the device powered by the technology that Egan licensed to help filter lithium from the brine using thirty membranes. Egan popped the lid of the contraption, which looked like an oversized guitar amp, and waved his hand in front of his nose. The smell of chlorine wafted through the air—far stronger than an average neighborhood pool.

What LiTAS actually makes is lithium chloride, which can be converted into the two types of lithium used to make EV batteries: lithium carbonate and lithium hydroxide. During our tour, Egan explained that EnergyX was working on a technology to cut out the middle step. LiTAS, though, had been chugging along for four months at the time of our visit, consistently filtering lithium without taking a break or needing any of the membranes to be changed, he and Amit said. I had no way of confirming what they said, so I asked for more information on the yield—that is, how much lithium in the brine they're able to extract. Egan demurred, describing it as a trade secret and saying I could find out when the government made its decision, which at that time was expected in only a few weeks.

I took notes about the chemistry and then remarked on the design of LiTAS, which evokes something Apple's Steve Jobs would have designed. Interestingly, Egan noted, that was the idea. "The style, the curves, the brushed stainless steel, the lighting. It doesn't look like what you'd expect," Egan said. "It has some swag to it, which is important to me."[68]

What's also important is trade secrets. Surveillance cameras watched over everything from the four corners of the shipping container. While not here, Egan had a local contracting company staffing the pilot facility. The cameras were designed to keep watch.

Outside, a small plaque is stamped to the hulk of a building where YLB used to process lithium. It commemorates the 2013 ceremony when Evo had christened the building. *Bolivia Industrializa con Dignidad y Soberania*, it reads. *Bolivia industrializes with dignity and sovereignty.*

Egan walked over: "We should get going. We have Rio Tinto at five thirty," he told Amit, before realizing he'd said this in front of me. Amit hesitated, then wiped sweat off his forehead.

"That's today? What slide deck are we using?"

"The combined technologies one," he replied.

Egan and I switched cars on the ride back so he could take his phone call with Amit. Traveling the 37 miles back to Uyuni, the sun setting in the distance behind us looked resplendent, calming even. It didn't faze me too much when suddenly the left rear tire exploded on the dirt road, the rubber flaps slapping to the ground. Gregorio, our new driver, got to changing the tire as I made friends with a group of llamas that were resting nearby. The salar's expanse spread out before us as the sun dropped in the west.

ON THE SECOND Wednesday in June, La Paz quietly announced on the Facebook page of the Energy Ministry that EnergyX and Argentina's Ecopetrol had been disqualified from the DLE race to produce Bolivia's vast lithium reserves. No reason was given. Egan and EnergyX declined to comment, and their social media accounts went silent.[69]

It emerged the next day that EnergyX had missed a routine deadline to submit preliminary brine-flow data. The reason seemed suspect, especially because EnergyX's pilot facility was literally sitting on a Bolivian military base. If the deadline had indeed been set from the beginning and was missed, couldn't a soldier have walked over and demanded the data? Cracks started to form in the company's leadership, who ignored phone calls.

Egan emerged weeks later determined to win back Bolivia's business. He held talks with Rio, Allkem, and other mining companies. The next month, a private equity firm said it would invest $450 million in EnergyX, but only after it launched a stock offering, something that was possible only if the company had actual customers. "I absolutely think we still have a chance in Bolivia," Egan told me. "If they have a change of heart and want to come back to use EnergyX as a service provider or have any type of business structure, we're open to that."[70]

Even while Egan's bravado returned, his rivals moved forward. Back in the United States, at Rhyolite Ridge, the fate of Tiehm's buckwheat grew more tense.

CHAPTER FIFTEEN

The Seedlings

About an hour south of Reno, amid the state's farmland and under the watchful gaze of mountains, a small greenhouse coddled hundreds of seedlings that ioneer nurtured as if they were gold. Bernard Rowe, ioneer's managing director (the equivalent of a chief executive officer) was my guide to the greenhouse, which sat on a complex owned by Comstock Seed, a Nevada-based agricultural consultancy.

Inside, the seedlings had been segmented depending on the site at Rhyolite Ridge from which they had been taken. The company, at pains to prove that it could save this small flower, spent more than $1 million on all the agricultural accoutrements to show Tiehm's buckwheat could thrive in soils not found in Rhyolite Ridge—that is to say, soils not high in concentrations of lithium and boron.

A full-time botanist hired by the company was watching over hundreds of small plastic containers in which she was germinating seeds inside the glass-enclosed space, the afternoon mountain sun beating down on them and us. The seeds were harvested from Tiehm's buckwheat samples in 2019 (state law let the company collect only 10 percent of any plant's available seeds) and frozen until the company took them out this year for germination.

"We are the solution to saving this flower," Rowe said. "It definitely has a much higher chance of survival, long-term survival, than if no one does anything to it. The government doesn't have the funding to be able to do this research for so many endangered species, but we're quite willing to do it."[1]

I asked Rowe, an Australian native, if he ever expected when his mining career started that he'd get to the point where he was spending so much time thinking about a plant, rather than building a mine itself. Mining companies are not accustomed to spending so much of their own time on nonmining activities. "No, I didn't," he replied, but then quickly pivoted to describe Tiehm's buckwheat as just another challenge to address. "I like challenge and I like problem solving."

I asked about the September 2020 incident when thousands of Tiehm's buckwheat died, some of which had been planted back at the site by the company after initial germination.[2] U.S. government scientists had said thirsty squirrels devoured them, though Patrick Donnelly and other conservationists disagreed.[3] While Rowe agreed that thirsty rodents were to blame, he and the company took on part of the blame.

"We grew these seedlings. We put them back in the ground, and we didn't protect them. We didn't do anything to keep the squirrels away, but maybe we should have," Rowe told me. He went on to describe how the company intended to install underground fencing when this generation of seeds was planted, as well as other safety measures that seemed perhaps overkill for a plant. But, I thought to myself, in an age of changing climate, animals will search out water wherever they can find it.

The year 2019 was particularly wet for Nevada's rolling western hills, and Tiehm's buckwheat thrived. What also thrived were rodents. Plenty of water means the animals got busy and their numbers grew. The next year, a drought slammed the area. "Suddenly there's not enough water or food to support these animals. So what did they do? They start eating things they don't typically eat. And that year, we had this herbivory."

Standing there in that greenhouse, I couldn't help but think how much the fate of this lithium mine was linked with this demure-looking flower. There were two mature Tiehm's buckwheats sitting there in large pots, grown under ideal circumstances and with the watchful hand of a trained botanist. But would that plant have survived out in the open without regular watering, shade, sun, food, and other creature comforts?

Even still, ioneer had slowly, over the years, realized that it needed to coexist with this buckwheat. A few weeks before my visit to the greenhouse, the company had filed a revised plan of operation with the Bureau of Land Management. Effectively, ioneer had changed its mine plan and now was telling federal regulators that it would not disturb the existing Tiehm's buckwheat populations.

"This new plan avoids all of the buckwheat, and then it has a buffer zone around them as well," Rowe said. "We had thought we could move some of the plants initially, but this new plan keeps them in place."

The new plan carved giant open pits out of Rhyolite Ridge that curved to avoid each of the six zones. It was just a proposal, and BLM could have rejected it, but inside the lengthy document were details on how the company planned to keep dust off leaves (regular watering) and keep bees and other pollinators in the area (build gardens nearby with other plants that pollinators love). But the plan itself revealed, whether on purpose or not, a tacit acknowledgment that ioneer thought the plants couldn't grow in other soils, despite spending lavishly to prove otherwise.

⚡

AS PATRICK DONNELLY geared up to fight ioneer's mine, the company had decided to hire botanists at the University of Nevada, Reno, to conduct an in-depth study of Tiehm's buckwheat in an attempt to show the flower could thrive if moved elsewhere.[4] It was a logical step, for presumably the study would show that the basic-looking plant could grow even if moved just down the road. Additionally, ioneer hired local Nevada scientists at the state's public land-grant university, a step that should have helped garner local support.

Beth Leger, a university botanist who earned a Ph.D. at the University of California, Riverside, conducted in-depth studies in 2020 of how bees, spiders, and other insects interacted with Tiehm's buckwheat at Rhyolite Ridge; how the plant responded to various temperatures and precipitation; and just how many of the plants were at the site.[5] From the beginning, ioneer seemed intent on using Leger's ongoing research to prove its point that the flowers could be moved and that they did not need to be listed as an endangered species by U.S. officials. Leger wanted to keep researching the plant, but ioneer repeatedly pushed for early results of the study, for which the company paid about $228,000, to be published.[6]

"I feel like maybe one very important thing isn't clear, and that's that these plants could die at any stage of this experiment," Leger wrote to ioneer in April 2020, pushing back at what she perceived as undue pressure to rush. "I'm not used to such a focus on in-progress research."[7]

Public universities are answerable to the public, which Donnelly knew. He began filing public-records requests for all documents related to Leger's research. And that's how he stumbled upon the behind-the-scenes tension between the scientists and the lithium company, including emails. Donnelly, seemingly, had outsmarted ioneer. The vast trove of more than five hundred pages of emails, memos, reports, and other documents showed that a consultant hired by ioneer expected Tiehm's buckwheat to be listed by federal officials as endangered and that a researcher at the university—whose name was redacted—thought it would take years at least to determine if Tiehm's buckwheat could ever be transplanted. But ioneer didn't have years, nor did an EV industry hungry for lithium.

"I wouldn't want them trying to frame our work in a way that would imply [an endangered species] listing is unnecessary, or that concern for the populations that would be impacted by mining is unfounded because they may be able to be relocated," the university researcher wrote to an ioneer consultant. "Even if we get encouraging initial results from the propagation and transplant efforts, we wouldn't know whether that is truly possible to establish a new population, potentially for years."[8]

Leger increasingly felt like a pawn in a much bigger game. "Ioneer's press people reached out AGAIN, they seemingly want to publish a blow-by-blow as the research goes on," she said in a February 2020 email. She pushed back hard when the company made another inquiry for an update on the research, saying she preferred to wait for "actual results."[9]

While Leger grew irked, ioneer grew alarmed that the flower could get even more federal attention. If it was labeled endangered, the flower could jeopardize the plan to extract lithium from Rhyolite Ridge. Leger's research could hold back that metaphorical tide. And the flower faced other problems besides mining; in late 2019, a cluster of Tiehm's buckwheat was run over by sheep hunters driving all-terrain vehicles.[10]

In July 2020, the Fish and Wildlife Service said that Donnelly and the CBD had presented "substantial scientific or commercial information" that Tiehm's buckwheat might require protection under the Endangered Species Act of 1973. "To ensure that the status reviews are comprehensive, we are requesting scientific and commercial data and other information regarding the species and factors that may affect their status," the agency wrote in the Federal Register. Based on that, the agency would then decide whether to label Jerry Tiehm's discovery as endangered.[11]

Leger's seventy-four-page study, published the following January, showed that in some cases the flowers might be transplantable, but that more studies were needed. Tiehm's buckwheat, the study said, "substantially contributes to and benefits from the high abundance and diversity of arthropods and pollinators found in our sampling areas. . . . Future work could determine whether other unoccupied sites can be found with conditions that can meet [the plant's] growth requirements at all life history stages."[12]

The report, which was heavily anticipated by federal regulators as well, was far from the slam-dunk that ioneer had hoped for. Indeed, it gave ammunition to U.S. authorities as they were considering whether to list Tiehm's buckwheat as endangered. Four months after Leger published her report, Reuters reported that President Biden was leaning toward importing metals from ally nations for the country's growing EV sector, a strategy that could sideline ioneer and other proposed U.S. mining projects.

The next month, in a report that found ioneer's mine would cause "permanent and irreversible damage" to Tiehm's buckwheat, the Fish and Wildlife Service proposed listing the flower as endangered. "The Service has determined, after a review of the best available scientific and commercial information, that the petitioned action to list Tiehm's buckwheat, a plant species native to Nevada in the United States, is warranted," the agency said.[13] Put simply, ioneer's own research had helped fuel the decision. Transplanting the flowers likely would fail, the agency added, given that Tiehm's buckwheat liked the lithium-rich soil at Rhyolite Ridge.[14] The listing wasn't final—the agency needed to solicit public comment—but it was a major blow against the company. Its stock fell by more than 10 percent in one day.[15]

The company had not obtained its permits and an endangered species listing could be detrimental to those efforts. Calaway and other executives had been planning to start construction in 2022 with the mine opening by the following year. Those plans evaporated. Instead, that December, the flower was declared officially endangered.[16] Research found, government officials said, that *Eriogonum tiehmii* loved the very type of soil found at Rhyolite Ridge.[17]

Yet if victory springs from the ashes of defeat, ioneer pivoted relatively quickly toward a plan that would save the flowers by building buffers around each cluster of them at the site while digging its mine. It's what Donnelly had described to me as "vacation on Buckwheat Island," and it was a plan that strove to honor what Calaway saw as his company's best path forward: ioneer would not touch one single specimen of the now officially endangered Tiehm's buckwheat. The expectation for the mine's opening was pushed to 2024.

"We could have easily just stayed with our argument, which is translocation, transplantation, protection is all that's needed. We still believe that's true. But we finally realized that we had a path forward where we don't have to touch the plants, any of them, and put a buffer around them and we can still make this work," Calaway had told me when we met a year earlier, indicating the buffer plan was already in the works.[18] "If that's not good enough, in the middle of nowhere, where there are no other issues being raised . . . let's just declare that America's off-limits to mining."

Even as he was fighting Donnelly and the Fish and Wildlife Service, Calaway was asking other federal regulators for money. The day before we met, Calaway and ioneer had announced they were close to receiving hundreds of millions of dollars' worth of loans from the U.S. Department of Energy's Advanced Technology Vehicles Manufacturing (ATVM) loan program, which had supported Tesla in the automaker's early days with a $465 million loan.[19]

The ATVM program went dormant under President Donald Trump before his successor, Joe Biden, revived it. Jigar Shah was hired from the private equity industry to run the program, which began the slow, methodical work of reviewing hundreds of loan applications from Piedmont Lithium, Ford Motor, Lithium Americas, ioneer, and others. While one part of the U.S. federal government was considering taking a step that could cripple ioneer's project, another part was mulling lending it a large sum. It seemed once again like the Washington silo effect—that one small sliver of the federal machine cared only about its own small sliver, not the whole.

Shah, the thoughtful and measured Department of Energy official who oversaw the loan program, didn't see an immediate disconnect but acknowledged the different roles. "I don't think it's confusing, per se," he told me. "I think each group has a different check that they're supposed to make. . . . My mandate is to find all the people who want to do a project and support them. And so, I'm doing that. There are other parts of the government whose job it is to make sure that we're protecting endangered species and Indigenous communities."[20]

And if there's conflict between the two agencies? Well, the White House could make the final decision, Shah explained. "We have the ability to give somebody a conditional commitment. And that commitment is conditional on them getting all the relevant permits and permissions that they need to start the project. So we wouldn't wire [money] until they met the conditions."

Four days after Tiehm's buckwheat was declared endangered, the U.S. Bureau of Land Management—which owns Rhyolite Ridge—decided to push ioneer's permitting process forward by issuing what's known as a Notice of Intent, a bit of Washington jargon that essentially signaled the project's final stage of permitting had begun.[21] It was the first lithium project for which Biden's administration had taken that step. By 2024, ioneer hoped to be digging its mine. As part of the process, ioneer, its botanists, contractors, engineers, and myriad other staff would have to prove the mine would not harm Tiehm's buckwheat.[22] In other words, they had to establish that Rhyolite Ridge would remain a paradise for those little flowers.

Epilogue

On a Friday morning in 2023 just before the Martin Luther King Jr. holiday weekend began in the United States, Jigar Shah and the U.S. Department of Energy said they would lend Calaway and ioneer up to $700 million to build the Rhyolite Ridge lithium project. For more than two years, department officials had pored over thousands of pages of loan application documents, including details of ioneer's agreement with Ford and the plans to protect Tiehm's buckwheat. While the loan was tied to the company's obtaining permits, publicly announcing it signaled a vote of confidence by the Biden administration in the project's fate.[1] It was Calaway's ioneer that became the first proposed U.S. lithium mine to catch the attention of Shah's loan program—and by extension that of Energy Secretary Jennifer Granholm and Biden himself. Each year, Shah said, the Rhyolite Ridge project would produce enough lithium to build 370,000 EVs and prevent the release of 1.3 million tonnes of CO_2, a key goal of the Paris Climate Accords.[2]

Shah first learned about the Tiehm's buckwheat controversy the same day he learned about the Rhyolite Ridge lithium project.[3] "This has been on my mind—and the minds of folks that are processing the loan—since day one. We wouldn't have moved forward . . . if we didn't think they had a path to building the facility." Importantly, Shah stressed that he had talked to the Fish and Wildlife Service and other federal agencies about the flower and its designation as an endangered species. He described ioneer's plans as a major step forward for the green energy transition and one that could produce lithium in what he called an environmentally responsible way.[4] The optics also mattered. Shah chose to lend money to ioneer before Piedmont Lithium, Lithium

Americas, or other projects. "Ioneer was very well prepared and very organized," Shah told me.

Calaway, not surprisingly, was thrilled. "The wind now feels like it's at our backs," he said.[5] "The government is sending a strong signal that it's time to let us go build this." While the company's 2020 estimate of $785 million for the mine's cost surely would need to be revised—largely due to post-pandemic inflation—the loan would cover a sizable chunk of it. The company's stock soared after the announcement.

"We're spending hundreds of millions of dollars to make sure we have the safest mining project in the United States," Calaway said. I asked how Tiehm's buckwheat had come up in the negotiations, aiming for more detail than Shah could provide. "The DOE is not decoupled from this issue. If they thought the plan of operation was to mow down these plants, I assure you they would not be moving our project forward. If the government didn't think we had a viable plan to protect an endangered species, well, we wouldn't have a Notice of Intent or be moving forward with things."

Donnelly, by contrast, was crushed. "This has been a pretty shitty way to start my Friday," he said.[6] He thought that while Shah and the Energy Department might *want* to lend $700 million to Calaway and ioneer, perhaps they would not be able to. The previous month, after Tiehm's buckwheat had been declared an endangered species, a curious line from the Fish and Wildlife Service appeared in the Federal Register. While the plan of operations from ioneer that had been revised in the summer of 2022 included more buffers to protect the flowers—"Buckwheat Island"—several clusters of them would be "concerningly close" to the quarry where lithium would be dug out. And while the flowers would be avoided, the mine plan itself would destroy as much as 38 percent of their critical habitat, where bees and spiders and other pollinators eat and drink and live.[7] To protect the flowers would require a buffer of at least 1,640 feet, but ioneer's mine plan showed the quarry getting as close as 13 feet to some clusters.[8]

"The Energy Department is putting the cart before the horse," Donnelly fumed. "The mine they are proposing simply will not move forward as planned. Most people actually care more about the buckwheat than they do an Australian mining company." Donnelly was betting that ioneer would fall flat in its attempts to get permits, even if it had convinced Shah's team to lend the money.

The funds were locked until ioneer proved the flower would be safe. A carrot had been dangled.[9] Would ioneer ultimately be able to claim it? "This company has said that yes, they're going to adhere to the highest, best practices for sustainable mining. But we want to make sure that happens," Granholm said.[10] The $1.2 million that ioneer had spent by that point on the flower's preservation—including on botanists and a new greenhouse capable of holding thirteen thousand seedlings and six hundred mature buckwheats—had helped. But in some ways, the harder work was just beginning and Donnelly was sharpening his knives.

⚡

THAT SAME MONTH, Bolivian officials chose a consortium led by the Chinese battery producer CATL to help them produce lithium from the Salar de Uyuni. Partnering with a U.S. firm had little appeal, as the Inflation Reduction Act would extend EV tax credits only to lithium produced in countries with U.S. Free Trade Agreements, and Bolivia had no such deal. The South American nation hoped it finally would be able to produce its own lithium to supply the world. But CATL had never produced lithium before, so there were risks. EnergyX's Teague Egan still was hoping to return to the country should CATL fail.[11] A few months later, General Motors gave Egan's startup a lifeline with a $50 million investment to fund five DLE demonstration plants across North and South America.[12] The deal gave the automaker right of first refusal for any lithium produced with EnergyX's technology, which Egan had tweaked to include DLE processes beyond membranes in order to operate in more regions of the world.

Less than two weeks after the U.S. Energy Department lent money to ioneer for its Nevada mine, the U.S. Interior Department said that no mining would be allowed on 225,504 acres in northern Minnesota for the next two decades, a region that included the proposed Twin Metals copper, cobalt, and nickel project. Officials in the Biden administration said they did not think it incongruous that they were blocking the Twin

Metals project while at the same time heralding the green energy transition. "The department sees the value in critical minerals and their critical importance to the future of this country," an administration official said. Pete Stauber, who represented Minnesota in the U.S. House of Representatives, was incensed. "If Democrats were serious about developing renewable energy sources and breaking China's stranglehold on the global market, they would be flinging open the doors to responsible mineral development here in the U.S.," he said.[13] Wall Street was similarly perplexed. "[I]f the U.S. intends to proceed with decarbonization, it will need copper, and blocking all domestic mine developments while expecting sufficient copper to be available may not be sensible. The U.S. may have to approve some projects," said the banking giant Credit Suisse.[14] Later in 2023, a U.S. judge rejected a request from Twin Metals to reinstate the Minnesota leases that Biden had canceled. Pressure, meanwhile, grew for the world to stop using artisanal cobalt. "How am I free if I know kids are still working in the cobalt mines in the Congo, making Teslas?" Kyrie Irving, the professional U.S. basketball player, said on social media.[15]

MP Materials and the Mountain Pass mine signed a deal for Sumitomo to sell its rare earths in Japan, but neither company released information for how many tonnes of the strategic minerals were at stake. MP Materials remained reliant on China for much of its revenue and the company's executives late in 2023 said they were struggling to calibrate their California rare earths refining equipment. John Burba's plans to make a portable DLE device drew interest from Exxon and Chevron, which were studying ways to filter lithium from water they already extracted alongside oil and natural gas.[16] Li-Cycle and Glencore said they would build a battery recycling hub in Italy, with Vietnam seen as the next possible expansion.[17] Perpetua Resources and the Nez Perce tribe agreed to settle their long-standing dispute over water quality, removing a key obstacle to John Paulson's goal of mining gold and antimony in Idaho.[18] In Alaska, Governor Mike Dunleavy, a Republican, asked the Supreme Court in 2023 to overturn federal regulators' veto of the Pebble Mine in a last-ditch effort to revive the moribund project.

Indigenous groups filed yet another lawsuit against the Thacker Pass lithium mining project, hoping to stop General Motors from ever buying the battery metal from the site. Yet construction of the mine had already begun.[19] Piedmont Lithium had admitted that its plans to develop an open-pit mine in North Carolina most likely wouldn't come to fruition until later in the decade, if ever.[20] The Snowdons and others had seemingly won, but the lithium remained there in the ground, beckoning miners of the future. Tesla broke ground on a Texas lithium refinery slated to become North America's largest processor of the battery material, although Albemarle was fast at work on its own rival complex in South Carolina.[21]

In June 2023, Albemarle became the world's first lithium company to complete an IRMA audit. Aimee Boulanger, IRMA's executive director, said a review of Albemarle's Chilean operations showed the company's "commitment to transparency and community engagement."[22] That announcement came two months after Chile's president, Gabriel Boric, said he would nationalize his country's vast lithium sector and impose the use of DLE. "This is the best chance we have at transitioning to a sustainable and developed economy. We can't afford to waste it," Boric said.[23] The move sparked global concerns that Chile would team up with Bolivia and Argentina to form a cartel for the battery metal, or what Bolivia's president, Luis Arce, called "a kind of lithium OPEC."[24]

In Arizona, Wendsler Nosie and Apache Stronghold continued their court battles against Rio Tinto and Resolution Copper, vowing to go all the way to the U.S. Supreme Court if necessary. Paradoxically, Biden administration attorneys kept defending Rio Tinto's plans in court even while Biden sought Indigenous support. While a handful of the San Carlos Apache had taken jobs with Resolution, Nosie continued to enjoy significant tribal support. He sent a letter to the tribal newspaper that read, in part: "I and so many others stand together and will not be used to destroy God's precious gifts to the world, the spirit of life."[25]

Meanwhile, a small company based in Vancouver, British Columbia, was promising to supply copper and nickel for the green energy transition without ever digging a hole in the ground. The Metals Co. aimed to vacuum mineral-rich, potato-sized nodules off the floor of the Pacific Ocean and process them into battery parts. Not surprisingly, the plan drew the ire of Greenpeace and other environmental groups who warned the practice would permanently harm whales and other aquatic species. "The sounds produced from mining operations, including from remotely operated vehicles on the seafloor, overlap with the frequencies at which cetaceans communicate," according to a peer-reviewed study.[26]

Despite attempts to find alternate ways to produce metals for the green energy transition, there was no way around the fact that mining is loud, dangerous, and disruptive and will remain so for the foreseeable future, a reality that continued to fuel the global battle over our collective future.

"I agree with those who say we must take no options off the table in our quest to mitigate the climate crisis already unfolding," Marco Lambertini, international director general of the World Wildlife Fund, said. "I share that grave sense of urgency. But we must not, once again, try to solve a problem while ignoring predicted consequences that could make the original problem even bigger. It is the very gravity of our current circumstances that requires us to act with utmost care for our planet's life-support system: nature."[27]

⚡

JAMES CALAWAY'S BUBBLE of pride burst less than a week after ioneer announced the government loan. One of the company's contractors had stored drilling equipment on the side of the road leading to Rhyolite Ridge, a violation of the exploratory permit that had been issued by federal regulators. The company apologized and vowed the error would not be repeated.[28] It was an untimely embarrassment so soon after Shah and the Department of Energy had lavished praise on ioneer.

Calaway and I had been set to visit Rhyolite Ridge together a few weeks later, but a snowstorm disrupted those plans. More than 2 feet of snow engulfed the region in and around Rhyolite Ridge, blanketing the dormant Tiehm's buckwheat plants. The massive storm caused a rare blizzard warning for Los Angeles, hundreds of miles to the south.[29] Instead of visiting the site, we met for lunch at a fast-casual restaurant in Houston. Tired and drawn, Calaway had recently returned from a planning session with fellow ioneer executives, and the multiday meetings had worn him down. Still, he spoke with optimism about the project and the permitting process.

Ford, which had agreed to buy much of ioneer's lithium from Rhyolite Ridge, had announced just days prior that it would build a $3.5 billion battery plant in Michigan with its Chinese partner CATL, the world's largest battery producer and the same company that had prevailed in Bolivia's lithium fight.[30] Ford's deal with ioneer, however, was to supply the automaker's BlueOvalSK joint venture in Kentucky. Calaway had built ioneer to wean the United States off Chinese supplies, not supply Chinese battery companies. "We, of course, immediately contacted Ford. They assured us that our material wasn't going to CATL," Calaway told me. "We've been pretty serious about keeping our material out of the hands of the Chinese."[31]

Beyond even the geopolitics, Calaway grew introspective about the environment. If he succeeded at Rhyolite Ridge, Calaway would have built not one but two lithium projects, an accomplishment that would ensure his role as titan of an industry central in the fight against climate change. Eight months prior, Calaway had welcomed the birth of his first grandson, an event that ushered back a flood of emotions and reminded him why he wanted to build Rhyolite Ridge in the first place. "What I want to do before I die is be confident that I've done everything I can possibly do to leave this place more livable for my children and grandchildren," he said.

I thought back to Jerry Tiehm's fateful drive in 1983 through Nevada's barren wilderness. His discovery that day had lain dormant for years, much like Tiehm's buckwheat through the winter months. But the bloom of the green energy revolution had made that plant emblematic of the choices and consequences facing our world as it struggles with how best to tackle the climate crisis.

At the end of one of our chats, I asked Tiehm what he thought of the inherent tensions in the fight over Rhyolite Ridge, its lithium, and the flower that bore his name. The botanist paused, as if to consider the weight of the matter, before responding: "If you find interesting habitats, you'll find interesting plants."

ACKNOWLEDGMENTS

Jack Kerouac once mused, "One day I will find the right words, and they will be simple." My deepest appreciation goes out to the many who shared their time and expertise for a narrative exploring a complex topic that is nevertheless of vital importance to every person on the planet.

I had the privilege of many long discussions with James Calaway, Patrick Donnelly, Aimee Boulanger, Payal Sampat, Richard Adkerson, Dr. John Burba, Dr. Wendsler Nosie, Chris Berry, Jerry Tiehm, Kathleen Quirk, Jon Evans, Warren and Sonya Snowdon, Max Wilbert, Jigar Shah, Mckinsey Lyon, Teague Egan, Joe Lowry, Keith Phillips, Chairman Terry Rambler, Senator Heidi Heitkamp, Emilie Nelson, Bernard Rowe, Ajay Kochhar, Becky Rom, James Litinsky, Eric Norris, Senator Lisa Murkowski, Rod Colwell, Mayor Mila Besich, and others.

A hearty thanks is due my editor and publisher, Julia Cheiffetz at One Signal, for her passion and wisdom, as well as to Abby Mohr and Nicholas Ciani for their support. Andrew Stuart saw the potential of this project from the beginning and fought tirelessly for it; I am grateful for his advocacy. Janine Pineo gave a young journalist his first industry job and years later provided crucial advice and edits for his first book. Janine: thank you. Marshall Burke, Judy Bergen, Erin Cavallaro, and Beth Enson provided invaluable feedback on early drafts, and Nicholas Jahr was a consummate fact-checker. Thank you also to Julie Witmer and Kathleen Rizzo.

At Reuters, I am indebted to Amran Abocar for many things, not the least of which was the opportunity to dive into the world of critical minerals. My thanks also to Tiffany Wu, Alessandra Galloni, Roni

Brown, Trevor Hunnicutt, Helen Reid, Clara Denina, Paul Lienert, Kevin Krolicki, Kieran Murray, Christian Plumb, Ben Klayman, Katy Daigle, Bud Seba, Joe White, Claudia Parsons, Dave Sherwood, Alex Villegas, Adam Jourdan, and many others.

A range of experts shared their insight for this project, including Dan Yergin, Jason Bordoff, Abby Wulf, Corby Anderson, Steve Enders, Colin Bennett, Jeff Green, David Deak, Andy Sabin, Jeff Marn, Scot Anderson, Jon Kellar, Peter Hannah, Roger Flynn, Adam Matthews, Jordan Roberts, Ryan Castilloux, Stan Trout, Roger Featherstone, Rod Eggert, David Sandalow, Michelle Michot Foss, and Dr. Shabbir Ahmed.

My thanks also to Jakob Stausholm, Marcelo Kim, Bold Baatar, Kent Masters, Chris Papagianis, Dan Poneman, Paul Graves, Jon Cherry, Tim Johnston, David Snydacker, Brian Menell, Will Adams, Eric Spomer, Robert Mintak, Dean DeBeltz, Andy Blackburn, Simon Moores, Andrew Miller, Ana Cristina Cabral Gardner, Rohitesh Dhawan, Mike Kowalski, and Melissa Sanderson, as well as Emily Hersh, Jean-Sebastien Jacques, Commissioner Chad Brown, Chairman Arlan Menendez, Sandra Rambler, Josh Kastrinsky, Lilly Yejin Lee, Senator Joe Manchin, and Representatives Pete Stauber, Betty McCollum, Guy Reschenthaler, and Eric Swalwell.

I'm grateful for the collaboration with Todd Malan, Matt Klar, Linda Hayes, Juan Carlos Cruz, Emily Olson, Kristi Golnar, Matt Sloutscher, Bruce Richardson, Kellee Khalil, Gary McKinney, Kathy Graul, Kim Ronkin Casey, Kelli Hopp-Michlosky, Martin Cej, Brian Risinger, Bethany Sam, Jamie Dolan, Jennifer Flake, Bobby Pollock, Will Baldwin, Susan Assadi, Valeria Arias Jaldin, Hugh Carpenter, Ben Schiltz, Aaron Mintzes, Will Falk, Jeremy Drucker, Darrin Lewis, Jan Morrill, Bonnie Gestring, Bill Erzar, Seraphine Rolando, Emily Flitter, Bunmi Ishola, Kate Ward, and Julie Tinari.

My life has been blessed with strong mentors, including Harvey Kail, Pat Burnes, Robin Reisig, Nick Lemann, Judith Crist, Reverend Leo Schuster, Philana Patterson, Greg McManus, Ruth Reitmeier, Jim and Jan Dolle, Erica and Mark DiBella, Ann Sexton, Dianne West, Jo-Ann Vatcher, Yolande Clark, and Reverend Thomas Clark. Thank you to my family and friends across New England, New York, North Dakota, Texas, New Mexico, and everywhere in between. Martin, this book would not have been possible without you (and Theo). I am thankful to my stepfather and father for pushing me to be the best person I can be.

My deepest gratitude goes to my mother and grandmothers, to whom this book is dedicated. *"Where you go, I will go. And where you stay, I will stay."*

NOTES

PROLOGUE: A DISCOVERY

1. Author's interview with Jerry Tiehm, August 10, 2022.
2. Author's interview with Jerry Tiehm, July 7, 2022.
3. Josh Ong, "Witness the First Commercial Cellular Call Being Made in 1983," *The Next Web*, April 17, 2013, thenextweb.com/news/call-history-witness-the-first-commercial-cellular-phone-call-being-made-in-1983.
4. Adele Peters, "In a Battle Between This Endangered Flower and a Lithium Mine, Who Should Win?" *Fast Company*, January 25, 2022, www.fastcompany.com/90714243/in-a-battle-between-this-endangered-flower-and-a-lithium-mine-who-should-win.
5. James L. Reveal, "New Nevada Entities and Combinations in *Eriogonum* (Polygonaceae)," *The Great Basin Naturalist*, April 30, 1985, www.jstor.org/stable/41712129.
6. U.S. Fish and Wildlife Service, "Species Status Assessment Report for *Eriogonum tiehmii* (Tiehm's Buckwheat), Version 2.0," May 2022, ecos.fws.gov/ServCat/DownloadFile/220616.
7. Author's interview with Jerry Tiehm, July 7, 2022.
8. U.S. Fish and Wildlife Service, "Species Status Assessment Report for *Eriogonum tiehmii* (Tiehm's Buckwheat), Version 2.0."
9. Bill King, "The Plight of *Eriogonum tiehmii*," *Sego Lily: The Newsletter of the Utah Native Plant Society*, Winter 2021, www.unps.org/segolily/Sego2021Winter.pdf.
10. Barbara Ertter, "Floristic Surprises in North America North of Mexico," *Annals of the Missouri Botanical Garden*, 2000 edition, ucjeps.berkeley.edu/floristic_surprises.html.
11. "U.S. Energy System Factsheet," Center for Sustainable Systems, accessed December 30, 2022, css.umich.edu/publications/factsheets/energy/us-energy-system-factsheet.

INTRODUCTION: A TURNING POINT

1. United Nations, UNFCC, "April 22 Paris Agreement Signing Ceremony in New York," press release, April 2, 2016, newsroom.unfccc.int/news/april-22-paris-agreement-signing-ceremony-in-new-york.
2. Doyle Rice, "175 Nations Sign Historic Paris Climate Deal on Earth Day," *USA Today*, April 22, 2016, www.usatoday.com/story/news/world/2016/04/22/paris-climate-agreement-signing-united-nations-new-york/83381218/.
3. The White House, "President Obama Marks an Historic Moment in Our Global Efforts to Combat Climate Change," press release, October 5, 2016,

obamawhitehouse.archives.gov/blog/2016/10/05/president-obama-marks-historic-moment-our-global-efforts-combat-climate-change.

4. International Energy Agency, "Global Energy-Related CO2 Emissions by Sector," official website, last updated October 26, 2022, www.iea.org/data-and-statistics/charts/global-energy-related-co2-emissions-by-sector.
5. U.S. Environmental Protection Agency's Office of Transportation and Air Quality, "Fast Facts: U.S. Transportation Sector Greenhouse Gas Emissions 1990–2020," official website, May 2022, nepis.epa.gov/Exe/ZyPDF.cgi?Dockey=P10153PC.pdf.
6. David Owen, "The Efficiency Dilemma," *The New Yorker*, December 13, 2010, www.newyorker.com/magazine/2010/12/20/the-efficiency-dilemma.
7. Raymond Zhong, "For Planet Earth, This Might Be the Start of a New Age," *The New York Times*, December 17, 2022, www.nytimes.com/2022/12/17/climate/anthropocene-age-geology.html.
8. International Energy Agency, "Executive Summary—the Role of Critical Minerals in Clean Energy Transitions—Analysis," official website, accessed January 7, 2023, www.iea.org/reports/the-role-of-critical-minerals-in-clean-energy-transitions/executive-summary.
9. International Energy Agency, "Global Supply Chains of EV Batteries," official website, accessed January 7, 2023, www.iea.org/reports/global-supply-chains-of-ev-batteries.
10. Rachel Coker, "The Nobel Journey of M. Stanley Whittingham: Distinguished Professor Earns Chemistry Prize for Lithium-ion Battery Development," *BingUNews*, May 6, 2020, www.binghamton.edu/news/story/2424/the-nobel-journey-of-m-stanley-whittingham; and EnergyFactor Europe by ExxonMobil, "Pioneer of Innovation: The Battery That Changed the World," official website, November 29, 2019, energyfactor.exxonmobil.eu/news/lithium-ion-whittingham/.
11. The Royal Swedish Academy of Sciences, "The Nobel Prize in Chemistry 2019," press release, October 9, 2019, www.nobelprize.org/prizes/chemistry/2019/press-release/.
12. Katrina Krämer, "The Lithium Pioneers," *Chemistry World*, October 17, 2019, www.chemistryworld.com/features/the-lithium-pioneers/4010510.article.
13. Evan Keuhnert and Alex Grant, "Big Lithium Will Be Built, but by Who? Why the Mining Industry Needs New People with New Ideas to Meet the Decarbonization Moment," *Mining Magazine*, March 8, 2022, www.miningmagazine.com/sustainability/news/1427933/big-lithium-will-be-built-but-by-who.
14. Science History Institute, "Rare Earth Elements and Why They Matter," 2019, www.sciencehistory.org/sites/default/files/rare-earth-elements-why-they-matter.pdf.
15. U.S. Department of Energy, Office of Energy Efficiency and Renewable Energy, "How Lithium-ion Batteries Work," official website, accessed February 20, 2023, www.energy.gov/eere/how-lithium-ion-batteries-work.
16. Author's interview with Dr. Shabbir Ahmed, December 16, 2021.
17. Argonne National Laboratory, "BatPac: Battery Manufacturing Cost Estimation," official website, accessed August 21, 2022, www.anl.gov/partnerships/batpac-battery-manufacturing-cost-estimation.
18. Chris Nelder, "Clean Energy 101: Electric Vehicle Charging for Dummies," RMI, June 10, 2019, rmi.org/electric-vehicle-charging-for-dummies/.
19. "2021 Tesla Model 3 Standard Range Plus RWD-Specifications and Price," EVSpecifications, accessed September 15, 2022, www.evspecifications.com/en/model/4ab310f.

20. John Voelcker, "EVs Explained: Consumption Versus Efficiency," *Car and Driver*, April 10, 2021, www.caranddriver.com/features/a36064484/evs-explained-consumption-versus-efficiency/.
21. "Tesla Model 3 Standard Range Plus," Electric Vehicle Database, accessed December 30, 2022, ev-database.org/car/1485/Tesla-Model-3-Standard-Range-Plus.
22. Fred Lambert, "Breakdown of Raw Materials in Tesla's Batteries and Possible Bottlenecks," *electrek*, November 1, 2016, electrek.co/2016/11/01/breakdown-raw-materials-tesla-batteries-possible-bottleneck/.
23. U.S. Geological Survey, "Minerals Commodity Summaries 2022—Lithium," accessed August 30, 2022, pubs.usgs.gov/periodicals/mcs2022/mcs2022-lithium.pdf.
24. Jonathon Davidson, "Eastern Resources Joins Chinese Lithium Giant to Target Lepidolite," *Market Index*, June 20, 2022, www.marketindex.com.au/news/eastern-resources-joins-chinese-lithium-giant-to-target-lepidolite.
25. "Minerals Commodity Summaries 2022—Copper," U.S. Geological Survey, accessed August 30, 2022, pubs.usgs.gov/periodicals/mcs2022/mcs2022-copper.pdf.
26. Wilda Asmarini, "Update 1—Indonesia Nickel Ore Export Ban to Remain—Mining Ministry Director," Reuters, June 3, 2020, www.reuters.com/article/indonesia-mining/update-1-indonesia-nickel-ore-export-ban-to-remain-mining-ministry-director-idUSL4N2DH17Q.
27. CreditSuisse, "US Inflation Reduction Act: A Tipping Point in Climate Action," official website, September 28, 2022, www.credit-suisse.com/about-us-news/en/articles/news-and-expertise/us-inflation-reduction-act-a-catalyst-for-climate-action-202211.html, 108.
28. U.S. Geological Survey, "Minerals Commodity Summaries 2022—Cobalt," accessed August 30, 2022, pubs.usgs.gov/periodicals/mcs2022/mcs2022-cobalt.pdf.
29. Amy Joi O'Donoghue, "Elon Musk's Quiet Success with Cobalt-Free EV Batteries at Tesla," *DeseretNews*, May 6, 2022, www.deseret.com/utah/2022/5/6/23060115/elon-musk-and-his-success-with-a-cobalt-free-ev-battery-at-tesla-congo-lithium-child-labor-abuse.
30. "Minerals Commodity Summaries 2022—Cobalt."
31. U.S. Geological Survey, "Minerals Commodity Summaries 2022—Rare Earths," accessed August 30, 2022, pubs.usgs.gov/periodicals/mcs2022/mcs2022-rare-earths.pdf.
32. Ben Blanchard, Michael Martina, and Tom Daly, "China Ready to Hit Back at U.S. with Rare Earths: Newspapers," Reuters, May 28, 2019, www.reuters.com/article/us-usa-trade-china-rareearth/china-ready-to-hit-back-at-u-s-with-rare-earths-newspapers-idUSKCN1SZ07V.
33. Ernest Scheyder, "Nevada Copper Starts Production at Mine in Western U.S.," Reuters, December 16, 2019, www.reuters.com/article/nevada-copper-mine-idUKL1N28N1T8.
34. Ernest Scheyder, "U.S. Faces Tough Choices in 2022 on Mines for Electric-Vehicle Metals," Reuters, December 22, 2021, www.reuters.com/markets/commodities/us-faces-tough-choices-2022-mines-electric-vehicle-metals-2021-12-22/.
35. U.S. Department of Energy, Office of Energy Efficiency and Renewable Energy, Vehicle Technologies Office, "FOTW#1124, March 9, 2020: U.S. All-Electric Vehicle Sales Level Off in 2019," official website, March 9, 2020, www.energy.gov/eere/vehicles/articles/fotw-1124-march-9-2020-us-all-electric-vehicle-sales-level-2019.

36. U.S. Department of Energy, "New Plug-In Electric Vehicle Sales in the United States Nearly Doubled from 2020 to 2021," official website, March 1, 2022, www.energy.gov/energysaver/articles/new-plug-electric-vehicle-sales-united-states-nearly-doubled-2020-2021.
37. Mike Colias, "U.S. EV Sales Jolted Higher in 2022 as Newcomers Target Tesla," *The Wall Street Journal*, January 6, 2023, www.wsj.com/articles/u-s-ev-sales-jolted-higher-in-2022-as-newcomers-target-tesla-11672981834.
38. "Tesla Q1 Earnings Call 2022 Transcript," Rev, April 21, 2022, www.rev.com/blog/transcripts/tesla-q1-earnings-call-2022-transcript.
39. Colias, "U.S. EV Sales Jolted Higher in 2022 as Newcomers Target Tesla."
40. Nivedita Balu and Maria Ponnezhath, "Tesla to Charge More for Cars in United States as Inflation Bites," Reuters, June 16, 2022, www.reuters.com/business/autos-transportation/tesla-hikes-us-prices-across-car-models-2022-06-16/.
41. Ernest Scheyder, "To Go Electric, America Needs More Mines. Can It Build Them?" Reuters, March 1, 2021, www.reuters.com/article/us-usa-mining-insight-idINKCN2AT39Z.
42. "Megafactories Hit 200 Mark," *Benchmark Minerals Magazine*, Q1 2021 edition, 28.
43. "China Controls Sway of Electric Vehicle Power Through Battery Chemicals, Cathode and Anode Production," Benchmark Source, May 6, 2020, source.benchmarkminerals.com/article/china-controls-sway-of-electric-vehicle-power-through-battery-chemicals-cathode-and-anode-production.
44. Sean McLain and Scott Patterson, "Rivian CEO Warns of Looming Electric-Vehicle Battery Shortage: Much of the Battery Supply Chain Isn't Built, Challenging an Industry Aiming to Sell Tens of Millions of EVs in Coming Years, RJ Scaringe Says," *The Wall Street Journal*, April 18, 2022, www.wsj.com/articles/rivian-ceo-warns-of-looming-electric-vehicle-battery-shortage-11650276000.
45. Joseph White, "China Has a 10,000 Euro Cost Advantage in Small EVs, Auto Suppliers Say," Reuters, January 5, 2023, www.reuters.com/business/autos-transportation/china-has-10000-euro-cost-advantage-small-evs-auto-supplier-says-2023-01-05/.
46. Ernest Scheyder, "Analysis: Biden's EV Minerals Cash Fruitless Without Permitting Reform," Reuters, October 24, 2022, www.reuters.com/markets/commodities/bidens-ev-minerals-cash-fruitless-without-permitting-reform-2022-10-24/.
47. Howard Gleckman, "The IRA's Green Energy Tax Credits Lose Their Punch Because They Try to Do Too Much," TaxVox: Business Taxes, August 17, 2022, www.taxpolicycenter.org/taxvox/iras-green-energy-tax-credits-lose-their-punch-because-they-try-do-too-much.
48. The White House, "Building Resilient Supply Chains, Revitalizing American Manufacturing, and Fostering Broad-Based Growth," official website, June 2021, www.whitehouse.gov/wp-content/uploads/2021/06/100-day-supply-chain-review-report.pdf.
49. Sarah Kaplan, "Biden Wants an All-Electric Fleet. The Question Is: How Will He Achieve It?" *The Washington Post*, January 28, 2021, www.washingtonpost.com/climate-solutions/2021/01/28/biden-federal-fleet-electric/.
50. Author's interview with Mark Senti, April 30, 2021.
51. Bill Carter, *Boom, Bust, Boom: A Story About Copper, the Metal That Runs the World* (New York: Simon & Schuster, 2012), 115.
52. Jesse Vega-Perkins, Joshua P. Newell, and Gregory Keoleian, "Map Electric Vehicle Impacts: Greenhouse Gas Emissions, Fuel Costs, and Energy Justice in

the United States," *Environmental Research Letters*, January 11, 2023, iopscience.iop.org/article/10.1088/1748-9326/aca4e6/pdf.

53. Reg Spencer, Timothy Hoff, and James Farr, "Lithium | 2H'22 Recharge: 'Giga-Demand' Needs Major Supply Growth," Canaccord Genuity note to clients, August 22, 2022.
54. Defense Logistics Agency, "About Strategic Materials," official website, accessed June 3, 2022, www.dla.mil/Strategic-Materials/About/.
55. Memorandum from U.S. Deputy Secretary of the Interior Katharine Sinclair MacGregor to Assistant to the President for Economic Policy Larry Kudlow, July 15, 2020, biologicaldiversity.org/programs/public_lands/pdfs/Department-of-the-Interior-Response-to-EO-13927.pdf.
56. Jeff Lewis, Yereth Rosen, Nichola Groom, and Ernest Scheyder, "Alaska's Pebble Mine Told to Offset Damage as Republican Opposition Grows," Reuters, August 24, 2020, www.reuters.com/article/us-usa-alaska-pebblemine-idUSKBN25K1W5.
57. Author's interview with Senator Joe Manchin, September 18, 2019.
58. Saeed Shah, "China Pursues Afghanistan's Mineral Wealth After U.S. Exit," *The Wall Street Journal*, March 14, 2022, www.wsj.com/articles/china-pursues-afghanistans-mineral-wealth-after-u-s-exit-11647172801.
59. Nicholas Bariyo, "In Congo, China Hits Roadblock in Global Race for Cobalt," *The Wall Street Journal*, March 12, 2022, www.wsj.com/articles/in-congo-china-hits-roadblock-in-global-race-forcobalt-11647081180.
60. "Spotlight: China's Lithium Business in Argentina and Chile," BNAmericas, September 15, 2022, www.bnamericas.com/en/features/spotlight-chinas-lithium-business-in-argentina-and-chile.
61. Neha Arora and Mayank Bhardwaj, "India Eyes Overseas Copper, Lithium Mines to Meet Domestic Shortfall," Reuters, January 11, 2023, www.yahoo.com/now/india-eyes-overseas-copper-lithium-111936828.html.
62. Andy Home, "Column: Europe Urgently Needs an Accelerator in Critical Metals Race," Reuters, May 1, 2022, www.reuters.com/markets/commodities/europe-urgently-needs-an-accelerator-critical-metals-race-2022-04-29/.
63. Peter Frankopan, *The Silk Roads: A New History of the World* (London: Bloomsbury, 2016), 318.
64. Niraj Chokshi and Kellen Browning, "Electric Cars Are Taking Off, but When Will Battery Recycling Follow?" *The New York Times*, December 21, 2022, www.nytimes.com/2022/12/21/business/energy-environment/battery-recycling-electric-vehicles.html.
65. Amitav Ghosh, *The Nutmeg's Curse: Parables for a Planet in Crisis* (London: John Murray, 2022).
66. Amos Hochstein, "Securing the Energy Transition," Center for Strategic and International Studies, October 29, 2021, www.csis.org/analysis/securing-energy-transition.
67. "The USA Hosts 24% of Global Lithium Resources but Benchmark Forecasts It Will Only Produce 3% of Global Requirements in 2030," Benchmark Mineral Intelligence, email newsletter, December 22, 2022.
68. Zachary J. Baum, et al., "Lithium-Ion Battery Recycling—Overview of Techniques and Trends," *ACS Energy Letters*, January 19, 2022, pubs.acs.org/doi/full/10.1021/acsenergylett.1c02602#, 715.
69. Melanie Burton, "Rio Tinto Reaches Historic Agreement with Juukan Gorge Group," Reuters, November 27, 2022, www.reuters.com/world/asia-pacific/rio-tinto-reaches-historic-agreement-with-juukan-gorge-group-2022-11-28/.

70. Gram Slattery and Marta Nogueira, "Brazil's Vale Dam Disaster Report Highlights Governance Shortcomings," Reuters, February 21, 2020, www.reuters.com/article/uk-vale-disaster-idINKBN20F2SM.
71. "Terrifying Moment of Brazil Dam Collapse Caught on Camera," *The Guardian*, February 1, 2019, www.youtube.com/watch?v=sKZUZQytads.
72. Moira Warburton et al., "The Looming Risk of Tailings Dams," Reuters, December 19, 2019, updated January 3, 2020, www.reuters.com/graphics/MINING-TAILINGS1/0100B4S72K1/index.html.
73. Alistair MacDonald, Kris Maher, and Kim Mackrael, "'Sense of Dread': How a Mining Disaster in Brazil Raised Alarms in Minnesota," *The Wall Street Journal*, October 14, 2019, www.wsj.com/articles/minnesotas-iron-range-likes-its-miners-a-deadly-brazil-disaster-is-giving-it-pause-11571064180.
74. John Eligon, Lynsey Chutel, and Ilan Godfrey, "The World Got Diamonds. A Mining Town Got Buried in Sludge," *The New York Times*, September 23, 2022, www.nytimes.com/2022/09/23/us/south-africa-diamond-mine-collapse.html.
75. John Kemp, "Critical Minerals and Mining Reform in the U.S.," Reuters, January 31, 2014, www.reuters.com/article/usa-mining-rare-earths/column-critical-minerals-and-mining-reform-in-the-u-s-kemp-idUSL5N0L52QP20140131.
76. Letter from U.S. Senator Lisa Murkowski et al. to U.S. Secretary of the Interior Deb Haaland and U.S. Secretary of Agriculture Tom Vilsack, November 14, 2022, www.murkowski.senate.gov/imo/media/doc/Letter%20to%20DOI_USDA%20on%20Sec.%2040206.pdf.
77. Angus Tweedie et al., "Electric Vehicle Transition: EVs Shifting from Regulatory to Supply-Chain-Driven Disruption," Citi GPS: Global Perspectives & Solutions, February 2021, icg.citi.com/icghome/what-we-think/citigps/insights/electric-vehicle-transition-20210216, 40.
78. Author's interview with Scot Anderson, October 21, 2022.
79. Helen Reid and Nelson Banya, "U.S. Bid for Battery Metals Has Africa Blind Spot," Reuters, December 9, 2022, www.reuters.com/markets/commodities/us-bid-battery-metals-has-africa-blind-spot-2022-12-09/.
80. Oralandar Brand-Williams, "Ford CEO Farley Calls for Making EVs More Affordable, Bringing Mining Back to US," *The Detroit News*, September 28, 2021, www.detroitnews.com/story/business/autos/ford/2021/09/25/ford-ceo-urges-making-evs-more-affordable-bringing-mining-back-us/5852516001/.

CHAPTER ONE: A CHOICE

1. Author's interview with James Calaway, November 11, 2021. Much of Calaway's history is based on this and subsequent interviews, as well as corroboration from contemporaneous news articles and other sources.
2. Chris King, "When Are Soft Rocks Tough, and Hard Rocks Weak?" Earth LearningIdea.com, accessed March 15, 2022, www.earthlearningidea.com/PD/312_Hard_soft_rocks.pdf.
3. "Tesla Overtakes Toyota to Become World's Most Valuable Carmaker," BBC News, July 1, 2020, www.bbc.com/news/business-53257933.
4. Yuka Obayashi and Ritsuko Shimizu, "Japan's Sumitomo to Focus on Battery Material Supply to Panasonic, Toyota," Reuters, September 13, 2018, www.reuters.com/article/us-sumitomo-mtl-min-strategy/japans-sumitomo-to-focus-on-battery-material-supply-to-panasonic-toyota-idUSKCN1LT1SN.
5. Buzz Aldrin, *Reaching for the Moon* (New York: HarperCollins, 2008).
6. Ioneer, "Rhyolite Ridge Lithium-Boron Project, Definitive Feasibility Study (DFS) Report," official website, accessed December 30, 2022, rhyolite-ridge

.ioneer.com/wp-content/uploads/2020/05/ioneer_DFS_Executive_Summary_Imperial_Units.pdf, 6.

7. Matt McGrath, "Climate Change: US Formally Withdraws from Paris Agreement," BBC News, November 4, 2020, www.bbc.com/news/science-environment-54797743.

CHAPTER TWO: SACRED SPACE

1. These events are recounted in Lauren Redniss's *Oak Flat: A Fight for Sacred Land in the American West* (New York: Random House, 2021). Additionally, they were relayed in a March 31, 2021, interview with Marlowe Cassadore, director of the San Carlos Apache Culture Center.
2. Redniss, *Oak Flat*, 41.
3. Ibid.
4. Diego Archuleta, "To the Editor of the New York Times," *The New York Times*, January 26, 1859, nyti.ms/3EiKHwk. Archuleta, a Mexican native, was appointed to his post as Indian agent in 1857 and reappointed by President Abraham Lincoln in 1865.
5. Redniss, *Oak Flat*, 18. Also author's interview with Dr. Wendsler Nosie, March 29, 2021.
6. Letter from San Carlos Apache Tribal Chairman Terry Rambler to U.S. Department of Agriculture's Tonto National Forest Supervisor Neil Bosworth, December 23, 2019.
7. Redniss, *Oak Flat*, 49.
8. San Carlos Apache Tribal Chairperson Kathleen W. Kitcheyan, "Oversight Hearing on the Problem of Methamphetamine in Indian Country," U.S. Senate Committee on Indian Affairs, official website, April 5, 2006, www.indian.senate.gov/sites/default/files/Kitcheyan040506.pdf.
9. "2020 Needs and Assets Report," First Things First: San Carlos Apache Region, official website, accessed December 15, 2022, www.firstthingsfirst.org/wp-content/uploads/2022/08/Regional-Needs-and-Assets-Report-2020-San-Carlos-Apache.pdf.
10. "Superior, Arizona, Demographics," Data Commons, Place Explorer, accessed October 14, 2022, datacommons.org/place/geoId/0471300?utm medium=explore&mprop=income&popt=Person&cpv=age%2CYears15 Onwards&hl=en.
11. Ibid.
12. "Copper in the USA: Bright Future—Glorious Past," Copper Development Association, official website, accessed December 30, 2022, www.copper.org/education/history/us-history.
13. Bill Carter, *Boom, Bust, Boom: A Story About Copper, the Metal That Runs the World* (New York: Simon & Schuster, 2012), 116.
14. "Copper in the USA: Bright Future—Glorious Past."
15. Dan Yergin et al., "The Future of Copper: Will the Looming Supply Gap Short-Circuit the Energy Transition?" S&P Global, official website, July 2022, cdn.ihsmarkit.com/www/pdf/1022/The-Future-of-Copper_Full-Report_SPGlobal.pdf, 9.
16. Ernest Scheyder, "Net Zero Climate Target Could Fail Without More Copper Supply," Reuters, July 14, 2022, www.reuters.com/markets/commodities/net-zero-climate-target-could-fail-without-more-copper-supply-report-2022-07-14/.
17. Yergin et al., "The Future of Copper."
18. Ibid.

19. Federal Register, vol. 20, no. 192, pp. 7336–37, October 1, 1955. Public Land Order 1229.
20. Federal Register, vol. 36, no. 187, p. 19029, September 25, 1971. Public Land Order 5132.
21. Matthew Philips, "Inside the Billion-Dollar Dig to America's Biggest Copper Deposit: Miners Are 7,000 Feet Down and They Aren't Turning Back," *Bloomberg Businessweek*, March 14, 2016, www.bloomberg.com/features/2016-arizona-copper-mine/.
22. CME Group, "Copper's Role in Growing Electric Vehicle Production," Reuters sponsored content, May 5, 2021, www.reuters.com/article/sponsored/copper-electric-vehicle.
23. Ernest Scheyder, "Arizona Mining Fight Pits Economy, EVs Against Conservation, Culture," Reuters, April 19, 2021, www.reuters.com/article/us-usa-mining-resolution-insight-idTRNIKBN2C612L.
24. U.S. Department of Agriculture, Tonto National Forest, "Draft EIS for Resolution Copper Project and Land Exchange," official website, accessed December 30, 2022, www.resolutionmineeis.us/documents/draft-eis.
25. Arizona State Climate Office, "Drought," official website, accessed December 20, 2022, azclimate.asu.edu/drought/.
26. Letter from San Carlos Apache Tribal Chairman Terry Rambler to U.S. Department of Agriculture's Tonto National Forest Supervisor Neil Bosworth, December 23, 2019.
27. U.S. Department of Agriculture, Tonto National Forest, "Draft EIS for Resolution Copper Project and Land Exchange," official website, accessed December 30, 2022, www.resolutionmineeis.us/documents/draft-eis.
28. Resolution Copper, "Project Profile," official website, accessed October 20, 2022, resolutioncopper.com/wp-content/uploads/2022/03/RTRC-Project-Profile-Fact-Sheet-600x800-FINAL.pdf.
29. The White House, "Statement by the President on H.R. 3979," press release, December 19, 2014, obamawhitehouse.archives.gov/the-press-office/2014/12/19/statement-president-hr-3979.
30. U.S. Congress, "Carl Levin and Howard P. 'Buck' McKeon National Defense Authorization Act for Fiscal Year 2015," official website, accessed December 30, 2022, www.congress.gov/113/plaws/publ291/PLAW-113publ291.pdf.
31. Author's interview with Bold Baatar, April 8, 2021.
32. Ibid.
33. "Historic Hotel Magma," official website, accessed April 9, 2021, www.hotelmagmasuperior.com/index.php/history.
34. Resolution Copper, "Project Overview," official website, accessed December 2, 2022, resolutioncopper.com/project-overview/.
35. Rio Tinto, "Resolution Copper Project Enters Next Phase of Public Consultation," official website, January 15, 2021, www.riotinto.com/en/news/releases/2021/Resolution-Copper-project-enters-next-phase-of-public-consultation.
36. CreditSuisse, "US Inflation Reduction Act: A Tipping Point in Climate Action," official website, September 28, 2022, www.credit-suisse.com/about-us-news/en/articles/news-and-expertise/us-inflation-reduction-act-a-catalyst-for-climate-action-202211.html, 148.
37. Author's interview with Mayor Mila Besich, March 29, 2021.
38. "Superior Unified School District," AZ School Report Cards, accessed December 30, 2022, azreportcards.azed.gov/Districts/detail/4440.
39. Resolution Copper, "Resolution Copper Fulfills Back-to-School Needs for Hundreds of Local Students and Teachers," official website, September 22,

2020, resolutioncopper.com/resolution-copper-fulfills-back-to-school-needs-for-hundreds-of-local-students-and-teachers/.
40. Associated Press, "Old Copper Smelter's Smokestack Is Demolished in Superior," November 11, 2018, apnews.com/article/73f90300fc9644b3b8eacc37639d1642.
41. Ryan Randazzo, "Mining Co. Conundrum: $2M to Destroy Historical Smelter or $12M to Preserve It," *The Arizona Republic,* October 23, 2015, www.azcentral.com/story/money/business/energy/2015/10/23/resolution-copper-mining-faces-decision-smelter-stack-superior-arizona/74237478/.
42. Author's interview with Darrin Lewis, March 30, 2021.
43. Superior Lumber & Hardware, Facebook post, December 17, 2021, www.facebook.com/people/Superior-Lumber-Hardware/100063807983409/.
44. D. F. Hammer and R. N. Webster, "Some Geologic Features of the Superior Area, Pinal County, Arizona," New Mexico Geological Society, 1962, www.resolutionmineeis.us/sites/default/files/references/hammer-webster-geologic-features-superior-1962.pdf.
45. Nosie portions based largely on author's interview with him, March 29, 2021.
46. "Authorities Investigating Vandalism at Sacred Apache Site," *Arizona Daily Star,* March 19, 2018, tucson.com/news/local/authorities-investigating-vandalism-at-sacred-apache-site/.
47. Dale Miles, "Oak Flat Is a Sacred Site? It Never Was Before. Former Tribe Historian: A Mining Shaft Was Built There in the 1970s with No Protest from the Tribe," *AZCentral,* July 23, 2015, www.azcentral.com/story/opinion/op-ed/2015/07/23/oak-flat-sacred/30587803/.
48. University of Arizona's Office of Native American Advancement, Initiatives and Research, "San Carlos Apache Tribe Community Profile," official website, accessed September 29, 2022, naair.arizona.edu/san-carlos-apache-indian-tribe.
49. Laurel Morales, "For the Navajo Nation, Uranium Mining's Deadly Legacy Lingers," NPR, April 10, 2016, www.npr.org/sections/health-shots/2016/04/10/473547227/for-the-navajo-nation-uranium-minings-deadly-legacy-lingers.
50. Peter H. Eichstaedt, *If You Poison Us: Uranium and Native Americans* (Santa Fe, N.M.: Red Crane Books, 1994).
51. Pope Francis, "Address of His Holiness Pope Francis to Participants at the Meeting Promoted by the Dicastery for Promoting Integral Human Development of the Mining Industry," Vatican, May 3, 2019, www.vatican.va/content/francesco/en/speeches/2019/may/documents/papa-francesco_20190503_incontro-industria-mineraria.html.
52. Carter, *Boom, Bust, Boom,* 161.
53. Joni Mitchell, "Big Yellow Taxi," official website, accessed February 20, 2023, jonimitchell.com/music/song.cfm?id=13.
54. Mark Mazzetti with Helene Cooper and Peter Baker, "Behind the Hunt for Bin Laden," *The New York Times,* May 2, 2011, www.nytimes.com/2011/05/03/world/asia/03intel.html?_r=2.
55. *American Experience: We Shall Remain,* Episode 4: "Geronimo," PBS, May 11, 2009, www-tc.pbs.org/wgbh/americanexperience/media/pdf/transcript/WeShallRemain_4_transcript.pdf.
56. Leandra A. Swanner, "Mountains of Controversy: Narrative and the Making of Contested Landscapes in Postwar American Astronomy," Harvard University doctoral dissertation, 2013, dash.harvard.edu/bitstream/handle/1/11156816/Swanner_gsas.harvard_0084L_10781.pdf?sequence=3&isAllowed=y.

57. U.S. Forest Service, "14 Day Stay Limit at National Forest Campgrounds and Dispersed Areas," official website, accessed December 16, 2022, www.fs.usda.gov/Internet/FSE_DOCUMENTS/fseprd491179.pdf.
58. McCain died in 2018 and his archives were sealed during the coronavirus pandemic.
59. Author's interview with Marlowe Cassadore, March 31, 2021.
60. Redniss, *Oak Flat*, 171.
61. Philips, "Inside the Billion-Dollar Dig to America's Biggest Copper Deposit."
62. Scheyder, "Arizona Mining Fight Pits Economy, EVs Against Conservation, Culture."
63. Nicholas K. Geranios, "Ferry County Gold Mine Opens After Decades of Wrangling," *The Seattle Times*, October 8, 2008, www.seattletimes.com/seattle-news/ferry-county-gold-mine-opens-after-decades-of-wrangling/.
64. U.S. Department of Agriculture, Tonto National Forest, "Draft EIS for Resolution Copper Project and Land Exchange," official website, accessed December 30, 2022, www.resolutionmineeis.us/documents/draft-eis.
65. Ernest Scheyder, "U.S. Copper Frenzy Grows as Rio Tinto Plans $1.5 Billion Utah Mine Expansion," Reuters, December 3, 2019, www.reuters.com/article/us-rio-tinto-plc-utah/u-s-copper-frenzy-grows-as-rio-tinto-plans-1-5-billion-utah-mine-expansion-idUSKBN1Y7272.
66. Ernest Scheyder, "U.S. Copper Projects Gain Steam Thanks to Electric Vehicle Trend," Reuters, January 24, 2019, www.reuters.com/article/us-usa-copper-electric-focus-idUSKCN1PI0GZ.
67. Tiffany Turnbull, "Destruction of Ancient Aboriginal Site Sparks Calls for Reform in Australia," Thomson Reuters Foundation, May 29, 2020, www.reuters.com/article/us-australia-rights-mining-feature-trfn/destruction-of-ancient-aboriginal-site-sparks-calls-for-reform-in-australia-idUSKBN2351UK.
68. Gregg Borschmann, Oliver Gordon, and Scott Mitchell, "Rio Tinto Blasting of 46,000-Year-Old Aboriginal Sites Compared to Islamic State's Destruction in Palmyra," *RN Breakfast*, Australian Broadcasting Commission, May 29, 2020, www.abc.net.au/news/2020-05-29/ken-wyatt-says-traditional-owners-tried-to-stop-rio-tinto-blast/12299944.
69. Ibid.
70. Rio Tinto, "Rio Tinto Executive Committee Changes," press release, September 12, 2020, www.riotinto.com/news/releases/2020/Rio-Tinto-Executive-Committee-changes.
71. The National Congress of American Indians, "Resolution #ABQ-19-062," press release, October 20, 2019, www.aph.gov.au/DocumentStore.ashx?id=e2510a7c-2d0f-485e-932a-8ac7588a051c&subId=690788.
72. Ibid.
73. Ernest Scheyder, "In Arizona, Rio Tinto CEO Seeks 'Win-Win' for Resolution Copper Project," Reuters, September 29, 2021, www.reuters.com/business/energy/arizona-rio-tinto-ceo-seeks-win-win-resolution-copper-project-2021-09-29/.
74. Praveen Menon, "Rio Tinto Has Not Given Up on $2.4 Billion Serbian Lithium Project," Reuters, December 15, 2022, www.reuters.com/article/rio-tinto-lithium-serbia/rio-tinto-has-not-given-up-on-2-4-billion-serbian-lithium-project-idUSKBN2SY22N.
75. Clara Denina, "Analysis—Rio Tinto Has Few Options to Save Serbia Lithium Mine, None Good," Reuters, January 24, 2022, www.reuters.com/article/rio-tinto-serbia/analysis-rio-tinto-has-few-options-to-save-serbia-lithium-mine-none-good-idUSKBN2JY1SZ.

76. "Rio Tinto Mines," Andalucia.com, accessed December 15, 2023, www.andalucia.com/province/huelva/riotinto/home.htm.
77. Rio Tinto, "Rio Tinto Releases External Review of Workplace Culture," press release, February 1, 2022, www.riotinto.com/news/releases/2022/Rio-Tinto-releases-external-review-of-workplace-culture.
78. Dalton Walker, "Joe Biden, Kamala Harris Meet with Tribal Leaders in Phoenix," *Indian Country Today*, October 8, 2020, indiancountrytoday.com/news/joe-biden-kamala-harris-head-to-phoenix-to-meet-with-tribal-leaders.
79. "Hundreds of Tribal and Indian Country Leaders Endorse Joe Biden for President," IndianZ.com, October 15, 2020, www.indianz.com/News/2020/10/15/hundreds-of-tribal-and-indian-country-leaders-endorse-joe-biden-for-president/.
80. U.S. Federal Election Commission records.
81. Ernest Scheyder, "Exclusive: Biden Campaign Tells Miners It Supports Domestic Production of EV Metals," Reuters, October 22, 2020, www.reuters.com/article/usa-election-mining/exclusive-biden-campaign-tells-miners-it-supports-domestic-production-of-ev-metals-idUSKBN27808B.
82. Brendan O'Brien, "Apache Tribe Marches to Protect Sacred Arizona Site from Copper Mine," Reuters, February 28, 2020, www.reuters.com/article/us-usa-oakflat-apache/apache-tribe-marches-to-protect-sacred-arizona-site-from-copper-mine-idUSKCN20M1QM.
83. Felicia Fonseca and Angeliki Kastanis, "Native American Votes Helped Secure Biden's Win in Arizona," Associated Press, November 19, 2020, apnews.com/article/election-2020-joe-biden-flagstaff-arizona-voting-rights-fa452fbd546fa00535679d78ac40b890.
84. U.S. Forest Service, "Tonto National Forest Releases Final Environmental Impact Statement Draft Decision for Resolution Copper Project and Land Exchange," press release, January 15, 2021, www.fs.usda.gov/detail/r3/home/?cid=fseprd858166.
85. Ibid.
86. Ibid.
87. Ernest Scheyder, "Trump Admin Set to Approve Arizona Land Swap for Mine Opposed by Native Americans," Reuters, December 7, 2020, www.reuters.com/article/us-usa-mining-resolution/trump-admin-set-to-approve-arizona-land-swap-for-mine-opposed-by-native-americans-idUSKBN28H0FW.
88. Patrick Reis and Greenwire, "Obama Admin, McCain Spar over Ariz. Copper Mine Bill," *The New York Times*, June 18, 2009, archive.nytimes.com/www.nytimes.com/gwire/2009/06/18/18greenwire-obama-admin-mccain-spar-over-ariz-copper-mine-72687.html.
89. Associated Press, "House Votes to Boost Huge Arizona Copper Mine," October 26, 2011, azcapitoltimes.com/news/2011/10/26/house-votes-to-boost-huge-arizona-copper-mine/.
90. Ryan Randazzo, "Sen. John McCain Visits Resolution Mine, Pledges Support," *Arizona Republic*, October 7, 2014, apnews.com/article/arizona-john-mccain-jeff-flake-forests-financial-markets-9acf7a87127757b11a080217561db1f1.
91. John McCain, "McCain: Why I'll Vote for Resolution Copper," *AZCentral*, October 15, 2014, www.azcentral.com/story/opinion/op-ed/2014/10/15/resolution-copper-arizona-mccain/17325487/.
92. Felicia Fonseca, "Apaches' Fight over Arizona Copper Mine Goes Before US Court," Associated Press, February 3, 2021, apnews.com/article/arizona-john-mccain-jeff-flake-forests-financial-markets-9acf7a87127757b11a080217561db1f1.

93. Shane Goldmacher, "Flake's Past as Lobbyist at Odds with His Image," *National Journal*, April 18, 2012, news.yahoo.com/flake-past-lobbyist-odds-image-181053586.html.
94. Fonseca, "Apaches' Fight over Arizona Copper Mine Goes Before US Court."
95. U.S. Department of the Interior, "Statement by Interior Secretary Sally Jewell on the National Defense Authorization Act for Fiscal Year 2015," press release, December 19, 2014, www.doi.gov/news/pressreleases/statement-by-interior-secretary-sally-jewell-on-the-national-defense-authorization-act-for-fiscal-year-2015.
96. Senator Bernie Sanders, "Sanders, Baldwin Introduce Bill to Stop Land Giveaway, Protect Native American Place of Worship," press release, November 5, 2015, www.sanders.senate.gov/press-releases/sanders-baldwin-introduce-bill-to-stop-land-giveaway-protect-native-american-place-of-worship/.
97. Jessica Swarner, "Did Obama Just Block the Sale of Sacred Apache Land to a Foreign Mining Company? Well . . . ," *Indian Country Today*, March 17, 2016, indiancountrytoday.com/archive/did-obama-just-block-the-sale-of-sacred-apache-land-to-a-foreign-mining-company-well.
98. Reuters, "Timeline—Rio Tinto's 26-Year Struggle to Develop a Massive Arizona Copper Mine," April 19, 2021, www.reuters.com/business/energy/rio-tintos-26-year-struggle-develop-massive-arizona-copper-mine-2021-04-19/.
99. Aluminum Corp. of China held roughly 15 percent of Rio Tinto's shares at the end of 2022, making it the company's largest shareholder.
100. Letter from San Carlos Apache Tribal Chairman Terry Rambler to U.S. Department of Agriculture's Tonto National Forest Supervisor Neil Bosworth, December 23, 2019.
101. Derek Francis, "Native Americans Sue Trump Administration over Rio Tinto's Arizona Copper Project," Reuters, January 13, 2021, www.reuters.com/world/us/native-americans-sue-trump-administration-over-rio-tintos-arizona-copper-project-2021-01-13/.
102. Ernest Scheyder, "Native Americans Say U.S. Does Not Own Land It Is About to Give to Rio Tinto," Reuters, January 14, 2021, www.reuters.com/article/us-usa-mining-resolution/native-americans-say-u-s-does-not-own-land-it-is-about-to-give-to-rio-tinto-idUSKBN29J2R9.
103. Reuters, "U.S. Judge Denies Native American Bid to Block Land Swap for Rio Tinto Copper Mine," January 14, 2021, www.reuters.com/business/legal/us-judge-denies-native-american-bid-block-land-swap-rio-tinto-copper-mine-2021-01-15.
104. Ernest Scheyder, "U.S. Judge Will Not Stop Land Transfer for Rio Tinto Mine in Arizona," Reuters, February 12, 2021, www.reuters.com/business/us-judge-will-not-stop-land-transfer-rio-tinto-mine-arizona-2021-02-12/.
105. Ibid.
106. Ernest Scheyder, "U.S. Appeals Court Hints at Support for Rio's Resolution Copper Mine," Reuters, October 22, 2021, www.reuters.com/legal/litigation/us-appeals-court-hints-support-rios-resolution-copper-mine-2021-10-22/.
107. Ibid.

CHAPTER THREE: RADICAL WORK

1. *Blood Diamond*, directed by Edward Zwick (Warner Bros. Pictures, 2006).
2. Author's interview with Michael J. Kowalski, January 23, 2023.
3. "Michael J. Kowalski Biography," 16th Nikkei Global Management Forum offi-

cial website, accessed January 15, 2023, www.ngmf.com/ngmf2014/speakers14.html.
4. Victoria Gomelsky, "Jewelers Divided over Use of Coral," *The New York Times*, December 8, 2009, www.nytimes.com/2009/12/08/business/global/08iht-rbogcoral.html.
5. Jasen Lee, "Utah's Kennecott Mines Silver, Gold for Tiffany & Co.," *DeseretNews*, March 13, 2012, www.deseret.com/2012/3/13/20499939/utah-s-kennecott-mines-silver-gold-for-tiffany-co.
6. "Top 10 Deep Open-Pit Mines," *Mining Technology*, September 26, 2013, www.mining-technology.com/features/feature-top-ten-deepest-open-pit-mines.
7. Nicholas K. Geranios, "Environmentalists Lash Out at Jewelry," Associated Press, April 27, 2004, www.ocala.com/story/news/2004/04/27/environmentalists-lash-out-at-jewelry/31304835007/.
8. Marc Gunther, "Green Gold?" CNN Money, September 3, 2008, money.cnn.com/2008/09/03/news/companies/gunther_gold.fortune/index2.htm.
9. Tiffany & Co., "Tiffany Blue: A Color So Famous, It's Trademarked," official website, accessed January 27, 2023, press.tiffany.com/our-story/tiffany-blue/.
10. *Washington Post* advertisement, March 24, 2004, A11.
11. Geranios, "Environmentalists Lash Out at Jewelry."
12. Michael J. Kowalski, "When Gold Isn't Worth the Price," *The New York Times*, November 6, 2015, www.nytimes.com/2015/11/07/opinion/when-gold-isnt-worth-the-price.html.
13. Author's interview with Michael J. Kowalski, January 23, 2023.
14. Tilde Herrera, "Jeweler Opposition to Bristol Bay Gold Grows," *GreenBiz*, February 14, 2011, www.greenbiz.com/article/jeweler-opposition-bristol-bay-gold-grows.
15. Joel Reynolds, "A Gem of an Ad: Tiffany's Applauds EPA for Action on Pebble Mine," *The Huffington Post*, March 6, 2014, www.huffpost.com/entry/a-gem-of-an-ad-tiffanys-a_b_4913482.
16. "IRMA Principles of Engagement," official website, accessed January 30, 2023, responsiblemining.net/wp-content/uploads/2018/09/IRMAPrinciplesofEngagement.pdf.
17. IRMA, "Finance," official website, accessed January 30, 2023, responsiblemining.net/what-you-can-do/finance/.
18. "Mind Your Mines: The Push to Make Mining Safer and Cleaner," *How to Save a Planet*, March 24, 2022, gimletmedia.com/shows/howtosaveaplanet/meheke2/mind-your-mines-the-push-to-make-mining, 13:00 mark.
19. Ibid., 21:30.
20. Ibid., 17:00.
21. Ibid., 17:40.
22. IRMA, "Standard Development Process," official website, accessed January 30, 2023, responsiblemining.net/what-we-do/standard/standard-development/.
23. IRMA, "IRMA—Stillwater Field Test," official website, October 2015, responsiblemining.net/wp-content/uploads/2018/09/IRMA_FieldTestReport_StillwaterMine.pdf.
24. IRMA, "IRMA—Anglo American Unki Mine Field Test Report," official website, November 2016, responsiblemining.net/wp-content/uploads/2018/09/Unki_Field_Test_Report_Nov2016.pdf.
25. Author's email with Aimee Boulanger, February 22, 2023.
26. "Mind Your Mines: The Push to Make Mining Safer and Cleaner," 20:00.
27. Tiffany & Co. Sustainability report 2016, 18.

28. IRMA, "Mines Under Assessment," official website, accessed January 30, 2023, responsiblemining.net/what-we-do/certification/mines-under-assessment/.
29. "Mind Your Mines: The Push to Make Mining Safer and Cleaner," 26:00.
30. Ibid., 24:00.
31. Author's interview with Aimee Boulanger, January 30, 2023.
32. Fred Lambert, "Tesla Releases List of Battery Material Suppliers, Confirms Long-Term Nickel Deal with Vale," *electrek*, May 6, 2022, electrek.co/2022/05/06/tesla-list-battery-material-suppliers-long-term-nickel-deal-vale/.
33. Ayanti Bera, "Ford Joins Global Initiative to Promote Responsible Mining," Reuters, February 15, 2021, www.reuters.com/article/us-fordmotor-mining/ford-joins-global-initiative-to-promote-responsible-mining-idUSKBN2AF1E9.
34. Ford Motor Company, "Ford Motor Company Is First American Automaker to Join Initiative Promoting Responsible Mining," press release, February 15, 2021, media.ford.com/content/fordmedia/fna/us/en/news/2021/02/15/ford-initiative-promoting-responsible-mining.html.
35. Author's interview with James Calaway, January 13, 2023.
36. Author's interview with Aimee Boulanger, January 30, 2023.

CHAPTER FOUR: THE LEAF BLOWER

1. Brian Palmer, "How Bad for the Environment Are Gas-Powered Leaf Blowers?" *The Washington Post*, September 16, 2013, www.washingtonpost.com/national/health-science/how-bad-for-the-environment-are-gas-powered-leaf-blowers/2013/09/16/8eed7b9a-18bb-11e3-a628-7e6dde8f889d_story.html.
2. Dennis Fitz et al., "Determination Particulate Emission Rates from Leaf Blowers," research paper presented to U.S. Environmental Protection Agency conference, accessed February 15, 2023, www3.epa.gov/ttnchie1/conference/ei15/session5/fitz.pdf.
3. Margaret Renkl, "The First Thing We Do, Let's Kill All the Leaf Blowers," *The New York Times*, October 25, 2021, www.nytimes.com/2021/10/25/opinion/leaf-blowers-california-emissions.html.
4. Edmunds, "Leaf Blower's Emissions Dirtier Than High-Performance Pick-Up Truck's, Says Edmunds' InsideLine.com," press release, December 6, 2011, www.edmunds.com/about/press/leaf-blowers-emissions-dirtier-than-high-performance-pick-up-trucks-says-edmunds-insidelinecom.html.
5. James Fallows, "Get Off My Lawn: How a Small Group of Activists (Our Correspondent Among Them) Got Leaf Blowers Banned in the Nation's Capital," *The Atlantic*, April 2019, www.theatlantic.com/magazine/archive/2019/04/james-fallows-leaf-blower-ban/583210/.
6. Tik Root, "California Set to Become First State to Ban Gasoline-Powered Lawn Equipment," *The Washington Post*, October 12, 2021, www.washingtonpost.com/climate-solutions/2021/10/12/california-newsom-law-equipment-pollution/.
7. Ibid.
8. Thomas Münzel et al., "Environmental Noise and the Cardiovascular System," *Journal of the American College of Cardiology*, February 13, 2018, www.sciencedirect.com/science/article/pii/S0735109717419309?via%253Dihub.
9. Palmer, "How Bad for the Environment Are Gas-Powered Leaf Blowers?"
10. The Home Depot, "The Home Depot Launches the Next Generation of Outdoor Power," press release, April 3, 2014, ir.homedepot.com/news-releases/2014/04-03-2014-014520700.

11. The Home Depot, "ONE+ 18V 100 MPH 280 CFM Cordless Battery Variable-Speed Jet Fan Leaf Blower with 4.0 Ah Battery and Charger," online sale page, accessed February 1, 2023, www.homedepot.com/p/RYOBI-ONE-18V-100-MPH-280-CFM-Cordless-Battery-Variable-Speed-Jet-Fan-Leaf-Blower-with-4-0-Ah-Battery-and-Charger-P2180/206451819.
12. Emma Bubola, "Europe Reaches Deal for Carbon Tax Law on Imports," *The New York Times*, December 13, 2022, www.nytimes.com/2022/12/13/world/europe/eu-carbon-tax-law-imports.html.
13. TTI, "Technical Data Sheet—Ryobi Lithium-Ion Battery Pack," accessed February 1, 2023, images.thdstatic.com/catalog/pdfImages/62/628a990d-1d88-478c-8829-43232ba26ae4.pdf.
14. Marcelo Rochabrun, "Peruvian Community Blocks Road Used by MMG Copper Mine, Source Says," Reuters, March 2, 2022, www.reuters.com/world/americas/peruvian-community-blocks-road-used-by-mmg-copper-mine-source-says-2022-03-02/.
15. Jon Emont, "EV Makers Confront the 'Nickel Pickle,'" *The Wall Street Journal*, June 4, 2023, www.wsj.com/articles/electric-vehicles-batteries-nickel-pickle-indonesia-9152b1f?page=1.

CHAPTER FIVE: A LONGING

1. Author's interview with Becky Rom, June 8, 2022.
2. Ibid.
3. Josephine Marcotty, "Loved and Loathed, Longtime Activist Has Drawn a Line in BWCA," Minneapolis *Star Tribune*, November 27, 2016, www.startribune.com/bwca-girl-guide-is-now-a-woman-warrior/403115576/?refresh=true.
4. Jack Brook, "Conservation vs. Copper: Minnesota Town Debates Its Future with a Mine," Pulitzer Center, July 7, 2020, pulitzercenter.org/stories/conservation-vs-copper-minnesota-town-debates-its-future-mine.
5. Ben Cohen, "'Canoe King of Ely' Bill Rom Dies," Minneapolis *Star Tribune*, January 22, 2008, www.startribune.com/canoe-king-of-ely-bill-rom-dies/14014121/.
6. Author's interview with Becky Rom, June 8, 2022.
7. International Joint Commission, "The Boundary Waters Treaty of 1909," official website, accessed February 20, 2023, www.ijc.org/sites/default/files/2018-07/Boundary%20Water-ENGFR.pdf.
8. Marcotty, "Loved and Loathed, Longtime Activist Has Drawn a Line in BWCA."
9. Ibid.
10. Author's interview with Becky Rom, June 8, 2022.
11. United States Department of the Interior, "Principal Deputy Solicitor Exercising the Authority of the Solicitor Pursuant to Secretarial Order 3345," official memorandum, December 22, 2017, www.doi.gov/sites/doi.gov/files/uploads/m-37040.pdf.
12. Daniel Gross, "Obscure Economic Indicator: The Price of Copper," *Slate*, November 11, 2005, slate.com/business/2005/11/obscure-economic-indicator-the-price-of-copper.html.
13. Christopher Cannon et al., "Bloomberg Billionaires Index," Bloomberg, March 1, 2017, www.bloomberg.com/billionaires/profiles/iris-fontbona/, #53, Iris Fontbona & Family.
14. "Twin Metals Mine, Minnesota," *Mining Technology*, accessed January 4, 2023, www.mining-technology.com/projects/twin-metals-minnesota-tmm-mine-minnesota/.

15. Author's interview with Becky Rom, June 8, 2022.
16. "The Ely Miner," Minnesota Digital Newspaper Hub (Minnesota Historical Society), accessed January 3, 2023, www.mnhs.org/newspapers/hub/ely-miner.
17. "It All Began with Mining: Ely Mines," Ely's Pioneer Museum, accessed January 3, 2023, assets.simpleviewinc.com/simpleview/image/upload/v1/clients/elymn/file_1131_ad6c7d48-9b73-4e2e-93e4-9e832ab8ded1.pdf.
18. Richard Helgerson, "Miner Tells How He Ran from Death in Tons of Falling Mud," *Minneapolis Sunday Tribune*, October 2, 1955.
19. "Closing of Pioneer Mine in 1967 Was No April Fool's Joke," *The Ely Echo*, accessed January 3, 2023, www.elyecho.com/articles/2017/03/31/closing-pioneer-mine-1967-was-no-april-fool%E2%80%99s-joke.
20. Dennis Anderson, "Defined by Its Complex History, Ely Is a Colorful Town Minnesota Is Lucky to Have," Minneapolis *Star Tribune*, February 4, 2022, www.startribune.com/ely-minnesota-history-bwca-town-mining-wilderness-canoe-superior-forest-dennis-anderson/600142997/.
21. James H. Stock and Jacob T. Bradt, "Analysis of Proposed 20-Year Mineral Leasing Withdrawal in Superior National Forest," *Ecological Economics*, August 2020, doi.org/10.1016/j.ecolecon.2020.106663.
22. Ibid.
23. U.S. Department of Agriculture, "Obama Administration Takes Steps to Protect Watershed of the Boundary Waters Canoe Wilderness Area," press release, December 15, 2016, www.usda.gov/media/press-releases/2016/12/15/obama-administration-takes-steps-protect-watershed-boundary-waters.
24. Ibid.
25. Hiroko Tabuchi and Steve Eder, "A Plan to Mine the Minnesota Wilderness Hit a Dead End. Then Trump Became President," *The New York Times*, June 25, 2019, www.nytimes.com/2019/06/25/climate/trump-minnesota-mine.html.
26. Ibid.
27. Dan Kraker, "Feds Give Twin Metals New Lease on NE Minn. Mining," MPR News, July 14, 2019, www.mprnews.org/story/2018/12/20/feds-move-to-formally-renew-leases-for-twin-metals-mine.
28. Tabuchi and Eder, "A Plan to Mine the Minnesota Wilderness Hit a Dead End. Then Trump Became President."
29. U.S. House Natural Resources Committee, "Oversight: Hybrid Full Committee Oversight Hearing Notice—June 23, 2021," official website, accessed June 23, 2021, naturalresources.house.gov/hearings/hybrid-full-committee-oversight-hearing-notice_june-23-2021.
30. Ernest Scheyder, "Exclusive—Biden Campaign Tells Miners It Supports Domestic Production of EV Metals," Reuters, October 22, 2023, www.reuters.com/article/usa-election-mining-idCNL1N2HD0RW.
31. Ibid.
32. Ibid.
33. Ernest Scheyder and Trevor Hunnicutt, "Exclusive: Biden Looks Abroad for Electric Vehicle Metals, in Blow to U.S. Miners," Reuters, May 25, 2021, www.reuters.com/business/energy/biden-looks-abroad-electric-vehicle-metals-blow-us-miners-2021-05-25/.
34. Ibid.
35. Ibid.
36. Andrea Shalal and Ernest Scheyder, "Biden Admin Still Undecided on Minnesota Copper Mine Project—Vilsack," Reuters, May 5, 2021, www.reuters.com/article/us-usa-biden-antofagasta-idCAKBN2CM1WS.

37. Trevor Hunnicutt and Ernest Scheyder, "Biden Administration Waiting for Legal Opinion Before Twin Metals Decision," Reuters, September 8, 2021, www.reuters.com/article/usa-mining-twinmetals-idCNL1N2QA2I4.
38. Ernest Scheyder, "U.S. Plan Would Block Antofagasta Minnesota Copper Mine," Reuters, October 20, 2021, www.reuters.com/business/environment/blow-twin-metals-us-proposes-mining-ban-boundary-waters-2021-10-20/.
39. Ashley Hackett, "The Biden Administration's Mining Study and the Future of Twin Metals, Explained," MinnPost, October 27, 2021, www.minnpost.com/national/2021/10/the-biden-administrations-mining-study-and-the-future-of-twin-metals-explained/.
40. Ernest Scheyder, "Biden Administration Kills Antofagasta's Minnesota Copper Project," Reuters, January 26, 2022, www.reuters.com/business/sustainable-business/biden-administration-kills-antofagastas-minnesota-copper-project-2022-01-26/.
41. Representative Pete Stauber, "Stauber Issues Statement Blasting Biden Administration for Political Decision on Twin Metals Permit," press release, January 26, 2022, stauber.house.gov/media/press-releases/stauber-issues-statement-blasting-biden-administration-political-decision-twin.
42. Ernest Scheyder, "U.S. Faces Tough Choices in 2022 on Mines for Electric-Vehicle Metals," Reuters, December 22, 2021, www.reuters.com/markets/commodities/us-faces-tough-choices-2022-mines-electric-vehicle-metals-2021-12-22.
43. Ibid.
44. Scheyder, "Biden Administration Kills Antofagasta's Minnesota Copper Project."
45. Julie Padilla, "Prepared Testimony Before US Senate Energy and Natural Resources Committee," official website, March 31, 2022, www.energy.senate.gov/services/files/C226ADF6-F7D7-4024-AA0B-12663870816E.
46. Ibid.
47. Ibid.
48. Ibid.
49. The White House, "Memorandum on Presidential Determination Pursuant to Section 303 of the Defense Production Act of 1950, as Amended," official website, March 31, 2022, www.whitehouse.gov/briefing-room/presidential-actions/2022/03/31/memorandum-on-presidential-determination-pursuant-to-section-303-of-the-defense-production-act-of-1950-as-amended/.
50. John S. Adams and Neil C. Gustafson, "Minnesota," *Encyclopaedia Britannica*, accessed November 9, 2022.
51. International Joint Commission, "The Boundary Waters Treaty of 1909," official website, accessed February 20, 2023, www.ijc.org/sites/default/files/2018-07/Boundary%20Water-ENGFR.pdf.
52. Ibid.
53. Author's interview with Twin Metals staff, June 7, 2022.
54. Ibid.
55. Jim L. Bower, *The Irresponsible Pursuit of Paradise* (Minneapolis: Levins Publishing, 2017).
56. Author's interview with Twin Metals staff, June 7, 2022.

CHAPTER SIX: A SINGLE POINT OF FAILURE

1. "Rental Space: 824 N Market St," Loopnet, accessed March 4, 2022, www.loopnet.com/Listing/824-N-Market-St-Wilmington-DE/19219572/.
2. Maureen Milford, "Companies Turn to Delaware to Survive Bankruptcy," *The News Journal*, September 19, 2014, www.delawareonline.com/story

/money/business/2014/09/19/companies-turn-delaware-survive-bankruptcy/15891887/.

3. *Molycorp Minerals LLC v. Debtors*, 15-11371 (U.S. Bankruptcy Court, District of Delaware), Document 374.
4. K. A. Gschneidner Jr. and J. Capellen, "Two Hundred Years of Rare Earths, 1787–1987," *Journal of the Less Common Metals*, January 1, 1987, www.osti.gov/biblio/6893525.
5. Lynas Rare Earths, "Did You Know—Rare Earths Magnets Mean Wind Turbines Are Now Highly Efficient?" official website, accessed November 15, 2022, lynasrareearths.com/products/how-are-rare-earths-used/wind-turbines.
6. U.S. Environmental Protection Agency, "Rare Earth Elements: A Review of Production, Processing, Recycling, and Associated Environmental Issues," official publication, January 17, 2013, cfpub.epa.gov/si/si_public_record_report.cfm?Lab=NRMRL&dirEntryId=251706.
7. Steve H. Hanke, "China Rattles Its Rare-Earth-Minerals Saber, Again," *National Review*, February 25, 2021, www.nationalreview.com/2021/02/china-rattles-its-rare-earth-minerals-saber-again/.
8. U.S. Geological Survey, "2011 Minerals Yearbook: Rare Earths," official publication, 2011, d9-wret.s3.us-west-2.amazonaws.com/assets/palladium/production/mineral-pubs/rare-earth/myb1-2011-raree.pdf, 2.
9. Royal Australian Chemical Institute, "Europium," official publication, 2011, raci.imiscloud.com/common/Uploaded%20files/Periodic%20files/424.pdf.
10. Katherine Bourzac, "Can the U.S. Rare-Earth Industry Rebound?" *MIT Technology Review*, October 29, 2010, www.technologyreview.com/2010/10/29/89827/can-the-us-rare-earth-industry-rebound/.
11. Joanne Abel Goldman, "The U.S. Rare Earth Industry: Its Growth and Decline," *The Journal of Policy History*, April 2014, 139–66.
12. Science History Institute, "The History and Future of Rare Earth Elements," official publication, accessed November 1, 2022, www.sciencehistory.org/learn/science-matters/case-of-rare-earth-elements-history-future.
13. Goldman, "The U.S. Rare Earth Industry: Its Growth and Decline."
14. Science History Institute, "The History and Future of Rare Earth Elements."
15. Stanley Reed, "Sweden Says It Has Uncovered a Rare Earth Bonanza," *The New York Times*, January 13, 2023, www.nytimes.com/2023/01/13/business/sweden-rare-earth-minerals.html.
16. U.S. Bureau of Mines, "1941 Minerals Yearbook," official publication, accessed November 15, 2022, www.usgs.gov/centers/national-minerals-information-center/bureau-mines-minerals-yearbook-1932-1993, 1,535.
17. Ibid.
18. U.S. Bureau of Mines, "1946 minerals yearbook," official publication, accessed November 15, 2022, www.usgs.gov/centers/national-minerals-information-center/bureau-mines-minerals-yearbook-1932-1993.
19. U.S. Bureau of Mines, "1947 Minerals Yearbook," official publication, accessed November 15, 2022, www.usgs.gov/centers/national-minerals-information-center/bureau-mines-minerals-yearbook-1932-1993, 1,275.
20. Nuclear Threat Initiative, "Aspara Research Reactor," archived version of website, accessed November 15, 2022, web.archive.org/web/20150419042039/http:/www.nti.org/facilities/818/.
21. Robert J. McMahon, "Food as a Diplomatic Weapon: The India Wheat Loan of 1951," *Pacific Historical Review*, August 1, 1987, doi.org/10.2307/3638663.
22. Harold B. Hinton, "Senate Votes India a $190,000,000 Loan to Buy U.S. Wheat,"

The New York Times, May 17, 1951, timesmachine.nytimes.com/timesmachine/1951/05/17/89438648.html?pageNumber=1.

23. Goldman, "The U.S. Rare Earth Industry: Its Growth and Decline."
24. Donald L. Fife, "U.S. Rare Earths: We Have and We Have Not," presentation to the RREs South Coast Geological Society Meeting, October 14, 2013, www.mineralsandminingadvisorycouncil.org/pdf/Rare-Earths.pdf.
25. Cindy Hurst, "China's Rare Earth Elements Industry: What Can the West Learn?" Institute for the Analysis of Global Security, March 2010, www.iags.org/rareearth0310hurst.pdf, 10.
26. J. C. Olson, D. R. Shawe, L. C. Pray, and W. N. Sharp, "Rare-Earth Mineral Deposits of the Mountain Pass District, San Bernardino County, California," U.S. Department of the Interior Geological Survey Professional Paper 261, 1954, pubs.usgs.gov/pp/0261/report.pdf.
27. Ibid., 5.
28. "Goodsprings Trail Feasibility Study: Clark County Nevada," official county publication, May 2009, cdn2.assets-servd.host/material-civet/production/images/documents/FINAL-REPORT_GOODSPRINGS-TRAIL-STUDY_COMPILED_Opt.pdf.
29. U.S. House Subcommittee on Mining and Natural Resources, "Mineral Exploration and Development Act of 1990," official publication, September 6, 1990, www.google.com/books/edition/Mineral_Exploration_and_Development_Act/156MPoL5gbAC?hl=en&gbpv=0.
30. Olson et al., "Rare-Earth Mineral Deposits of the Mountain Pass District, San Bernardino County, California."
31. Ibid., 5.
32. Ibid.
33. "Marx Hirsch, 76, Ex-Mining Chief; Retired Molybdenum Head, Rare-Earth Specialist, Dies," *The New York Times*, August 26, 1964, www.nytimes.com/1964/08/26/archives/marx-hirsch-76-exmining-chief-retired-molybdenum-head-rareearth.html.
34. Ira U. Cobleigh, "Moly's Minerals," *The Commercial and Financial Chronicle*, November 25, 1954, fraser.stlouisfed.org/title/1339#555990, 4.
35. "Southern California's Rare-Earth Bonanza," *Engineering and Mining Journal*, January 1952, archive.org/details/sim_engineering-and-mining-journal_1952-01_153_1/page/100/mode/2up, 100.
36. Ibid.
37. Ibid.
38. Goldman, "The U.S. Rare Earth Industry: Its Growth and Decline."
39. "Processing Ores," *Encyclopedia Britannica*, accessed February 20, 2023, www.britannica.com/science/rare-earth-element/Processing-ores.
40. Hurst, "China's Rare Earth Elements Industry: What Can the West Learn?" 4–5.
41. Goldman, "The U.S. Rare Earth Industry: Its Growth and Decline."
42. Ibid.
43. U.S. Geological Survey, "Minerals Yearbook: Rare Earths," for each year.
44. Goldman, "The U.S. Rare Earth Industry: Its Growth and Decline."
45. Yelong Han, "An Untold Story: American Policy Toward Chinese Students in the United States, 1949–1955," *The Journal of American–East Asian Relations*, Spring 1993, www.jstor.org/stable/23612667.
46. Hepeng Jia, "Xu Guangxian: A Chemical Life," *Chemistry World*, March 25, 2009, www.chemistryworld.com/news/xu-guangxian-a-chemical-life/3004348.article.
47. Goldman, "The U.S. Rare Earth Industry: Its Growth and Decline."

48. Hurst, "China's Rare Earth Elements Industry: What Can the West Learn?" 11.
49. Goldman, "The U.S. Rare Earth Industry: Its Growth and Decline."
50. Ezra F. Vogel, *Deng Xiaoping and the Transformation of China* (Cambridge, MA: Belknap Press of Harvard University Press, 2013), 551.
51. Andreas Kluth, "China's Got the Dysprosium. That's a Problem," Bloomberg, January 9, 2023, www.bloomberg.com/opinion/articles/2023-01-09/china-s-way-ahead-in-the-rare-earths-race-an-ill-omen-for-global-stability.
52. Hurst, "China's Rare Earth Elements Industry: What Can the West Learn?" 11.
53. Ibid.
54. Goldman, "The U.S. Rare Earth Industry: Its Growth and Decline."
55. Ibid.
56. Ibid.
57. Robert Pear, "With New Budget, Domestic Spending Is Cut $24 Million," *The New York Times*, April 27, 1996, www.nytimes.com/1996/04/27/us/with-new-budget-domestic-spending-is-cut-24-million.html.
58. U.S. Geological Survey, "2009 Minerals Yearbook: California," official publication, 2009, d9-wret.s3.us-west-2.amazonaws.com/assets/palladium/production/mineral-pubs/rare-earth/myb1-2011-raree.pdf.
59. U.S. House Committee on Science and Technology, "Hearing on Rare Earth Minerals and 21st Century Industry," official publication, March 16, 2010, www.govinfo.gov/content/pkg/CHRG-111hhrg55844/pdf/CHRG-111hhrg55844.pdf, 70.
60. Ibid.
61. Marc Humphries, "Rare Earth Elements: The Global Supply Chain," Congressional Research Service, September 30, 2010, www.everycrsreport.com/files/20100930_R41347_280a374dedfad91970bb123b0a05180bd8f18159.pdf, page.
62. Simony Parry and Ed Douglas, "In China, the True Cost of Britain's Clean, Green Wind Power Experiment: Pollution on a Disastrous Scale," DailyMail Online, January 26, 2011, www.dailymail.co.uk/home/moslive/article-1350811/In-China-true-cost-Britains-clean-green-wind-power-experiment-Pollution-disastrous-scale.html.
63. Buqing Zhong, Lingqing Wang, Tao Liang, and Baoshan Xing, "Pollution Level and Inhalation Exposure of Ambient Aerosol Fluoride as Affected by Polymetallic Rare Earth Mining and Smelting in Baotou, North China," *Atmospheric Environment*, August 10, 2017, www.sciencedirect.com/science/article/abs/pii/S1352231017305216.
64. Tim Maughan, "The Dystopian Lake Filled by the World's Tech Lust," BBC, April 2, 2015, www.bbc.com/future/article/20150402-the-worst-place-on-earth.
65. Hurst, "China's Rare Earth Elements Industry: What Can the West Learn?" 16.
66. Keith Bradsher, "Main Victims of Mines Run by Gangsters Are Peasants," *The New York Times*, December 30, 2010, www.nytimes.com/2010/12/30/business/global/30smugglebar.html.
67. Eric Charles Nystrom, "Mojave: From Neglected Space to Protected Place, an Administrative History of Mojave National Preserve," National Park Service History, April 5, 2005, www.nps.gov/parkhistory/online_books/moja/adhi8.htm, Chapter Eight: Resource Management.
68. Brooks Mencher, "U.S. Rare Earth Mine Revived," *SFGate*, November 21, 2012, www.sfgate.com/opinion/article/U-S-rare-earth-mine-revived-4057911.php.
69. Marla Cone, "Desert Lands Contaminated by Toxic Spills," *Los Angeles Times*, April 24, 1997, www.latimes.com/archives/la-xpm-1997-04-24-mn-51903-story.html.

70. Nystrom, "Mojave: From Neglected Space to Protected Place, an Administrative History of Mojave National Preserve."
71. Ibid.
72. John Tkacik, "Magnequench: CFIUS and China's Thirst for U.S. Defense Technology," Heritage Foundation, May 2, 2008, www.heritage.org/asia/report/magnequench-cfius-and-chinas-thirst-us-defense-technology.
73. Nystrom, "Mojave: From Neglected Space to Protected Place, an Administrative History of Mojave National Preserve."
74. Mike Alberti, "Digging a Deep Hole: Rare Earths Debacle Puts U.S. Trade Policy Under Scrutiny," *Remapping Debate*, January 11, 2011, www.remappingdebate.org/article/digging-deep-hole-rare-earths-debacle-puts-us-trade-policy-under-scrutiny/page/0/1.
75. "Molycorp to Submit 30-Year Plan," *Baker Valley News*, May 13, 1999, archived on Molycorp legacy website, accessed November 30, 2022, web.archive.org/web/20010726034224/http://www.molycorp.com/lan_news-01.html.
76. Mencher, "U.S. Rare Earth Mine Revived."
77. Ernest Scheyder and Ben Klayman, "General Motors Returns to Rare Earth Magnets with Two U.S. Deals," Reuters, December 9, 2021, www.reuters.com/business/general-motors-sets-rare-earth-magnet-supply-deals-with-two-us-suppliers-2021-12-09/.
78. Neal E. Boudette and Coral Davenport, "G.M. Will Sell Only Zero-Emission Vehicles by 2035," *The New York Times*, January 28, 2021 (updated October 1, 2021), www.nytimes.com/2021/01/28/business/gm-zero-emission-vehicles.html.
79. Andrew Leonard, "How G.M. Helped China to World Magnet Domination," *Salon*, August 31, 2010, www.salon.com/2010/08/31/china_neodymium_domination/.
80. U.S. Senate Committee on Banking, Housing, and Urban Affairs, "A Review of the CFIUS Process for Implementing the Exon-Florio Amendment," October 2005, www.govinfo.gov/content/pkg/CHRG-109shrg33310/html/CHRG-109shrg33310.htm.
81. Office of the Under Secretary of Defense (Acquisition, Technology & Logistics), Deputy Under Secretary of Defense (Industrial Policy), "Foreign Sources of Supply—Annual Report of United States Defense Industrial Base Capabilities and Acquisitions of Defense Items and Components Outside the United States," official publication, accessed January 2, 2023, www.hsdl.org/?view&did=713562, 4.
82. Scheyder and Klayman, "General Motors Returns to Rare Earth Magnets with Two U.S. Deals."
83. Keith Bradsher, "Challenging China in Rare Earth Mining," *The New York Times*, April 21, 2010, www.nytimes.com/2010/04/22/business/energy-environment/22rare.html.
84. ChevronTexaco, "ChevronTexaco Announces Agreement to Acquire Unocal," press release, April 4, 2005, chevroncorp.gcs-web.com/news-releases/news-release-details/chevrontexaco-announces-agreement-acquire-unocal.
85. Bradsher, "Challenging China in Rare Earth Mining."
86. John Miller and Anjie Zheng, "Molycorp Files for Bankruptcy Protection," *The Wall Street Journal*, June 25, 2015, www.wsj.com/articles/this-article-also-appears-in-daily-bankruptcy-review-a-publication-from-dow-jones-co-1435219007.
87. Bradsher, "Challenging China in Rare Earth Mining."
88. Peter Smith, Jonathan Soble, and Leslie Hook, "Japan Secures Rare Earths Deal with Australia," *Financial Times*, November 24, 2010, www.ft.com/content/63a18538-f773-11df-8b42-00144feab49a.

89. Ernest Scheyder, "Lynas Touts Its Independence from China in Push for Rare Earths Growth," Reuters, June 6, 2019, www.reuters.com/article/us-usa-rareearths-lynas-corp/lynas-touts-its-independence-from-china-in-push-for-rare-earths-growth-idUSKCN1T7255.
90. Keith Bradsher, "China Said to Widen Its Embargo of Minerals," *The New York Times*, October 19, 2010, www.nytimes.com/2010/10/20/business/global/20rare.html.
91. Sarah McBride, "Rare Earth Producer Molycorp Wins OK for Mine," Reuters, December 13, 2010, www.reuters.com/article/molycorp-california-idCNN1321376420101213.
92. James B. Kelleher, "Molycorp in Talks with More JV Partners: CEO," Reuters, December 30, 2010, www.reuters.com/article/us-molycorp-ceo/molycorp-in-talks-with-more-jv-partners-ceo-idUKTRE6BT46820101230.
93. Shirley Jahad, "New 'Call of Duty: Black Ops 2' Video Game Parallels US Quest to Rise in Rare Earths Metals Industry," KPCC, May 31, 2012, www.kpcc.org/2012-05-31/rare-earths-are-key-ingredients-high-tech-age-and.
94. Kelleher, "Molycorp in Talks with More JV Partners: CEO."
95. Rohit Gupta, "Molycorp Counting on Project Phoenix, New Demand: Incremental Production Could Help Molycorp Break Even This Year," TheStreet, March 26, 2014, www.thestreet.com/markets/emerging-markets/molycorp-counting-on-project-phoenix-new-demand-1557070.
96. Julie Gordon, "Update 4—Molycorp Speeds Up Plan to Boost Rare Earth Supply," Reuters, October 20, 2011, www.reuters.com/article/molycorp/update-4-molycorp-speeds-up-plan-to-boost-rare-earth-supply-idUSN1E79I1RB20111020.
97. Julie Gordon, "Molycorp Buys Neo Material for C$1.3 Billion," Reuters, March 8, 2012, www.reuters.com/article/us-molycorp/molycorp-buys-neo-material-for-c1-3-billion-idUSBRE82800T20120309.
98. Sarah McBride, "Update 2—Rare Earth Producer Molycorp Wins OK for Mine," Reuters, December 13, 2010, www.reuters.com/article/molycorp-california-idCNN1321376420101213.
99. Author's interview with a former Molycorp executive.
100. John W. Miller and Annie Zheng, "Molycorp Files for Bankruptcy Protection," *The Wall Street Journal*, June 25, 2015, www.wsj.com/articles/this-article-also-appears-in-daily-bankruptcy-review-a-publication-from-dow-jones-co-1435219007.
101. Reuters, "Update 2—Molycorp CEO Quits Amid SEC Investigation," December 11, 2012, www.reuters.com/article/molycorp-ceoresignation/update-2-molycorp-ceo-quits-amid-sec-investigation-idUKL4N09L65R20121211.
102. Molycorp Inc., "Form 10-Q for the Third Quarter of 2012," U.S. Securities and Exchange Commission public filing, www.sec.gov/Archives/edgar/data/1489137/000148913712000008/mcp930201210q.htm, 30.
103. Jim Steinberg, "EPA Fines San Bernardino County's Molycorp $27,300," *San Bernardino Sun*, April 21, 2014, www.sbsun.com/2014/04/21/epa-fines-san-bernardino-countys-molycorp-27300/.
104. Gupta, "Molycorp Counting on Project Phoenix, New Demand."
105. *Molycorp Minerals LLC v. Debtors*, 15-11371 (U.S. Bankruptcy Court, District of Delaware), Document 1.
106. Neo Performance Materials, "Molycorp, Inc. Emerges from Chapter 11 as Neo Performance Materials," press release, August 31, 2016, www.globenewswire.com/news-release/2016/08/31/868672/0/en/Molycorp-Inc-Emerges-from-Chapter-11-as-Neo-Performance-Materials.html.

107. Peg Brickley, "Molycorp Defeats Effort to Delay Chapter 11 Exit Plan Hearings," *The Wall Street Journal*, March 30, 2016, www.wsj.com/articles/molycorp-defeats-effort-to-delay-chapter-11-exit-plan-hearings-1459365802?mod=Searchresults_pos1&page=1.
108. Ibid.
109. Ibid.
110. Peg Brickley, "Brickley's Take: Molycorp's Rare Earths Money Pit," *The Wall Street Journal*, August 30, 2016, www.wsj.com/articles/brickleys-take-molycorps-rare-earths-money-pit-1472493505?mod=Searchresults_pos20&page=1.
111. Peg Brickley, "California's Mountain Pass Mine to be Auctioned in Bankruptcy: Former Molycorp Mine Is Major U.S. Source of Rare Earths; Auction Has Opening Offer of $40 Million," *The Wall Street Journal*, February 1, 2017, www.wsj.com/articles/californias-mountain-pass-mine-to-be-auctioned-in-bankruptcy-1485955874.
112. Ibid.
113. Ibid.
114. Peg Brickley, "Brickley's Take: JHL, QVT Steal a March on Mountain Pass Mine," *The Wall Street Journal*, May 9, 2017, www.wsj.com/articles/brickleys-take-jhl-qvt-steal-a-march-on-mountain-pass-mine-1494270396.
115. *Molycorp Minerals LLC v. Debtors*, 15-11371 (U.S. Bankruptcy Court, District of Delaware), Document 338.
116. *Molycorp Minerals LLC v. Debtors*, 15-11371 (U.S. Bankruptcy Court, District of Delaware), Document 333.
117. Peg Brickley, "Clarke Challenges JHL Bid for Mountain Pass Mine: Virginia Entrepreneur Says Rival Bid Is Supported by 'Substantial Chinese Investment,' Posing Regulatory Risk," *The Wall Street Journal*, June 13, 2017, www.wsj.com/articles/clarke-challenges-jhl-bid-for-mountain-pass-mine-1497397842.
118. Shearman & Sterling, "Final CFIUS Regulations Implement Significant Changes by Broadening Jurisdiction and Updating Scope of Reviews," *Shearman & Sterling Perspectives*, January 14, 2020, www.shearman.com/perspectives/2020/01/final-cfius-regulations-implement-changes-by-broadening-jurisdiction-and-updating-scope-of-reviews.
119. *Molycorp Minerals LLC v. Debtors*, 15-11371 (U.S. Bankruptcy Court, District of Delaware), Document 374.
120. Ibid.
121. Author's interview with Jim Litinsky, January 30, 2020.
122. Author's interview with Stan Trout, December 17, 2019.
123. MP Materials Corp., "Form 10-Q for the Second Quarter of 2022," U.S. Securities and Exchange Commission public filing, s25.q4cdn.com/570172628/files/doc_financials/2022/q2/MP-Materials-2Q-2022-10Q-as-Filed.pdf, 8.
124. MP Materials Corp., "Form 10-Q for the Third Quarter of 2021," U.S. Securities and Exchange Commission public filing, www.sec.gov/ix?doc=/Archives/edgar/data/0001801368/000180136821000046/mp-20210930.htm, Note 3.
125. Ernest Scheyder, "U.S. Rare Earths Miner MP Materials to Go Public in $1.47 Billion Deal," Reuters, July 15, 2020, www.reuters.com/article/us-mp-materials-ipo/u-s-rare-earths-miner-mp-materials-to-go-public-in-1-47-billion-deal-idUSKCN24G1WT.
126. Ibid.
127. Sam Boughedda, "MP Materials Stock Drops Following Grizzly Research Short Report," Investing.com, October 26, 2021, www.investing.com/news/stock-market-news/mp-materials-stock-drops-following-grizzly-research-short-report-2655805.

128. "MP Materials Corp. (NYSE: MP): Rare Earth Shenanigans in Chamath Backed Company Will Likely Cost Investors Dearly," Grizzly Research, October 26, 2021, grizzlyreports.com/Research/MP%20Materials%20Corp.pdf, 10.
129. Ernest Scheyder, "American Quandary: How to Secure Weapons-Grade Minerals Without China," Reuters, April 22, 2020, www.reuters.com/article/us-usa-rareearths-insight/american-quandary-how-to-secure-weapons-grade-minerals-without-china-idUSKCN2241KF.
130. Ibid.
131. Reuters, "California's MP Materials Wins Pentagon Funding for Rare Earths Facility," April 22, 2020, www.reuters.com/article/usa-rareearths-mpmaterials/californias-mp-materials-wins-pentagon-funding-for-rare-earths-facility-idUSL2N2CA2NO.
132. Ernest Scheyder, "Pentagon Halts Rare Earths Funding Program Pending 'Further Research,'" Reuters, May 22, 2020, www.reuters.com/article/us-usa-rareearths-exclusive/exclusive-pentagon-halts-rare-earths-funding-program-pending-further-research-idUSKBN22Y1VC.
133. Ernest Scheyder, "Pentagon Resumes Rare Earths Funding Program After Review," Reuters, July 21, 2020, www.reuters.com/article/us-usa-rareearths/pentagon-resumes-rare-earths-funding-program-after-review-idUSKCN24M2Z4.
134. Anastasia Lyrchikova and Gleb Stolyarov, "Russia Has $1.5 Billion Plan to Dent China's Rare Earth Dominance," Reuters, August 12, 2020, www.reuters.com/article/russia-rareearths/russia-has-1-5-billion-plan-to-dent-chinas-rare-earth-dominance-idUSL8N2F73F4.
135. Demetri Sevastopulo, Tom Mitchell, and Sun Yu, "China Targets Rare Earth Export Curbs to Hobble US Defence Industry," *Financial Times*, February 16, 2021, www.ft.com/content/d3ed83f4-19bc-4d16-b510-415749c032c1.
136. Ernest Scheyder, "Exclusive U.S. Bill Would Block Defense Contractors from Using Chinese Rare Earths," Reuters, January 14, 2022, www.reuters.com/business/energy/exclusive-us-bill-would-block-defense-contractors-using-chinese-rare-earths-2022-01-14/.
137. Ernest Scheyder, "U.S. House Bill Would Give Tax Credit for Rare Earth Magnets," Reuters, August 10, 2021, www.reuters.com/article/usa-mining-washington-idCNL1N2PD2DD.
138. John Kemp, "Critical Minerals and Mining Reform in the U.S.," Reuters, January 31, 2014, www.reuters.com/article/usa-mining-rare-earths/column-critical-minerals-and-mining-reform-in-the-u-s-kemp-idUSL5N0L52QP20140131.

CHAPTER SEVEN: BRIGHT GREEN LIES?

1. Jacob Pramuck, "Trump Signs Executive Order Aiming to Slash Regulations," CNBC, January 30, 2017, www.cnbc.com/2017/01/30/trump-set-to-sign-executive-order-aiming-to-slash-regulations.html.
2. Ibid.
3. Nolan D. McCaskill and Matthew Nussbaum, "Trump Signs Executive Order Requiring That for Every One New Regulation, Two Must Be Revoked," *Politico*, January 30, 2017, politico.com/story/2017/01/trump-signs-executive-order-requiring-that-for-every-one-new-regulation-two-must-be-revoked-234365.
4. Mike Soraghan, "Interior Lawyer Knows Colorado," *The Denver Post*, December 4, 2006, www.denverpost.com/2006/12/04/interior-lawyer-knows-colorado/.

5. David Bernhardt, *You Report to Me: Accountability for the Failing Administrative State* (New York: Encounter Books, 2023), 129.
6. U.S. Deputy Secretary of the Interior David Bernhardt, "Order No. 3355," official publication, August 31, 2017, www.doi.gov/sites/doi.gov/files/elips/documents/3355_-_streamlining_national_environmental_policy_reviews_and_implementation_of_executive_order_13807_establishing_discipline_and_accountability_in_the_environmental_review_and_permitting_process_for.pdf.
7. Bernhardt's successor, Deb Haaland, revoked the order in 2021: Kurt Repanshek, "Interior Secretary Reverses Many of Trump Administration's Energy Actions," *National Parks Traveler*, April 16, 2021, www.nationalparkstraveler.org/2021/04/interior-secretary-reverses-many-trump-administrations-energy-actions.
8. Lithium Americas, "Independent Technical Report for the Thacker Pass Project, Humboldt County, Nevada, USA," filed with the U.S. Securities and Exchange Commission, May 17, 2018, www.sec.gov/Archives/edgar/data/1440972/000156459018013979/lac-ex991_8.htm.
9. Antonio Lara, et al., "Natural Clays with an Inherent Uranium Component That Nevertheless Sequester Uranium from Contaminated Water," *Journal of Environmental Science and Health*, November 8, 2018, www.ncbi.nlm.nih.gov/pmc/articles/PMC6447444.
10. "Lithium Americas Thacker Pass," Desert Fog blog, accessed July 15, 2022, desertfog.org/projects/lithium-mining-in-the-mojave-and-great-basin-deserts/exploration-sites/lithium-americas-thacker-pass/.
11. Ibid.
12. Author's interview with Jon Evans, November 18, 2022.
13. Lithium Americas, "Western Lithium Announces Name Change to Lithium Americas and Provides Corporate Update," press release, March 22, 2016, www.lithiumamericas.com/news/-western-lithium-announces-name-change-to-lithium-americas--and-provides-corporate-update.
14. "Lithium Americas Thacker Pass."
15. Lithium Americas, "Annual Information Form," public filing, March 15, 2022, www.lithiumamericas.com/_resources/pdf/investors/AIF/2021.pdf?v=0.137.
16. Western Lithium, "Western Lithium Secures US$5.5 Million from Strategic Investor Orion Mine Finance," press release, September 23, 2013, www.globenewswire.com/en/news-release/2013/09/23/1343344/0/en/Western-Lithium-Secures-US-5-5-Million-From-Strategic-Investor-Orion-Mine-Finance.html.
17. Diane Cardwell and Clifford Krauss, "Frack Quietly, Please: Sage Grouse Is Nesting," *The New York Times*, July 19, 2014, www.nytimes.com/2014/07/20/business/energy-environment/disparate-interests-unite-to-protect-greater-sage-grouse.html.
18. *Bartell Ranch LLC et al. v. Ester M. McCullough et al.*, 3:21-cv-00080 (U.S. District Court, Nevada), Document 202.
19. Ibid.
20. Ibid.
21. Letter from Senators Catherine Cortez Masto and Jacky Rosen to U.S. Secretary of the Interior David Bernhardt, April 3, 2020, www.rosen.senate.gov/wp-content/uploads/sites/default/files/2020-04/Rosen%20CCM%20letter%20to%20DOI%20on%20suspending%20public%20comment%20periods%20during%20COVID-19.pdf.
22. Loda was asked for comment about the emails. He declined to comment

in a message conveyed through the U.S. Bureau of Land Management's Winnemucca District Office public affairs specialist.

23. *Bartell Ranch LLC et al. v. Ester M. McCullough et al.*, Document 200.
24. Ernest Scheyder, "Lithium Americas Moves Closer to Nevada Mine Approval," Reuters, January 20, 2020, www.reuters.com/article/us-usa-mining-lithium-americas/lithium-americas-moves-closer-to-nevada-mine-approval-idUSKBN1ZJ1WP.
25. Ernest Scheyder, "China's Ganfeng to Take Control of Argentina Lithium Project," Reuters, February 7, 2020, www.reuters.com/article/lithium-americas-ganfeng-lithium/chinas-ganfeng-to-take-control-of-argentina-lithium-project-idUSL1N2A704J.
26. *Bartell Ranch LLC et al. v. Ester M. McCullough et al.*, Document 202.
27. Ibid.
28. U.S. Bureau of Land Management, "Thacker Pass Lithium Mine Project: Final Environmental Impact Statement," official publication, December 4, 2020, eplanning.blm.gov/public_projects/1503166/200352542/20030633/250036832/Thacker%20Pass_FEIS_Chapters1-6_508.pdf, 2–8.
29. Ibid., Table 4.18, 4–109.
30. *Bartell Ranch LLC et al. v. Ester M. McCullough et al.*, Document 1.
31. Ibid.
32. Ibid.
33. Scott Sonner, "Nevada Rancher Sues to Block Lithium Mine Near Oregon Border," Associated Press, February 18, 2021, nbc16.com/newsletter-daily/nevada-rancher-sues-to-block-lithium-mine-near-oregon-border.
34. Ivan Penn and Eric Lipton, "The Lithium Gold Rush: Inside the Race to Power Electric Vehicles," *The New York Times*, May 6, 2021, www.nytimes.com/2021/05/06/business/lithium-mining-race.html.
35. Bill McKibben, "It's Not the Heat, It's the Damage: Two Questions Lie at the Heart of the Climate Crisis," *The New Yorker*, August 4, 2021, www.newyorker.com/news/annals-of-a-warming-planet/its-not-the-heat-its-the-damage.
36. Penn and Lipton, "The Lithium Gold Rush: Inside the Race to Power Electric Vehicles."
37. Ernest Scheyder, "U.S. Judge Rules Lithium Americas May Excavate Nevada Mine Site," Reuters, July 26, 2021, www.reuters.com/business/environment/us-judge-rules-lithium-americas-may-excavate-nevada-mine-site-2021-07-24/.
38. Ernest Scheyder, "Native Americans Win Ruling to Join Lawsuit Against Lithium Americas Project," Reuters, July 29, 2021, www.reuters.com/legal/litigation/native-americans-win-ruling-join-lawsuit-against-lithium-americas-project-2021-07-28.
39. Author's interview with Gary McKinney, February 2, 2023.
40. Derrick Jensen, Lierre Keith, and Max Wilbert, *Bright Green Lies: How the Environmental Movement Lost Its Way and What We Can Do About It* (Rhinebeck, N.Y.: Monkfish Book Publishing, 2021).
41. Derrick Jensen, Lierre Keith, and Max Wilbert, "It's Time for Us All to Stand Up Against Big 'Sister,'" *Feminist Current*, October 5, 2019, www.feministcurrent.com/2019/10/05/its-time-for-us-all-to-stand-up-against-big-sister/.
42. Jennifer Solis, "Feds Slap Fines on Thacker Pass Protestors," *Nevada Current*, September 29, 2021, www.nevadacurrent.com/2021/09/29/feds-slap-fines-on-thacker-pass-protestors/.
43. Ernest Scheyder, "Lithium Americas Expects Court Ruling on Nevada Lithium Mine by Autumn," Reuters, February 25, 2022, www.reuters.com/legal

/transactional/lithium-americas-expects-court-ruling-nevada-lithium-mine-by-autumn-2022-02-25.

44. Ernest Scheyder, "Exclusive—Lithium Americas Delays Nevada Mine Work After Environmental Lawsuit," Reuters, June 11, 2021, www.reuters.com/business/environment/exclusive-lithium-americas-delays-nevada-mine-work-after-environmentalist-2021-06-11.
45. Lithium Americas, "Annual Information Form," public filing, March 15, 2022, www.lithiumamericas.com/_resources/pdf/investors/AIF/2021.pdf?v=0.137, 41–42.
46. The average concentration of lithium in Chile's Salar de Atacama, one of the world's largest active lithium sources, is about 1,500 parts per million: Carolina F. Cubillos et al., "Microbial Communities from the World's Largest Lithium Reserve, Salar de Atacama, Chile: Life at High LiCl Concentrations," *Journal of Geophysical Research: Biogeosciences*, December 3, 2018, agupubs.onlinelibrary.wiley.com/doi/full/10.1029/2018JG004621#:~:text=Abstract,leading%20producer%20of%20lithium%20products.
47. Jensen, Keith, and Wilbert, "It's Time for Us All to Stand Up Against Big 'Sister.'"
48. Associated Press, "New Zealand River's Personhood Status Offers Hope to Māori," August 15, 2022, www.usnews.com/news/world/articles/2022-08-15/new-zealand-rivers-personhood-status-offers-hope-to-maori.
49. Author's interviews with Max Wilbert, August 12–13, 2022.
50. Elaine Sciolino, *Persian Mirrors: The Elusive Face of Iran* (New York: Free Press, 2000, 2005), 282.
51. Jensen, Keith, and Wilbert, "It's Time for Us All to Stand Up Against Big 'Sister.'"
52. Jael Holzman, "How an 'Anti-Trans' Group Split the Fight Against a Lithium Mine," *E&E News*, January 27, 2022, www.eenews.net/articles/how-an-anti-trans-group-split-the-fight-against-a-lithium-mine/.
53. Ibid.
54. Ibid.
55. Jennifer Solis, "BLM's Rediscovery of Massacre Site Renews Calls for Halt of Lithium Project," *Nevada Current*, September 6, 2022, www.nevadacurrent.com/2022/09/06/blms-rediscovery-of-massacre-site-renews-calls-for-halt-of-lithium-mine-project/.
56. Tom Kertscher, "Fact-Checking Whether Senate Hopeful Adam Laxalt Helped Oil Industry Then Got Campaign Money from It," Politifact, August 12, 2022, www.politifact.com/factchecks/2022/aug/12/catherine-cortez-masto/fact-checking-whether-senate-hopeful-adam-laxalt-h/.
57. Senator Catherine Cortez Masto, "Cortez Masto Applauds Investments She Secured in the Bipartisan Infrastructure Law to Boost Domestic Battery Manufacturing and Supply Chains," press release, May 2, 2022, www.cortezmasto.senate.gov/news/press-releases/cortez-masto-applauds-investments-she-secured-in-the-bipartisan-infrastructure-law-to-boost-domestic-battery-manufacturing-and-supply-chains.
58. Ernest Scheyder, "Update 1—U.S. Senator Manchin Promises to Block Mining Royalty Plan," Reuters, October 14, 2021, www.reuters.com/article/usa-mining-royalties-idAFL1N2RA2X5.
59. Nathaniel Phillipps, "Westside Residents Need Local Opportunity, Not Distant Mining Jobs," *Nevada Current*, December 7, 2021, www.nevadacurrent.com/2021/12/07/westside-residents-need-local-opportunity-not-distant-mining-jobs/.

60. "We were very happy to welcome Senator Cortez Masto @SenCortezMasto to tour the Lithium Nevada Research & Process Testing Facility in Reno today," tweet from Lithium Americas Twitter account, September 27, 2019, twitter.com/lithiumamericas/status/1177675777782865922.
61. Ernest Scheyder, "Lithium Americas Trims Production Target, Budget for Nevada Mine," Reuters, September 25, 2019, www.reuters.com/article/usa-mining-lithium-americas/lithium-americas-trims-production-target-budget-for-nevada-mine-idINL2N26E1RP.
62. Lithium Nevada, a Lithium Americas company, "Newsletter December 2019," corporate publication, www.lithiumamericas.com/_resources/thacker-pass/LAC-LNC-Thacker-Pass-Newsletter-Dec-17-2019.pdf.
63. Lithium Nevada, a Lithium Americas company, "2021 Q4 Newsletter," corporate publication, www.lithiumamericas.com/_resources/thacker-pass/LNC-Thacker-Pass-Newsletter-Q4-2021.pdf.
64. The White House, "FACT SHEET: Securing a Made in America Supply Chain for Critical Minerals," official publication, February 22, 2022, www.whitehouse.gov/briefing-room/statements-releases/2022/02/22/fact-sheet-securing-a-made-in-america-supply-chain-for-critical-minerals/.
65. Andy Home, "US Green Metals Push Needs a Revamp of Gold-Rush Mining Law," Reuters, February 25, 2022, www.reuters.com/article/usa-mining-ahome/us-green-metals-push-needs-a-revamp-of-gold-rush-mining-law-andy-home-idUSKBN2KU1HG.
66. Scheyder, "Update 1—U.S. Senator Manchin Promises to Block Mining Royalty Plan."
67. Author's interview with Jon Evans, November 18, 2022.
68. Joseph Menn, "Chinese Posed as Texans on Social Media to Attack Rare Earths Rivals," *The Washington Post*, June 28, 2022, www.washingtonpost.com/technology/2022/06/28/china-misinformation-rare-earths/.
69. Tim Burmeister, "Lithium Americas Signs Agreement with Local Tribe," *Elko Daily*, October 25, 2022, elkodaily.com/mining/lithium-americas-signs-agreement-with-local-tribe/article_a7e6d900-5418-11ed-9e4f-1f9853aa0ad0.html.
70. Ernest Scheyder, "GM to Help Lithium Americas Develop Nevada's Thacker Pass Mine," Reuters, January 31, 2023, www.reuters.com/markets/commodities/gm-lithium-americas-develop-thacker-pass-mine-nevada-2023-01-31/.
71. Ernest Scheyder, "U.S. Judge Orders Waste Rock Study for Thacker Pass Lithium Project," Reuters, February 7, 2023, www.reuters.com/legal/us-judge-orders-fresh-review-part-lithium-americas-nevada-permit-2023-02-07/.
72. Daniel Rothberg, "'We're Just Somebody Little': Amid Plans to Mine Lithium Deposit, Indigenous, Rural Communities Find Themselves at the Center of the Energy Transition," *The Nevada Independent*, June 20, 2021, thenevadaindependent.com/article/were-just-somebody-little-rural-indigenous-communities-on-the-frontlines-of-energy-transition-amid-plans-to-mine-major-lithium-deposit.

CHAPTER EIGHT: A REBIRTH

1. "Yellow Pine, Idaho, Population 2023," World Population Review, accessed December 15, 2023, worldpopulationreview.com/us-cities/yellow-pine-id-population.
2. "Yellow Pine Post Office 83677," PostOfficeHours.com, postofficeshours.com/id/yellow-pine/yellow-pine.

3. "Music & Harmonica Festival," Village of Yellow Pine, www.yellowpinefestival.org/.
4. "1950 Census of Populations: Volume 1. Number of Inhabitants, Idaho," www2.census.gov/library/publications/decennial/1950/population-volume-1/vol-01-15.pdf.
5. U.S. Geological Survey, "Antimony," official publication, 2017, pubs.usgs.gov/pp/1802/c/pp1802c.pdf.
6. U.S. Department of the Interior, National Park Service, "National Register of Historic Places Inventory Nomination Form," June 8, 1987, history.idaho.gov/wp-content/uploads/2018/09/Stibnite_Historic_District_87001186.pdf.
7. "Thunder Mountain, Idaho," Western Mining History, accessed October 31, 2022, westernmininghistory.com/towns/idaho/thunder-mountain/.
8. U.S. Department of the Interior, National Park Service, "National Register of Historic Places Inventory Nomination Form," https://history.idaho.gov/wp-content/uploads/2018/09/Stibnite_Historic_District_87001186.pdf.
9. Ibid.
10. Susan van den Brink et al., "Resilience in the Antimony Supply Chain," *Resources, Conservation and Recycling*, August 10, 2022, www.sciencedirect.com/science/article/pii/S0921344922004219#bib0054.
11. U.S. Department of the Interior, National Park Service, "National Register of Historic Places Inventory Nomination Form."
12. Ibid.
13. "Moving Day at Stibnite," *Payette Lake Star*, October 3, 1963, portal.laserfiche.com/Portal/DocView.aspx?id=44152&repo=r-d76fb24e.
14. Associated Press, "Mobil Sells Mine," May 1, 1986, www.nytimes.com/1986/05/01/business/mobil-sells-mine.html.
15. Midas Gold, "Stibnite Gold Project: Feasibility Study Technical Report," official publication, January 27, 2021, perpetuaresources.com/wp-content/uploads/2021/06/2021-01-27-feasibility-study.pdf.
16. U.S. Geological Survey, "Antimony."
17. Idaho State Historical Society, "Idaho's State Motto," official publication, accessed November 2, 2022, history.idaho.gov/wp-content/uploads/0134.pdf.
18. Author's interview with Mckinsey Lyon, August 15, 2022.
19. Thomas Bulfinch, *Bulfinch's Mythology* (New York: HarperCollins, 1991), 43.
20. Perpetua Resources, "Midas Gold Announces Name Change to Perpetua Resources and Approved NASDAQ Listing," press release, February 16, 2021, www.investors.perpetuaresources.com/investors/news/2021/midas-gold-announces-name-change-to-perpetua-resources-and-approved-nasdaq-listing.
21. Author's interview with Mckinsey Lyon, August 15, 2022.
22. Midas Gold, "Stibnite Gold Project: Feasibility Study Technical Report," 15.
23. David Blackmon, "Perpetua, Ambri Ink Key Antimony Supply Deal to Boost Liquid Metal Battery Tech," *Forbes*, August 14, 2021, www.forbes.com/sites/davidblackmon/2021/08/14/perpetua-ambri-ink-key-antimony-supply-deal-to-boost-liquid-metal-battery-tech/?sh=47aa1a476afd.
24. Jack Healy and Mike Baker, "As Miners Chase Clean-Energy Minerals, Tribes Fear a Repeat of the Past," *The New York Times*, December 27, 2021, www.nytimes.com/2021/12/27/us/mining-clean-energy-antimony-tribes.html.
25. Ibid.
26. Ibid.
27. Perpetua Resources, "U.S. Forest Service Chooses Perpetua Resources' Proposed Stibnite Gold Project as Preferred Alternative," press release, Octo-

ber 28, 2022, www.prnewswire.com/news-releases/us-forest-service-chooses-perpetua-resources-proposed-stibnite-gold-project-as-preferred-alternative-301661983.html.

28. Author's interviews with Aimee Boulanger, January 10, 2023.
29. Senator Martin Heinrich, "Heinrich, Risch Introduce Bipartisan Legislation to Remove Hurdles for Good Samaritans to Clean Up Abandoned Hardrock Mines," press release, February 3, 2022, www.heinrich.senate.gov/newsroom/press-releases/heinrich-risch-introduce-bipartisan-legislation-to-remove-hurdles-for-good-samaritans-to-clean-up-abandoned-hardrock-mines-.
30. Midas Gold, "Midas Gold to Enter Strategic Relationship with Paulson & Co. and Raise C$55.2 million," press release, February 22, 2016, www.globenewswire.com/news-release/2016/02/22/1330827/0/en/Midas-Gold-to-Enter-Strategic-Relationship-With-Paulson-Co-and-Raise-C-55-2-Million.html.
31. Midas Gold, "Consolidated Financial Statements for the Years Ended December 31, 2015, and 2014," public filing, February 26, 2016, perpetuaresources.com/wp-content/uploads/2021/06/2015-q4-fs.pdf.
32. Midas Gold, "Midas Gold Complements Its Leadership Team with New Appointments," press release, September 20, 2016, midasgoldcorp.com/investors/news/2016/midas-gold-complements-its-leadership-team-with-new-appointments/.
33. "About Perpetua Resources," corporate website, accessed February 20, 2023, perpetuaresources.com/about/.
34. Midas Gold Corp., "Paulson & Co. Provides Notice of Intention to Exercise Convertible Notes in Midas Gold," press release, August 26, 2020, www.newswire.ca/news-releases/paulson-amp-co-provides-notice-of-intention-to-exercise-convertible-notes-in-midas-gold-857031914.html.
35. Ibid.
36. Gregory Zuckerman, "Trade Made Billions on Subprime: John Paulson Bet Bid on Drop in Housing Values," *The Wall Street Journal*, January 15, 2008, www.wsj.com/articles/SB120036645057290423?mod=article_inline.
37. Kip McDaniel, "The Obsession of John Paulson," *Chief Investment Officer*, December 10, 2013, www.ai-cio.com/news/the-obsession-of-john-paulson/.
38. Gregory Zuckerman, "Worried About Your Tax Bill? Hedge Fund Star John Paulson Owes $1 Billion," *The Wall Street Journal*, April 11, 2018, www.wsj.com/articles/worried-about-your-tax-bill-hedge-fund-star-john-paulson-owes-1-billion-1523458528.
39. Nicole Mordant, "Hedge Fund Paulson & Co. Declares War on Poor Gold Mining Returns," Reuters, September 26, 2017, www.reuters.com/article/us-mining-gold-paulson/hedge-fund-paulson-co-declares-war-on-poor-gold-mining-returns-idUSKCN1C12OJ.
40. Ibid.
41. Author's interview with Marcelo Kim, June 22, 2022.
42. U.S. Department of Defense, "DoD Issues $24.8M Critical Minerals Award to Perpetua Resources," press release, December 19, 2022, www.defense.gov/News/Releases/Release/Article/3249350/dod-issues-248m-critical-minerals-award-to-perpetua-resources/.
43. PebbleWatch, "Pebble Project," accessed February 20, 2023, pebblewatch.com/pebble-project/.
44. Reuters, "Factbox—History of Alaska's Pebble Mine Project: A Long-Running Saga," August 25, 2020, www.reuters.com/article/usa-alaska-pebblemine-history/factbox-history-of-alaskas-pebble-mine-project-a-long-running-saga-idUSL1N2FR1JK.

45. Ernest Scheyder, "Alaska's Pebble Mine Told to Offset Damage as Republican Opposition Grows," Reuters, August 24, 2020, www.reuters.com/article/us-usa-alaska-pebblemine/alaskas-pebble-mine-told-to-offset-damage-as-republican-opposition-grows-idUSKBN25K1W5.
46. Juliet Eilperin and Brady Dennis, "Obama Blocked This Controversial Alaskan Gold Mine. Trump Just Gave It New Life," *The Washington Post*, October 27, 2021, www.washingtonpost.com/news/energy-environment/wp/2017/05/12/obama-blocked-this-controversial-alaskan-gold-mine-trump-just-gave-it-new-life/.
47. Edwin Dobb, "Alaska's Clash over Salmon and Gold Goes National," *National Geographic*, November 18, 2012, www.nationalgeographic.com/science/article/121116-bristol-bay-alaska-salmon-gold-pebble-mine-science-nation.
48. Powell Michael and Jo Becker, "Palin's Hand Seen in Battle over Mine in Alaska," *The New York Times*, October 22, 2008, www.nytimes.com/2008/10/22/us/politics/22mining.html.
49. Bill Carter, *Boom, Bust, Boom: A Story About Copper, the Metal That Runs the World* (New York: Simon & Schuster, 2012), 121.
50. Dobb, "Alaska's Clash over Salmon and Gold Goes National."
51. Ibid.
52. Ibid.
53. Reuters, "Factbox—History of Alaska's Pebble Mine Project: A Long-Running Saga."
54. Eilperin and Dennis, "Obama Blocked This Controversial Alaskan Gold Mine. Trump Just Gave It New Life."
55. Ernest Scheyder, "EPA Breathes New Life into Controversial Alaska Mining Project," Reuters, June 26, 2019, www.reuters.com/article/us-usa-alaska-mine/epa-breathes-new-life-into-controversial-alaska-mining-project-idUSKCN1TR35G.
56. Yereth Rosen, "U.S. Army Corps Poised to Recommend Approval of Alaska's Pebble Mine," Reuters, July 20, 2020, www.reuters.com/article/us-usa-alaska-mine/u-s-army-corps-poised-to-recommend-approval-of-alaskas-pebble-mine-idUSKCN24L2UC.
57. Reuters, "Danish PM Says Trump's Idea of Selling Greenland to U.S. Is Absurd," August 18, 2019, www.reuters.com/article/uk-usa-trump-greenland-idUKKCN1V80M2.
58. Tweet from the account of Donald Trump Jr., @DonaldJTrumpJr, August 4, 2020, twitter.com/DonaldJTrumpJr/status/1290723762523045888?s=20.
59. Author's interview with Andrew Sabin, August 20, 2020.
60. Annie Karni, "Trump Signs Landmark Land Conservation Bill," *The New York Times*, August 4, 2020, www.nytimes.com/2020/08/04/us/politics/trump-land-conservation-bill.html.
61. Tucker Carlson, "Alaska's Pebble Mine Could Significantly Harm Fishing and the Environment," Fox News, August 14, 2020, www.foxnews.com/video/6181326417001#sp=show-clips.
62. Ibid.
63. U.S. Army Corps of Engineers, "Army Finds Pebble Mine Project Cannot Be Permitted as Proposed," press release, August 24, 2020, www.army.mil/article/238426/army_finds_pebble_mine_project_cannot_be_permitted_as_proposed.
64. Scheyder, "Alaska's Pebble Mine Told to Offset Damage as Republican Opposition Grows."

65. Reuters, "Doubts Grow Alaska's Pebble Mine Can Satisfy New Regulatory Hurdles, Shares Tumble," August 25, 2020, www.reuters.com/article/us-usa-alaska-pebblemine/doubts-grow-alaskas-pebble-mine-can-satisfy-new-regulatory-hurdles-shares-tumble-idUSKBN25L26A.
66. Martin Kaste, "This Pebble Is Stirring a Whole Lot of Controversy in Alaska," NPR, January 22, 2014, www.npr.org/2014/01/22/265035184/this-pebble-is-stirring-a-whole-lot-of-controversy-in-alaska.
67. Author's interview with Ron Thiessen, March 6, 2022.
68. Reuters, "Alaska Mining Project CEO Criticizes U.S. EPA Veto Suggestion," December 2, 2022, www.reuters.com/legal/litigation/alaska-mining-project-ceo-criticizes-us-epa-veto-suggestion-2022-12-02/.
69. Reuters, "Conservationists Move to Permanently Protect Areas Around Proposed Alaskan Mine," December 22, 2022, www.reuters.com/business/environment/conservationists-move-permanently-protect-areas-around-proposed-alaskan-mine-2022-12-22/.
70. KTVB, "Twin Brothers Pass Away in Valley County Plane Crash", August 18, 2022, www.ktvb.com/article/news/local/twin-brothers-pass-away-valley-county-plane-crash/277-92d886db-925c-48bb-9446-7db97a5a742f.

CHAPTER NINE: LONELY ARE THE BRAVE

1. Center for Biological Diversity, "More Than 17,000 Rare Nevada Wildflowers Destroyed: Tiehm's Buckwheat, Under Review for Federal Protection, Loses up to 40% of Population," press release, September 16, 2020, biologicaldiversity.org/w/news/press-releases/more-17000-rare-nevada-wildflowers-destroyed-2020-09-16/.
2. Author's text messages with Patrick Donnelly, December 15, 2022.
3. Adam Federman, "'This Is the Wild West Out Here': How Washington Is Bending Over Backward for Mining Companies in Nevada at the Expense of Environmental Rules," *Politico*, February 9, 2020, www.typeinvestigations.org/investigation/2020/02/09/this-is-the-wild-west-out-here/.
4. LinkedIn profile of Daniel R. Patterson, accessed January 15, 2023, www.linkedin.com/in/dpatterson2/.
5. Federman, "'This Is the Wild West Out Here.'"
6. Author's interview with Patrick Donnelly, August 11, 2022.
7. John Smith, "Whistleblower Puts Nevada BLM's Chummy Industry Relationships in the Spotlight," *Nevada Independent*, February 9, 2020, thenevadaindependent.com/article/whistleblower-puts-nevada-blms-chummy-industry-relationships-in-the-spotlight.
8. Dan Patterson, "Supplement to Information Disclosed to the U.S. Office of Special Counsel," whistleblower complaint, October 4, 2019, s3.documentcloud.org/documents/6768915/Nevada-Whisteblower-Complaint.pdf, 1.
9. Ibid., 13.
10. Smith, "Whistleblower Puts Nevada BLM's Chummy Industry Relationships in the Spotlight."
11. Tweet from Twitter account of Dan Patterson, @DanPattersonUSA, mobile.twitter.com/DanPattersonUSA/status/1254095825371709440.
12. Patterson, "Supplement to Information Disclosed."
13. Center for Biological Diversity, "Emergency Petition to the U.S. Fish and Wildlife Service to List Tiehm's Buckwheat (*Eriogonum tiehmii*) Under the Endangered Species Act as an Endangered or Threatened Species and to Concurrently Designate Critical Habitat," petition to U.S. Department of the Inte-

rior, October 7, 2019, www.biologicaldiversity.org/species/plants/pdfs/Tiehms-buckwheat-petition-to-FWS.pdf.

14. Author's interview with Patrick Donnelly, August 11, 2022.
15. CBD, "Emergency Petition," 4.
16. Ibid., 28.
17. Ibid.
18. Center for Biological Diversity, "Lawsuit Aims to Protect Rare Nevada Wildflower from Exploratory Mining," press release, October 30, 2019, biologicaldiversity.org/w/news/press-releases/lawsuit-aims-protect-rare-nevada-wildflower-exploratory-mining-2019-10-30/.
19. Ioneer, "Mine Plan of Operations / Nevada Reclamation Permit Application: Rhyolite Ridge Lithium-Boron Project, Esmeralda County, Nevada," official corporate filing to U.S. Bureau of Land Management, July 2022.
20. Ernest Scheyder, "As Lithium Prices Drop, Private Equity Investors Hunt for Deals," Reuters, November 22, 2019, www.reuters.com/article/us-mining-lithium-investment/as-lithium-prices-drop-private-equity-investors-hunt-for-deals-idUSKBN1XW24N.
21. Ioneer, "Successful Completion of A$40 Million Placement," press release, November 22, 2019, wcsecure.weblink.com.au/pdf/INR/02176241.pdf.
22. Ibid.
23. Center for Biological Diversity, "Agreement Protects Rare Nevada Wildflower from Mine Exploration: Tiehm's Buckwheat Still Threatened by Proposed Open-Pit Mine," press release, January 3, 2020, biologicaldiversity.org/w/news/press-releases/agreement-protects-rare-nevada-wildflower-mine-exploration-2020-01-03/.
24. Ernest Scheyder, "Lithium Americas Moves Closer to Nevada Mine Approval," Reuters, January 20, 2020, www.reuters.com/article/usa-mining-lithium-americas-idINL1N29P0F0.
25. Alice Yu, "Lithium and Cobalt CBS December 2022—Lithium Prices Pressured; Cobalt Down," S&P Global Market Intelligence, December 26, 2022, www.spglobal.com/marketintelligence/en/news-insights/research/lithium-and-cobalt-cbs-december-2022-lithium-prices-pressured-cobalt-down.
26. Ernest Scheyder, "Lithium Developer Ioneer Forecasts High Margins for Nevada Project," Reuters, April 29, 2020, www.reuters.com/article/ioneer-lithium-usa-idUKL1N2CH33Y.
27. Terell Wilkins, "Rare Wildflowers in Nevada Destroyed, 40% of World Population Ruined," *Reno Gazette Journal*, September 23, 2020, www.rgj.com/story/news/2020/09/23/40-percent-worlds-population-rare-nevada-wildflowers-tiehms-buckwheat-destroyed/5820913002/.
28. Ioneer, "ioneer Enters into 12-Month Employement Agreement with Chairman Mr James D. Calaway," July 2, 2020, https://wcsecure.weblink.com.au/pdf/INR/02250712.pdf.
29. Ioneer, "ioneer's Plan of Operations for Rhyolite Ridge Lithium-Boron Project Accepted by BLM," August 31, 2020, https://wcsecure.weblink.com.au/pdf/INR/02274700.pdf.
30. Letter from Patrick Donnelly and Dr. Naomi Fraga to Douglas Furtado, U.S. Bureau of Land Management, September 15, 2020, www.biologicaldiversity.org/programs/public_lands/pdfs/Tiehms-buckwheat-large-scale-destruction-incident-letter-20200916.pdf.
31. Center for Biological Diversity, "More Than 17,000 Rare Nevada Wildflowers Destroyed."

32. Wilkins, "Rare Wildflowers in Nevada Destroyed, 40% of World Population Ruined."
33. Letter from Donnelly and Fraga to Furtado.
34. Wilkins, "Rare Wildflowers in Nevada Destroyed, 40% of World Population Ruined."
35. Blake Apgar, "More Than 17,000 Rare Nevada Wildflowers Destroyed," *Las Vegas Review-Journal*, September 16, 2020, www.reviewjournal.com/local/local-nevada/more-than-17k-rare-nevada-wildflowers-destroyed-2122795/.
36. Ioneer, "Overwhelming Scientific Validation Overrides False and Misleading Claims Regarding Tiehm's Buckwheat," official website, accessed February 21, 2023, rhyolite-ridge.ioneer.com/wp-content/uploads/2021/06/Tiehms-Buckwheat-Destruction-Comparison-Statements_0616.pdf.
37. Reuters, "Rodents, Not Mining, Caused Damage to Nevada Wildflowers, Says Government Agency," December 4, 2020, www.reuters.com/article/us-ioneer-nevada-wildflowers/rodents-not-mining-caused-damage-to-nevada-wildflowers-says-government-agency-idUSKBN28E2WL.
38. From an email obtained by the author.
39. Ernest Scheyder, "Exclusive: Biden Campaign Tells Miners It Supports Domestic Production of EV Metals," Reuters, October 22, 2020, www.reuters.com/article/usa-election-mining/exclusive-biden-campaign-tells-miners-it-supports-domestic-production-of-ev-metals-idUSKBN27808B.
40. U.S. Federal Election Commission donation reports on both individuals.
41. Ernest Scheyder, "U.S. to List Nevada Flower as Endangered, Dealing Blow to Lithium Mine," Reuters, June 3, 2021, www.reuters.com/article/usa-mining-ioneer-idCNL2N2NL1DO.
42. Ernest Scheyder, "To Go Electric, America Needs More Mines. Can It Build Them?" Reuters, March 1, 2021, www.reuters.com/article/us-usa-mining-insight/to-go-electric-america-needs-more-mines-can-it-build-them-idUSKCN2AT39Z.
43. From an email obtained by the author.
44. Ibid.
45. Amy Alonzo, "Threatened by Mining, Nevada's Rare Tiehm's Buckwheat Listed as Endangered," *Reno Gazette Journal*, December 14, 2022, www.rgj.com/story/news/2022/12/14/nevadas-tiehms-buckwheat-threatened-by-lithium-declared-endangered/69728977007/.
46. Elizabeth Leger, Jamey McClinton, and Robert Shriver, "Ecology of *Eriogonum tiehmii*: A Report on Arthropod Diversity, Abundance, and the Importance of Pollination for Seed Set; Plant-Soil Relationships; Greenhouse Propagation and a Seedling Transplant Experiment; and Wild Population Demography," University of Nevada, Reno, report, January 2021.
47. Jael Holzman, "Lithium Miner Rips Its Own Research in ESA Fight," *E&E News*, December 17, 2021, www.eenews.net/articles/lithium-miner-rips-its-own-research-in-esa-fight/.
48. Ernest Scheyder, "Rare Flower to Get Protected Zone Near ioneer's Nevada Lithium Mine," Reuters, February 3, 2022, www.reuters.com/business/environment/us-regulators-preserve-acreage-near-ioneers-lithium-mine-site-2022-02-02.
49. Ernest Scheyder, "Australia's ioneer Says U.S. Gov't Loan Application Moves Forward," Reuters, December 19, 2021, www.reuters.com/markets/commodities/australias-ioneer-says-us-govt-loan-application-moves-forward-2021-12-19/.
50. Ernest Scheyder, "Update 2—Sibanye Stillwater Buys Half of ioneer's Nevada

Lithium Project in $490 Million Deal," Reuters, September 15, 2021, www.reuters.com/article/usa-mining-ioneer-idAFL1N2QH34A.

51. Reuters, "Australia's ioneer Signs Lithium Offtake Deal with South Korea's Ecopro," June 29, 2021, www.reuters.com/article/ioneer-deals-ecorpo/australias-ioneer-signs-lithium-offtake-deal-with-south-koreas-ecopro-idUSL3N2OC0RA.
52. Michael Wayland, "Ford Plans to Produce 2 Million EVs Annually, Generate 10% Operating Profit by 2026," CNBC, March 2, 2022, www.cnbc.com/2022/03/02/ford-plans-to-produce-2-million-evs-generate-10percent-operating-profit-by-2026.html.
53. Ernest Scheyder, "Ford Chairman Praises CEO, Mulls Lithium Venture," Reuters, March 12, 2019, www.reuters.com/article/us-ceraweek-energy-ford-motor/ford-chairman-praises-ceo-mulls-lithium-venture-idUSKBN1QT209.
54. Ernest Scheyder, "CERAWEEK—As EV Demand Rises, Biden Officials Warm to New Mines," Reuters, March 11, 2021, www.reuters.com/business/ceraweek-ev-demand-rises-biden-officials-warm-new-mines-2022-03-11/.
55. Secretary Jennifer Granholm virtual speech to Securing America's Future Energy, March 9, 2021.
56. Ernest Scheyder and Steve Holland, "Biden Voices Support for New U.S. Mines, if They Don't Repeat Past Sins," Reuters, February 22, 2022, www.reuters.com/business/energy/biden-set-tout-us-progress-critical-minerals-production-2022-02-22/.
57. Calculation assumes lithium prices of $20,000 per tonne.
58. Ernest Scheyder, "Ford Inks Argentina Lithium Supply Deal with Lake Resources," Reuters, April 11, 2022, www.reuters.com/business/autos-transportation/ford-inks-argentina-lithium-supply-deal-with-lake-resources-2022-04-11/.
59. Ernest Scheyder, "Ford to Buy Lithium from ioneer for U.S. EV Battery Plant," Reuters, July 21, 2021, www.reuters.com/business/autos-transportation/ford-buy-lithium-ioneer-american-ev-battery-plant-2022-07-21/.
60. Author's interview with James Calaway, January 13, 2023.
61. Tweet from Patrick Donnelly's Twitter account, July 21, 2022, twitter.com/BitterWaterBlue/status/1550131044321353729.
62. "Edward Abbey," University of Montana's Wilderness Connect, accessed January 15, 2023, wilderness.net/learn-about-wilderness/edward-abbey.php.
63. Ibid.
64. Ibid.
65. Video obtained by author.
66. Isla Binnie and Gloria Dickie, "Factbox: '30-by-30': Key Takeaways from the COP15 Biodiversity Summit," Reuters, December 19, 2022, www.reuters.com/business/environment/30-by-30-key-takeaways-cop15-biodiversity-summit-2022-12-19/.
67. Michael Barbaro et al., "Consider the Burying Beetle (or Else)," *The New York Times*, January 6, 2023, www.nytimes.com/2023/01/06/podcasts/the-daily/biodiversity-cop15-montreal.html?showTranscript=1.
68. Evan Halper, "Is Sustainable Mining Possible? The EV Revolution Depends on It," *The Washington Post*, August 11, 2022, www.washingtonpost.com/business/2022/08/11/electric-vehicle-nickel-mine/.
69. Ioneer, "Mine Plan of Operations / Nevada Reclamation Permit Application."
70. Ibid.
71. Ibid.
72. Ibid.

73. Ioneer, "Ioneer and Caterpillar Complete Definitive Agreement Regarding Autonomous Haul Trucks at Rhyolite Ridge," press release, September 15, 2022, rhyolite-ridge.ioneer.com/ioneer-and-caterpillar-complete-definitive-agreement-regarding-autonomous-haul-trucks-at-rhyolite-ridge/.
74. Ioneer, "Mine Plan of Operations / Nevada Reclamation Permit Application."
75. Ibid.

CHAPTER TEN: THE NEIGHBORS

1. Ronnie W. Faulkner, "William J. Gaston (1778–1844)," North Carolina History Project, accessed January 10, 2023, northcarolinahistory.org/encyclopedia/william-j-gaston-1778-1844/.
2. William Gaston, "Address Delivered Before the Philanthropic and Dialectic Societies, at Chapel Hill: June 20, 1832," University of North Carolina, archive.org/details/addressdelivered00gaston/page/14/mode/2up?q=economy.
3. Ibid.
4. "Paul Edward Hastings," FindaGrave.com, accessed January 15, 2023, www.findagrave.com/memorial/32343630/paul-edward-hastings.
5. The account of Paul Hastings and his descendants is drawn from interviews on July 15, 2021, and October 17, 2022, with Sonya Snowdon and Warren Snowdon, with corroboration from property records and vital statistics.
6. "Carpenter and Hastings Tin Mine," Diggings.com, accessed December 15, 2022, thediggings.com/mines/27012.
7. Gaston County, North Carolina, property tax records.
8. Kristen Korosec, "Tesla Delivers Nearly 500,000 Vehicles in 2020," TechCrunch, January 2, 2021, techcrunch.com/2021/01/02/tesla-delivers-nearly-500000-vehicles-in-2020.
9. "Tesla 2020 Battery Day Transcript September 22," Rev, September 23, 2020, www.rev.com/blog/transcripts/tesla-2020-battery-day-transcript-september-22.
10. Ibid.
11. Ibid.
12. Ibid.
13. This paragraph is based on sources close to Elon Musk. Neither Tesla nor Musk responded to multiple interview requests.
14. Scott Patterson and Amrith Ramkumar, "America's Battery-Powered Car Hopes Ride on Lithium. One Producer Paves the Way," *The Wall Street Journal*, March 10, 2021, www.wsj.com/articles/americas-battery-powered-car-hopes-ride-on-lithium-one-producer-paves-the-way-11615311932.
15. The White House, "Fact Sheet: The Biden-Harris Electric Vehicle Charging Action Plan," press release, December 13, 2021, www.whitehouse.gov/briefing-room/statements-releases/2021/12/13/fact-sheet-the-biden-harris-electric-vehicle-charging-action-plan/.
16. Flyer obtained by author.
17. Author's interview with Hugh Carpenter and Will Baldwin, July 15, 2021.
18. Author's interview with Emilie Nelson, July 15, 2021.
19. Brandy Beard, "Call of the Wild," *Gaston Gazette*, November 23, 2018, https://www.gastongazette.com/story/news/local/2018/11/23/nc-wildlife-rehab-providing-safe-space-for-injured-wildlife/8305149007/.
20. Piedmont said it was not aware if one of its contracted landmen made the alleged threat, adding it did not approve or condone it.

21. WCP Resources Ltd., "Resignation of Managing Director," press release, January 15, 2016, piedmontlithium.com/wp-content/uploads/160115_resignation_of_managing_director-1-1.pdf.
22. WCP Resources Ltd., "Strategic Landholding Secured in Historic Lithium Producing Region in USA," press release, September 27, 2016, piedmontlithium.com/wp-content/uploads/160927_strategic-USA-landholding-secured-in-historic-lithium-producing-region.pdf.
23. WCP Resources Ltd., "Senior Wall Street Mining Executive Appointed as Managing Director & CEO," press release, July 4, 2017, piedmontlithium.com/wp-content/uploads/170706_wcp_senior_wall_street_mining_executive_appointed_as_md___ceo-1.pdf.
24. Author's interview with Keith Phillips, February 22, 2019.
25. Ibid.
26. Katherine Towers and Andrew Main, "ASIC Probe Bans Mochkin," *Australian Financial Review*, December 4, 2001, www.afr.com/politics/asic-probe-bans-mochkin-20011204-j88xt.
27. Ernest Scheyder, "In Push to Supply Tesla, Piedmont Lithium Irks North Carolina Neighbors," Reuters, July 21, 2021, www.reuters.com/business/energy/push-supply-tesla-piedmont-lithium-irks-north-carolina-neighbors-2021-07-20/.
28. Ibid.
29. Ernest Scheyder, "N. Carolina County Slaps Moratorium on Mining as Piedmont Lithium Plans Project," Reuters, November 15, 2021, www.reuters.com/world/us/n-carolina-county-slaps-moratorium-mining-piedmont-lithium-plans-project-2021-08-06/.
30. Scheyder, "In Push to Supply Tesla, Piedmont Lithium Irks North Carolina Neighbors."
31. Ibid.
32. Ernest Scheyder, "Update 1—Piedmont Lithium Delays Timeline to Supply Tesla," Reuters, August 2, 2021, www.reuters.com/article/usa-mining-piedmont-lithium-idCNL1N2P91B0.
33. Scheyder, "N. Carolina County Slaps Moratorium on Mining as Piedmont Lithium Plans Project."
34. Catherine Clifford, "Elon Musk Says Tesla May Have to Get into the Lithium Business Because Costs Are So 'Insane,'" CNBC, April 8, 2022, www.cnbc.com/2022/04/08/elon-musk-telsa-may-have-get-into-mining-refining-lithium-directly.html.
35. Ernest Scheyder, "North Carolina County Zoning Changes to Affect Piedmont Lithium Project," Reuters, September 29, 2021, www.reuters.com/legal/litigation/north-carolina-county-zoning-changes-affect-piedmont-lithium-project-2021-09-28.
36. Ken Lemon, "Piedmont Lithium CEO: Mining Operation Is Safe for Residents," WSOC TV, August 31, 2022, www.wsoctv.com/news/local/piedmont-lithium-ceo-mining-operation-is-safe-residents/74OAMMYXTVHHPDRZ72RJ7GYUKY/?fbclid=IwAR2Vk6xOZLdVwQWKrSIMCQ2enM-yPaDsS1fqGGImx-kz4BzoMR_nkr73MGg.
37. David Shepardson and Ernest Scheyder, "Biden Awards $2.8 Billion to Boost U.S. Minerals Output for EV Batteries," Reuters, October 19, 2022, www.reuters.com/markets/us/us-awards-28-billion-ev-battery-grid-projects-2022-10-19/.
38. Ernest Scheyder, "Piedmont Lithium Looks Abroad amid North Carolina Uncertainty," Reuters, June 22, 2022, www.reuters.com/markets/commodities

/piedmont-lithium-looks-abroad-amid-north-carolina-uncertainty-2022-06-22/.

39. Author's interview with Eric Norris, September 27, 2022.
40. U.S. Patent Application Publication Number US 2021/0207243 A1.
41. Ernest Scheyder, "Tesla's Nevada Lithium Plan Faces Stark Obstacles on Path to Production," Reuters, September 23, 2020, www.reuters.com/article/us-tesla-batteryday-lithium-idUKKCN26E3G1.
42. Reuters, "Tesla Considering Lithium Refinery in Texas, Seeks Tax Relief," September 9, 2022, www.reuters.com/technology/tesla-considering-lithium-refinery-texas-2022-09-09/.
43. Ernest Scheyder, "Albemarle Calls for High Lithium Prices to Fuel EV Industry Growth," Reuters, January 24, 2023, www.reuters.com/markets/commodities/albemarle-expects-lithium-prices-remain-high-fuel-fresh-supply-2023-01-24/.
44. ExxonMobil figures are based on 2022 daily production of 2.4 million barrels, per corporate figures, contrasted with daily global liquid fuels production of 99.95 million barrels, per U.S. Energy Information Administration data.
45. Shepardson and Scheyder, "Biden Awards $2.8 Billion to Boost U.S. Minerals Output for EV Batteries."
46. The White House, "Remarks by President Biden on the Bipartisan Infrastructure Law," official website, October 19, 2022, www.whitehouse.gov/briefing-room/speeches-remarks/2022/10/19/remarks-by-president-biden-on-the-bipartisan-infrastructure-law-6/.
47. Colin Huguley, "Piedmont Lithium Pegs Its Investment in Gaston County Mine Project at More Than $100M," *Charlotte Business Journal*, August 25, 2022, www.bizjournals.com/charlotte/news/2022/08/25/piedmont-lithium-gaston-county-mine-100-million.html?utm_source=sy&utm_medium=nsyp&utm_campaign=yh&fbclid=IwAR1lznHC6z5_yLUDgwiHBeR_a3Hqrv5WfAmv5jXUAbRmuZmI18UJmLHdtNM.

CHAPTER ELEVEN: "ELECTRICITY MEANS COPPER"

1. Bryant Park Corporation, "Horticulture," official website, accessed on February 21, 2023, bryantpark.org/the-park/horticulture.
2. NYC Parks, "Bryant Park: William Earl Dodge History," official website, accessed February 21, 2023, www.nycgovparks.org/parks/bryant-park/monuments/389.
3. Carlos A. Schwantes, *Vision & Enterprise: Exploring the History of Phelps Dodge Corporation* (Tucson: University of Arizona Press, 2000), 44.
4. Ibid., 31.
5. Kim Kelly, *Fight Like Hell* (New York: One Signal, 2022), 95.
6. Phelps Dodge, "Morenci," official corporate document, accessed February 21, 2023, docs.azgs.az.gov/OnlineAccessMineFiles/M-R/MorenciMineGreenleeT4SR29ESec16-5.pdf.
7. Ibid.
8. Copper Development Association Inc., "Copper in the Arts," official website, accessed February 23, 2023, www.copper.org/consumers/arts/2015/april/thomas-edison.html.
9. Google Arts & Culture, "Cubic Foot of Copper," accessed February 23, 2023, artsandculture.google.com/asset/cubic-foot-of-copper-tiffany-co/UAFPdpVEj6IDDQ?hl=en.

10. Edmund Morris, *Edison* (New York: Random House, 2019), 124.
11. Freeport-McMoRan Form 10-K Annual Report for 2021, 10.
12. Ibid., 9.
13. Robert Chilicky and Gerald Hunt, *Images of America: Clifton and Morenci Mining District* (Charleston, S.C.: Arcadia Publishing, 2015), 36.
14. Ibid.
15. Ibid., 121.
16. Walter Mares, "U.S. 191 to Be Rerouted Around FMI Morenci Copper Mine," *The Copper Era*, February 25, 2015, www.eacourier.com/copper_era/news/u-s-to-be-rerouted-around-fmi-morenci-copper-mine/article_e0b3489a-bc36-11e4-b941-2fae514b31d0.html.
17. Melanie Burton, "Copper Takes Aim at COVID-19 with Virus-Killer Coatings," Reuters, May 8, 2020, www.reuters.com/article/us-health-coronavirus-copper-antimicrobi/copper-takes-aim-at-covid-19-with-virus-killer-coatings-idUSKBN22K0RX.
18. Freeport-McMoRan Form 10-K Annual Report for 2021, 39.
19. Author's interview with Richard Adkerson, December 2, 2022.
20. Ibid.
21. Bonnie Gestring, "U.S. Operating Copper Mines: Failure to Capture and Treat Wastewater," Earthworks, accessed February 23, 2023, www.congress.gov/116/meeting/house/110436/documents/HHRG-116-II06-20200205-SD036.pdf.
22. Freeport's average total compensation for all employees in 2021 (other than the CEO, Adkerson) was $77,036, according to corporate filings with the U.S. Securities and Exchange Commission. For the same year, U.S. Census Bureau data show a median national income of $70,784.
23. Freeport-McMoRan, "Transforming Tomorrow Together: Community Partnership Panel Meeting Summary," corporate document, accessed February 23, 2023, www.freeportinmycommunity.com/uploads/Q4_Meeting_Notes_Summary_2018_Greenlee.pdf.
24. U.S. Congress, "H.R. 429-Reclamation Projects Authorization and Adjustment Act of 1992," October 30, 1992, www.congress.gov/bill/102nd-congress/house-bill/429.
25. U.S. Department of the Interior, "People Land & Water," internal newsletter, npshistory.com/publications/doi/plw/v4n6.pdf.
26. Ibid.
27. Lawrence Blaskey, "Payment Made to Tribe to Secure Water for Morenci," *Eastern Arizona Courier*, January 5, 1999, www.eacourier.com/news/payment-made-to-tribe-to-secure-water-for-morenciby-lawrence-blaskey-eastern-arizona-courier-january/article_fc9d8d04-ea8c-522e-a8c3-ba82ca5770f4.html.
28. U.S. Department of the Interior, "People Land & Water."
29. Greg Hahne, "San Carlos Apache Tribe Reaches Preliminary Agreement for Rio Verde Foothills Community Water," KJZZ, kjzz.org/content/1831921/san-carlos-apache-tribe-reaches-preliminary-agreement-rio-verde-foothills-community.
30. Author's interview with Chairman Terry Rambler, April 5, 2021.
31. "John McCain's Pallbearers: 5 Fast Facts You Need to Know," heavy.com, accessed February 23, 2023, heavy.com/news/2018/08/john-mccain-pallbearers/.
32. Author's interview with Richard Adkerson, December 2, 2022.
33. Andrew Ross Sorkin and Ian Austen, "Phelps Dodge and Freeport-McMoRan Agree to Merge to Form Market Leader," *The New York Times*, November 20,

2006, www.nytimes.com/2006/11/20/business/worldbusiness/20iht-copper.3599828.html.

34. Author's interview with Richard Adkerson, December 2, 2022.
35. Kelly, *Fight Like Hell*, 98–99.
36. Author's interview with Richard Adkerson, December 2, 2022.
37. Freeport-McMoRan, "Webcast to Discuss FCX Acquisition of PXP and MMR 11 AM," conference call transcript, December 5, 2012.
38. Christopher Swann and Kevin Allison, "Freeport's Deals Epitomize Industry's Conflicts of Interest," Reuters Breakingviews, December 5, 2012, archive.nytimes.com/dealbook.nytimes.com/2012/12/05/freeports-deals-epitomize-industrys-conflicts-of-interest/.
39. James B. Stewart, "Freeport-McMoRan Battles the Oil Slump," *The New York Times*, January 21, 2016, www.nytimes.com/2016/01/22/business/energy-environment/freeport-mcmoran-battles-the-oil-slump.html.
40. Russ Wiles, "Moffett Resigns as Freeport-McMoRan Chairman," *The Arizona Republic*, www.azcentral.com/story/money/business/2015/12/28/moffett-resigns-freeport-mcmoran-chairman/77971352/.
41. Ibid.
42. Author's interview with Richard Adkerson, December 2, 2022.
43. Stewart, "Freeport-McMoRan Battles the Oil Slump."
44. Antoine Gara, "Freeport-McMoRan Exits Disastrous Foray into Gulf of Mexico Amid Pressure from Carl Icahn," *Forbes*, September 13, 2016, www.forbes.com/sites/antoinegara/2016/09/13/freeport-mcmoran-exits-disastrous-foray-into-gulf-of-mexico-oil-amid-pressure-from-carl-icahn/?sh=2c24532419f1.
45. Ben Miller and Olivia Pulsinelli, "Freeport-McMoRan to Sell California Oil and Gas Assets for $742M," *Houston Business Journal*, October 17, 2016, www.bizjournals.com/houston/news/2016/10/17/freeport-mcmoran-to-sell-california-oil-and-gas.html.
46. Freeport-McMoRan, "Freeport-McMoRan Announces Agreement to Sell a 13% Interest in Morenci Mine for $1.0 Billion in Cash," press release, February 15, 2016, www.businesswire.com/news/home/20160214005059/en/Freeport-McMoRan-Announces-Agreement-to-Sell-a-13-Interest-in-Morenci-Mine-for-1.0-Billion-in-Cash.
47. Golder Associates, "Environmental and Social Impact Assessment," consultant's report for Tenke Fungurume Mining S.A.R.L., March 2007, www3.dfc.gov/environment/eia/tenke/Executive%20Summary-Long-Apr9.pdf#page=58.
48. Dionne Searcey, Michael Forsythe, and Eric Lipton, "A Power Struggle over Cobalt Rattles the Clean Energy Revolution," *The New York Times*, November 20, 2021, www.nytimes.com/2021/11/20/world/china-congo-cobalt.html?.
49. Author's interview with Richard Adkerson, December 2, 2022.
50. Anet Josline Pinto and Denny Thomas, "Freeport to Sell Prized Tenke Copper Mine to China Moly for $2.65 Billion," Reuters, May 9, 2016, www.reuters.com/article/us-freeport-mcmoran-tenke-cmoc/freeport-to-sell-prized-tenke-copper-mine-to-china-moly-for-2-65-billion-idUSKCN0Y015U.
51. Freeport-McMoRan Second Quarter Earnings Call Transcript, 2016.
52. Author's interview with Melissa Sanderson, February 3, 2023.
53. David Stanway, "China's Belt and Road Plans Losing Momentum as Opposition, Debt Mount—Study," Reuters, September 29, 2021, www.reuters.com/world/china/chinas-belt-road-plans-losing-momentum-opposition-debt-mount-study-2021-09-29/.

54. Searcey, Forsythe, and Lipton, "A Power Struggle over Cobalt Rattles the Clean Energy Revolution."
55. Nicholas Niarchos, "The Dark Side of Congo's Cobalt Rush," *The New Yorker*, May 24, 2021, www.newyorker.com/magazine/2021/05/31/the-dark-side-of-congos-cobalt-rush.
56. Pratima Desai, "Explainer: Costs of Nickel and Cobalt Used in Electric Vehicle Batteries," Reuters, February 3, 2022, www.reuters.com/business/autos-transportation/costs-nickel-cobalt-used-electric-vehicle-batteries-2022-02-03/.
57. Ibid.
58. Helen Reid, "Microsoft Calls for 'Coalition' to Improve Congo's Informal Cobalt Mines," Reuters, February 8, 2023, www.reuters.com/markets/commodities/microsoft-calls-coalition-improve-congos-informal-cobalt-mines-2023-02-08/.
59. Siddharth Kara, *Cobalt Red: How the Blood of the Congo Powers Our Lives* (New York: St. Martin's, 2023), 126.
60. Thomas Catenacci, "Biden Turns to Country with Documented Child Labor Issues for Green Energy Mineral Supplies: 'It's Egregious,'" Fox News, December 16, 2022, www.foxnews.com/politics/biden-turns-country-documented-child-labor-green-energy-mineral-supplies-its-egregious.
61. Reid, "Microsoft Calls for 'Coalition' to Improve Congo's Informal Cobalt Mines."
62. Searcey, Forsythe, and Lipton, "A Power Struggle over Cobalt Rattles the Clean Energy Revolution."
63. Hyunjoo Jin and Paul Lienert, "Iron Man Elon Musk Places His Tesla Battery Bets," Reuters, April 27, 2022, www.reuters.com/business/autos-transportation/iron-man-elon-musk-places-his-tesla-battery-bets-2022-04-27/.
64. U.S. Department of State, "Secretary Blinken at an MOU Signing with Democratic Republic of the Congo Vice Prime Minister and Foreign Minister Christophe Lutundula and Zambian Foreign Minister Stanley Kakubo," press release, December 13, 2022, www.state.gov/secretary-blinken-at-an-mou-signing-with-democratic-republic-of-the-congo-vice-prime-minister-and-foreign-minister-christophe-lutundula-and-zambian-foreign-minister-stanley-kakubo/.
65. U.S. Representative Pete Stauber, "Stauber Statement on Biden's Northern Minnesota Mining Ban," press release, January 26, 2023.
66. Philip Pullella and Paul Lorgerie, "'Hands off Africa,' Pope Francis Tells Rich World," Reuters, February 1, 2023, www.reuters.com/world/africa/popes-visit-shine-spotlight-war-ravaged-dr-congo-2023-01-31/.
67. Clara Denina, Helen Reid, and Ernest Scheyder, "Analysis: Miners Face Talent Crunch as Electric Vehicles Charge Up Metals Demand," Reuters, December 10, 2021, www.reuters.com/article/mining-education-analysis-idCAKBN2IP10R.
68. Author's interview with Kathleen Quirk, June 30, 2022.
69. Reuters, "U.S. Worker Shortage Denting Freeport-McMoRan's Copper Output," January 25, 2023, www.reuters.com/markets/commodities/freeport-mcmoran-quarterly-profit-falls-lower-copper-price-2023-01-25/.

CHAPTER TWELVE: THE ENTREPRENEUR

1. "Past Weather in Houston, Texas, USA—April 2017," TimeAndDate.com, accessed January 21, 2022, www.timeanddate.com/weather/usa/houston/historic?month=4&year=2017.

2. KHOU, "Train Car Carrying Lithium Batteries Explodes Near Downtown Houston," April 23, 2017, www.khou.com/article/news/local/train-car-carrying-lithium-batteries-explodes-near-downtown-houston/285-433576556.
3. Sophia Beausoleil, "Lithium Batteries Cause Train Car Explosion in NE Houston," Click2Houston.com, April 23, 2017, www.click2houston.com/news/2017/04/24/lithium-batteries-causes-train-car-explosion-in-ne-houston/.
4. Gareth Tredway, "Train Car Carrying Used Batteries Bursts into Flames," *Automotive Logistics*, April 26, 2017, www.automotivelogistics.media/train-car-carrying-used-batteries-bursts-into-flames/18117.article.
5. Marina Smith, "Union Pacific Train Car Carrying Used Lithium Ion Batteries Explodes and Catches Fire Near Downtown Houston, Texas," Metropolitan Engineering Consulting & Forensics Expert Engineers blog, April 27, 2017, metroforensics.blogspot.com/2017/04/union-pacific-train-car-carrying-used.html.
6. U.S. Department of Transportation, Research and Special Programs Administration, "Hazardous Materials Incident Report, Incident Id: E-2017060716," official publication, June 29, 2017.
7. Victoria Hutchinson, "Li-Ion Battery Energy Storage Systems: Effect of Separation Distances Based on a Radiation Heat Transfer Analysis," Worcester Polytechnic Institute graduate independent study research project, June 12, 2017, www.wpi.edu/sites/default/files/docs/Departments-Programs/Fire-Protection/Final_ESS_Report.pdf.
8. Tredway, "Train Car Carrying Used Batteries Bursts into Flames."
9. U.S. Environmental Protection Agency's Office of Resource Conservation and Recovery, "An Analysis of Lithium-Ion Battery Fires in Waste Management and Recycling," official publication, July 2021, www.epa.gov/system/files/documents/2021-08/lithium-ion-battery-report-update-7.01_508.pdf, 19.
10. David Shepardson, "U.S. Bars Lithium Batteries as Cargo on Passenger Aircraft," Reuters, February 27, 2019, www.reuters.com/article/us-usa-airlines-safety/u-s-bars-lithium-batteries-as-cargo-on-passenger-aircraft-idUSKCN1QG1XI.
11. U.S. Environmental Protection Agency, Office of Resource Conservation and Recovery, "An Analysis of Lithium-Ion Battery Fires in Waste Management and Recycling," 27.
12. Reuters, "Fire Dies Down on Ship Carrying Luxury Cars, with Little Left to Burn," February 21, 2022, www.reuters.com/world/europe/fire-dies-down-ship-carrying-luxury-cars-with-little-left-burn-2022-02-21/.
13. Lufthansa Cargo, "From 31 August: Restrictions for Air Transport of Lithium Batteries," official publication, accessed February 21, 2023, lufthansa-cargo.com/documents/20184/746434/Tabelle_EN_02.pdf/1fbfe705-b787-4558-8844-b7dacc2dab49.
14. Reuters, "Fire Dies Down on Ship Carrying Luxury Cars, with Little Left to Burn."
15. Hutchinson, "Li-Ion Battery Energy Storage Systems."
16. Aaron Gordon, "New York City Bill to Ban Reuse of Lithium Ion Batteries Is 'Absolutely Crazy,' Right-to-Repair Advocates Warn," *Vice*, November 17, 2022, www.vice.com/en/article/dy7eka/new-york-city-bill-to-ban-reuse-of-lithium-ion-batteries-is-absolutely-crazy-right-to-repair-advocates-warn.
17. Author's interview with Michelle Michot Foss, October 3, 2019.
18. U.S. Department of Energy, Office of Energy Efficiency & Renewable Energy, "U.S. Plug-In Electric Vehicle Sales by Model," official publication, accessed February 21, 2023, afdc.energy.gov/data/10567.
19. United Nations Institute for Training and Research, "The Global E-Waste

Monitor 2020," official publication, accessed February 21, 2023, ewastemonitor .info/gem-2020/.

20. Emily Barone, "Your Junk Drawer Full of Small, Unused Electronics Is a Big Climate Problem," *Time*, October 21, 2022, time.com/6223653/electronic -waste-climate-change/.
21. Niraj Chokshi and Kellen Browning, "Electric Cars Are Taking Off, but When Will Battery Recycling Follow?" *The New York Times*, December 21, 2022, www.nytimes.com/2022/12/21/business/energy-environment/battery -recycling-electric-vehicles.html.
22. Pérez de Solay participated in a lithium panel on March 9, 2022, at the CERA-Week conference in Houston.
23. Platform for Acclerating the Circluar Economy/World Economic Forum, "A New Circular Vision for Electronics, Time for a Global Reboot," official publication, January 2019, www3.weforum.org/docs/WEF_A_New_Circular _Vision_for_Electronics.pdf, 5.
24. Madeline Stone, "As Electric Vehicles Take Off, We'll Need to Recycle Their Batteries," *National Geographic*, May 28, 2021, www.nationalgeographic.com /environment/article/electric-vehicles-take-off-recycling-ev-batteries.
25. Benjamin Spreche et al., "Life Cycle Inventory of the Production of Rare Earths and the Subsequent Production of NdFeB Rare Earth Permanent Magnets," *Environmental Science & Technology*, 48 (7) (February 27, 2014): 3951–58, pubs.acs.org/doi/10.1021/es404596q.
26. Andy Home, "Humble Aluminium Can Shows a Circular Economy Won't Be Easy," Reuters, March 26, 2021, www.reuters.com/business/energy/humble -aluminium-can-shows-circular-economy-wont-be-easy-andy-home-2021-03-26/.
27. James Morton Turner, "Recycling Lead-Acid Batteries Is Easy. Why Is Recycling Lithium-Ion Batteries Hard?" CleanTechnica, July 24, 2022, cleantechnica.com/2022/07/24/recycling-lead-acid-batteries-is-easy-why-is -recycling-lithium-ion-batteries-hard/.
28. Maria Virginia Olano, "Chart: China Is Trouncing the US on Battery Recycling," Canary Media, June 17, 2022, www.canarymedia.com/articles/batteries /chart-china-is-trouncing-the-us-on-battery-recycling.
29. Baum et al., "Lithium-Ion Battery Recycling—Overview of Techniques and Trends," American Chemical Society, accessed February 21, 2023, pubs.acs .org/doi/pdf/10.1021/acsenergylett.1c02602.
30. Ibid.
31. Author's interview with Lisa Jackson, September 27, 2019.
32. "Environmental Responsibility Report: 2017 Progress Report, Covering Fiscal Year 2016," Apple, accessed February 21, 2023, images.apple.com/environment /pdf/Apple_Environmental_Responsibility_Report_2017.pdf, 16.
33. William Gallagher, "Apple Wins UN Climate Action Award for Environmental Work," AppleInsider.com, September 26, 2019, appleinsider.com /articles/19/09/26/apple-wins-un-climate-action-award-for-environmental -work.
34. Stephen Nellis, "Apple Buys First-Ever Carbon-Free Aluminum from Alcoa–Rio Tinto Venture," Reuters, December 5, 2019, www.reuters.com/article/us -apple-aluminum/apple-buys-first-ever-carbon-free-aluminum-from-alcoa -rio-tinto-venture-idUSKBN1Y91RQ.
35. Author's interview with Jon Kellar, October 1, 2019.
36. Reuters, "Apple Pushes Recycling with Robot, but Mined Metals Still Needed," January 10, 2020, www.reuters.com/article/usa-minerals-recycling/apple -pushes-recycling-with-robot-but-mined-metals-still-needed-idUSL1N298151.

37. Apple, "Apple Expands the Use of Recycled Materials Across Its Products," press release, April 19, 2022, www.apple.com/newsroom/2022/04/apple-expands-the-use-of-recycled-materials-across-its-products/.
38. Ibid.
39. Author's interview with Corby Anderson, October 1, 2019.
40. Author's interview with Ajay Kochhar, November 18, 2022.
41. Reuters, "Glencore Investing $200 Mln in Battery Recycler Li-Cycle," May 5, 2022, www.reuters.com/business/sustainable-business/glencore-investing-200-mln-battery-recycler-li-cycle-2022-05-05/.
42. Tim Higgins, "One of the Brains Behind Tesla May Have a New Way to Make Electric Cars Cheaper," *The Wall Street Journal*,, August 29, 2020, www.wsj.com/articles/one-of-the-brains-behind-tesla-found-a-new-way-to-make-electric-cars-cheaper-11598673630?mod=e2tw.
43. Paul Lienert, "Battery Recycling Firm Redwood Raises $700 Mln from Big Fund Managers," Reuters, July 28, 2021, www.reuters.com/business/finance/battery-recycling-firm-redwood-raises-700-mln-big-fund-managers-2021-07-28/.
44. Daniel Yergin, *The New Map* (New York: Penguin Press, 2020), 327.
45. Matt Blois, "Cathode Projects Advance in North America: Redwood Materials Will Supply a Panasonic Battery Factory," November 17, 2022, cen.acs.org/energy/energy-storage-/Cathode-projects-advance-North-America/100/i41.
46. Tom Randall and Bloomberg, "Tesla Co-Founder Has a Plan to Become King of EV Battery Materials—in the U.S.," *Fortune*, September 14, 2021, fortune.com/2021/09/14/tesla-cofounder-jb-straubel-redwood-materials-battery-materials/.
47. Author's interview with Ajay Kochhar, November 18, 2022.
48. Ernest Scheyder, "U.S. to Loan Li-Cycle $275 Million for New York Recycling Plant," Reuters, February 27, 2023, www.reuters.com/business/sustainable-business/us-loan-li-cycle-375-million-new-york-recycling-plant-2023-02-27/.
49. Baum et al., "Lithium-Ion Battery Recycling—Overview of Techniques and Trends."
50. Ibid.
51. Author's interview with Ajay Kochhar, June 30, 2022.
52. Katerina Rosova, "Li-Cycle: Sustainable Lithium-Ion Battery Recycling Technology," InnovationNewsNetwork, May 10, 2022, www.innovationnewsnetwork.com/li-cycle-sustainable-lithium-ion-battery-recycling-technology/21097.
53. Joshua Franklin, "Battery Recycler Li-Cycle to Go Public in Deal with Peridot SPAC," Reuters, February 16, 2021, www.reuters.com/article/peridot-acqsn-ma-licycle/battery-recycler-li-cycle-to-go-public-in-deal-with-peridot-spac-idUSL8N2KI6LE.
54. Reuters, "Glencore Investing $200 Mln in Battery Recycler Li-Cycle."
55. Baum et al., "Lithium-Ion Battery Recycling—Overview of Techniques and Trends."
56. Kenneth Rapoza, "China Quits Recycling U.S. Trash as Sustainable Start-Up Makes Strides," *Forbes*, January 10, 2021, www.forbes.com/sites/kenrapoza/2021/01/10/china-quits-recycling-us-trash-as-sustainable-start-up-makes-strides/?sh=147200625a56.
57. Ernest Scheyder, "Li-Cycle to Build EV Battery Recycling Plant in Alabama," Reuters, September 8, 2021, www.reuters.com/technology/li-cycle-build-ev-battery-recycling-plant-alabama-2021-09-08/.
58. Cameron Murray, "Li-Cycle Opens Third Battery Recycling Facility at

'Strategic' Southwest US Location," EnergyStorageNews, May 18, 2022, www.energy-storage.news/li-cycle-opens-third-battery-recycling-facility-at-strategic-southwest-us-location.

59. Allied Market Research, "Lithium-Ion Battery Recycling Market to Reach $38.21 Bn, Globally, by 2030 at 36.0% CAFR: Allied Market Research," press release, July 19, 2021, www.prnewswire.com/news-releases/lithium-ion-battery-recycling-market-to-reach-38-21-bn-globally-by-2030-at-36-0-cagr-allied-market-research-886028135.html.
60. Casey Crownhart, "This Is Where Tesla's Former CTO Thinks Battery Recycling Is Headed," *MIT Technology Review*, January 17, 2023, www.technologyreview.com/2023/01/17/1066915/tesla-former-cto-battery-recycling/.

CHAPTER THIRTEEN: GREEN TECHNOLOGY

1. The White House, "President Biden Hosts a Roundtable on Securing Critical Minerals for a Future Made in America," official video via YouTube, February 22, 2022, www.youtube.com/watch?v=DYZfC8JNsZ0.
2. The White House, "Executive Order on Strengthening American Leadership in Clean Cars and Trucks," press release, August 5, 2021, www.whitehouse.gov/briefing-room/presidential-actions/2021/08/05/executive-order-on-strengthening-american-leadership-in-clean-cars-and-trucks/.
3. Greg Grandin, *Fordlandia: The Rise and Fall of Henry Ford's Forgotten Jungle City* (New York: Macmillan, 2010).
4. The lake has no outlet.
5. Peter Valdes-Dapena, "This California Desert Could Hold the Key to Powering All of America's Electric Cars," CNNBusiness, May 11, 2022, www.cnn.com/2022/05/11/business/salton-sea-lithium-extraction/index.html.
6. Sophie Parker et al., "Potential Lithium Extraction in the United States: Environmental, Economic, and Policy Implications," Nature Conservancy, August 2022, www.scienceforconservation.org/assets/downloads/Lithium_Report_FINAL.pdf.
7. Some of these DLE technologies had worked in tandem with evaporation ponds in Argentina and China, but none as of late 2023 had worked independently.
8. California Governor's Office, "Governor Newsom Joins President Biden to Uplift California's Vision for an Inclusive, Sustainable, Clean Energy Economy in Lithium Valley," press release, February 22, 2022, www.gov.ca.gov/2022/02/22/governor-newsom-joins-president-biden-to-uplift-californias-vision-for-an-inclusive-sustainable-clean-energy-economy-in-lithium-valley/.
9. Ernest Scheyder, "U.S. Steps Away from Flagship Lithium Project with Buffett's Berkshire," Reuters, October 5, 2023, www.reuters.com/markets/us/us-steps-away-flagship-lithium-project-with-berkshire-2022-10-05/.
10. Emails obtained by author.
11. Scheyder, "U.S. Steps Away from Flagship Lithium Project with Buffett's Berkshire."
12. T. D. Palmer et al., "Geothermal Development of the Salton Trough, California and Mexico," U.S. Department of Commerce, January 1, 1975, www.osti.gov/biblio/5107191.
13. William Stringfellow and Patrick Dobson, "Technology for the Recovery of Lithium from Geothermal Brines," *Energies*, October 18, 2021, doi.org/10.3390/en14206805.
14. Ernest Scheyder, "GM Shakes Up Lithium Industry with California Geothermal Project," Reuters, July 2, 2021, www.reuters.com/business/autos

-transportation/gm-shakes-up-lithium-industry-with-california-geothermal-project-2021-07-02/.

15. Ibid.
16. Dow Chemical Company, "Visualizing Our History," corporate website, accessed February 21, 2023, corporate.dow.com/en-us/about/company/history/timeline.html.
17. "Leland Doan Dies at 79," *Ann Arbor News*, April 5, 1974, aadl.org/node/83745.
18. Doan was also at the helm during the napalm saga, one of Dow Chemical's darkest chapters.
19. This account and related portions were relayed by Dr. John Burba during multiple interviews, and based on reflections from Bill Bauman.
20. John M. Lee and William C. Bauman, "US-4116856-A-Recovery of Lithium from Brines," UnifiedPatents portal, accessed February 21, 2023, portal.unifiedpatents.com/patents/patent/US-4116856-A.
21. John Burba, "Lithium—the Key to Our Energy Transformation," Innovation News Network, April 13, 2021, www.innovationnewsnetwork.com/lithium/10672/.
22. J. D. Bailey, "Albemarle Celebrates 50 Years in Magnolia," *Banner-News*, July 19, 2019, www.magnoliabannernews.com/news/2019/jul/19/albemarle-celebrates-50-years-magnolia/.
23. DuPont has also used the patents: DuPont, "Separation of Lithium from Liquid Media," accessed February 21, 2023, www.dupont.com/water/periodic-table/lithium.html.
24. "FMC: Hombre Muerto Lithium Output," GlassOnline.com, February 5, 1998, www.glassonline.com/fmc-hombre-muerto-lithium-output/.
25. Apple, "Apple Presents iPod," press release, October 23, 2001, www.apple.com/newsroom/2001/10/23Apple-Presents-iPod/.
26. Elsa Wenzel, "Simbol Mining Raises Funds for 'Zero-Waste' Lithium Extraction," CNET, August 11, 2008, www.cnet.com/culture/simbol-mining-raises-funds-for-zero-waste-lithium-extraction/.
27. EnergySource, "EnergySource's First Geothermal Plant in Imperial Valley Lauded for Creating Jobs, Boosting the Economy, Delivering Clean Energy to 50,000 Homes; Second Plant to Follow," press release, May 18, 2012, www.businesswire.com/news/home/20120518005065/en/EnergySource%E2%80%99s-First-Geothermal-Plant-in-Imperial-Valley-Lauded-for-Creating-Jobs-Boosting-the-Economy-Delivering-Clean-Energy-to-50000-Homes-Second-Plant-to-Follow.
28. Sammy Roth, "Tesla Offered $325 Million for Salton Sea Startup," *The Desert Sun*, June 8, 2016, www.desertsun.com/story/tech/science/energy/2016/06/08/tesla-offered-325-million-salton-sea-startup/84913572/.
29. Wenzel, "Simbol Mining Raises Funds for 'Zero-Waste' Lithium Extraction."
30. Roth, "Tesla Offered $325 Million for Salton Sea Startup."
31. Alexander Richter, "Simbol Materials Succeeds in Producing Lithium from Geothermal Brine," Think GeoEnergy, October 11, 2013, www.thinkgeoenergy.com/simbol-materials-succeeds-in-producing-lithium-from-geothermal-brine/.
32. Letter from Elon Musk to Dr. John Burba, June 21, 2014.
33. Ibid.
34. Interview with Dr. John Burba, November 2, 2022. This account was corroborated by multiple parties.
35. Ibid.

36. Neither Tesla, nor its chief executive, Elon Musk, responded to multiple interview requests.
37. Rockwood was bought by Albemarle in 2014.

CHAPTER FOURTEEN: AN ELUSIVE PRIZE

1. Danny Ramos and Mitra Taj, "Explainer: Bolivia's 'Evo'—Socialist Icon or Would-be Dictator?" Reuters, October 18, 2019, www.reuters.com/article/us-bolivia-election-candidates-explainer/explainer-bolivias-evo-socialist-icon-or-would-be-dictator-idUSKBN1WX158.
2. NationMaster, "Countries Compared," accessed February 21, 2023, www.nationmaster.com/country-info/stats/Geography/Land-area/Sq.-km.
3. U.S. Central Intelligence Agency, "Bolivia," World Factbook, accessed February 21, 2023, www.cia.gov/the-world-factbook/countries/bolivia/.
4. Clifford Krauss, "Green-Energy Race Draws an American Underdog to Bolivia's Lithium," *The New York Times*, December 16, 2021, www.nytimes.com/2021/12/16/business/energy-environment/bolivia-lithium-electric-cars.html.
5. Adolfo Arranz and Marco Hernandez, "When China Wanted Silver from the Rest of the World," *South China Morning Post*, February 6, 2019, www.scmp.com/news/china/article/2184313/when-china-wanted-silver-rest-world.
6. Dennis Flynn and Arturo Giráldez, "Born with a 'Silver Spoon': The Origin of World Trade in 1571," *Journal of World History*, Fall 1995, www.jstor.org/stable/20078638.
7. Tony Hillerman, "Old Knowledge from the New World: Indian Givers: How the Indians of the Americas Transformed the World, by Jack Weatherford," *Los Angeles Times*, December 11, 1998, articles.latimes.com/1988-12-11/books/bk-144_1_indian-knowledge.
8. Patrick Greenfield, "How Silver Turned Potosi into 'the First City of Capitalism,'" *The Guardian*, March 21, 2016, www.theguardian.com/cities/2016/mar/21/story-of-cities-6-potosi-bolivia-peru-inca-first-city-capitalism.
9. John Maxwell Hamilton, "The Glory That Was Once Potosi," *The New York Times*, May 29, 1977, www.nytimes.com/1977/05/29/archives/the-glory-that-was-once-potosi-the-glory-that-was-once-potosi.html.
10. Adam Smith, *The Wealth of Nations*, Chapter 11.
11. Lawrence Wright, "Lithium Dreams: Can Bolivia Become the Saudi Arabia of the Electric-Car Era?" *The New Yorker*, March 15, 2010, www.newyorker.com/magazine/2010/03/22/lithium-dreams.
12. Marcelo Rochabrun and Santiago Limachi, "In Bolivia's Silver Mountain, Artisanal Miners Turn to Coca and the Devil," Reuters, May 30, 2022, www.reuters.com/world/americas/bolivias-silver-mountain-artisanal-miners-turn-coca-devil-2022-05-30/.
13. "Uyuni," *Encyclopedia Brittanica*, accessed February 21, 2023, www.britannica.com/place/Uyuni.
14. Lisa M. Hamilton, "The Quinoa Quarrel: Who Owns the World's Greatest Superfood?" *Harper's*, accessed February 21, 2023, harpers.org/archive/2014/05/the-quinoa-quarrel/.
15. NASA, "An Expanse of White in Bolivia," Earth Observatory, accessed February 21, 2023, earthobservatory.nasa.gov/images/84853/an-expanse-of-white-in-bolivia.
16. Wright, "Lithium Dreams."

17. Ian Failes, "Crafting Crait: ILM's VFX Supe on How Rian Johnson Wanted to Go 'Redder, Redder, Redder,'" VFXBlog, January 1, 2018, vfxblog.com/2018/01/01/crafting-crait-ilms-vfx-supe-on-how-rian-johnson-wanted-to-go-redder-redder-redder/.
18. Anthony Breznican, "Rian Johnson Reveals Details of New Plant in *The Last Jedi* Trailer," *Entertainment Weekly*, April 14, 2017, ew.com/movies/2017/04/14/star-wars-rian-johnson-last-jedi-planet/.
19. "Uyuni Info," Sala De Uyuni tourism website, accessed February 21, 2023, www.salardeuyuni.com/info.
20. "Increase in Tin Mining," *Encyclopedia Britannica*, accessed February 21, 2023, www.britannica.com/place/Bolivia/Increase-in-tin-mining.
21. Argus Media, "Gas-Rich Bolivia Loses Fight for Sea Access," October 1, 2018, www.argusmedia.com/en/news/1764389-gasrich-bolivia-loses-fight-for-sea-access.
22. Bloomberg, "President Energy Finds Oil in Paraguay's Chaco Basin," October 20, 2014, www.epmag.com/president-energy-finds-oil-paraguays-chaco-basin-757736.
23. Daniel Hofer, "Borax Production in Rio Grande," Daniel in Bolivia blog, September 24, 2010, danielinbolivia.wordpress.com/2010/09/24/borax-production-in-rio-grande_ulexit_-daniel-hofer-bolivia-bolivien-blog-fotograf-serie-fotos-documentary-photographer-salar_de_uyuni_bolivia_bolivien_fotoserie_fotos/.
24. Argus Media, "Gas-Rich Bolivia Loses Fight for Sea Access."
25. S. L. Rettig, B. F. Jones, and F. Risacher, "Geochemical Evolution of Brines in the Salar of Uyuni, Bolivia," *Chemical Geology*, April 1, 1980, www.sciencedirect.com/science/article/pii/0009254180901163.
26. Wright, "Lithium Dreams."
27. Ronn Pineo, "Progress in Bolivia: Declining the United States Influence and the Victories of Evo Morales," *Journal of Developing Societies*, December 2016, www.researchgate.net/publication/312406225_Progress_in_Bolivia_Declining_the_United_States_Influence_and_the_Victories_of_Evo_Morales.
28. Wright, "Lithium Dreams."
29. Diego Ore, "Bolivia Set to Build Large Lithium Plant in Uyuni," Reuters, September 30, 2009, www.reuters.com/article/bolivia-lithium/bolivia-set-to-build-large-lithium-plant-in-uyuni-idUKN3021269020090930.
30. Wright, "Lithium Dreams."
31. Ibid.
32. Ore, "Bolivia Set to Build Large Lithium Plant in Uyuni."
33. Mitra Taj, "In the New Lithium 'Great Game,' Germany Edges Out China in Bolivia," Reuters, January 28, 2019, www.reuters.com/article/bolivia-lithium-germany/in-the-new-lithium-great-game-germany-edges-out-china-in-bolivia-idUKL1N1ZL0I1.
34. Ibid.
35. Daniel Ramos, "Bolivia Picks Chinese Partner for $2.3 Billion Lithium Projects," Reuters, www.reuters.com/article/us-bolivia-lithium-china/bolivia-picks-chinese-partner-for-2-3-billion-lithium-projects-idUSKCN1PV2F7.
36. Argus Media, "Bolivia Scraps Lithium Deal with Germany's ACI," November 4, 2019, www.argusmedia.com/en/news/2008429-bolivia-scraps-lithium-deal-with-germanys-aci.
37. Ibid.
38. Adam Jourdan, "Exclusive: Bolivia's New Lithium Tsar Says Country Should Go It Alone," Reuters, January 15, 2020, www.reuters.com/article/us-bolivia

-lithium-exclusive/exclusive-bolivias-new-lithium-tsar-says-country-should -go-it-alone-idUSKBN1ZE2DW.

39. Ernest Scheyder, "New Lithium Technology Can Help the World Go Green—If It Works," Reuters, April 7, 2022, www.reuters.com/article/mining-lithium -technology-focus-idCAKCN2LZ25R.
40. Marcelo Rochabrun, "Legendary Lithium Riches from Bolivia's Salt Flats May Still Just Be a Mirage," Reuters, May 23, 2022, www.reuters.com/markets /commodities/legendary-lithium-riches-bolivias-salt-flats-may-still-just-be -mirage-2022-05-23/.
41. "Bolivia's Lithium Mining Dilemma," BBC News, September 10, 2008, news.bbc .co.uk/1/hi/business/7607624.stm.
42. Associated Press, "Republic Agrees to Buy Alamo Rent-A-Car for $625 Million in Stock," November 7, 1996, apnews.com/article/880c8e23dd9bc1 7e655a9f28a63cfbb1.
43. "Teague Egan," Sports Agent Blog, accessed February 21, 2023, sportsagent blog.com/interview-with-the-agent/teague-egan/.
44. Ibid.
45. Sam Adams, "Swang," Genius.com lyrics, accessed February 21, 2023, genius .com/Sam-adams-swang-lyrics.
46. T. J. Simers, "Teague Egan, the Student Agent with the Golf Cart, Could be Taking USC on a Dangerous Ride," *Los Angeles Times*, November 29, 2010, www.latimes.com/archives/la-xpm-2010-nov-29-la-sp-simers-20101130 -story.html.
47. Ibid.
48. "Teague Egan," Sports Agent Blog.
49. Ibid.
50. ESPN, "Oregon Ducks v. USC Trojans, October 31, 2010," score statistics, www.espn.com/college-football/game/_/gameId/303030030.
51. Tom Pelissero, "Dillon Baxter Seeks Chance at NFL After Growing Up," *USA Today*, April 5, 2014, www.usatoday.com/story/sports/nfl/2014/04/05/dillon -baxter-usc-baker-university-nfl-draft/7356305/.
52. Holly Anderson, "Teague Egan's Agent Certification Revoked; Trojans Rejoice," SBNation.com, December 3, 2010, www.sbnation.com/ncaa-football /2010/12/3/1853768/teague-egan-agent-certification-revoked-nflpa-dillon -baxter.
53. Teague Egan, "Making Kindness Cool," TEDxBergamo, www.vexplode.com/en /tedx/making-kindness-cool-teague-egan-tedxbergamo/?t=00:18:22.
54. Krauss, "Green-Energy Race Draws an American Underdog to Bolivia's Lithium."
55. Author's interview with Teague Egan, January 5, 2022.
56. Ibid.
57. Ernest Scheyder, "Albemarle Unfazed by Chilean Election, Cites 'Unique' Lithium Contract," Reuters, December 23, 2021, www.reuters.com/markets /commodities/albemarle-unfazed-by-chilean-election-cites-unique-lithium -contract-2021-12-23/.
58. Loverly, "About Loverly," accessed February 21, 2023, loverly.com/about-us.
59. Wright, "Lithium Dreams."
60. U.S. Geological Survey, "Lithium," official publication, accessed February 21, 2023, pubs.usgs.gov/periodicals/mcs2023/mcs2023-lithium.pdf.
61. Krauss, "Green-Energy Race Draws an American Underdog to Bolivia's Lithium."
62. "EnergyX Will Support Health and Education Infrastructure in the Potosi

and Uyuni Regions of Bolivia Through a Multi-Year Funding Commitment," ElPotosi.net, May 5, 2022, elPotosi.net/local/20220505_energyx-apoyara-la-infraestructura-de-salud-y-educacion-en-las-regiones-de-potosi-y-uyuni-de-bolivia-a-traves-de-un-compromiso-de-financiacion-plurianual.html.

63. Author's interview with Teague Egan, May 6, 2022.
64. Daniel Brett, "Bolivian Fight Club: Honor Mother Earth, Beat Thy Neighbor at the World's Wildest Ritual Mass Brawl," Noble Sapien, September 26, 2021, noblesapien.com/body/bolivian-fight-club-beat-thy-neighbor-honor-mother-earth/.
65. Rochabrun and Limachi, "In Bolivia's Silver Mountain, Artisanal Miners Turn to Coca and the Devil."
66. "Bolivian Bus Crash Kills 13," *The Sydney Morning Herald*, May 3, 2008, www.smh.com.au/world/bolivian-bus-crash-kills-13-20080503-2ahb.html.
67. Chantel Delulio, "This Glamping Experience on the Bolivian Salt Flats Drops You into Your Own Personal Adventure Serial," Fodor's Travel, August 15, 2019, www.fodors.com/world/south-america/bolivia/experiences/news/this-glamping-experience-on-the-bolivian-salt-flats-drops-you-into-your-own-personal-adventure-serial.
68. Author's interview with Teague Egan, May 5, 2022.
69. Marcelo Rochabrun, "American Startup EnergyX Out of Bolivian Lithium Race," Reuters, June 8, 2022, www.reuters.com/markets/commodities/american-startup-energyx-out-bolivian-lithium-race-2022-06-09/.
70. Ernest Scheyder, "Lithium Startup EnergyX Gets $450 Mln Investment Tied to IPO Plans," Reuters, July 22, 2022, www.reuters.com/markets/us/lithium-startup-energyx-gets-450-mln-investment-tied-ipo-plans-2022-07-22/.

CHAPTER FIFTEEN: THE SEEDLINGS

1. Author's interview with Bernard Rowe, August 12, 2022.
2. Terell Wilkins, "Rare Wildflowers in Nevada Destroyed, 40% of World Population Ruined," *Reno Gazette Journal*, September 23, 2020, www.rgj.com/story/news/2020/09/23/40-percent-worlds-population-rare-nevada-wildflowers-tiehms-buckwheat-destroyed/5820913002/.
3. Reuters, "Rodents, Not Mining, Caused Damage to Nevada Wildflowers, Says Government Agency," December 4, 2020, www.reuters.com/article/us-ioneer-nevada-wildflowers/rodents-not-mining-caused-damage-to-nevada-wildflowers-says-government-agency-idUSKBN28E2WL.
4. Scott Sonner, "AP Exclusive: Rare Wildflower Could Jeopardize Lithium Mine," Associated Press, August 4, 2020, apnews.com/article/ap-top-news-deserts-technology-reno-business-3ab59bbc4fd6e6c602b4b6d037ec7f12.
5. Elizabeth Leger, Jamey McClinton, and Robert Shriver, "Ecology of *Eriogonum tiehmii*: A Report on Arthropod Diversity, Abundance, and the Importance of Pollination for Seed Set; Plant-Soil Relationships; Greenhouse Propagation and a Seedling Transplant Experiment; and Wild Population Demography," University of Nevada, Reno, report, January 2021.
6. Sonner, "AP Exclusive: Rare Wildflower Could Jeopardize Lithium Mine."
7. Ibid.
8. Leger files were obtained via public records request.
9. Ibid.
10. Ibid.
11. Federal Register, vol. 85, no. 141, July 22, 2020, 44265–67.
12. Ibid.

13. U.S. Fish & Wildlife Service, "Endangered and Threatened Wildlife and Plants; Finding on a Petition to List the Tiehm's Buckwheat as Threatened or Endangered," official website, June 4, 2021, www.fws.gov/species-publication-action/endangered-and-threatened-wildlife-and-plants-finding-petition-list.
14. Federal Register, vol. 86, no. 106, June 4, 2021, 29975–77.
15. Federal Register, vol. 87, no. 241, December 16, 2022, 77368, 77401.
16. Ibid.
17. Ibid.
18. Author's interview with James Calaway, December 20, 2021.
19. Ernest Scheyder, "Australia's ioneer Says U.S. Gov't Loan Application Moves Forward," Reuters, December 19, 2021, www.reuters.com/markets/commodities/australias-ioneer-says-us-govt-loan-application-moves-forward-2021-12-19/.
20. Author's interview with Jigar Shah, March 10, 2022.
21. Federal Register, vol. 87, no. 241, December 20, 2022, 77879–80.
22. Ioneer, "Ioneer's Rhyolite Ridge Project Advances into Final Stage of Permitting," press release, December 19, 2022, www.prnewswire.com/news-releases/ioneers-rhyolite-ridge-project-advances-into-final-stage-of-permitting-301706219.html.

EPILOGUE

1. Ioneer, "U.S. Department of Energy Offers Conditional Commitment for a Loan of Up to US$700 Million for the Rhyolite Ridge Project," press release, January 13, 2023, www.prnewswire.com/news-releases/us-department-of-energy-offers-conditional-commitment-for-a-loan-of-up-to-us700-million-for-the-rhyolite-ridge-project-301721334.html?tc=eml_cleartime.
2. Jigar Shah, "5 Big Things About Rhyolite Ridge, LPO's Latest Critical Materials Project Conditional Commitment," U.S. Department of Energy's YouTube page, January 26, 2023, www.youtube.com/watch?v=TAN8JtzxmSo.
3. Author's interview with Jigar Shah, January 13, 2023.
4. Tweet from Jigar Shah's Twitter account @JigarShahDC, January 13, 2023, twitter.com/JigarShahDC/status/1613901652649738247?s=20&t=syt1u5mEUJ7TLI3i2DqNOQ.
5. Author's interview with James Calaway, January 13, 2023.
6. Author's interview with Patrick Donnelly, January 13, 2023.
7. Federal Register, vol. 87, no. 241, December 16, 2022, 77368.
8. Ibid.
9. U.S. Department of Energy's Loan Programs Office, "LPO Announces Conditional Commitment to Ioneer Rhyolite Ridge to Advance Domestic Production of Lithium and Boron, Boost U.S. Battery Supply Chain," press release, January 13, 2023, www.energy.gov/lpo/articles/lpo-announces-conditional-commitment-ioneer-rhyolite-ridge-advance-domestic-production.
10. Associated Press, "Nevada Lithium Mine Gets $700 Million Conditional Loan from Dept. of Energy," January 13, 2023, www.2news.com/news/nevada-lithium-mine-gets-700-million-conditional-loan-from-dept-of-energy/article_cce8bd7e-936d-11ed-92bf-531c93138755.html.
11. Daniel Ramos, "Bolivia Taps Chinese Battery Giant CATL to Help Develop Lithium Riches," Reuters, January 20, 2023, www.reuters.com/technology/bolivia-taps-chinese-battery-giant-catl-help-develop-lithium-riches-2023-01-20.
12. John Rosevear, "General Motors Will Lead a $50 Million Funding Round for Lithium Extraction Startup EnergyX," CNBC, April 11, 2023, www.cnbc.com/2023/04/11/general-motors-energyx-investment.html.

13. Ernest Scheyder, "U.S. Bans Mining in Parts of Minnesota, Dealing Latest Blow to Antofagasta's Copper Project," Reuters, January 26, 2023, www.reuters.com/legal/litigation/us-blocks-mining-parts-minnesota-dealing-latest-blow-antofagastas-copper-project-2023-01-26/.
14. CreditSuisse, "US Inflation Reduction Act: A Tipping Point in Climate Action," September 28, 2022, www.credit-suisse.com/about-us-news/en/articles/news-and-expertise/us-inflation-reduction-act-a-catalyst-for-climate-action-202211.html, 109.
15. Samir Mehdi, "'How Am I Free if My Brothers Work in Mines for Tesla?': Kyrie Irving Contemplates His Own Freedoms Following Mavs Loss," *The Sports Rush*, March 9, 2023, thesportsrush.com/nba-news-how-am-i-free-if-my-brothers-work-in-mines-for-tesla-kyrie-irving-contemplates-his-own-freedom-following-mavs-loss/.
16. Ernest Scheyder, "Inside the Race to Remake Lithium Extraction for EV Batteries," Reuters, June 16, 2023, www.reuters.com/markets/commodities/inside-race-remake-lithium-extraction-ev-batteries-2023-06-16/.
17. Elena Vardon, "Glencore and Li-Cycle Plan to Build Battery Recycling Hub In Italy," *The Wall Street Journal*, May 10, 2023, www.wsj.com/articles/glencore-and-li-cycle-plan-to-build-battery-recycling-hub-in-italy-58960d31.
18. Perpetua Resources press release, "Perpetua Resources and Nez Perce Tribe Reach Agreement in Principle Under the Clean Water Act," June 20, 2023, www.prnewswire.com/news-releases/perpetua-resources-and-nez-perce-tribe-reach-agreement-in-principle-under-the-clean-water-act-301854763.html.
19. Matthew Daly, "Biden Administration Clarifies 1872 Mining Law; Says Huge Nevada Lithium Mine Can Proceed," Associated Press, May 16, 2023, apnews.com/article/mining-lithium-nevada-thacker-rosemont-decision-c7e251ef3994dfea4f2dff58322ff4ac.
20. Reuters, "North Carolina Seeks More Info for Piedmont Lithium Mine Permit Review," May 31, 2023, www.reuters.com/markets/commodities/north-carolina-seeks-more-info-piedmont-lithium-mine-permit-review-2023-05-30/.
21. Reuters, "Elon Musk and Tesla Break Ground on Massive Texas Lithium Refinery," May 9, 2023, www.reuters.com/business/autos-transportation/tesla-plans-produce-lithium-1-mln-vehicles-texas-refinery-elon-musk-2023-05-08/.
22. Albemarle Press Release, "Albemarle Becomes First Lithium Producer to Complete Independent Audit and Publish IRMA Report," June 20, 2023, www.prnewswire.com/news-releases/albemarle-becomes-first-lithium-producer-to-complete-independent-audit-and-publish-irma-report-301855202.html/.
23. Alexandra Sharp, "Chile's White Gold Rush: In a Move to Nationalize Lithium, Santiago Could Freeze Vital Foreign Capital Investments," *Foreign Policy*, April 21, 2023, foreignpolicy.com/2023/04/21/chile-lithium-reserves-albemarle-sqm-nationalize-boric-santiago/.
24. Ciara Nugent, "What Would Happen if South America Formed an OPEC for Lithium," *Time*, April 28, 2023, time.com/6275197/south-america-lithium-opec/.
25. Wendsler Nosie, letter to the editor, *Apache Messenger*, May 10, 2023.
26. Helen Reid, "Deep-Sea Mining May Disrupt Whale Communication, Study Finds," Reuters, February 14, 2023, www.yahoo.com/now/1-deep-sea-mining-may-185200258.html.
27. "The Future Is Circular," World Wildlife Fund, November 15, 2022, wwfint.awsassets.panda.org/downloads/the_future_is_circular___sintefminerals finalreport_nov_2022__1__1.pdf.

28. Ioneer, "Ioneer Permitting Violation," press release, January 19, 2023, company-announcements.afr.com/asx/inr/5c3e46e2-9776-11ed-b701-befebebb5124.pdf.
29. Max Matza, "Los Angeles Sees First Blizzard Warnings Since 1989," BBC News, February 24, 2023, www.bbc.com/news/world-us-canada-64753583.
30. Claire Bushey, "Ford to License Electric Vehicle Battery Tech from China's CATL," *Financial Times*, February 13, 2023, www.ft.com/content/08f08895-0ea0-40da-af31-2d29e2ae62e9.
31. Author's interview with James Calaway, February 24, 2023.

INDEX

Page numbers in *italics* refer to maps.

ABOUT THE AUTHOR

Ernest Scheyder is a senior correspondent for Reuters covering the green energy transition and the minerals that undergird it. He previously covered the U.S. shale oil revolution, politics, and the environment, and held roles at the Associated Press and the *Bangor Daily News*. A native of Maine, Scheyder is a graduate of the University of Maine and Columbia Journalism School. Visit his website at ErnestScheyder.com.